It's okay, I'll protect you!

Pretty Girl

Chin

Squinty-eyed

Alien

KOYOHARU GOTOUGE

Hi, everyone! I'm Gotouge and this is volume 22! Thank you to everyone involved! Recently, I've been thinking about ways to address an extraterrestrial lifeform furtively invading the earth. I was thinking that if aliens replaced my family and friends, I might be able to tell by establishing a made-up code word...but if the aliens have a device or natural ability that allows them to read minds, then what could I do?! Solving one problem just leads to another!! The Earth Defense Corps never sleeps! ★ If you watch too many science fiction films, you start thinking like this, so be careful! When I ran out of midmorning snacks, my assistant gave me some!

DEMON SLAYER:
KIMETSU NO YAIBA
VOLUME 22
Shonen Jump Edition

Story and Art by
KOYOHARU GOTOUGE

KIMETSU NO YAIBA
© 2016 by Koyoharu Gotouge
All rights reserved. First published in Japan
in 2016 by SHUEISHA Inc., Tokyo. English
translation rights arranged by SHUEISHA Inc.

TRANSLATION John Werry

ENGLISH ADAPTATION Stan!

TOUCH-UP ART & LETTERING John Hunt

DESIGN Jimmy Presler

EDITOR Mike Montesa

Printed in the U.S.A

Published by VIZ Media, LLC
P.O. Box 77010
San Francisco, CA 94107

10 9 8 7 6 5 4 3 2 1
First printing, June 2021

viz.com

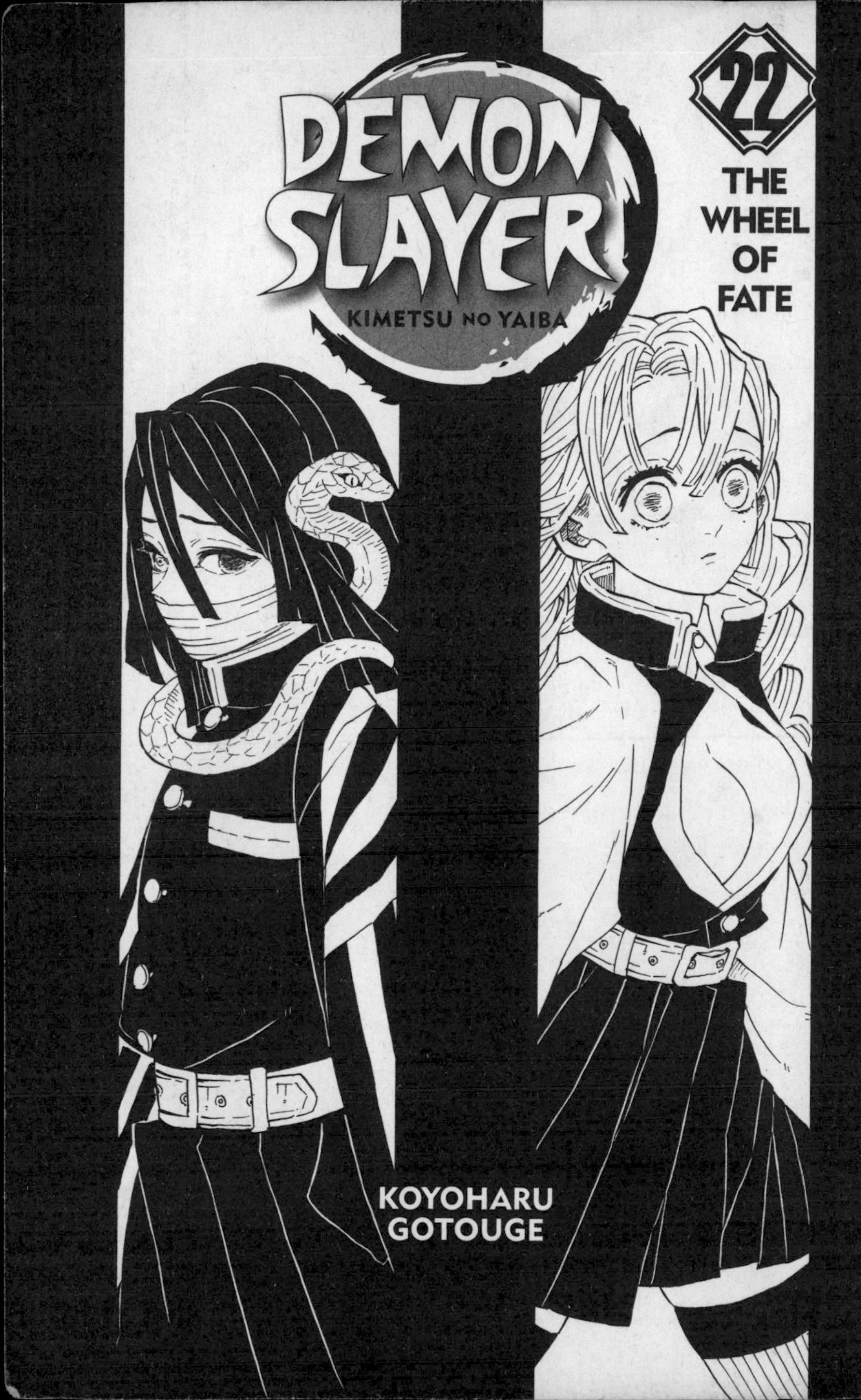
DEMON SLAYER
KIMETSU NO YAIBA
22
THE WHEEL OF FATE
KOYOHARU GOTOUGE

CHARACTERS

TANJIRO KAMADO

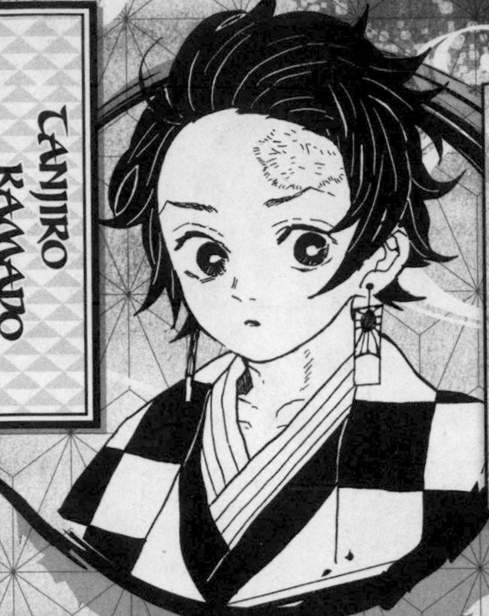

A kind boy who saved his sister and now aims to avenge his family. He can smell the scent of demons and an opponent's weakness.

NEZUKO KAMADO

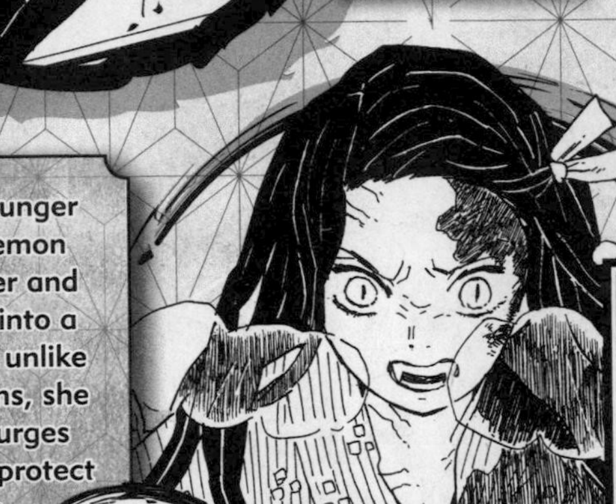

Tanjiro's younger sister. A demon attacked her and turned her into a demon. But unlike other demons, she fights her urges and tries to protect Tanjiro.

STORY

In Taisho-era Japan, young Tanjiro makes a living selling charcoal. One day, demons kill his family and turn his younger sister Nezuko into a demon. Tanjiro and Nezuko set out to find a way to return Nezuko to human form and defeat Kibutsuji, the demon who killed their family!

After joining the Demon Slayer Corps, Tanjiro meets Tamayo and Yushiro—demons who oppose Kibutsuji—who provide a clue to how Nezuko may be turned back into a human. Nezuko manifests the ability to withstand sunlight, so Kibutsuji attacks Ubuyashiki Mansion. The Demon Slayers suffer many sacrifices, but they kill all the upper-rank demons and eventually succeed in forcing Kibutsuji above ground from inside Infinity Castle!! The Hashira attack with all their remaining strength, and Tanjiro collapses after an attack by Kibutsuji!!

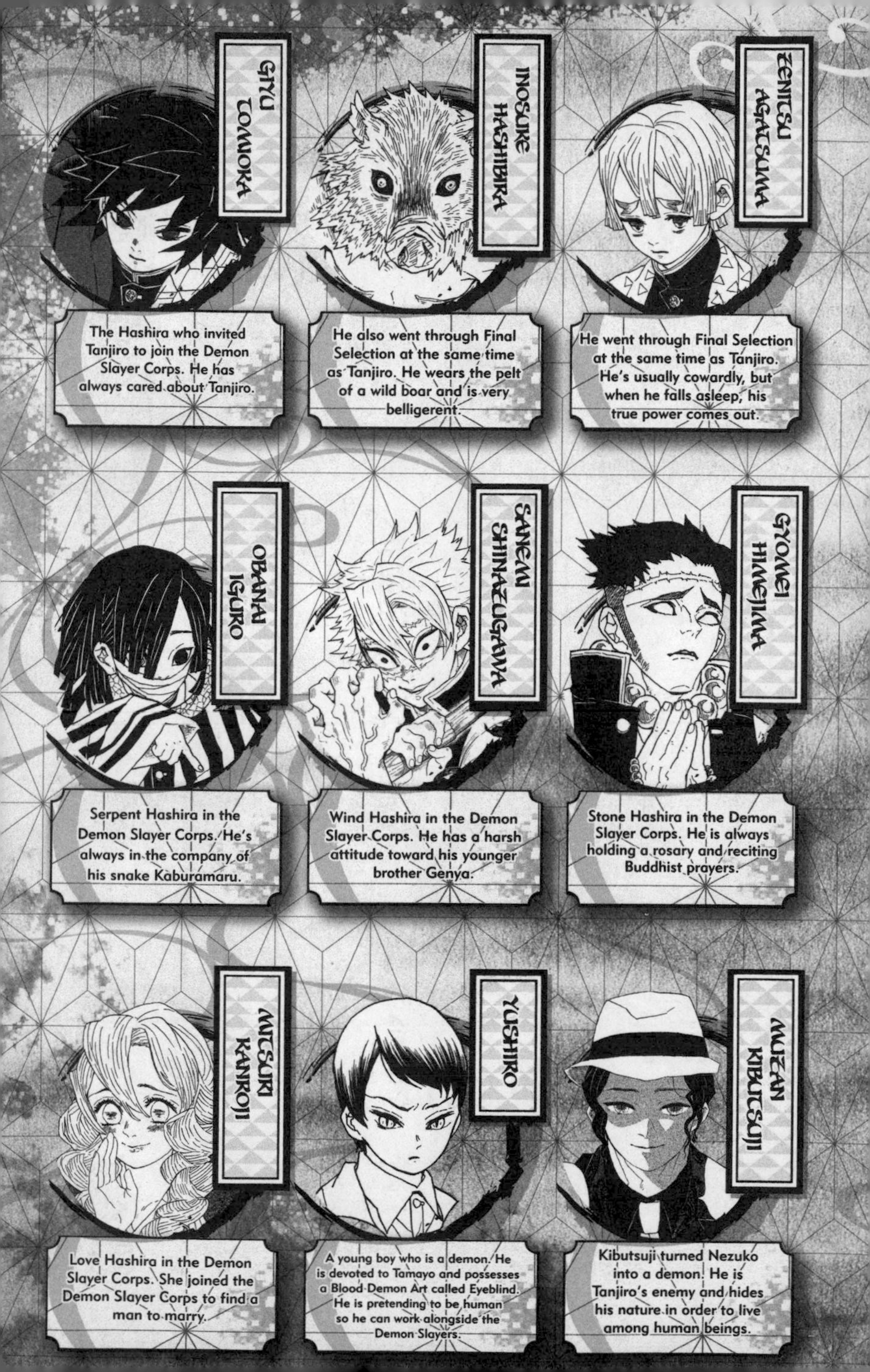
ZENITSU AGATSUMA
He went through Final Selection at the same time as Tanjiro. He's usually cowardly, but when he falls asleep, his true power comes out.
INOSUKE HASHIBIRA
He also went through Final Selection at the same time as Tanjiro. He wears the pelt of a wild boar and is very belligerent.
GIYU TOMIOKA
The Hashira who invited Tanjiro to join the Demon Slayer Corps. He has always cared about Tanjiro.
GYOMEI HIMEJIMA
Stone Hashira in the Demon Slayer Corps. He is always holding a rosary and reciting Buddhist prayers.
SANEMI SHINAZUGAWA
Wind Hashira in the Demon Slayer Corps. He has a harsh attitude toward his younger brother Genya.
OBANAI IGURO
Serpent Hashira in the Demon Slayer Corps. He's always in the company of his snake Kaburamaru.
MUZAN KIBUTSUJI
Kibutsuji turned Nezuko into a demon. He is Tanjiro's enemy and hides his nature in order to live among human beings.
YUSHIRO
A young boy who is a demon. He is devoted to Tamayo and possesses a Blood Demon Art called Eyeblind. He is pretending to be human so he can work alongside the Demon Slayers.
MITSURI KANROJI
Love Hashira in the Demon Slayer Corps. She joined the Demon Slayer Corps to find a man to marry.

CONTENTS

DEMON SLAYER!
KIMETSU NO YAIBA

22

THE WHEEL
OF FATE

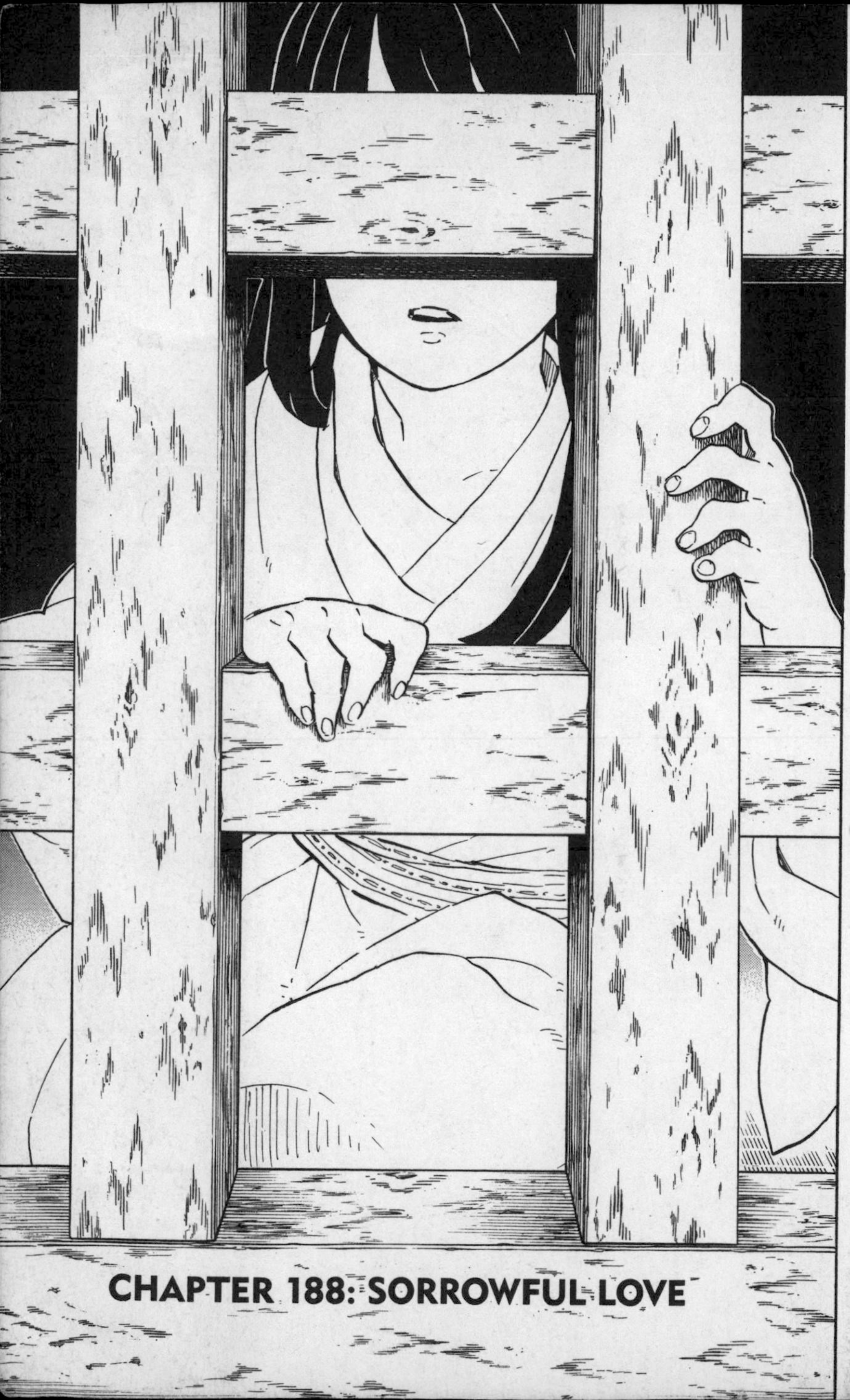

CHAPTER 188: SORROWFUL LOVE

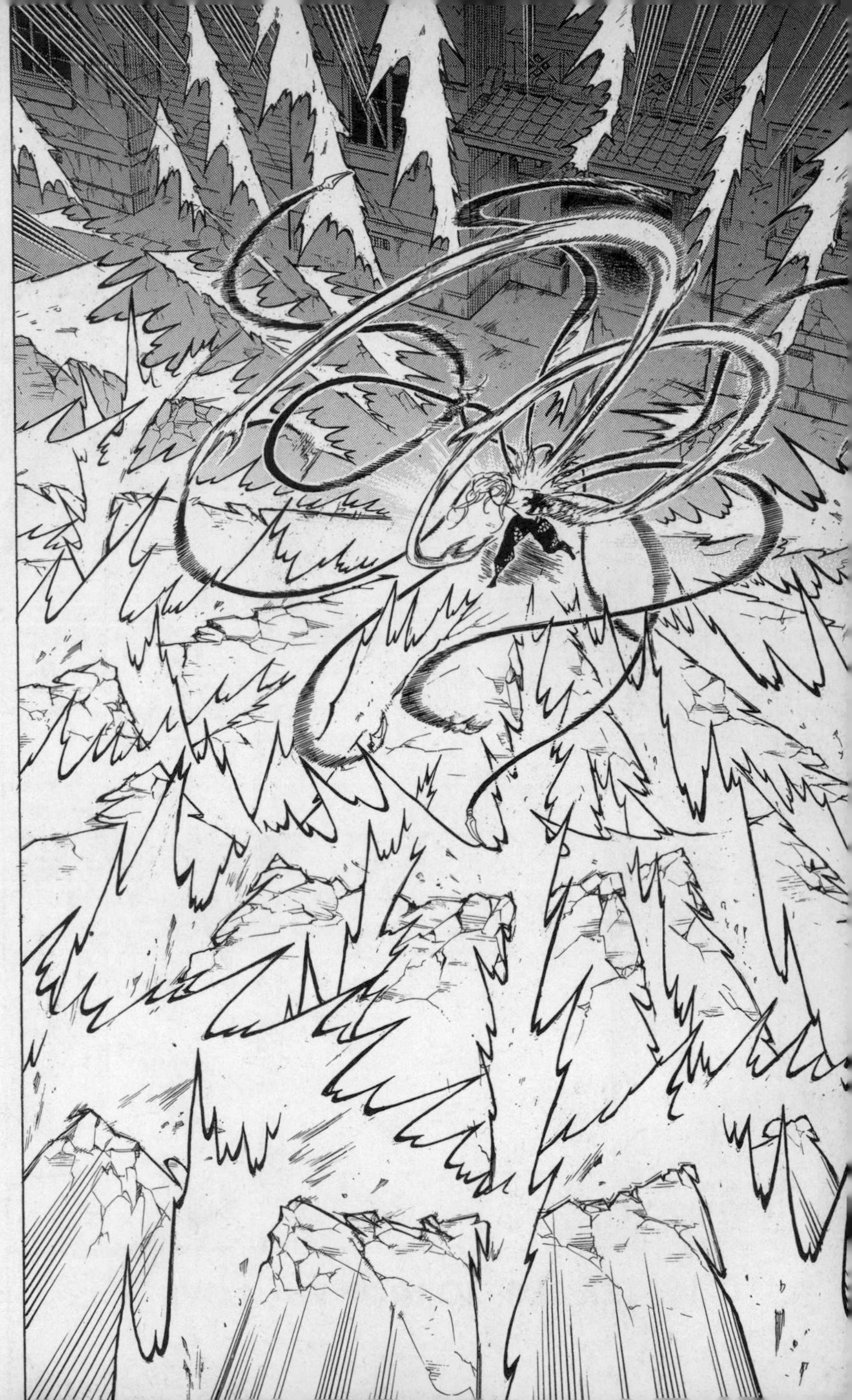

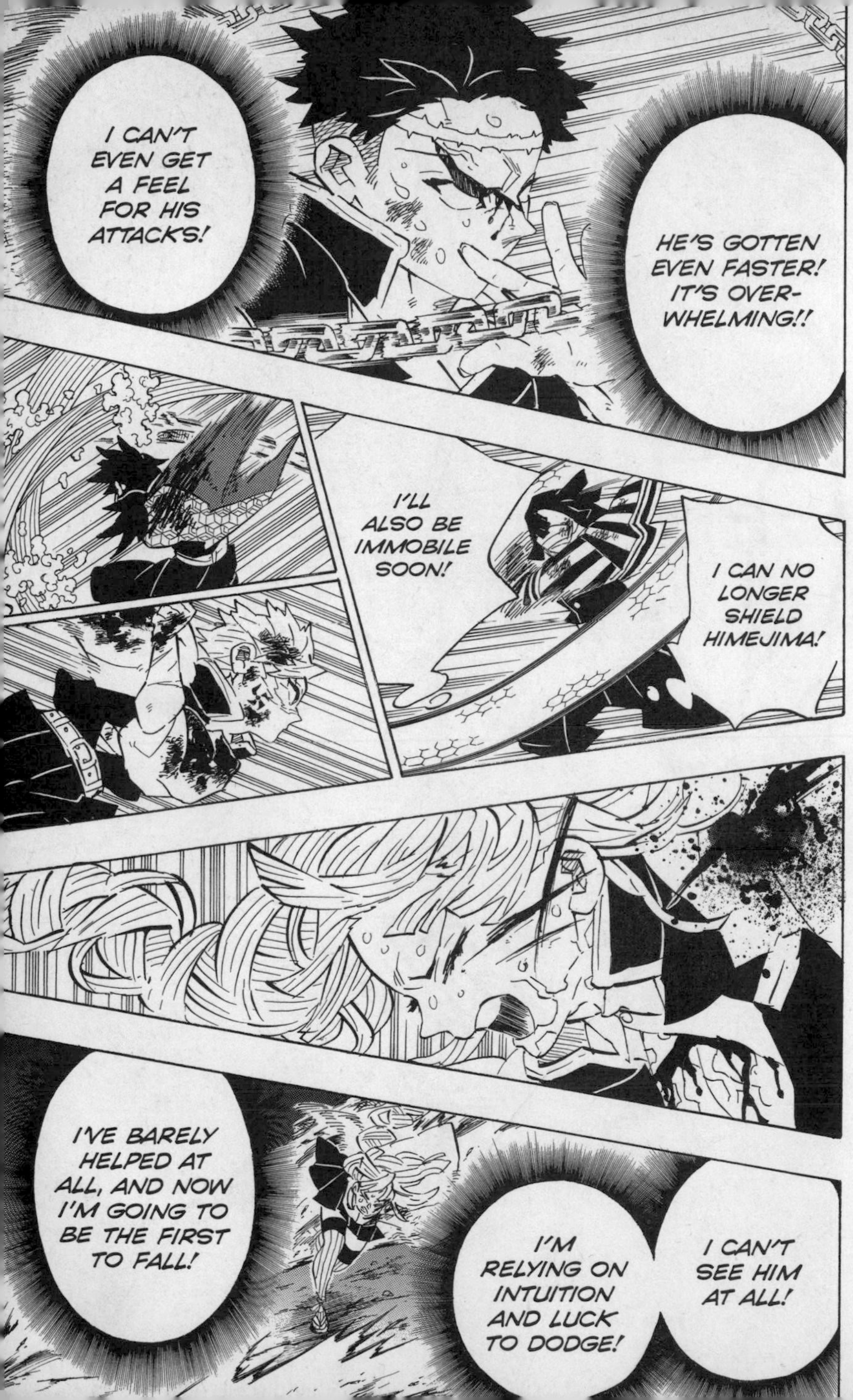
HE'S GOTTEN EVEN FASTER! IT'S OVER-WHELMING!!
I CAN'T EVEN GET A FEEL FOR HIS ATTACKS!
I CAN NO LONGER SHIELD HIMEJIMA!
I'LL ALSO BE IMMOBILE SOON!
I CAN'T SEE HIM AT ALL!
I'M RELYING ON INTUITION AND LUCK TO DODGE!
I'VE BARELY HELPED AT ALL, AND NOW I'M GOING TO BE THE FIRST TO FALL!

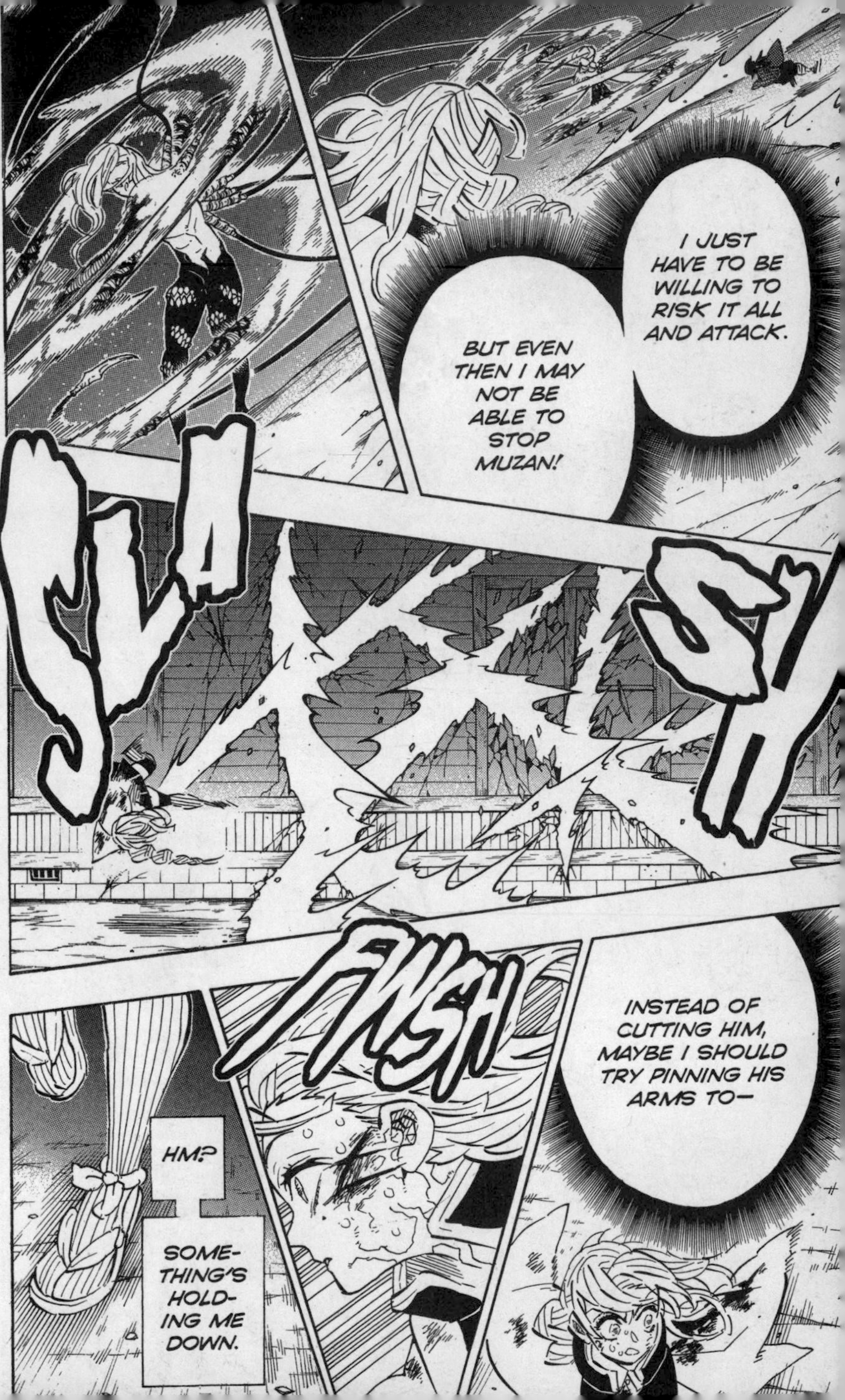
I JUST HAVE TO BE WILLING TO RISK IT ALL AND ATTACK.
BUT EVEN THEN I MAY NOT BE ABLE TO STOP MUZAN!
SLASH
INSTEAD OF CUTTING HIM, MAYBE I SHOULD TRY PINNING HIS ARMS TO—
FWSH
HM?
SOME-THING'S HOLD-ING ME DOWN.

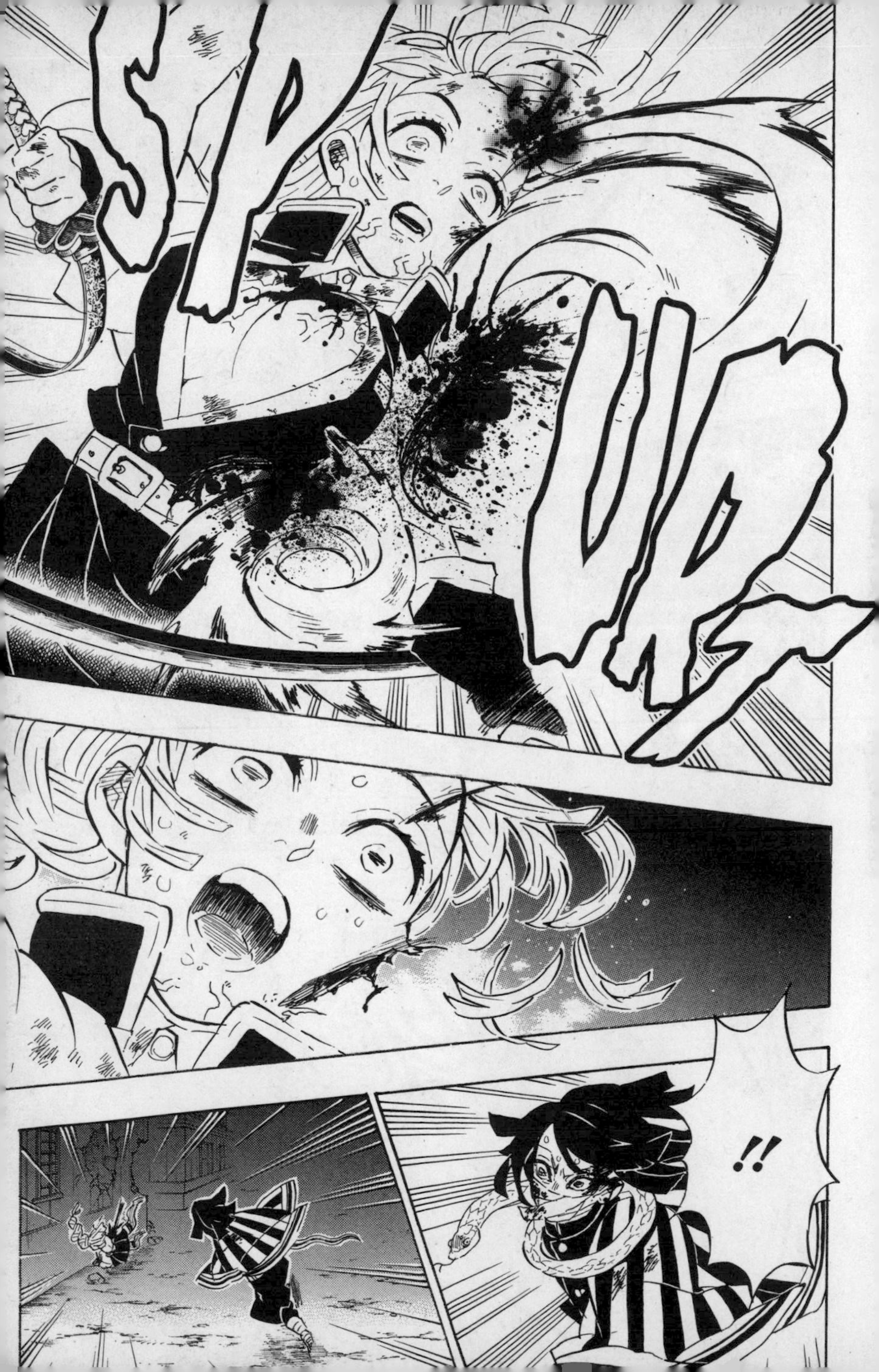
SPLUT
!!

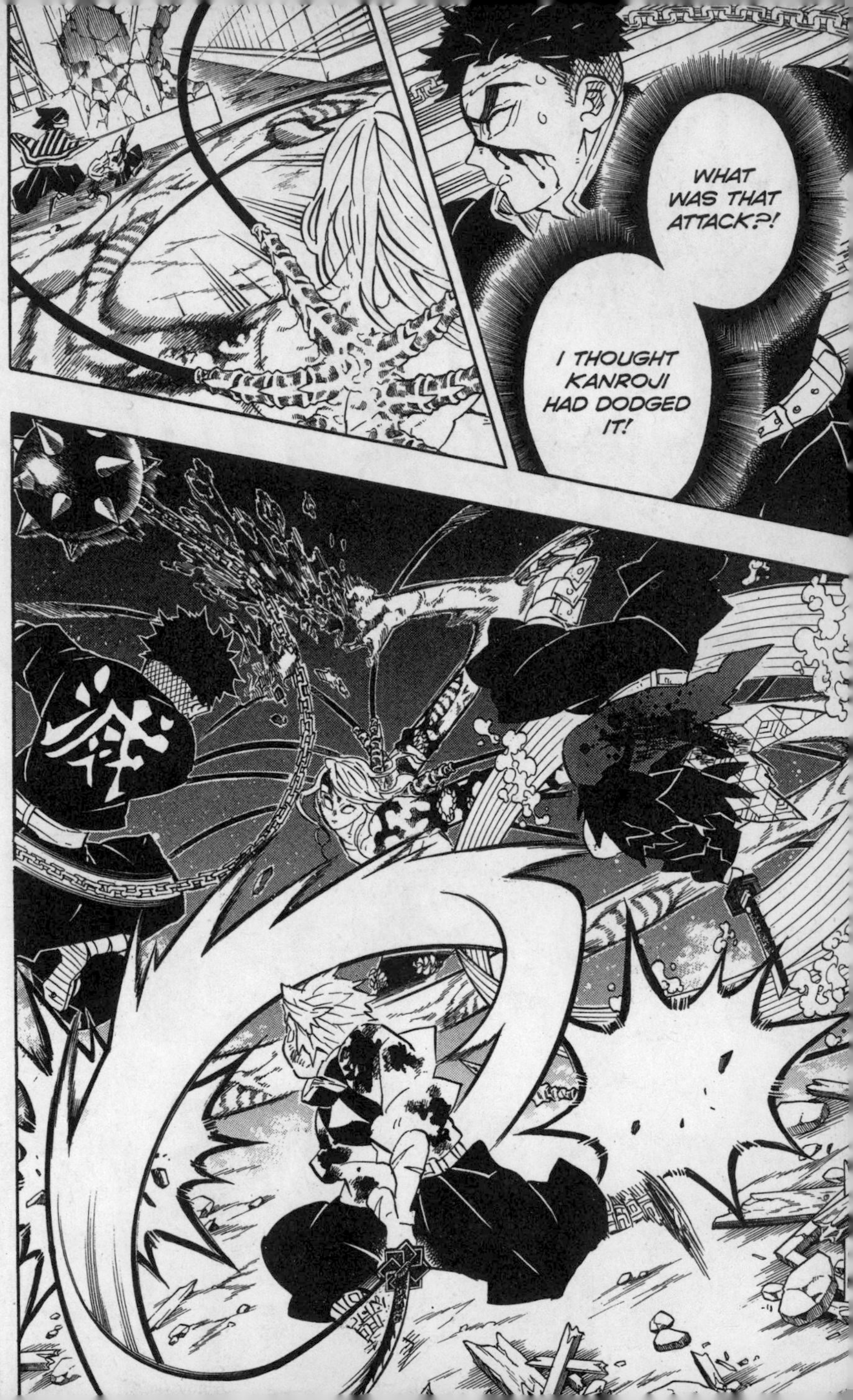
WHAT WAS THAT ATTACK?!
I THOUGHT KANROJI HAD DODGED IT!

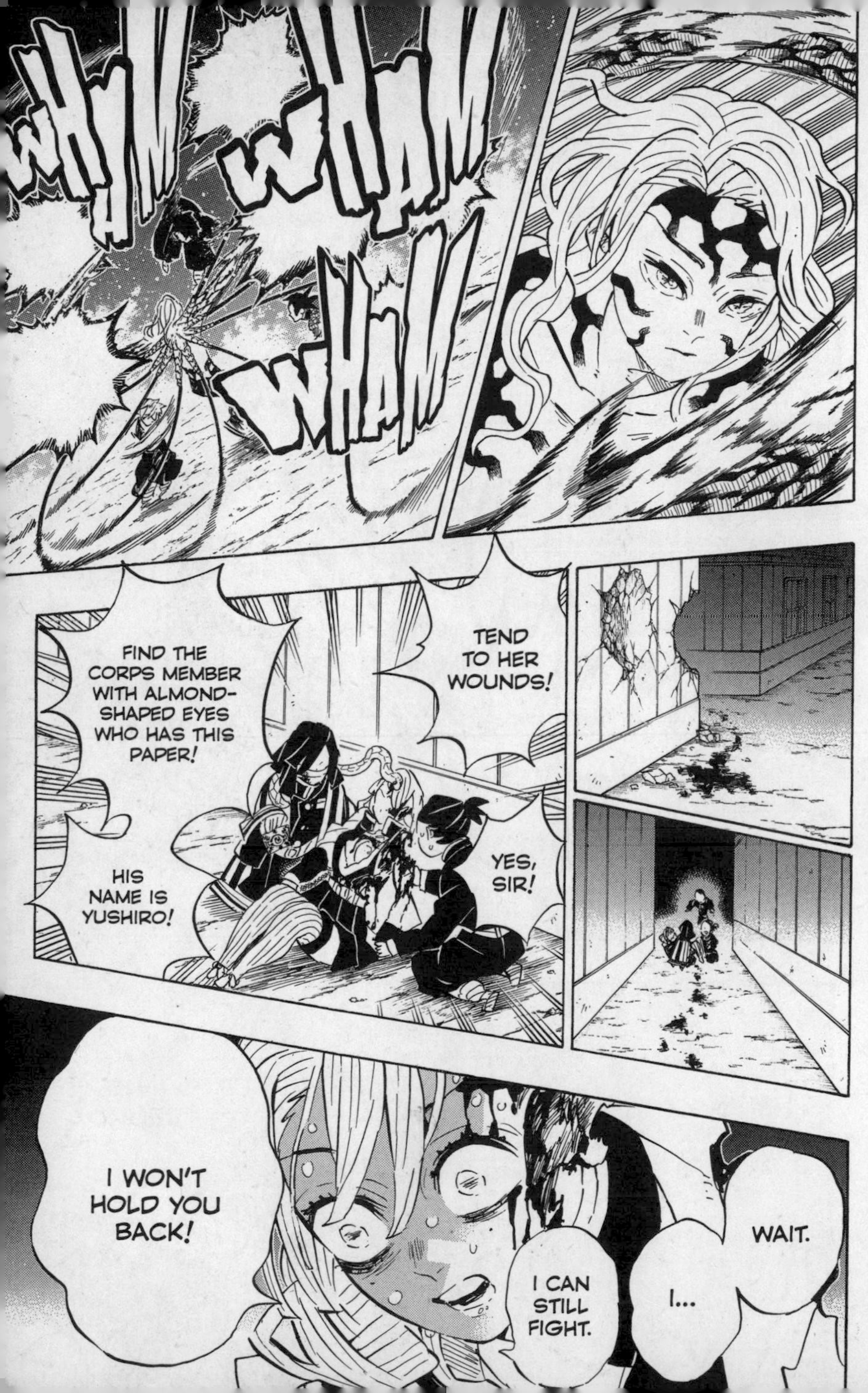
WHAM
WHAM
WHAM
TEND TO HER WOUNDS!
FIND THE CORPS MEMBER WITH ALMOND-SHAPED EYES WHO HAS THIS PAPER!
YES, SIR!
HIS NAME IS YUSHIRO!
WAIT.
I...
I CAN STILL FIGHT.
I WON'T HOLD YOU BACK!

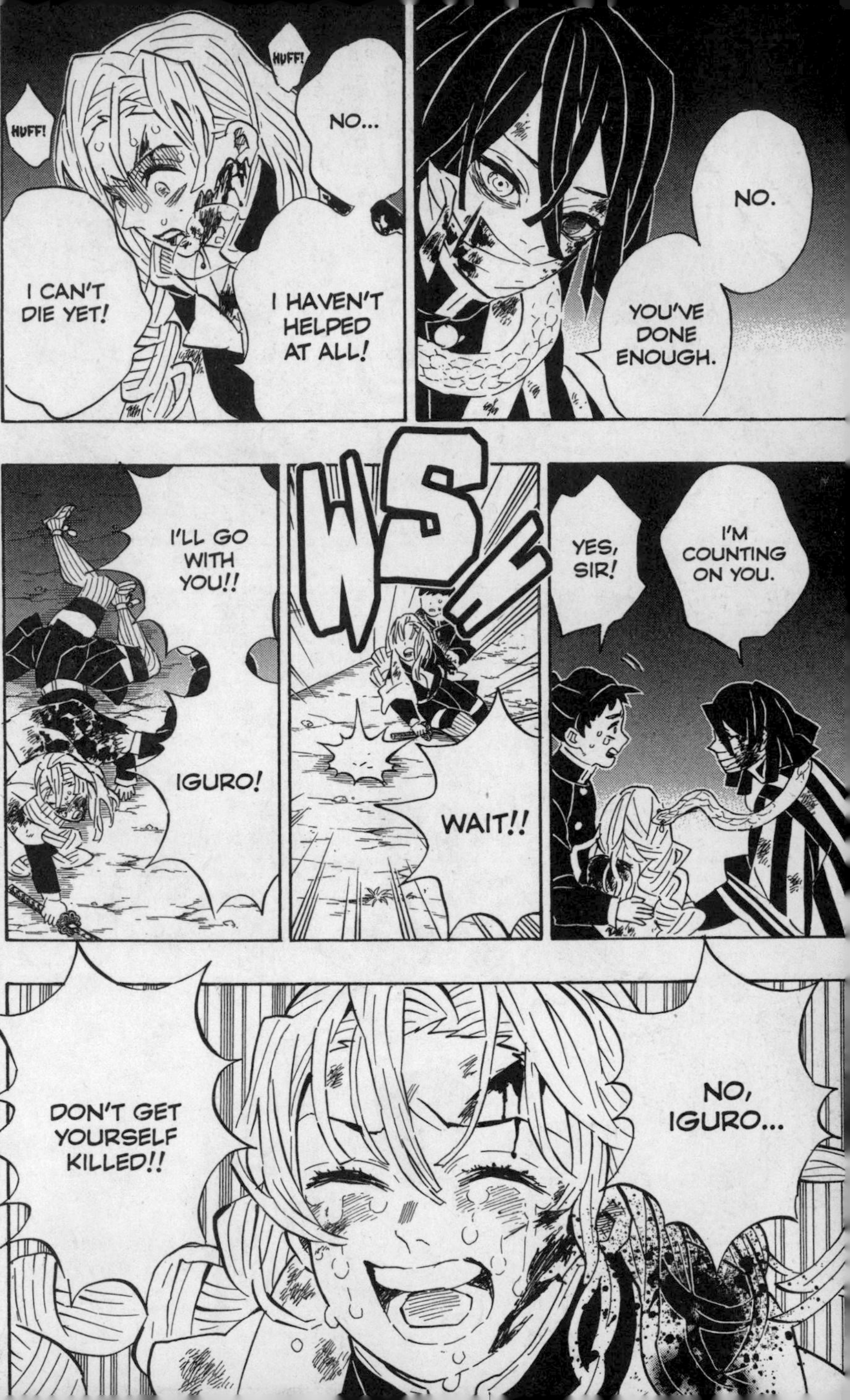
NO.
YOU'VE DONE ENOUGH.
HUFF!
HUFF!
NO...
I HAVEN'T HELPED AT ALL!
I CAN'T DIE YET!
I'M COUNTING ON YOU.
YES, SIR!
WSH
WAIT!!
I'LL GO WITH YOU!!
IGURO!
NO, IGURO...
DON'T GET YOURSELF KILLED!!

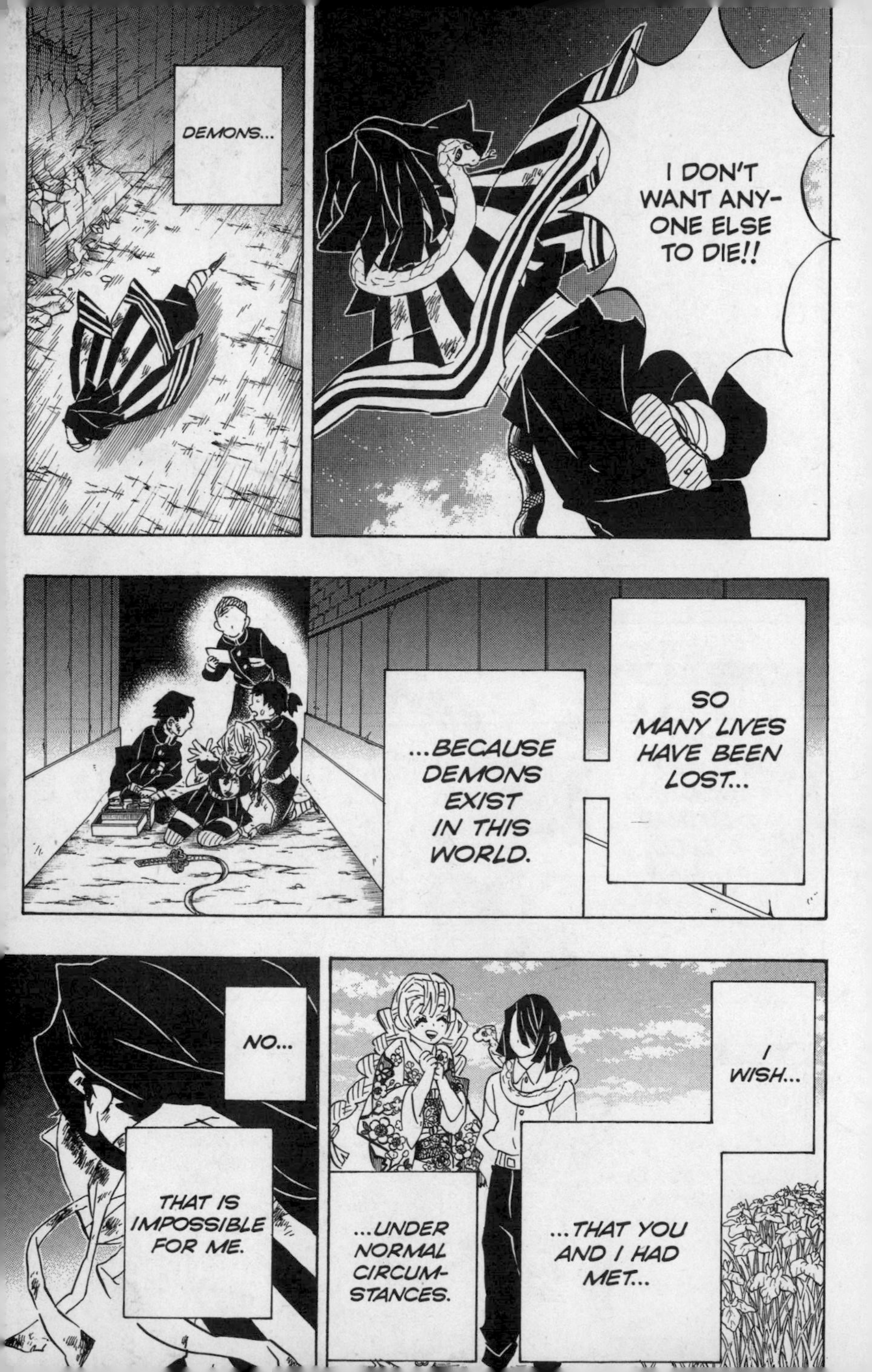
I DON'T WANT ANY-ONE ELSE TO DIE!!
DEMONS...
SO MANY LIVES HAVE BEEN LOST...
...BECAUSE DEMONS EXIST IN THIS WORLD.
I WISH...
...THAT YOU AND I HAD MET...
...UNDER NORMAL CIRCUM-STANCES.
NO...
THAT IS IMPOSSIBLE FOR ME.

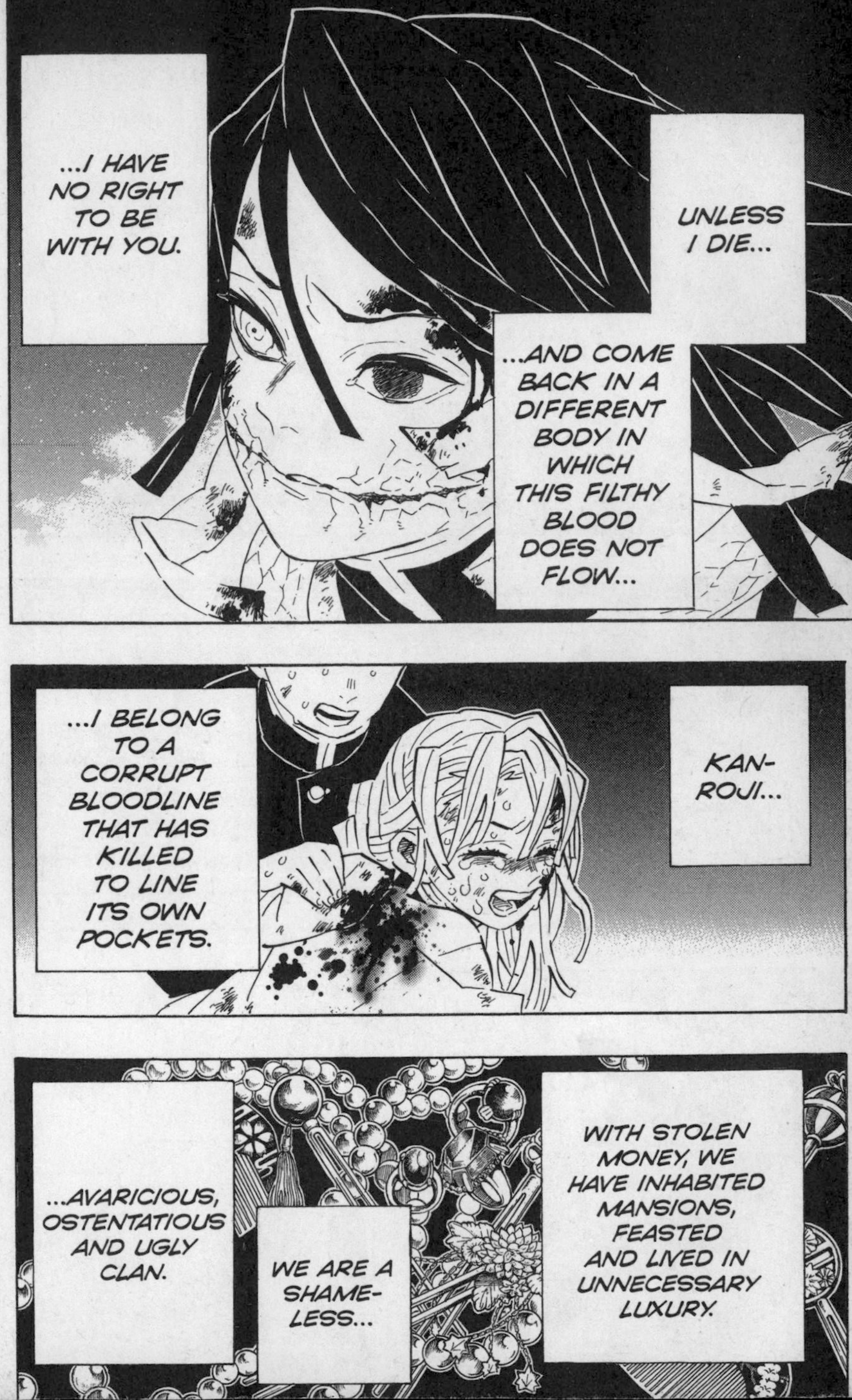
UNLESS I DIE...
...AND COME BACK IN A DIFFERENT BODY IN WHICH THIS FILTHY BLOOD DOES NOT FLOW...
...I HAVE NO RIGHT TO BE WITH YOU.
KAN-ROJI...
...I BELONG TO A CORRUPT BLOODLINE THAT HAS KILLED TO LINE ITS OWN POCKETS.
WITH STOLEN MONEY, WE HAVE INHABITED MANSIONS, FEASTED AND LIVED IN UNNECESSARY LUXURY.
WE ARE A SHAME-LESS...
...AVARICIOUS, OSTENTATIOUS AND UGLY CLAN.

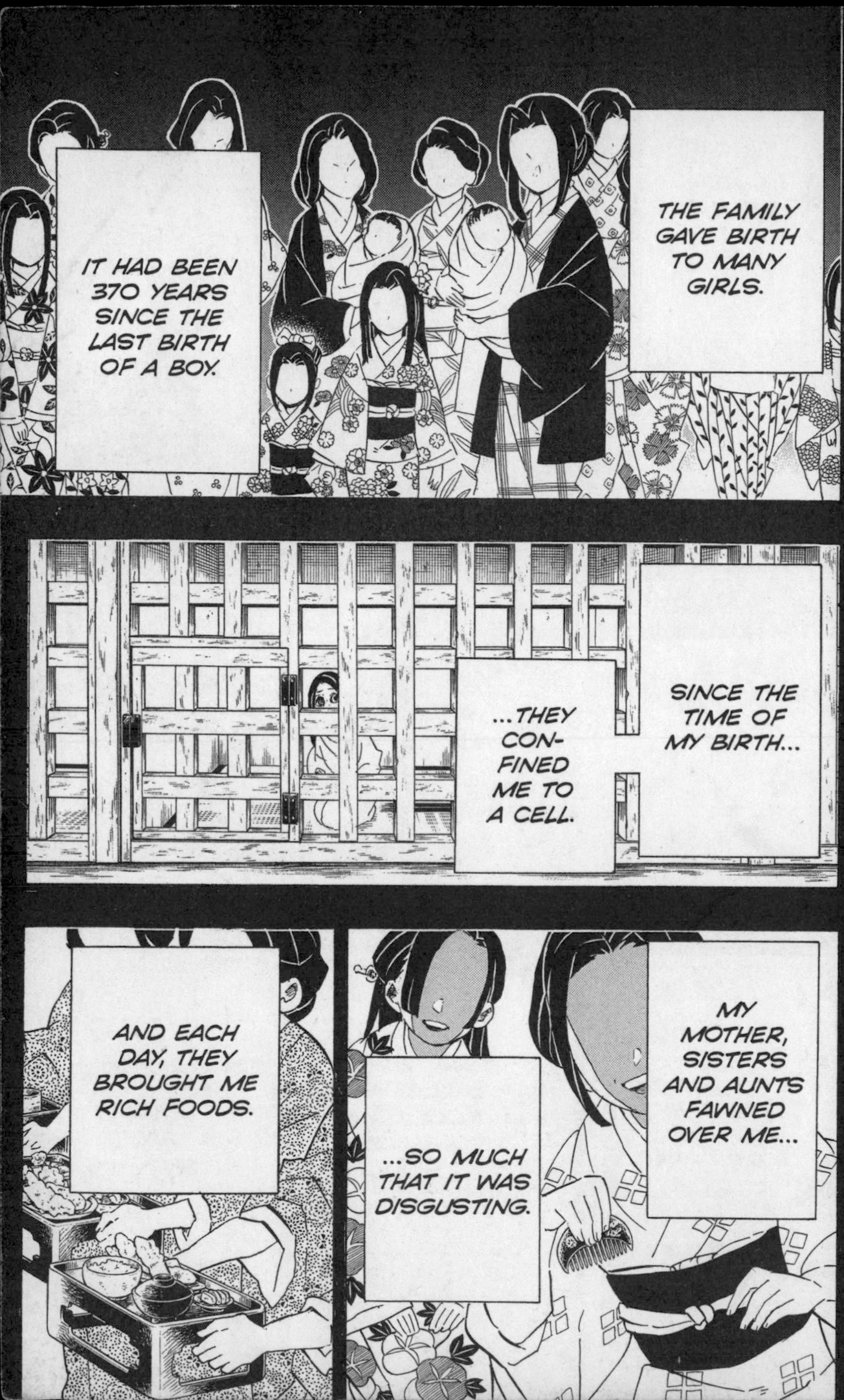
THE FAMILY GAVE BIRTH TO MANY GIRLS.
IT HAD BEEN 370 YEARS SINCE THE LAST BIRTH OF A BOY.
SINCE THE TIME OF MY BIRTH...
...THEY CONFINED ME TO A CELL.
MY MOTHER, SISTERS AND AUNTS FAWNED OVER ME...
...SO MUCH THAT IT WAS DISGUSTING.
AND EACH DAY, THEY BROUGHT ME RICH FOODS.

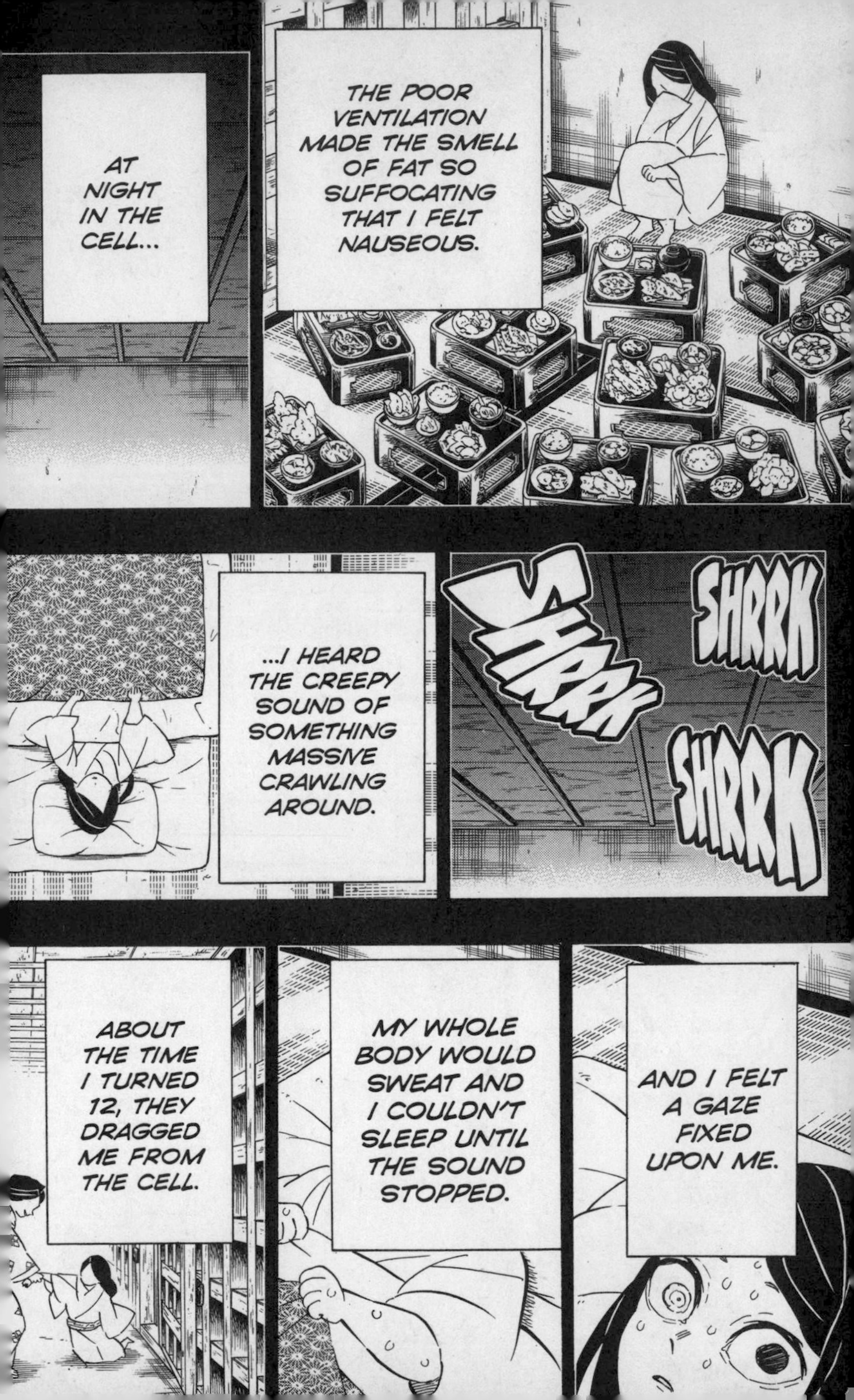
THE POOR VENTILATION MADE THE SMELL OF FAT SO SUFFOCATING THAT I FELT NAUSEOUS.
AT NIGHT IN THE CELL...
SHRRK
SHRRK
SHRRK
...I HEARD THE CREEPY SOUND OF SOMETHING MASSIVE CRAWLING AROUND.
AND I FELT A GAZE FIXED UPON ME.
MY WHOLE BODY WOULD SWEAT AND I COULDN'T SLEEP UNTIL THE SOUND STOPPED.
ABOUT THE TIME I TURNED 12, THEY DRAGGED ME FROM THE CELL.

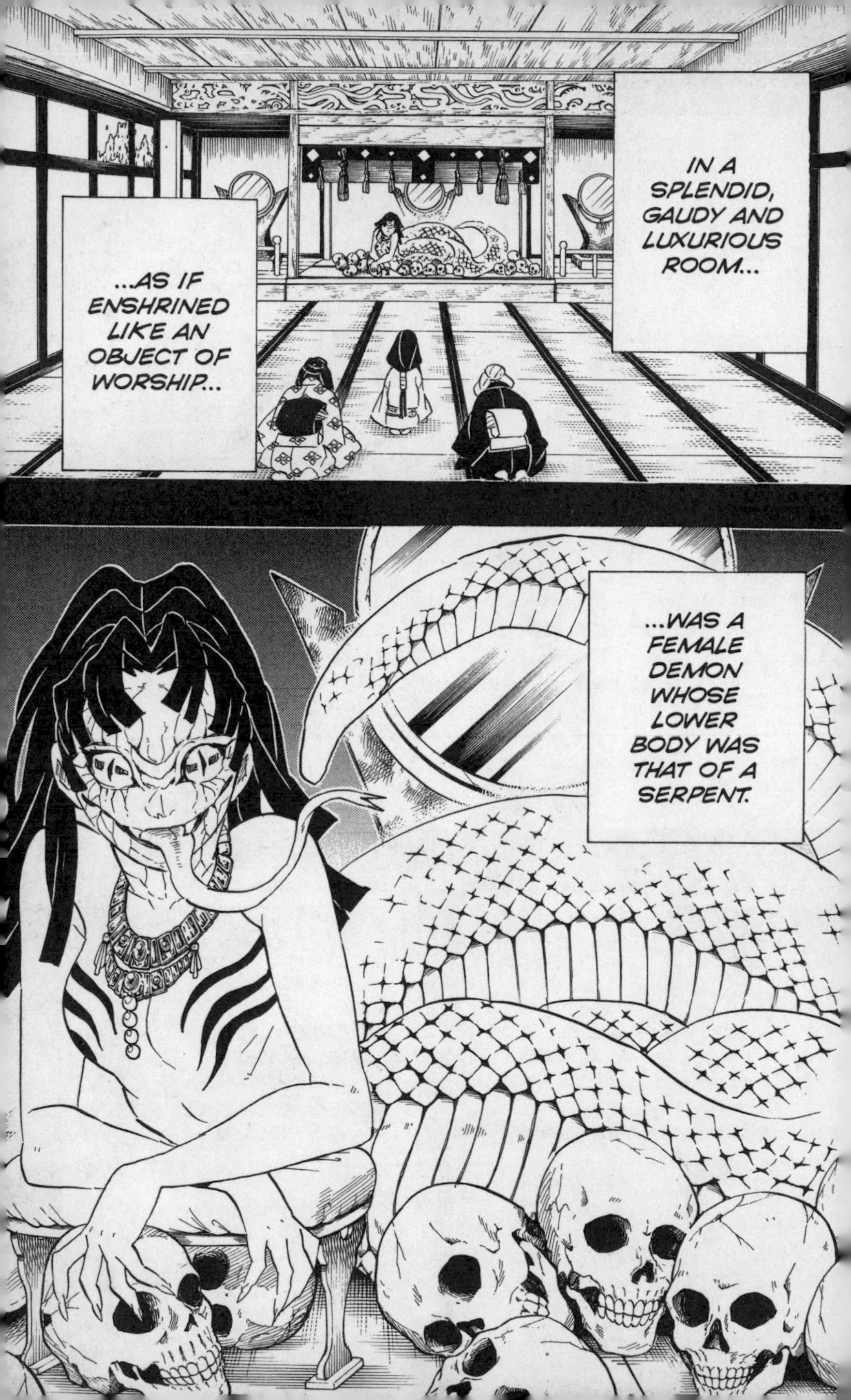
IN A SPLENDID, GAUDY AND LUXURIOUS ROOM...
...AS IF ENSHRINED LIKE AN OBJECT OF WORSHIP...
...WAS A FEMALE DEMON WHOSE LOWER BODY WAS THAT OF A SERPENT.

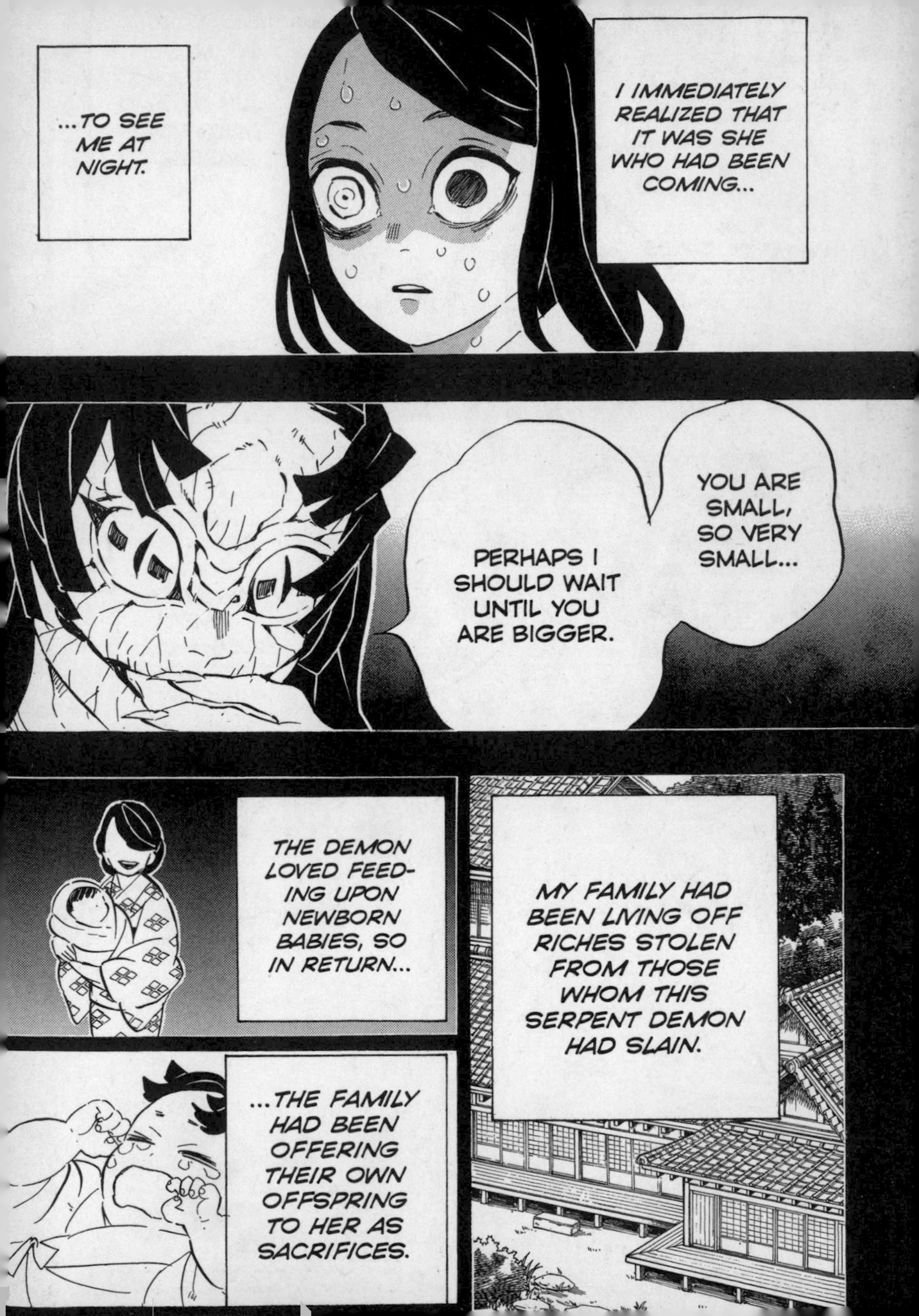
I IMMEDIATELY REALIZED THAT IT WAS SHE WHO HAD BEEN COMING...
...TO SEE ME AT NIGHT.
YOU ARE SMALL, SO VERY SMALL...
PERHAPS I SHOULD WAIT UNTIL YOU ARE BIGGER.
MY FAMILY HAD BEEN LIVING OFF RICHES STOLEN FROM THOSE WHOM THIS SERPENT DEMON HAD SLAIN.
THE DEMON LOVED FEED-ING UPON NEWBORN BABIES, SO IN RETURN...
...THE FAMILY HAD BEEN OFFERING THEIR OWN OFFSPRING TO HER AS SACRIFICES.

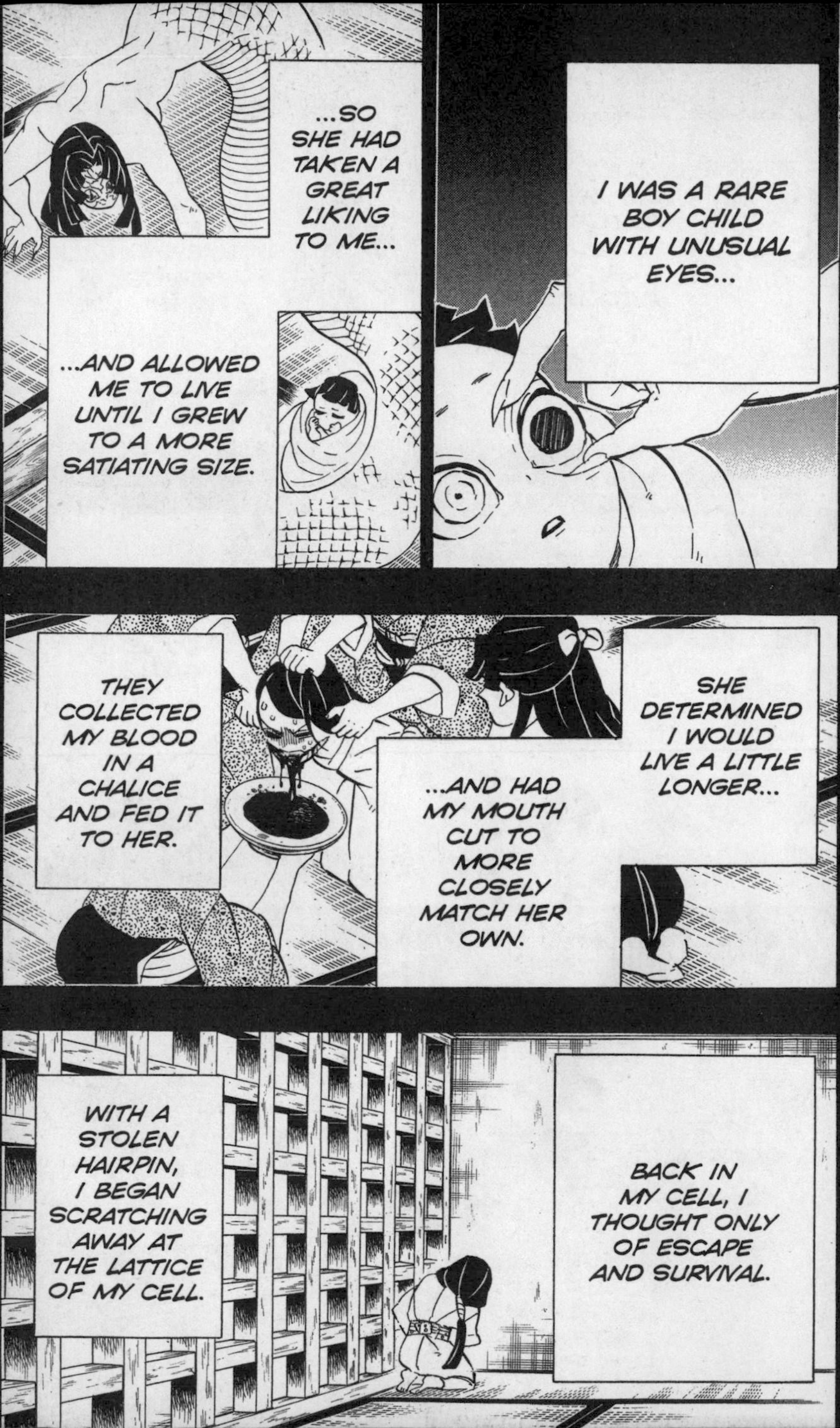

I WAS A RARE BOY CHILD WITH UNUSUAL EYES...
...SO SHE HAD TAKEN A GREAT LIKING TO ME...
...AND ALLOWED ME TO LIVE UNTIL I GREW TO A MORE SATIATING SIZE.
SHE DETERMINED I WOULD LIVE A LITTLE LONGER...
...AND HAD MY MOUTH CUT TO MORE CLOSELY MATCH HER OWN.
THEY COLLECTED MY BLOOD IN A CHALICE AND FED IT TO HER.
BACK IN MY CELL, I THOUGHT ONLY OF ESCAPE AND SURVIVAL.
WITH A STOLEN HAIRPIN, I BEGAN SCRATCHING AWAY AT THE LATTICE OF MY CELL.

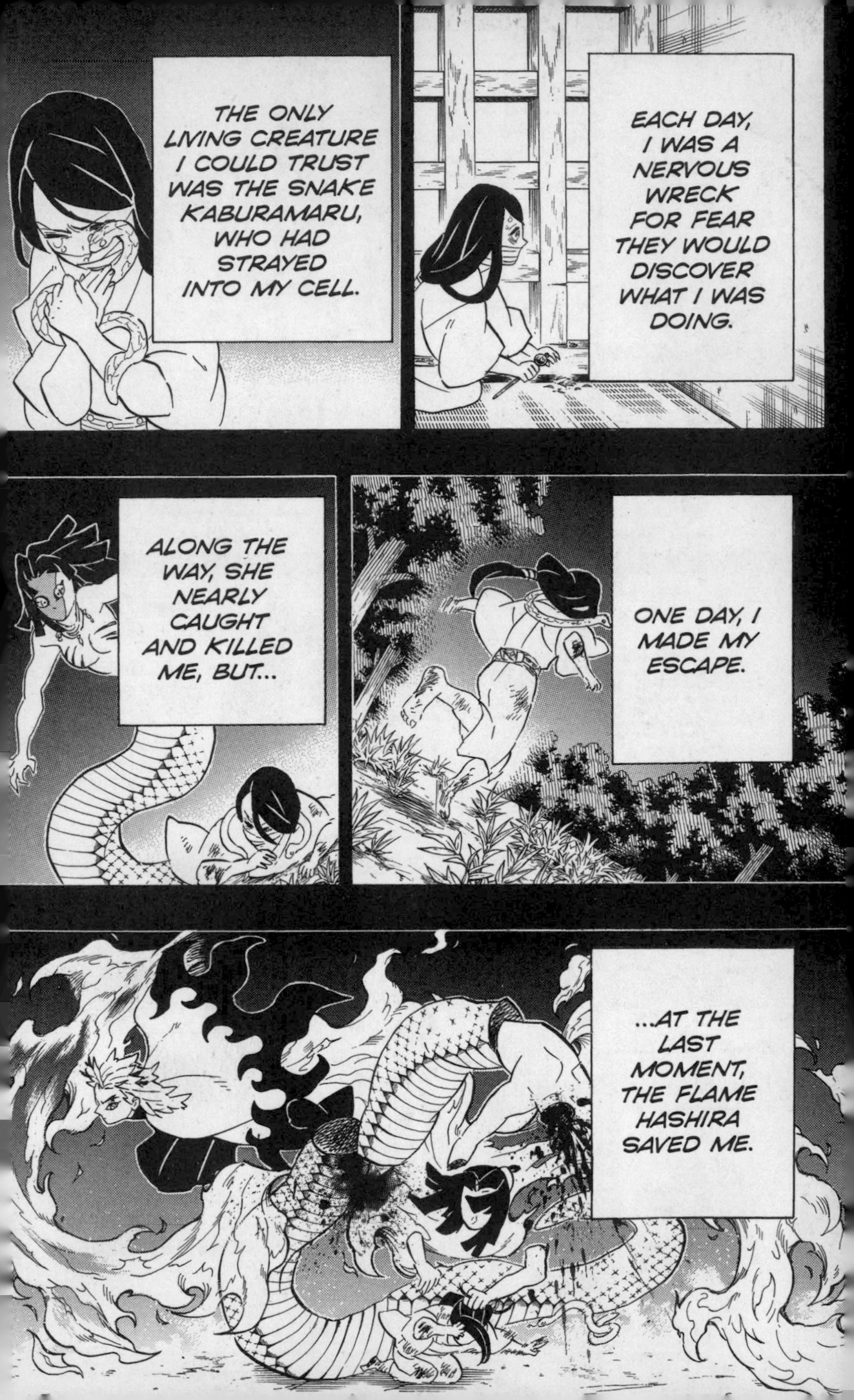
EACH DAY, I WAS A NERVOUS WRECK FOR FEAR THEY WOULD DISCOVER WHAT I WAS DOING.
THE ONLY LIVING CREATURE I COULD TRUST WAS THE SNAKE KABURAMARU, WHO HAD STRAYED INTO MY CELL.
ONE DAY, I MADE MY ESCAPE.
ALONG THE WAY, SHE NEARLY CAUGHT AND KILLED ME, BUT...
...AT THE LAST MOMENT, THE FLAME HASHIRA SAVED ME.

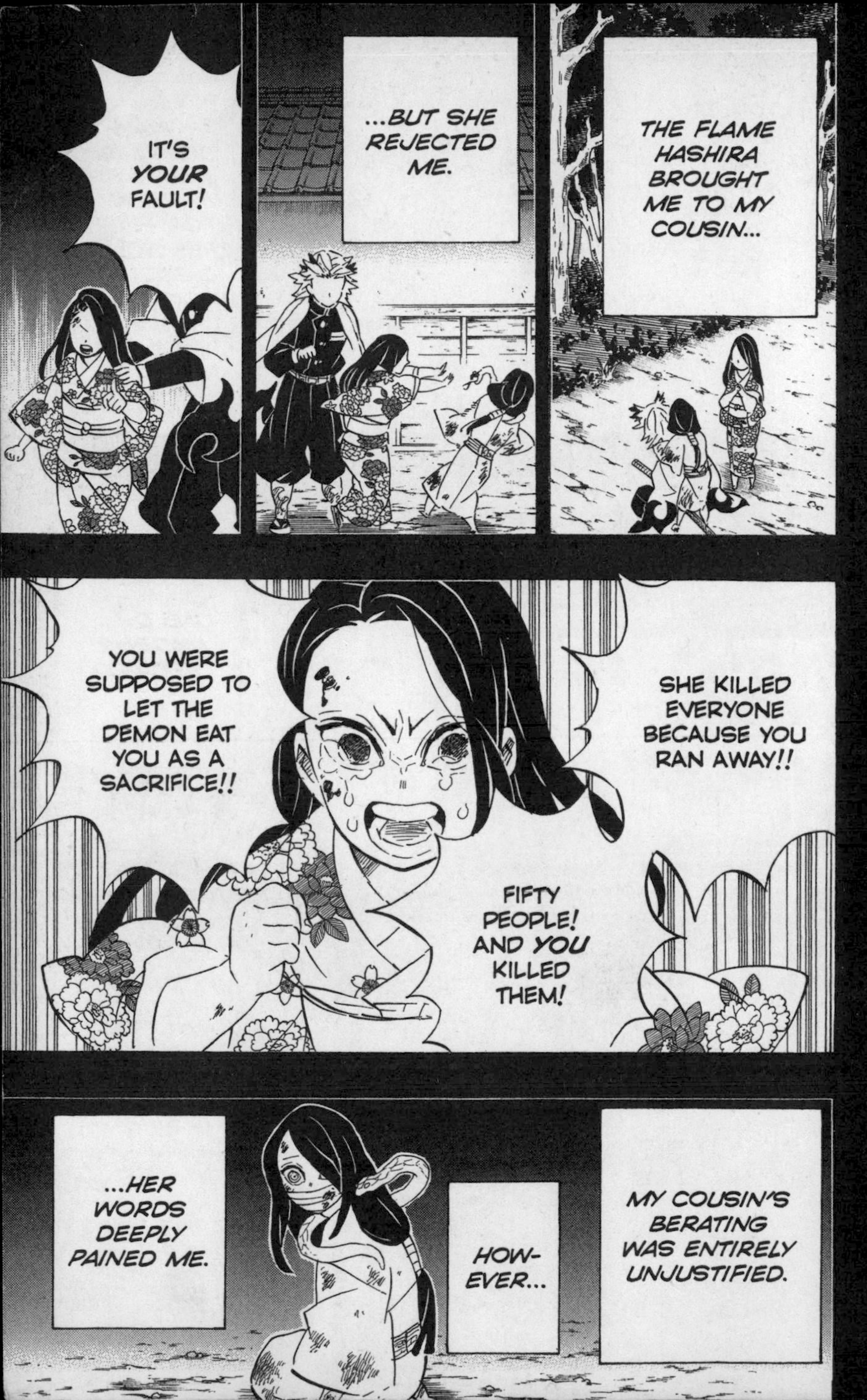
THE FLAME HASHIRA BROUGHT ME TO MY COUSIN...
...BUT SHE REJECTED ME.
IT'S *YOUR* FAULT!
SHE KILLED EVERYONE BECAUSE YOU RAN AWAY!!
YOU WERE SUPPOSED TO LET THE DEMON EAT YOU AS A SACRIFICE!!
FIFTY PEOPLE! AND *YOU* KILLED THEM!
MY COUSIN'S BERATING WAS ENTIRELY UNJUSTIFIED.
HOW-EVER...
...HER WORDS DEEPLY PAINED ME.

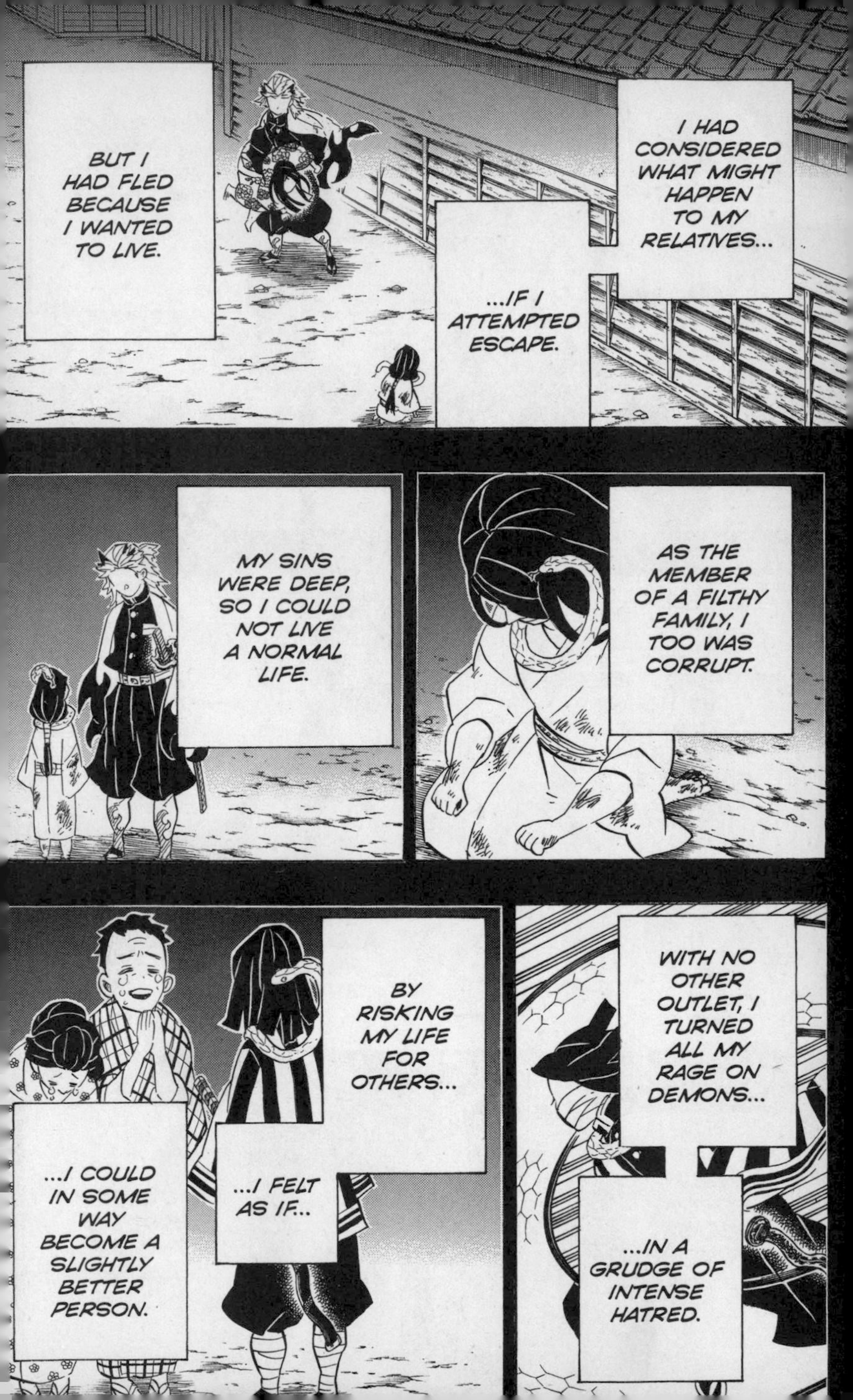
I HAD CONSIDERED WHAT MIGHT HAPPEN TO MY RELATIVES...
...IF I ATTEMPTED ESCAPE.
BUT I HAD FLED BECAUSE I WANTED TO LIVE.
AS THE MEMBER OF A FILTHY FAMILY, I TOO WAS CORRUPT.
MY SINS WERE DEEP, SO I COULD NOT LIVE A NORMAL LIFE.
WITH NO OTHER OUTLET, I TURNED ALL MY RAGE ON DEMONS...
...IN A GRUDGE OF INTENSE HATRED.
BY RISKING MY LIFE FOR OTHERS...
...I FELT AS IF...
...I COULD IN SOME WAY BECOME A SLIGHTLY BETTER PERSON.

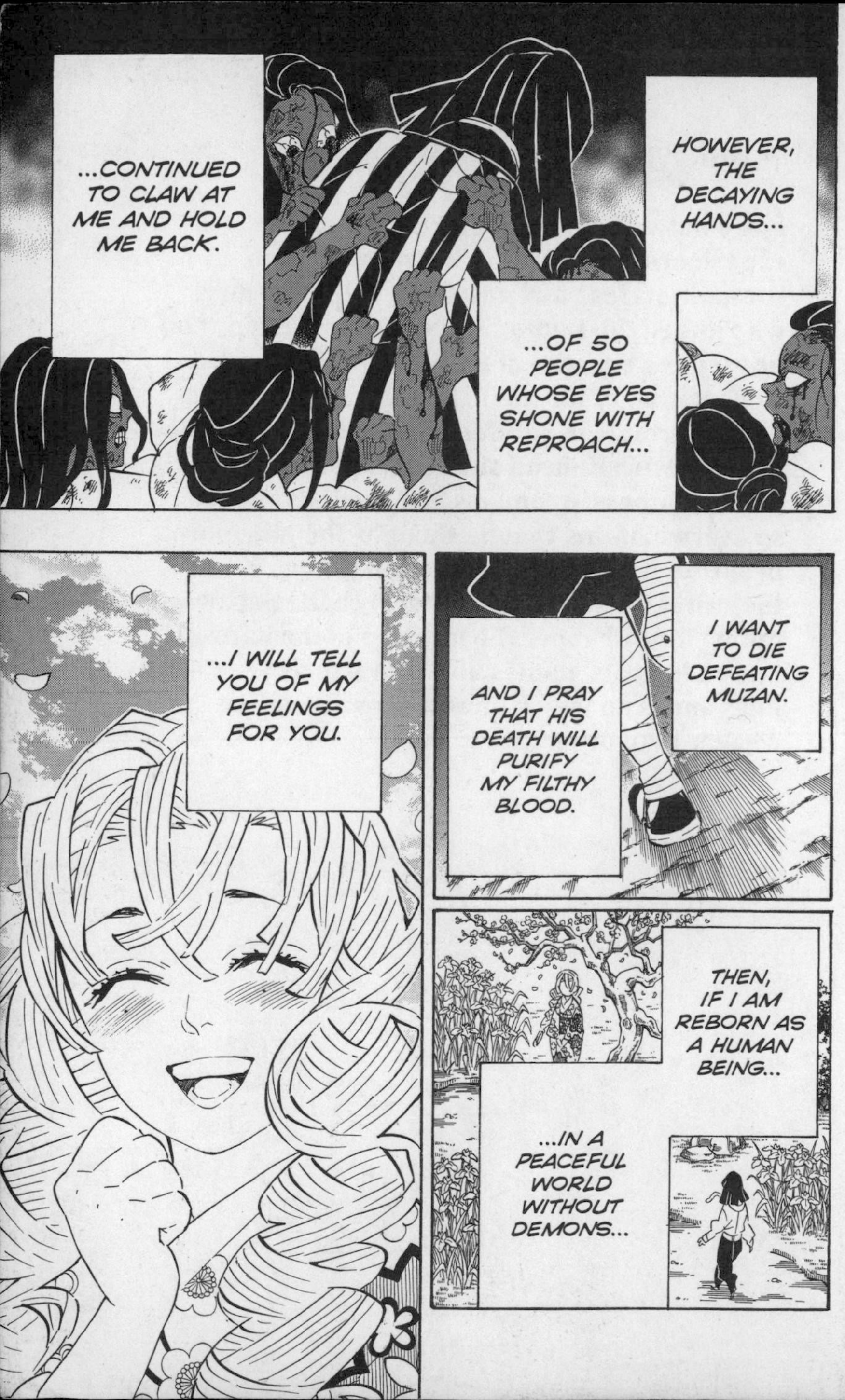
HOWEVER, THE DECAYING HANDS...
...OF 50 PEOPLE WHOSE EYES SHONE WITH REPROACH...
...CONTINUED TO CLAW AT ME AND HOLD ME BACK.
I WANT TO DIE DEFEATING MUZAN.
AND I PRAY THAT HIS DEATH WILL PURIFY MY FILTHY BLOOD.
THEN, IF I AM REBORN AS A HUMAN BEING...
...IN A PEACEFUL WORLD WITHOUT DEMONS...
...I WILL TELL YOU OF MY FEELINGS FOR YOU.

TAISHO WHISPERS

Iguro has difficulty with girls. Due to his experiences growing up, he was unable to conquer his fear and animosity. Plus, the girls who joined the Demon Slayer Corps often put on brave faces because of their sad backgrounds, so he felt sorry for them, making him uncomfortable in a different way. He was startled when Mitsuri Kanroji suddenly spoke to him. Her brightness, openness and kindness were so overwhelming that he thought she was more beautiful than anyone else. Even though it was their first time meeting, Mitsuri chattered away, telling him all about the makeup of the Kanroji family, her cats' names and characteristics, their likes and even which ones were stronger or weaker than others.

Talking fervently about her darling cats (4) →

Learning everything about her cats at their first meeting

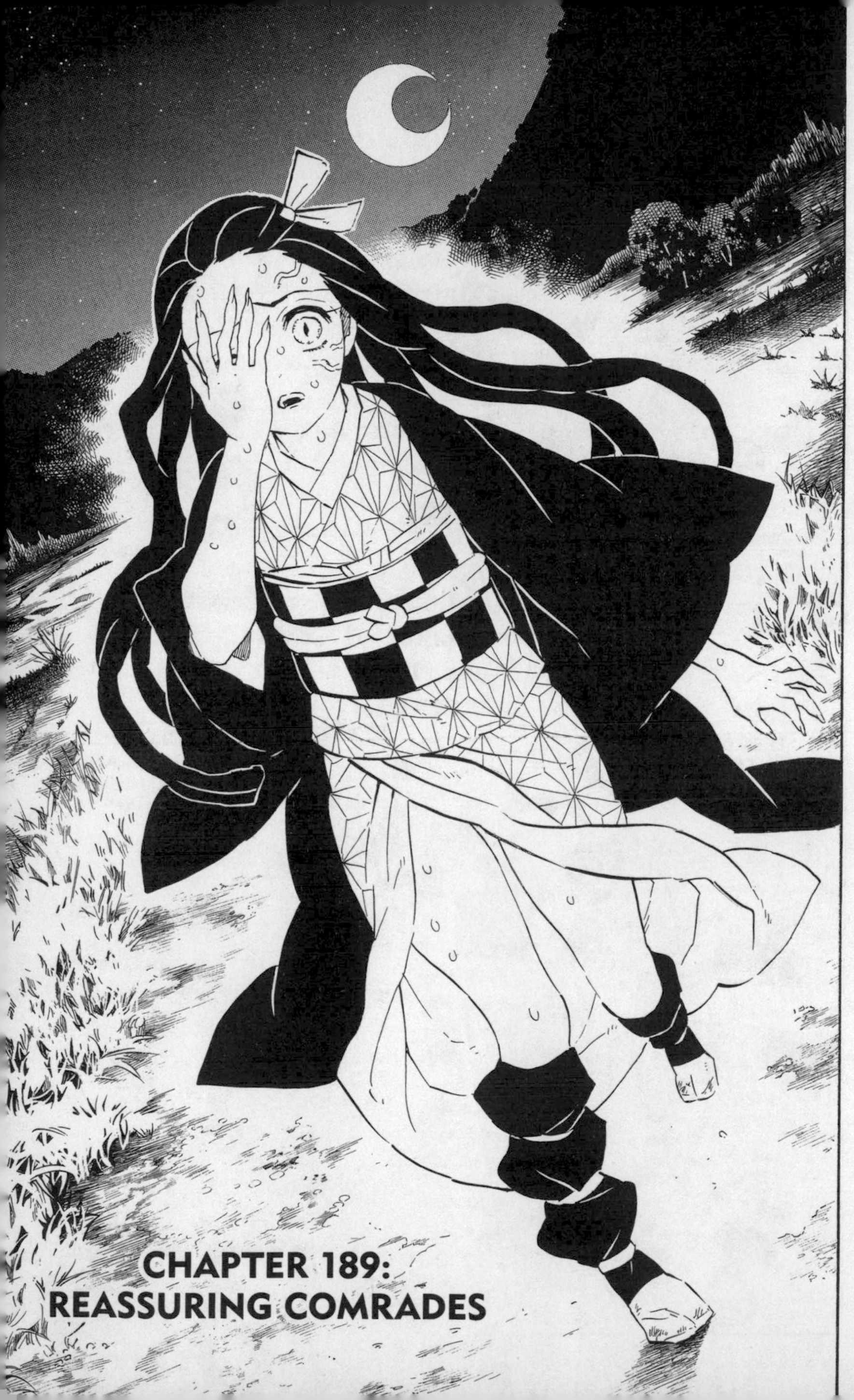
CHAPTER 189:
REASSURING COMRADES

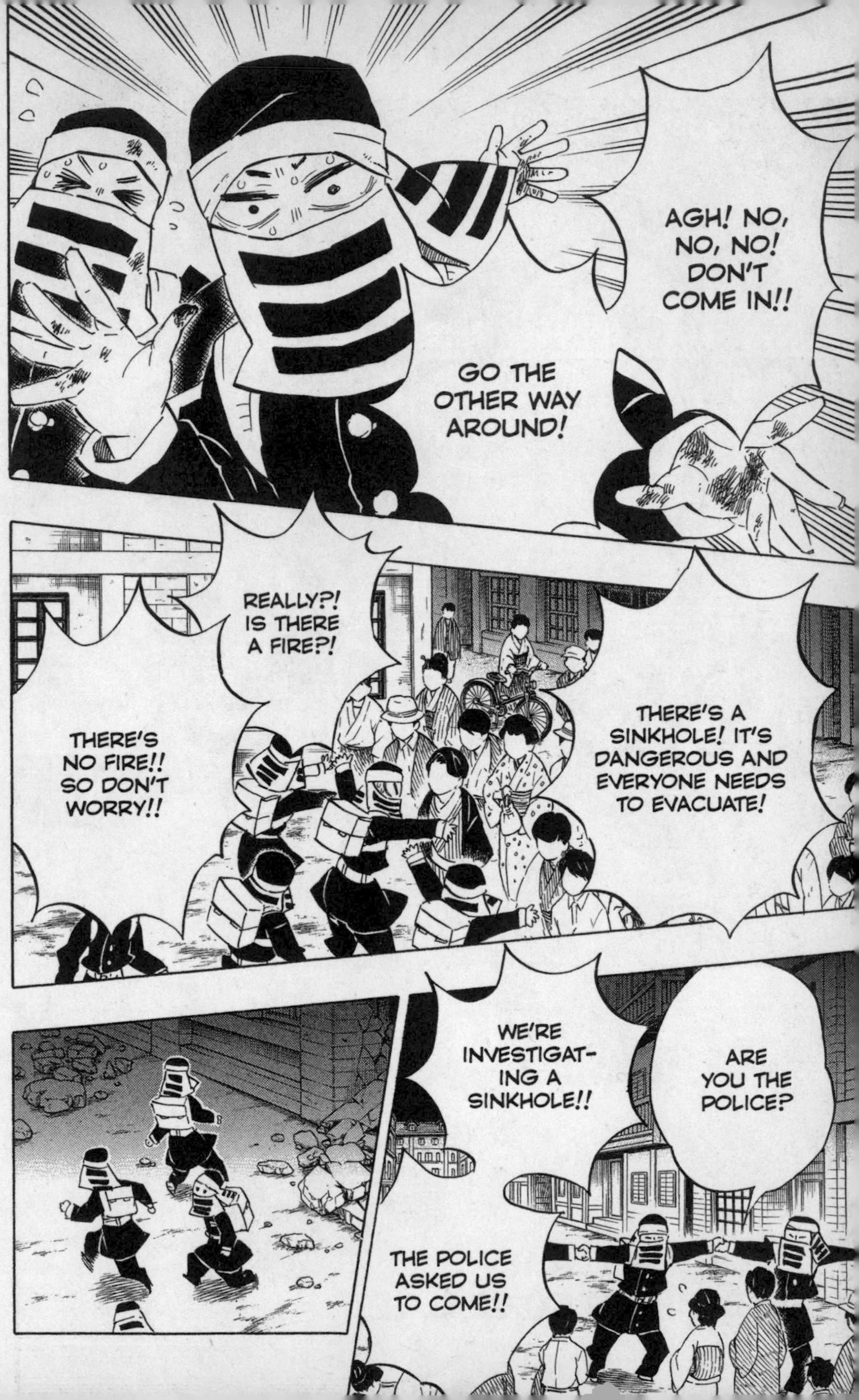
AGH! NO, NO, NO! DON'T COME IN!!
GO THE OTHER WAY AROUND!
REALLY?! IS THERE A FIRE?!
THERE'S NO FIRE!! SO DON'T WORRY!!
THERE'S A SINKHOLE! IT'S DANGEROUS AND EVERYONE NEEDS TO EVACUATE!
ARE YOU THE POLICE?
WE'RE INVESTIGAT-ING A SINKHOLE!!
THE POLICE ASKED US TO COME!!

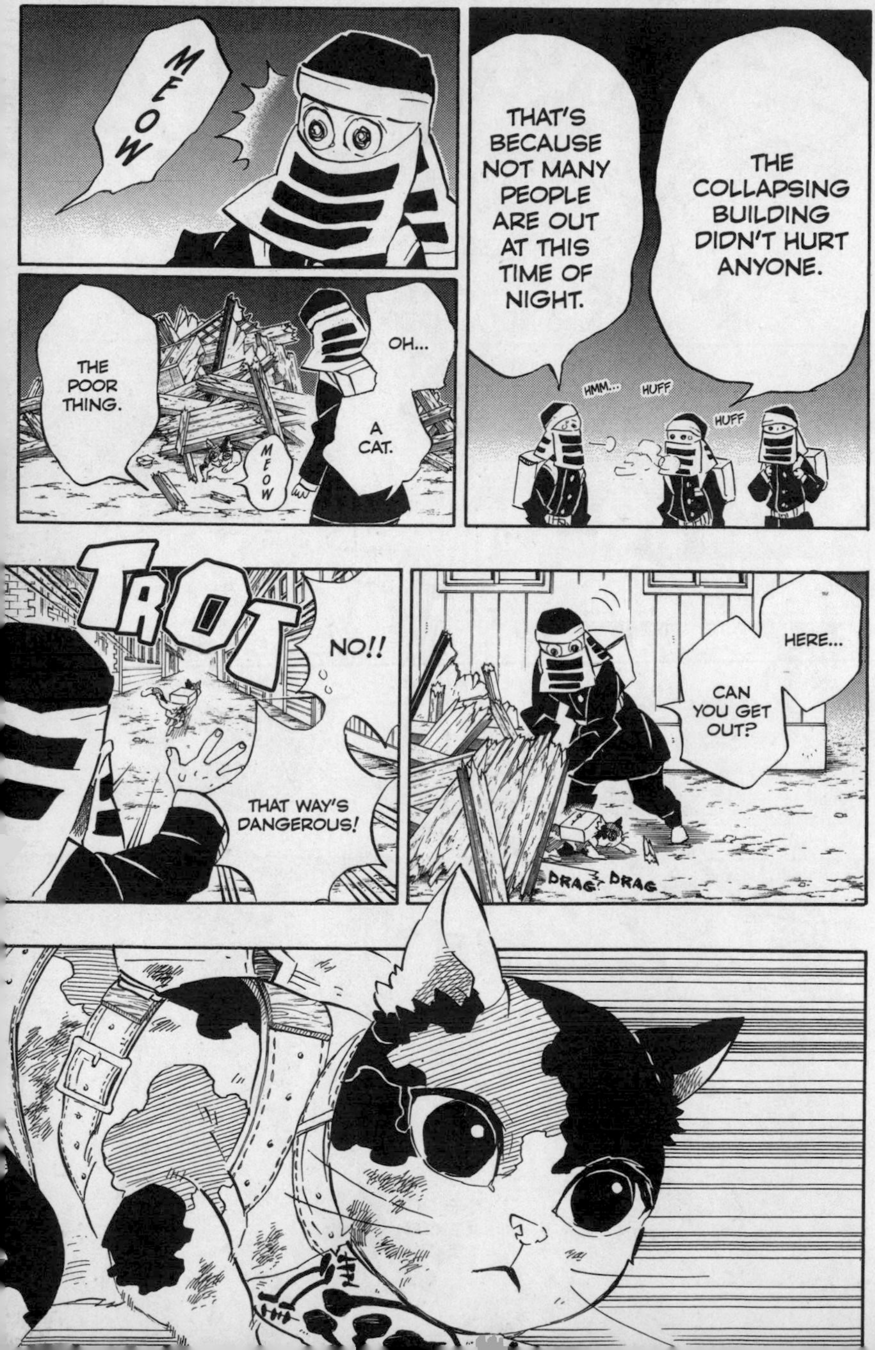
THE COLLAPSING BUILDING DIDN'T HURT ANYONE.
THAT'S BECAUSE NOT MANY PEOPLE ARE OUT AT THIS TIME OF NIGHT.
HMM...
HUFF
HUFF
MEOW
OH...
A CAT.
MEOW
THE POOR THING.
HERE...
CAN YOU GET OUT?
DRAG DRAG
TROT
NO!!
THAT WAY'S DANGEROUS!

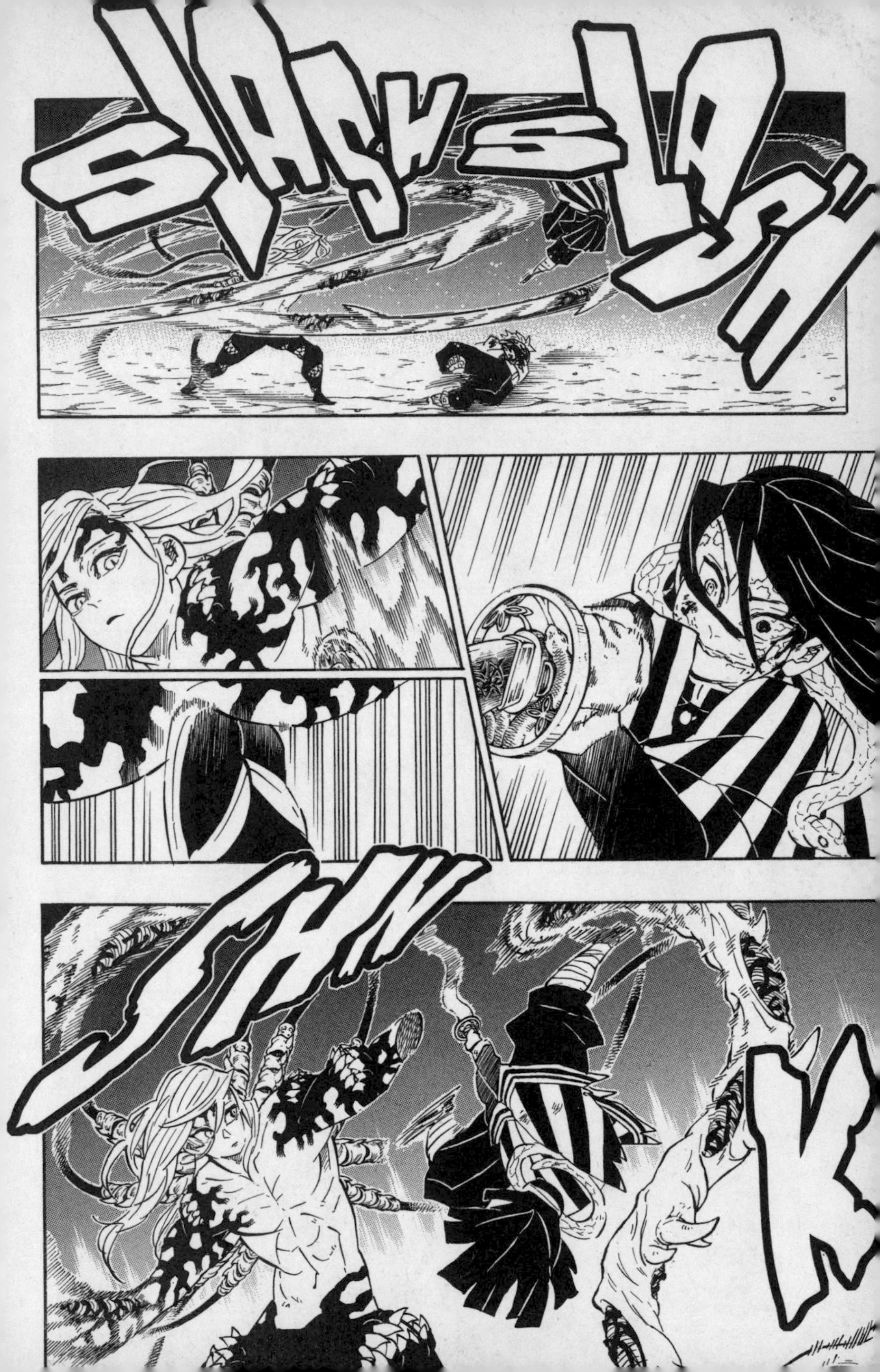
SLASH SLASH

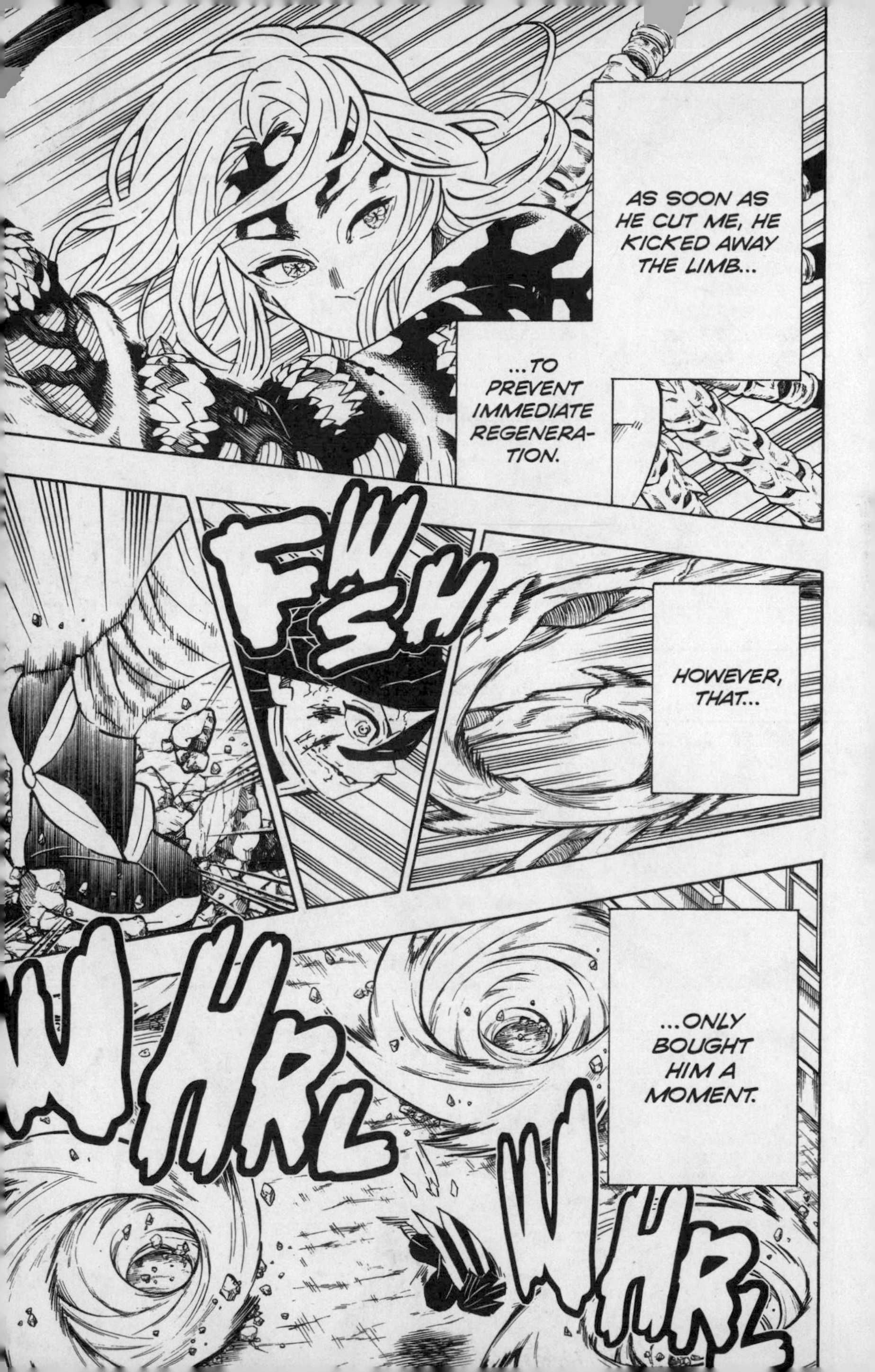
AS SOON AS HE CUT ME, HE KICKED AWAY THE LIMB...
...TO PREVENT IMMEDIATE REGENERA-TION.
HOWEVER, THAT...
FWSH
...ONLY BOUGHT HIM A MOMENT.
WHRL
WHR

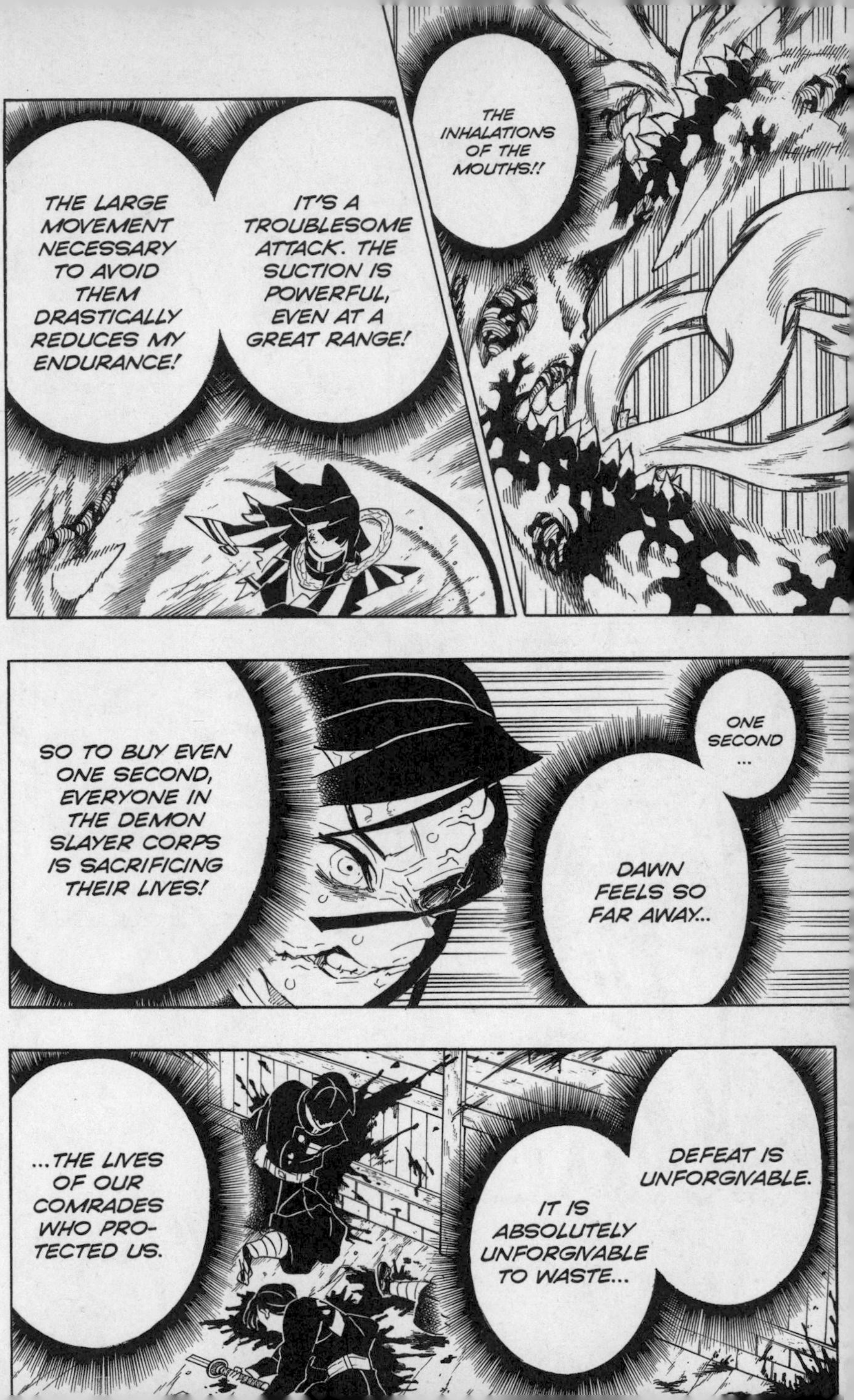
THE INHALATIONS OF THE MOUTHS!!
IT'S A TROUBLESOME ATTACK. THE SUCTION IS POWERFUL, EVEN AT A GREAT RANGE!
THE LARGE MOVEMENT NECESSARY TO AVOID THEM DRASTICALLY REDUCES MY ENDURANCE!
ONE SECOND ...
DAWN FEELS SO FAR AWAY...
SO TO BUY EVEN ONE SECOND, EVERYONE IN THE DEMON SLAYER CORPS IS SACRIFICING THEIR LIVES!
DEFEAT IS UNFORGIVABLE.
IT IS ABSOLUTELY UNFORGIVABLE TO WASTE...
...THE LIVES OF OUR COMRADES WHO PROTECTED US.

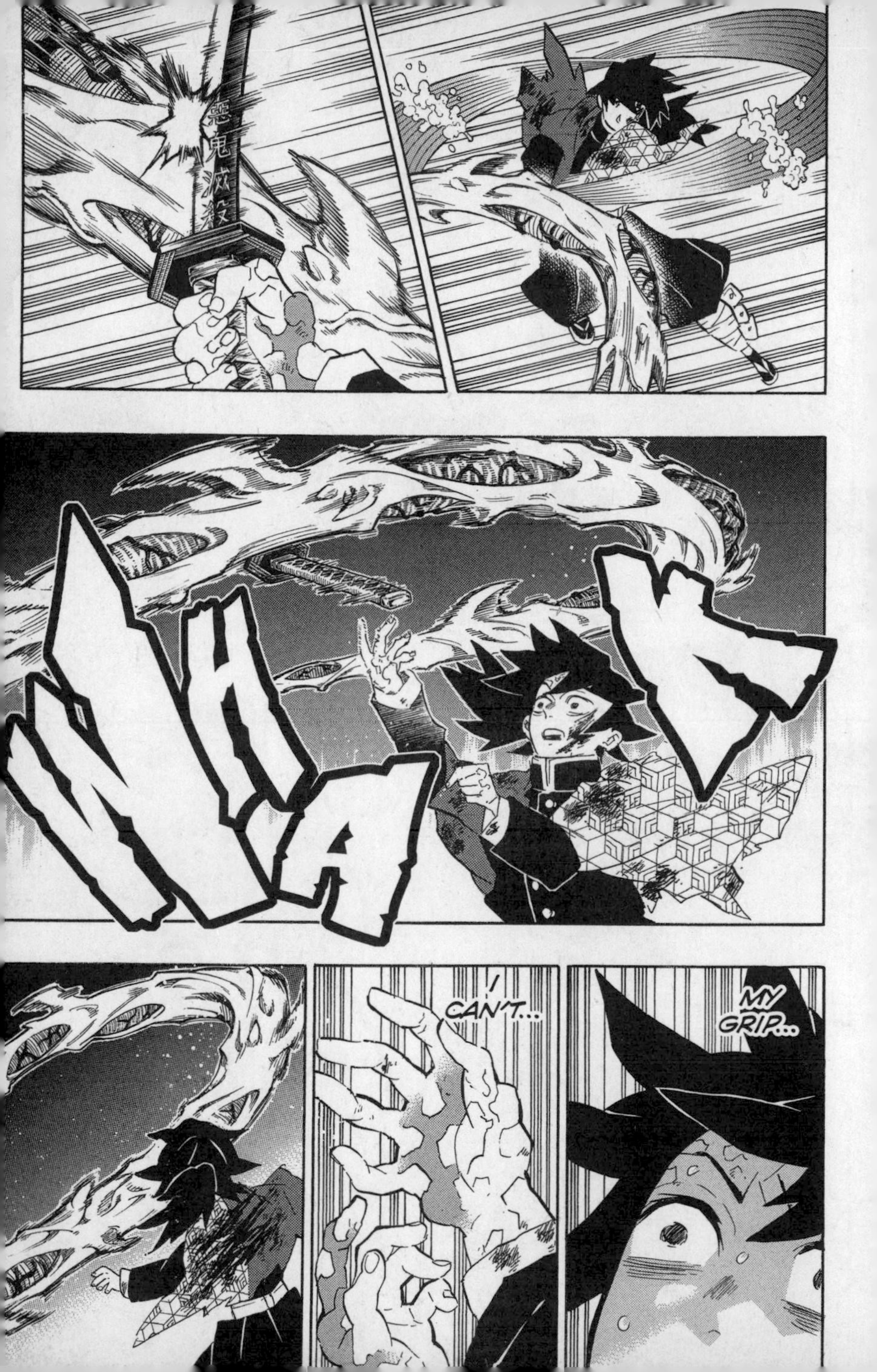
悪鬼滅殺
WHA
MY GRIP...
I CAN'T...

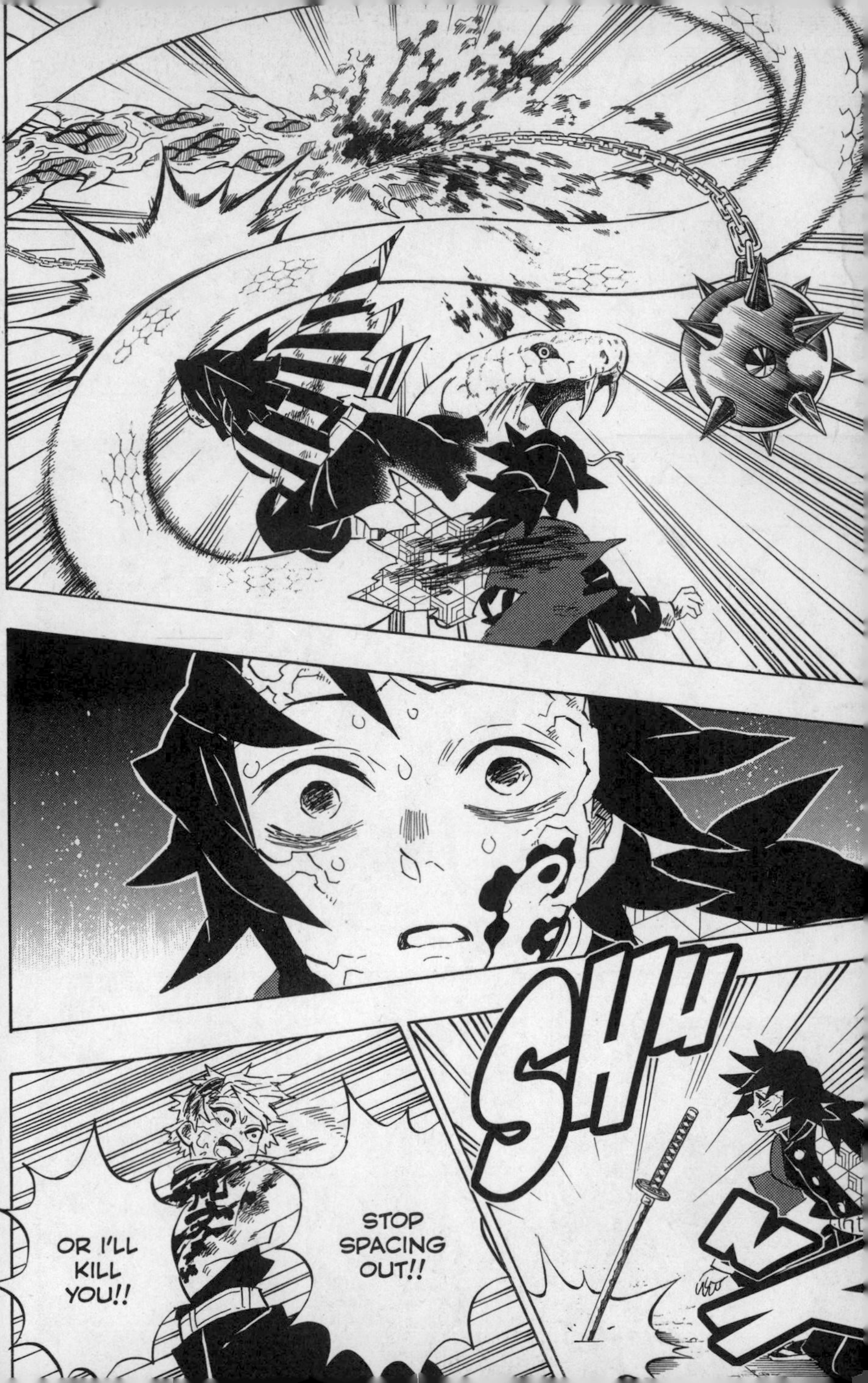
SHU
STOP SPACING OUT!!
OR I'LL KILL YOU!!

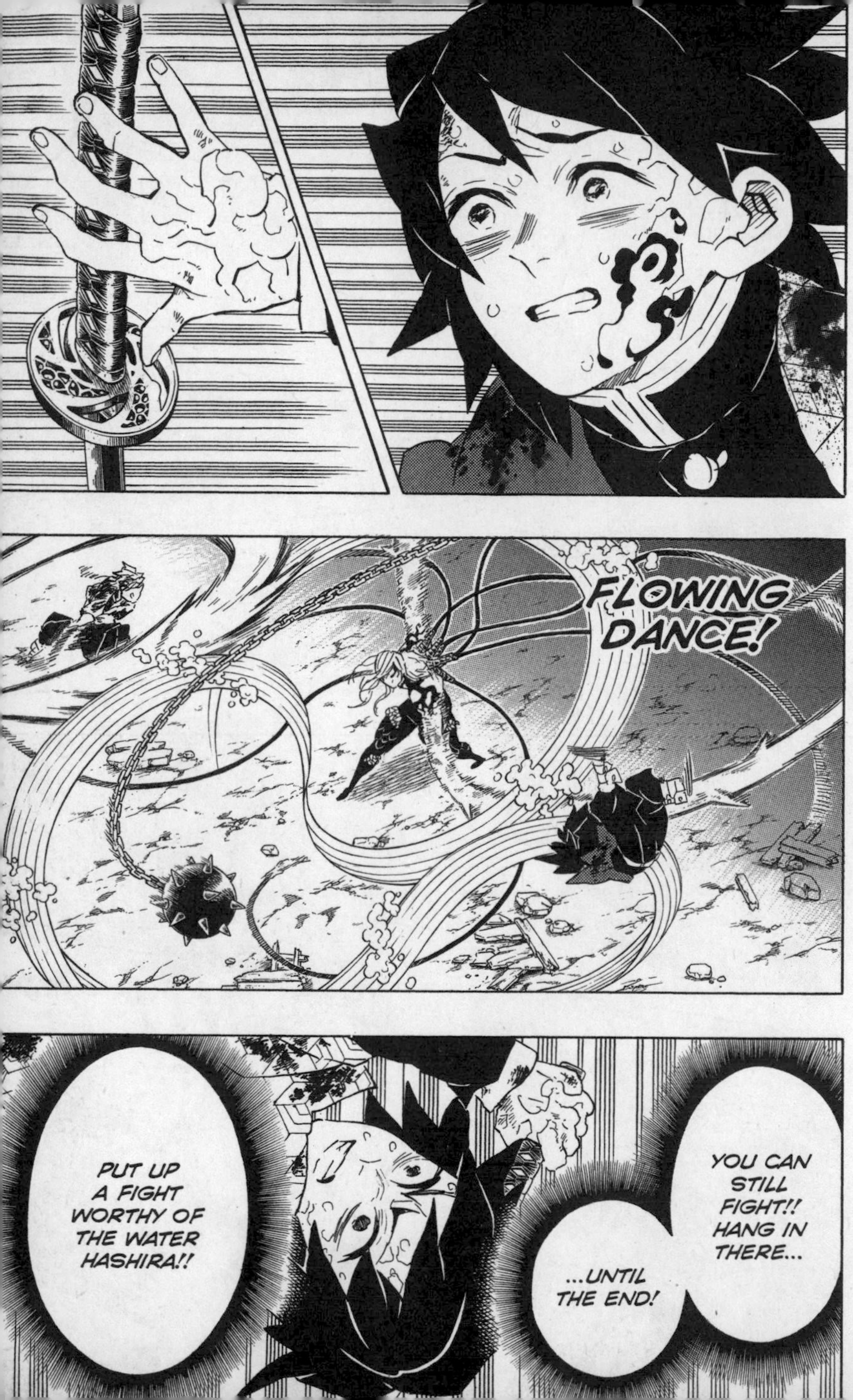
FLOWING DANCE!
YOU CAN STILL FIGHT!! HANG IN THERE...
...UNTIL THE END!
PUT UP A FIGHT WORTHY OF THE WATER HASHIRA!!

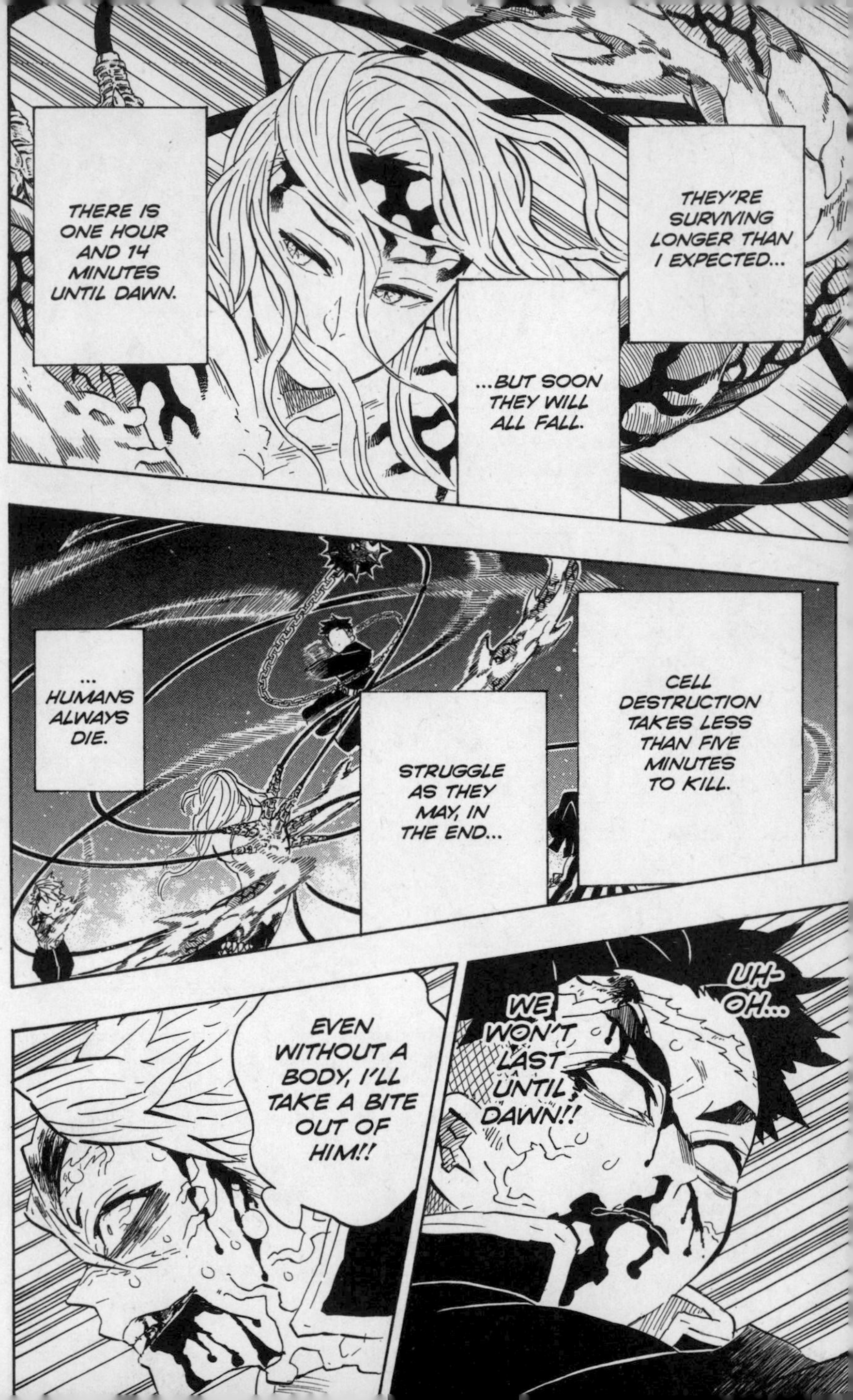
THEY'RE SURVIVING LONGER THAN I EXPECTED...
...BUT SOON THEY WILL ALL FALL.
THERE IS ONE HOUR AND 14 MINUTES UNTIL DAWN.
CELL DESTRUCTION TAKES LESS THAN FIVE MINUTES TO KILL.
STRUGGLE AS THEY MAY, IN THE END...
... HUMANS ALWAYS DIE.
UH-OH...
WE WON'T LAST UNTIL DAWN!!
EVEN WITHOUT A BODY, I'LL TAKE A BITE OUT OF HIM!!

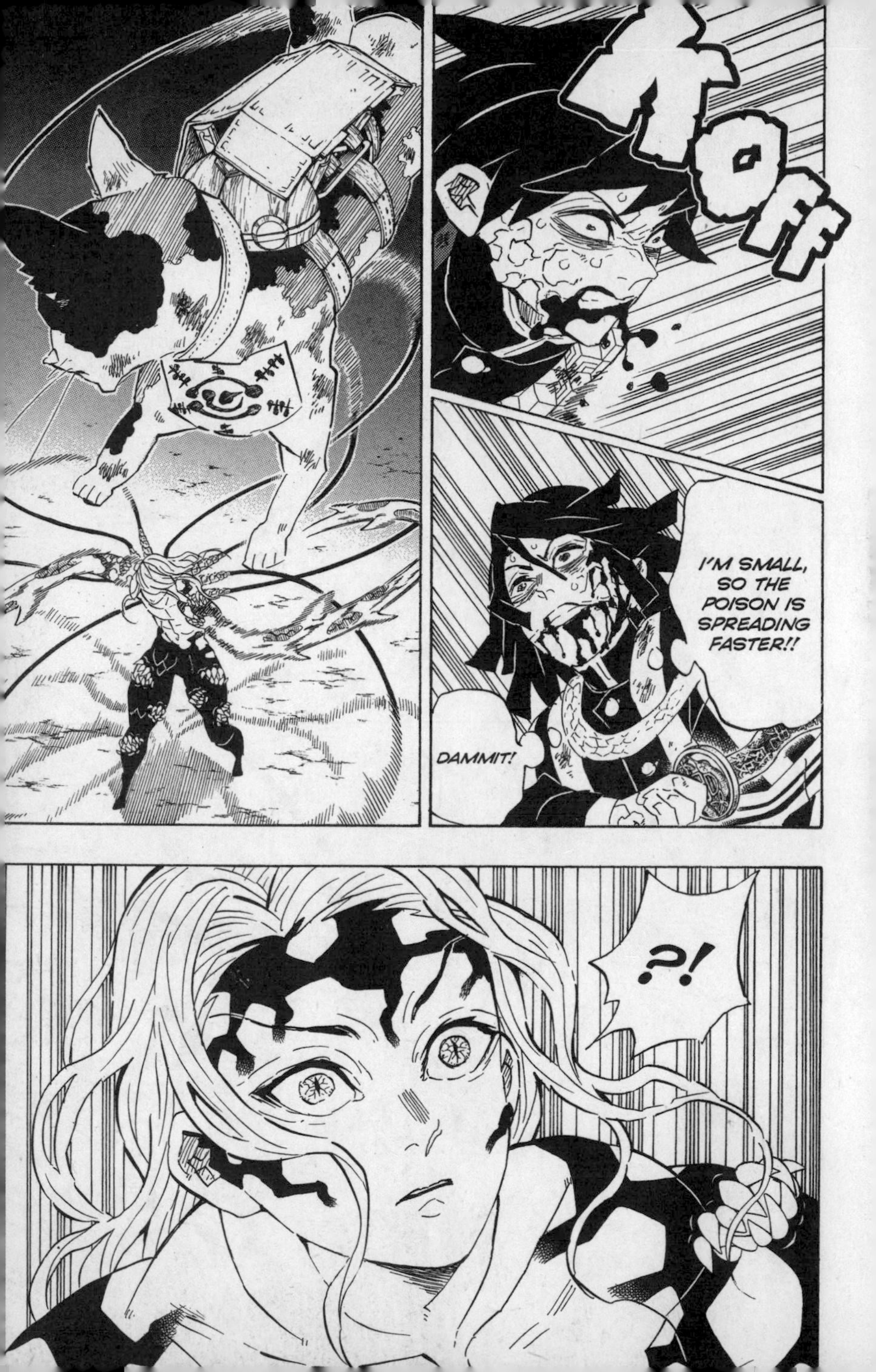
KOFF
I'M SMALL, SO THE POISON IS SPREADING FASTER!!
DAMMIT!
?!

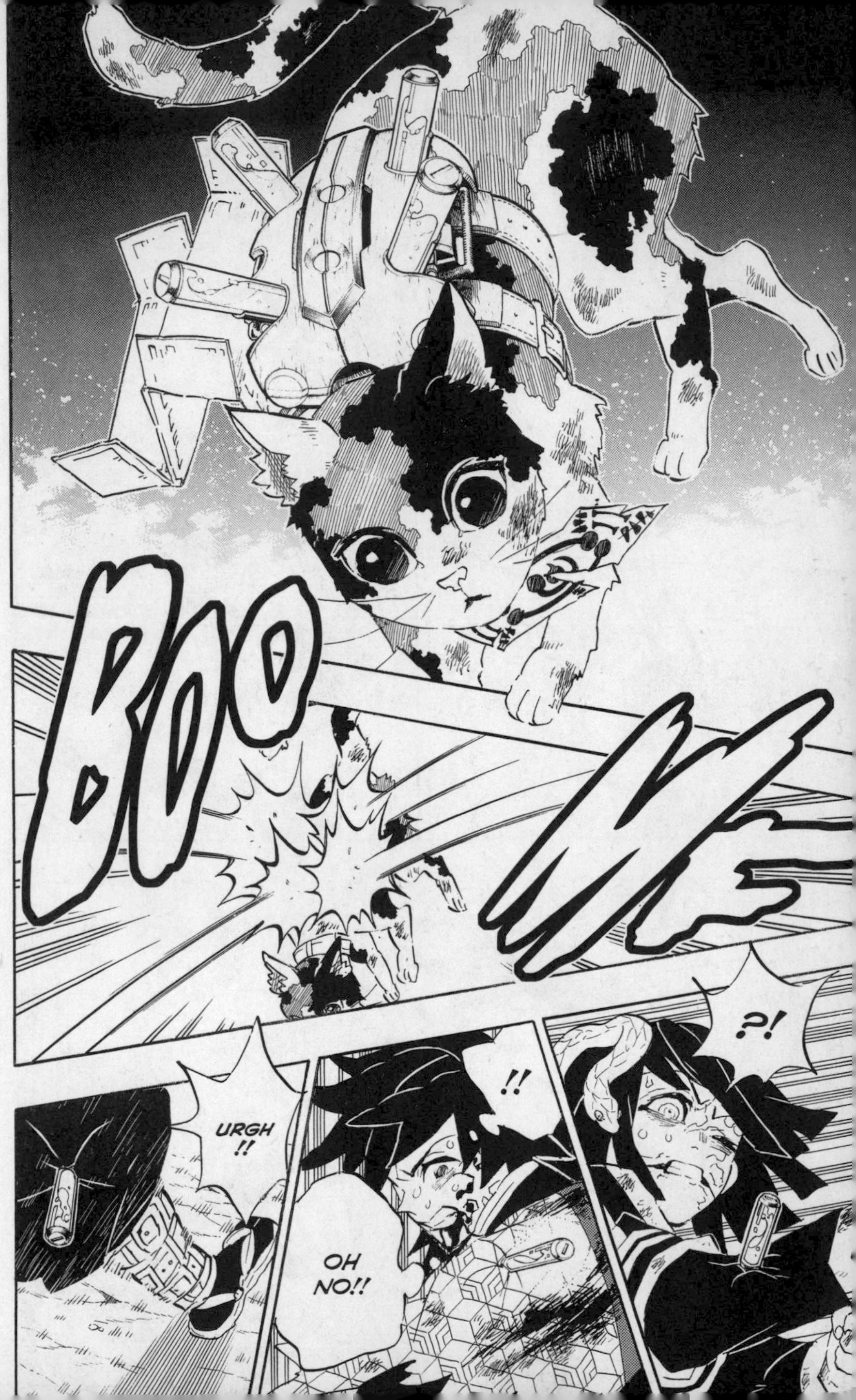
BOOM
?!
!!
OH NO!!
URGH !!

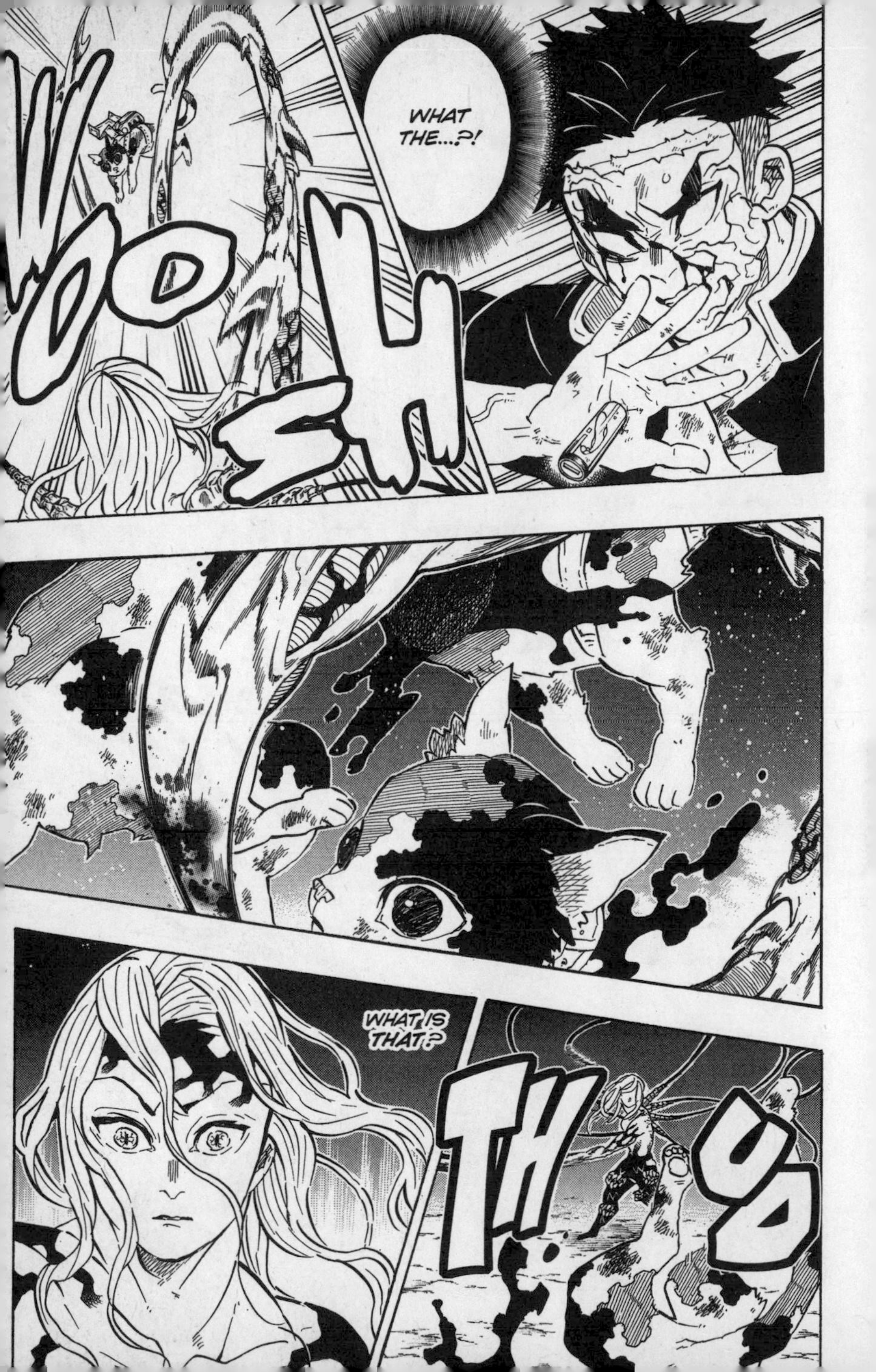
WHAT THE...?!
WOOSH
THUD
WHAT IS THAT?

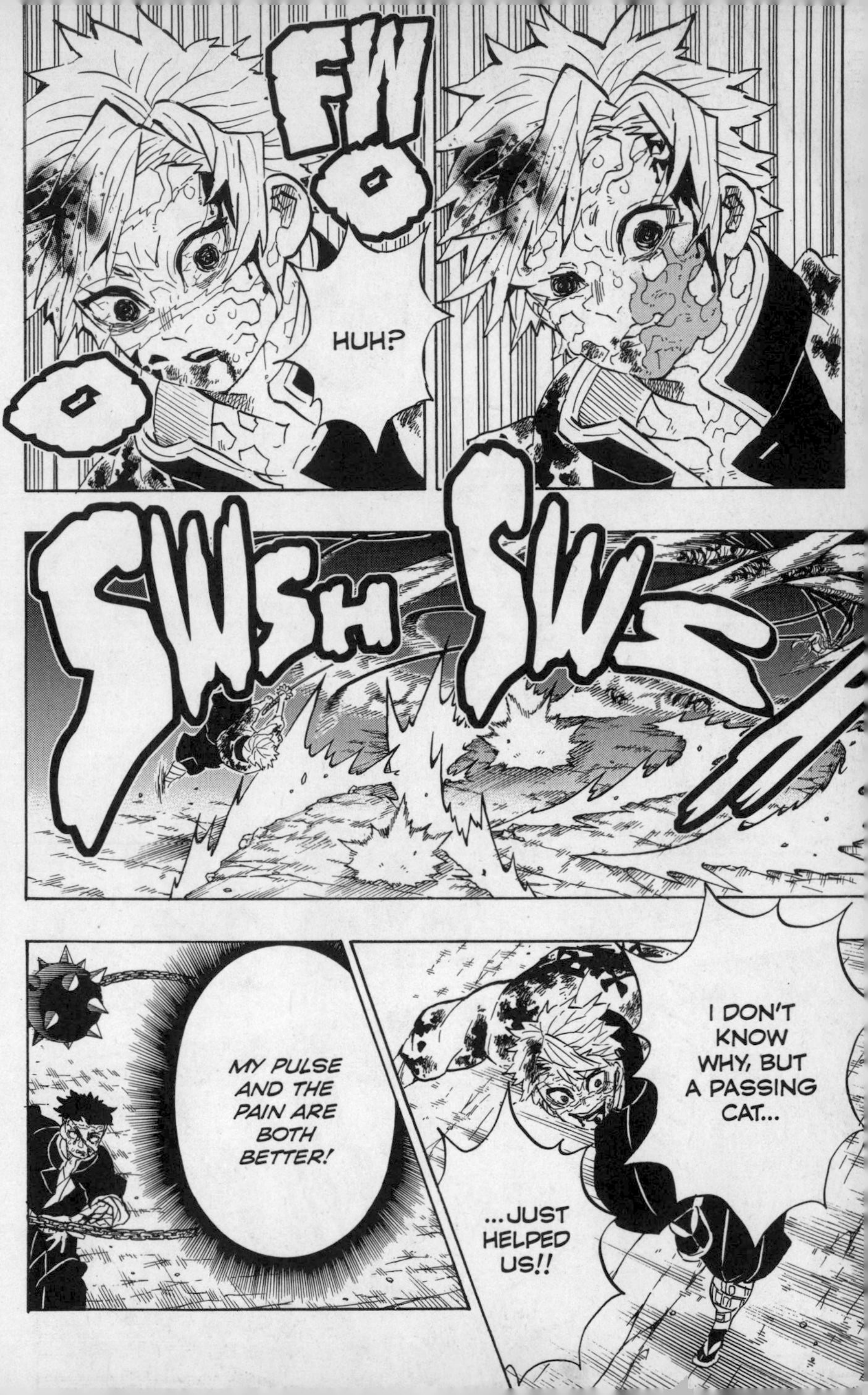
FW
HUH?
FWSH
I DON'T KNOW WHY, BUT A PASSING CAT...
...JUST HELPED US!!
MY PULSE AND THE PAIN ARE BOTH BETTER!

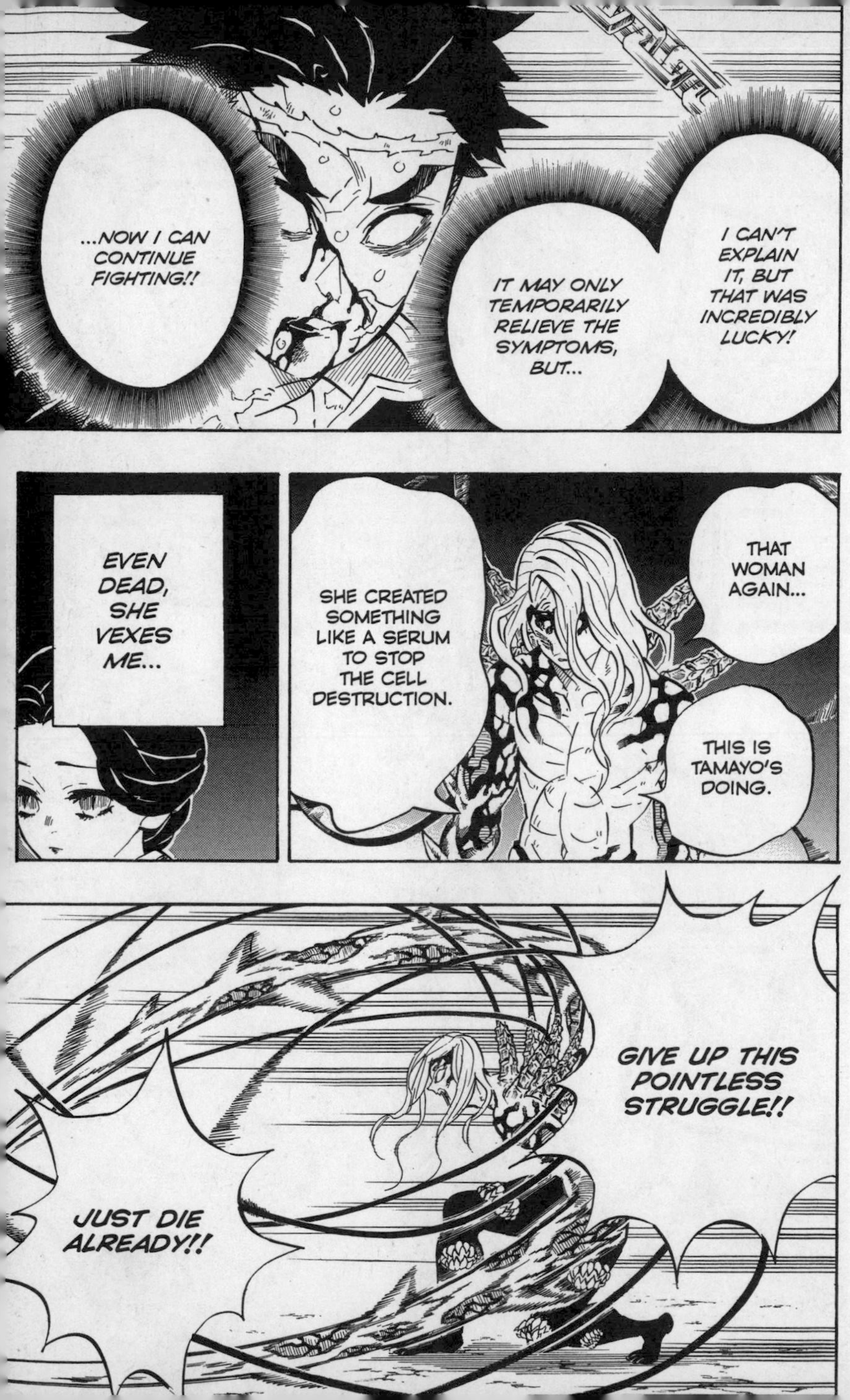
I CAN'T EXPLAIN IT, BUT THAT WAS INCREDIBLY LUCKY!
IT MAY ONLY TEMPORARILY RELIEVE THE SYMPTOMS, BUT...
...NOW I CAN CONTINUE FIGHTING!!
THAT WOMAN AGAIN...
THIS IS TAMAYO'S DOING.
SHE CREATED SOMETHING LIKE A SERUM TO STOP THE CELL DESTRUCTION.
EVEN DEAD, SHE VEXES ME...
GIVE UP THIS POINTLESS STRUGGLE!!
JUST DIE ALREADY!!

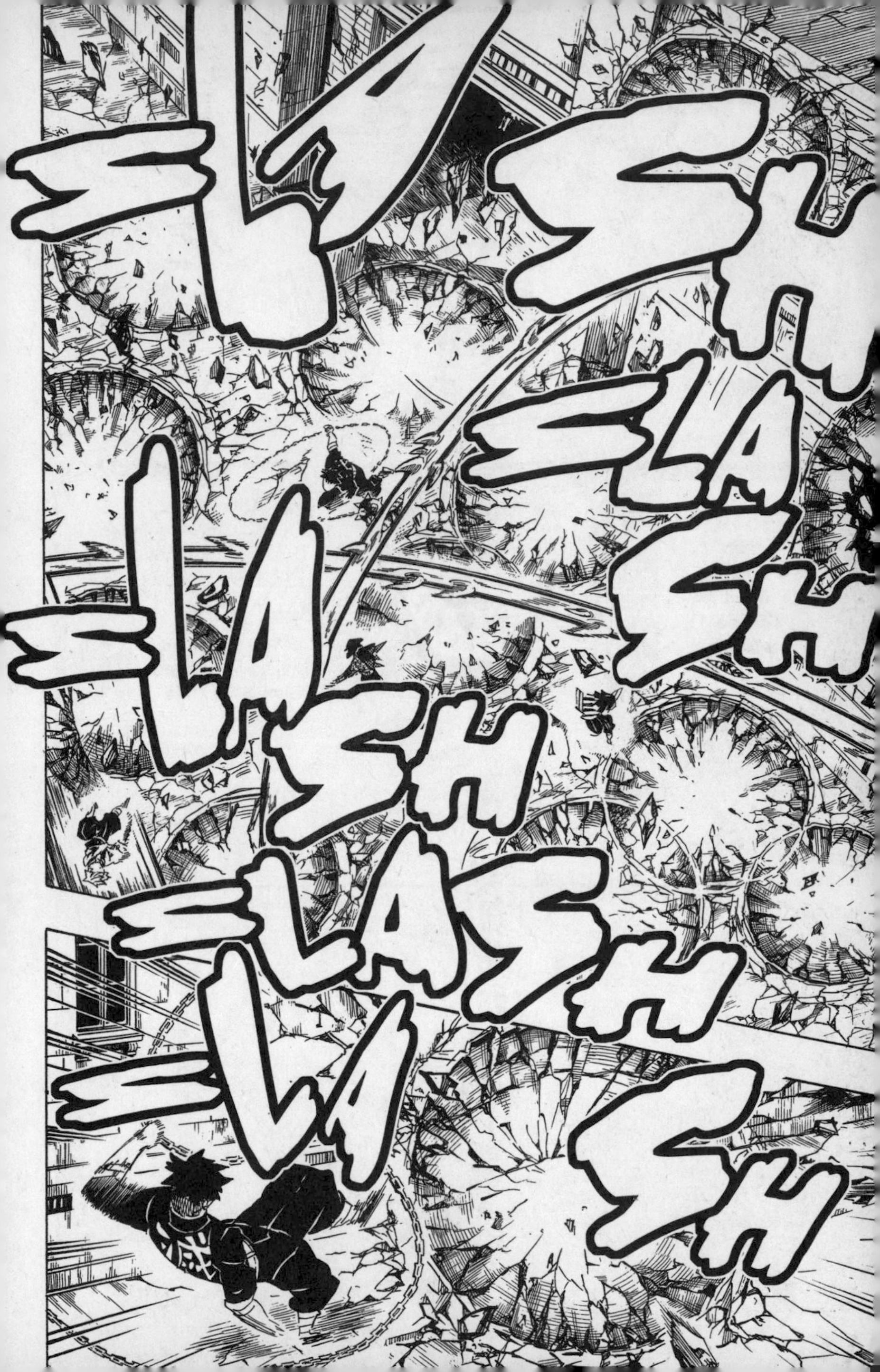
SLASH
SLASH
SLASH
SLASH
SLASH

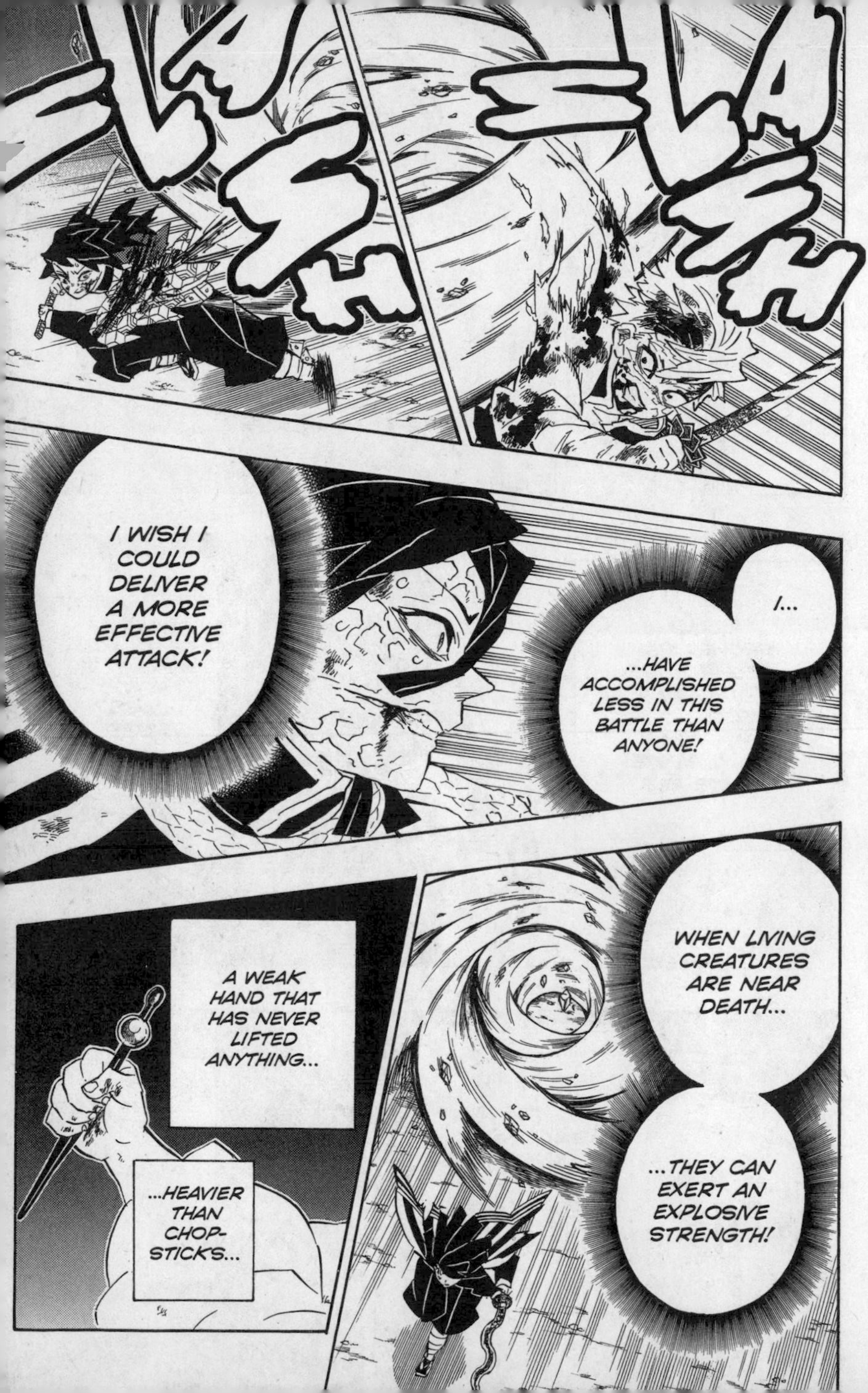
SLASH
SLASH
I...
...HAVE ACCOMPLISHED LESS IN THIS BATTLE THAN ANYONE!
I WISH I COULD DELIVER A MORE EFFECTIVE ATTACK!
WHEN LIVING CREATURES ARE NEAR DEATH...
...THEY CAN EXERT AN EXPLOSIVE STRENGTH!
A WEAK HAND THAT HAS NEVER LIFTED ANYTHING...
...HEAVIER THAN CHOP-STICKS...

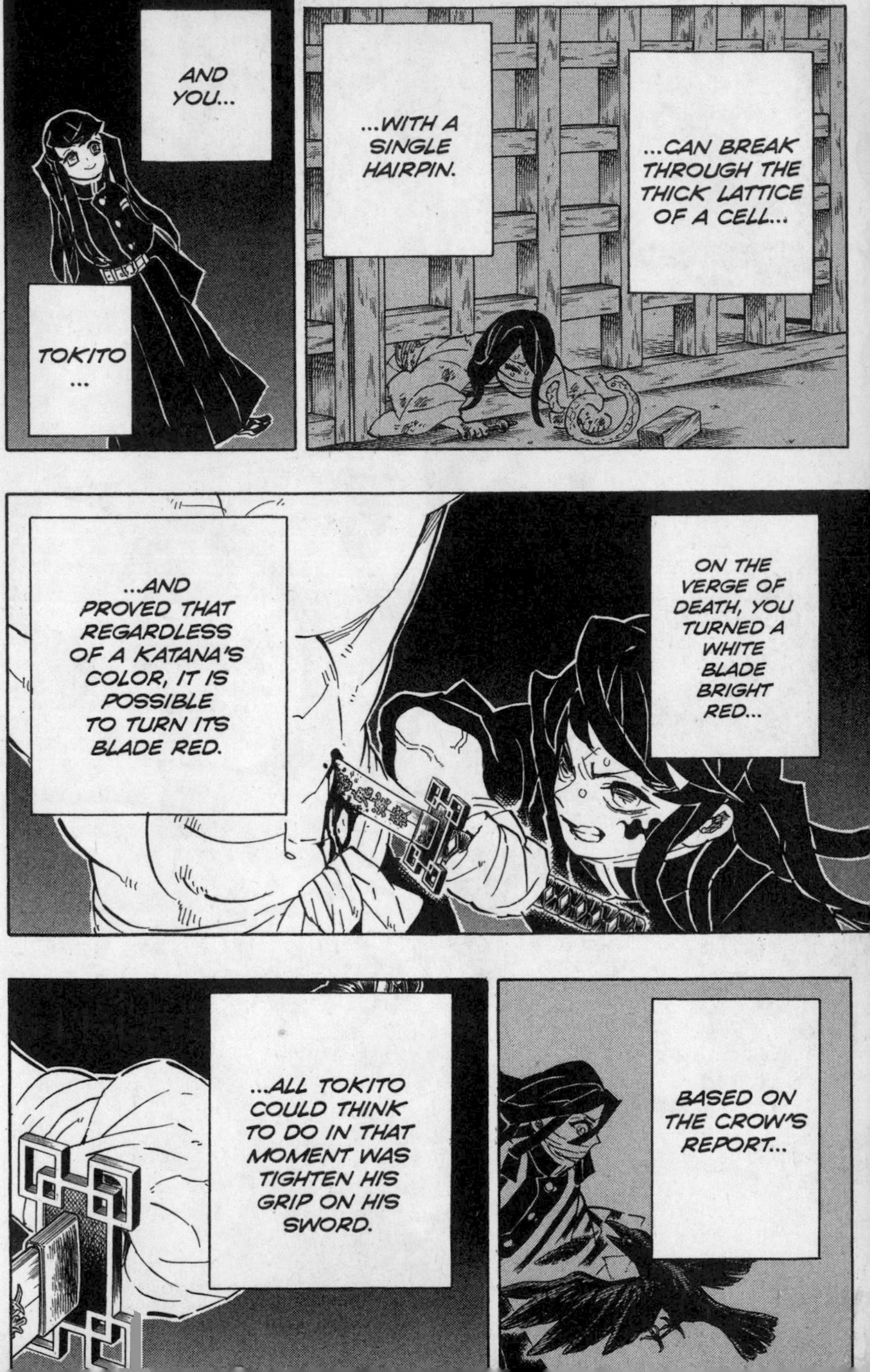
...CAN BREAK THROUGH THE THICK LATTICE OF A CELL...
...WITH A SINGLE HAIRPIN.
AND YOU...
TOKITO ...
ON THE VERGE OF DEATH, YOU TURNED A WHITE BLADE BRIGHT RED...
...AND PROVED THAT REGARDLESS OF A KATANA'S COLOR, IT IS POSSIBLE TO TURN ITS BLADE RED.
BASED ON THE CROW'S REPORT...
...ALL TOKITO COULD THINK TO DO IN THAT MOMENT WAS TIGHTEN HIS GRIP ON HIS SWORD.

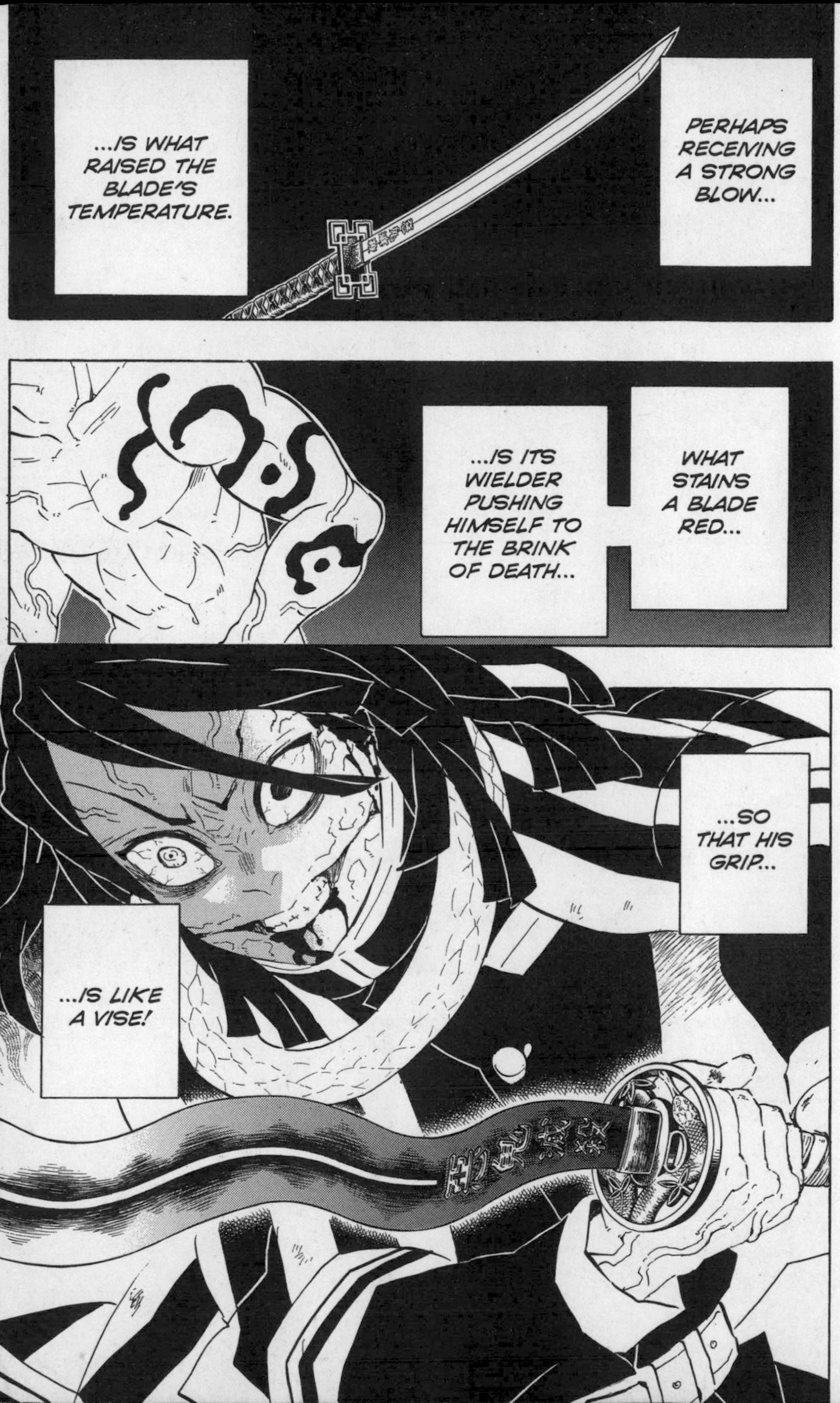
PERHAPS RECEIVING A STRONG BLOW...
...IS WHAT RAISED THE BLADE'S TEMPERATURE.
WHAT STAINS A BLADE RED...
...IS ITS WIELDER PUSHING HIMSELF TO THE BRINK OF DEATH...
...SO THAT HIS GRIP...
...IS LIKE A VISE!

Can't unsheathe. Seriously. It's impossible.
Iguro's scabbard is leather. Otherwise, he wouldn't be able to unsheathe his sword due to its wavy shape.
Open-sided scabbard
Tecchin's son Gantetsu made it.
Akkimessatsu
Like this.
Iguchi
Fastens with weak magnets
Wraps around the blade

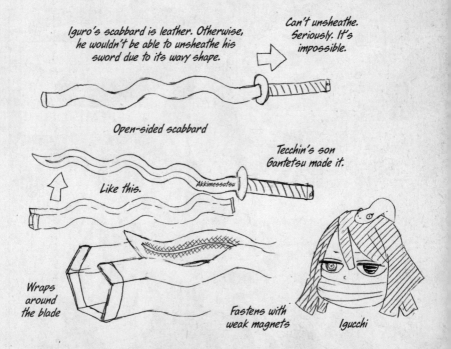

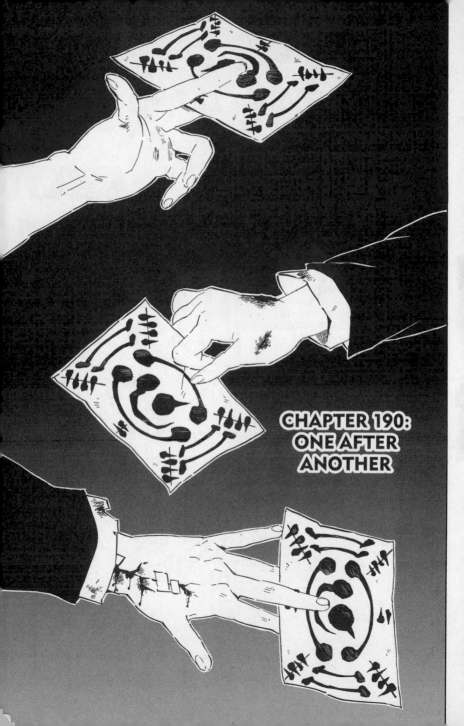

CHAPTER 190:
ONE AFTER
ANOTHER

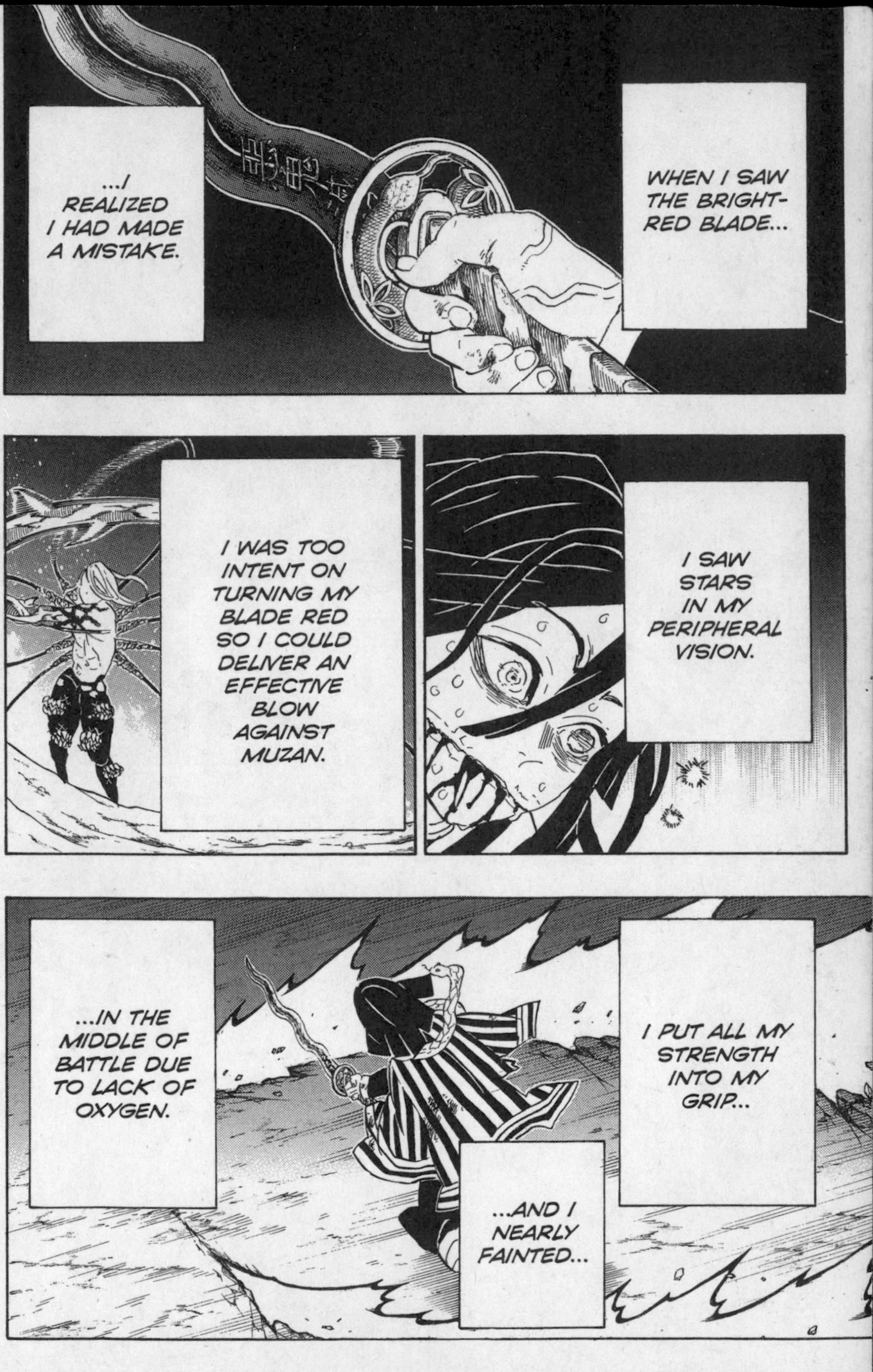
WHEN I SAW THE BRIGHT-RED BLADE...
...I REALIZED I HAD MADE A MISTAKE.
I SAW STARS IN MY PERIPHERAL VISION.
I WAS TOO INTENT ON TURNING MY BLADE RED SO I COULD DELIVER AN EFFECTIVE BLOW AGAINST MUZAN.
I PUT ALL MY STRENGTH INTO MY GRIP...
...AND I NEARLY FAINTED...
...IN THE MIDDLE OF BATTLE DUE TO LACK OF OXYGEN.

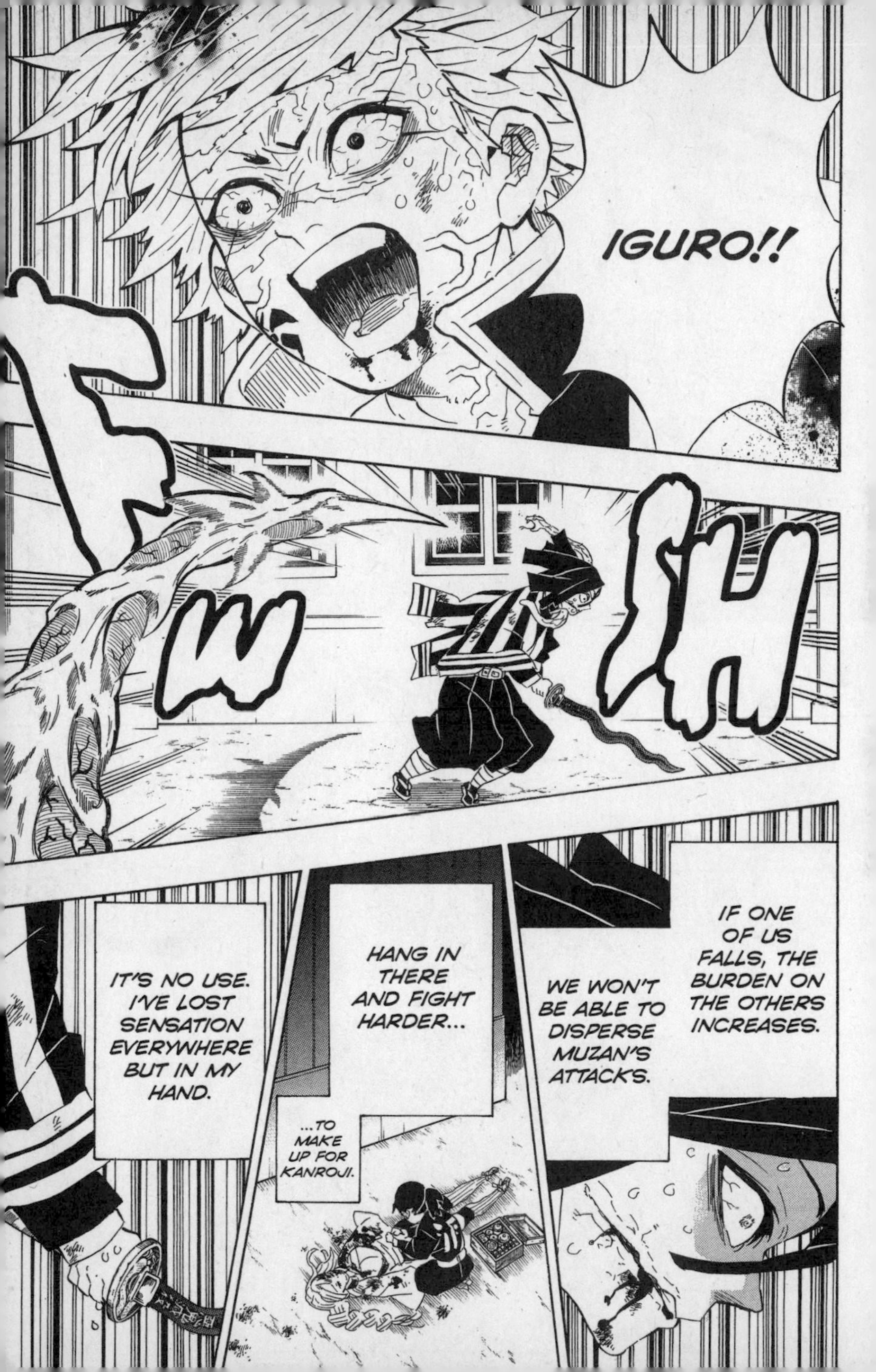
IGURO!!
IF ONE OF US FALLS, THE BURDEN ON THE OTHERS INCREASES.
WE WON'T BE ABLE TO DISPERSE MUZAN'S ATTACKS.
HANG IN THERE AND FIGHT HARDER...
...TO MAKE UP FOR KANROJI.
IT'S NO USE. I'VE LOST SENSATION EVERYWHERE BUT IN MY HAND.

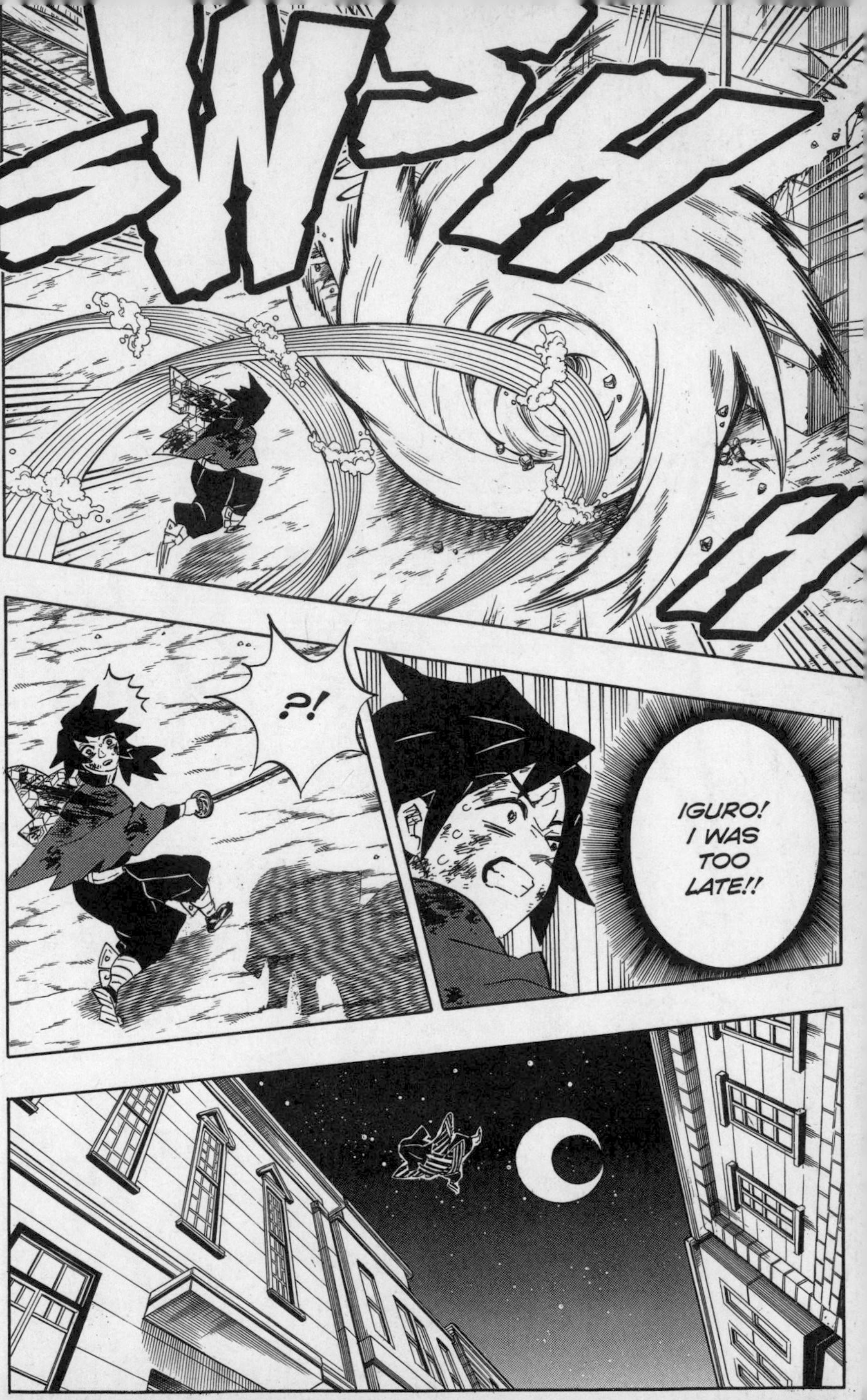
IGURO! I WAS TOO LATE!!
?!

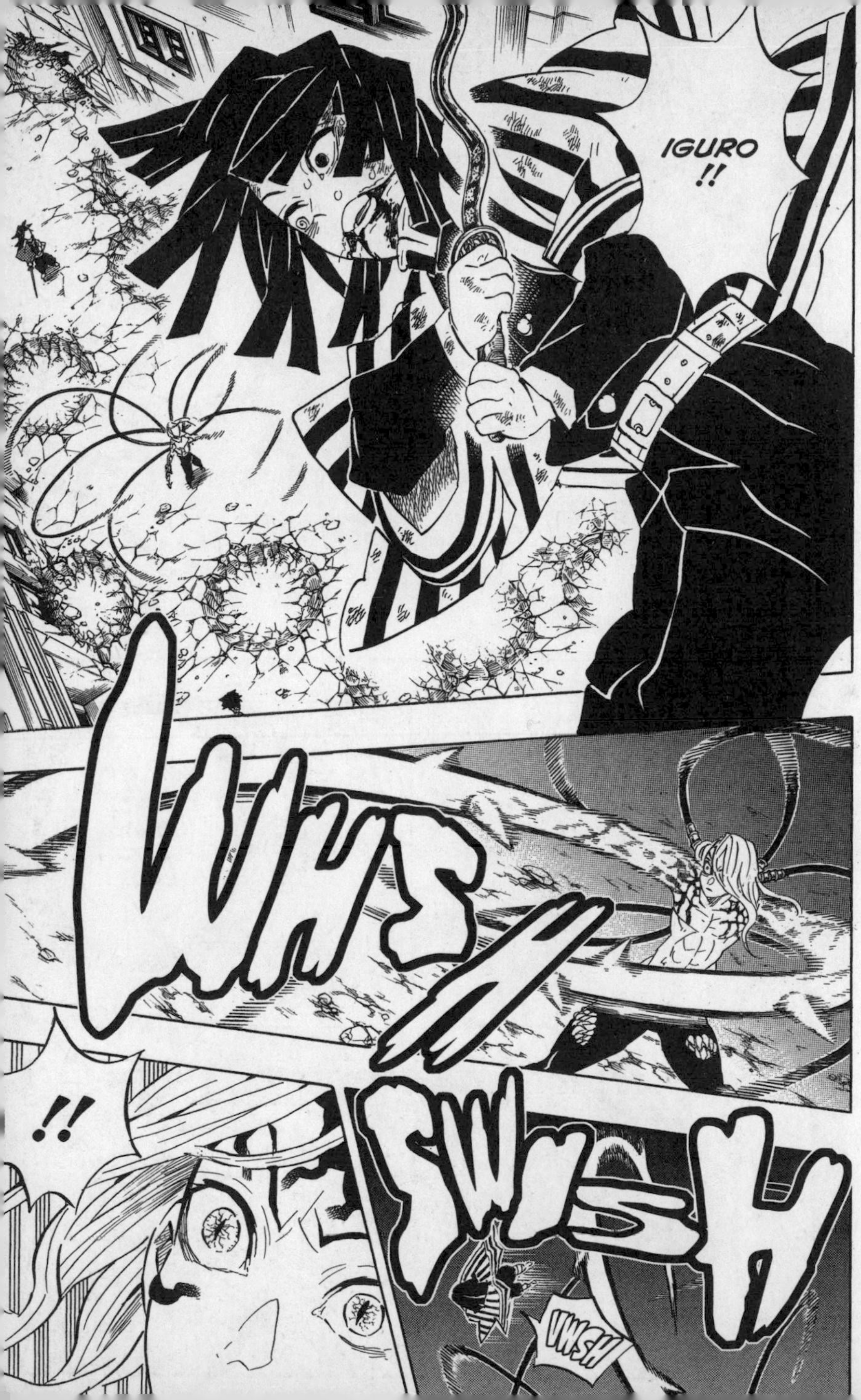
IGURO !!
WHSH
SWISH
WHSH
!!

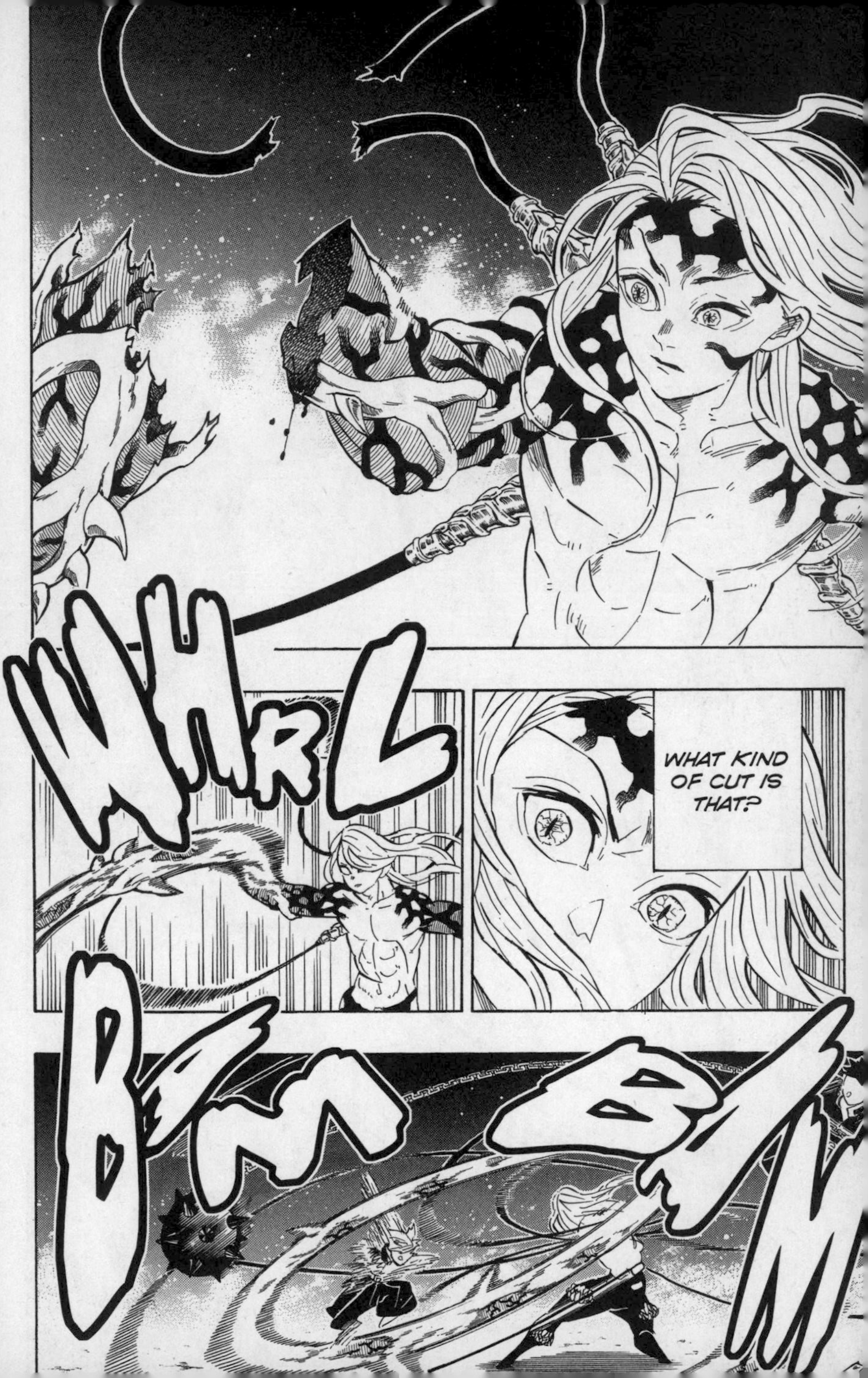
WHAT KIND OF CUT IS THAT?

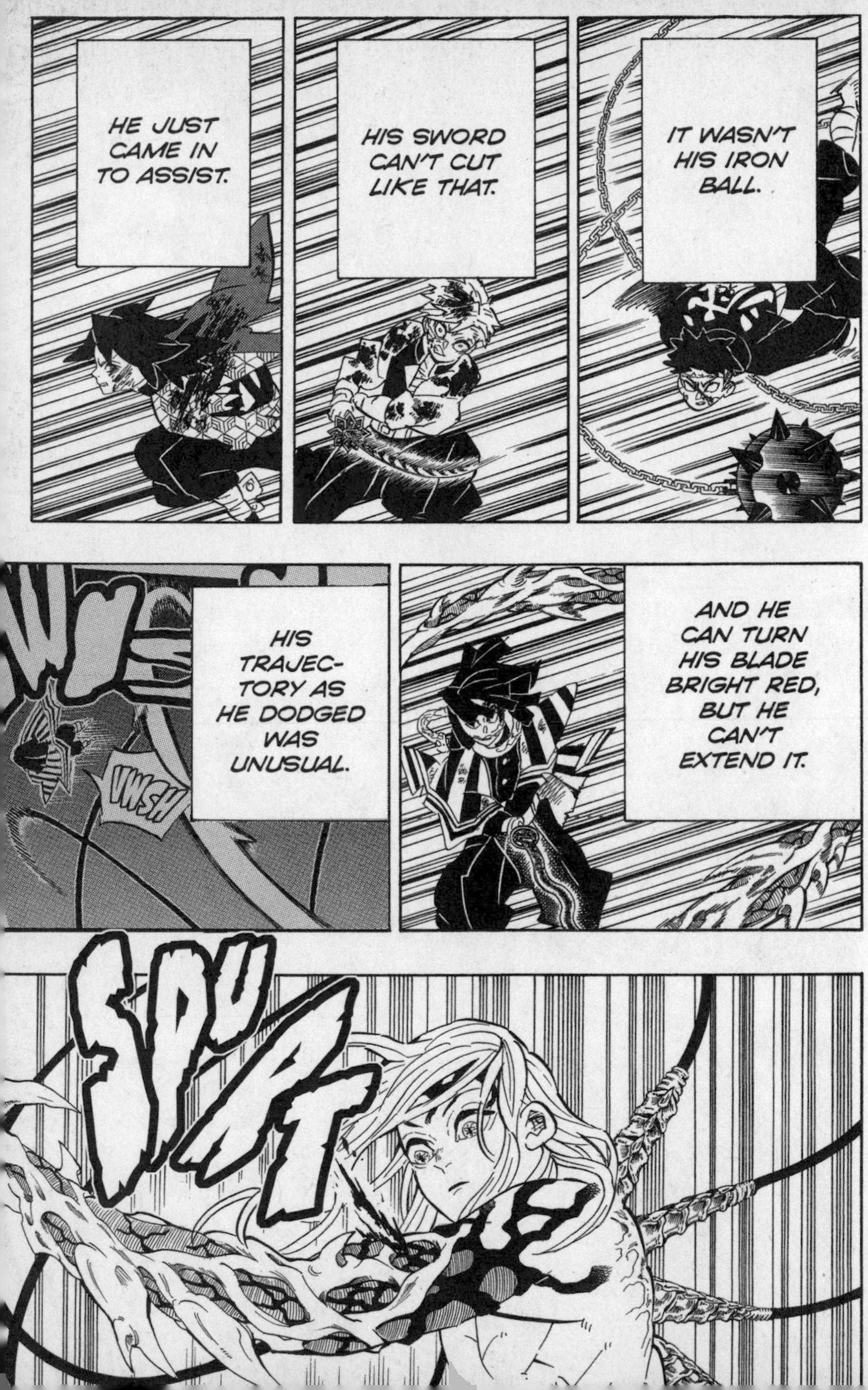
IT WASN'T HIS IRON BALL.
HIS SWORD CAN'T CUT LIKE THAT.
HE JUST CAME IN TO ASSIST.
AND HE CAN TURN HIS BLADE BRIGHT RED, BUT HE CAN'T EXTEND IT.
HIS TRAJECTORY AS HE DODGED WAS UNUSUAL.
VWSH
SPLAT

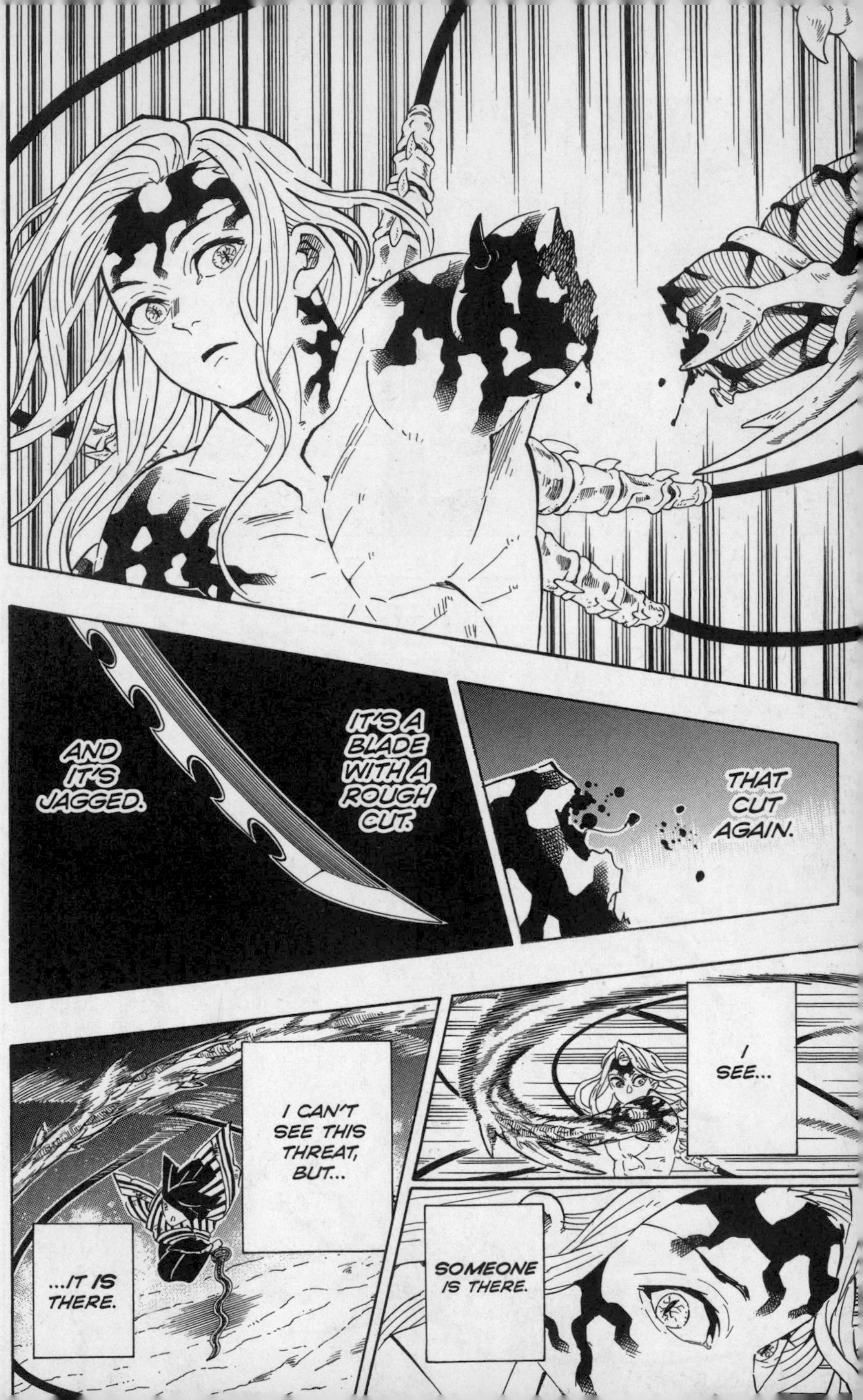
THAT CUT AGAIN.
IT'S A BLADE WITH A ROUGH CUT.
AND IT'S JAGGED.
I SEE...
SOMEONE IS THERE.
I CAN'T SEE THIS THREAT, BUT...
...IT IS THERE.

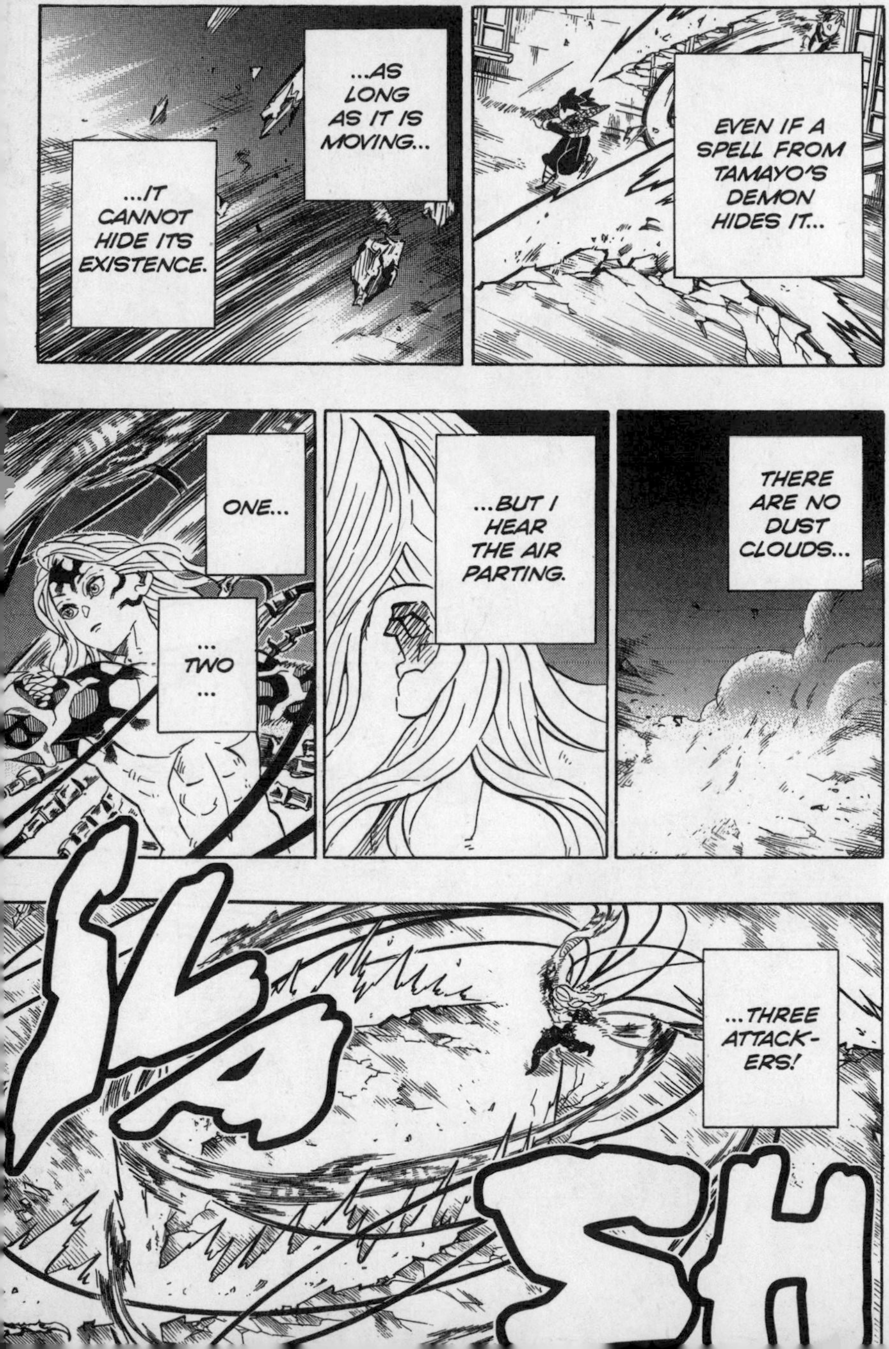
EVEN IF A SPELL FROM TAMAYO'S DEMON HIDES IT...
...AS LONG AS IT IS MOVING...
...IT CANNOT HIDE ITS EXISTENCE.
THERE ARE NO DUST CLOUDS...
...BUT I HEAR THE AIR PARTING.
ONE...
... TWO ...
...THREE ATTACKERS!

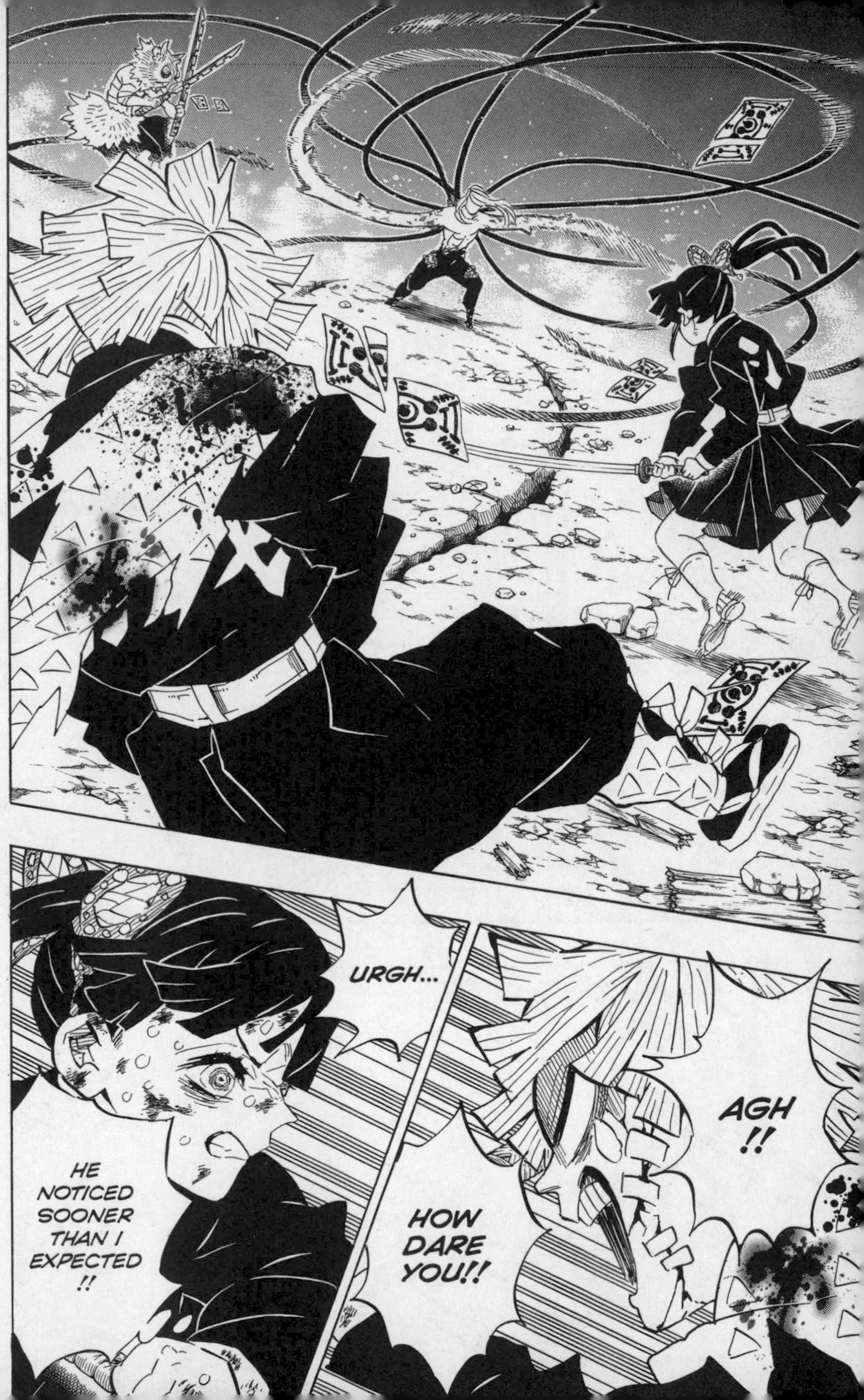
AGH!!
HOW DARE YOU!!
URGH...
HE NOTICED SOONER THAN I EXPECTED!!

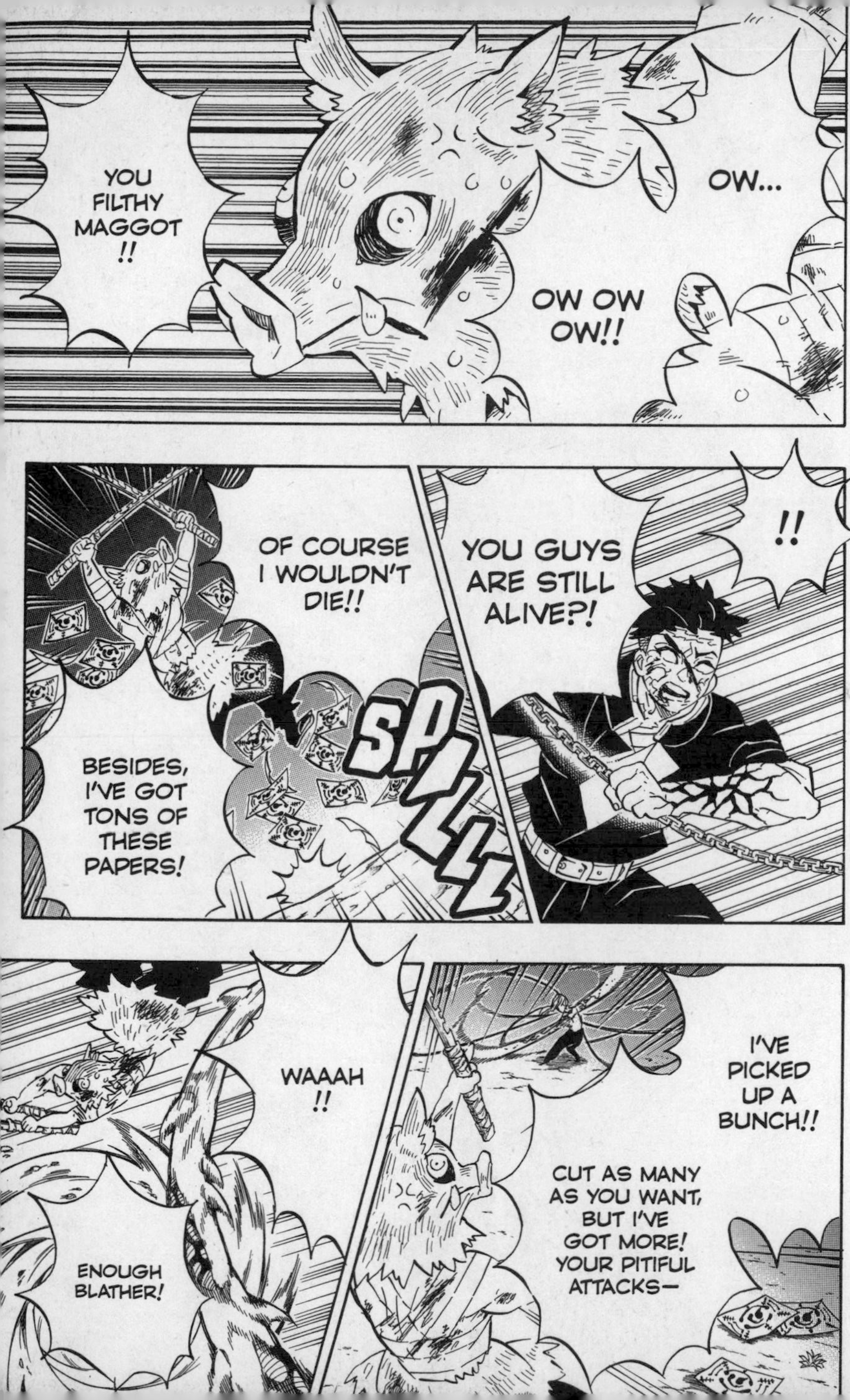
OW...
OW OW OW!!
YOU FILTHY MAGGOT!!
!!
YOU GUYS ARE STILL ALIVE?!
OF COURSE I WOULDN'T DIE!!
SPILL
BESIDES, I'VE GOT TONS OF THESE PAPERS!
I'VE PICKED UP A BUNCH!!
CUT AS MANY AS YOU WANT, BUT I'VE GOT MORE! YOUR PITIFUL ATTACKS—
WAAAH!!
ENOUGH BLATHER!

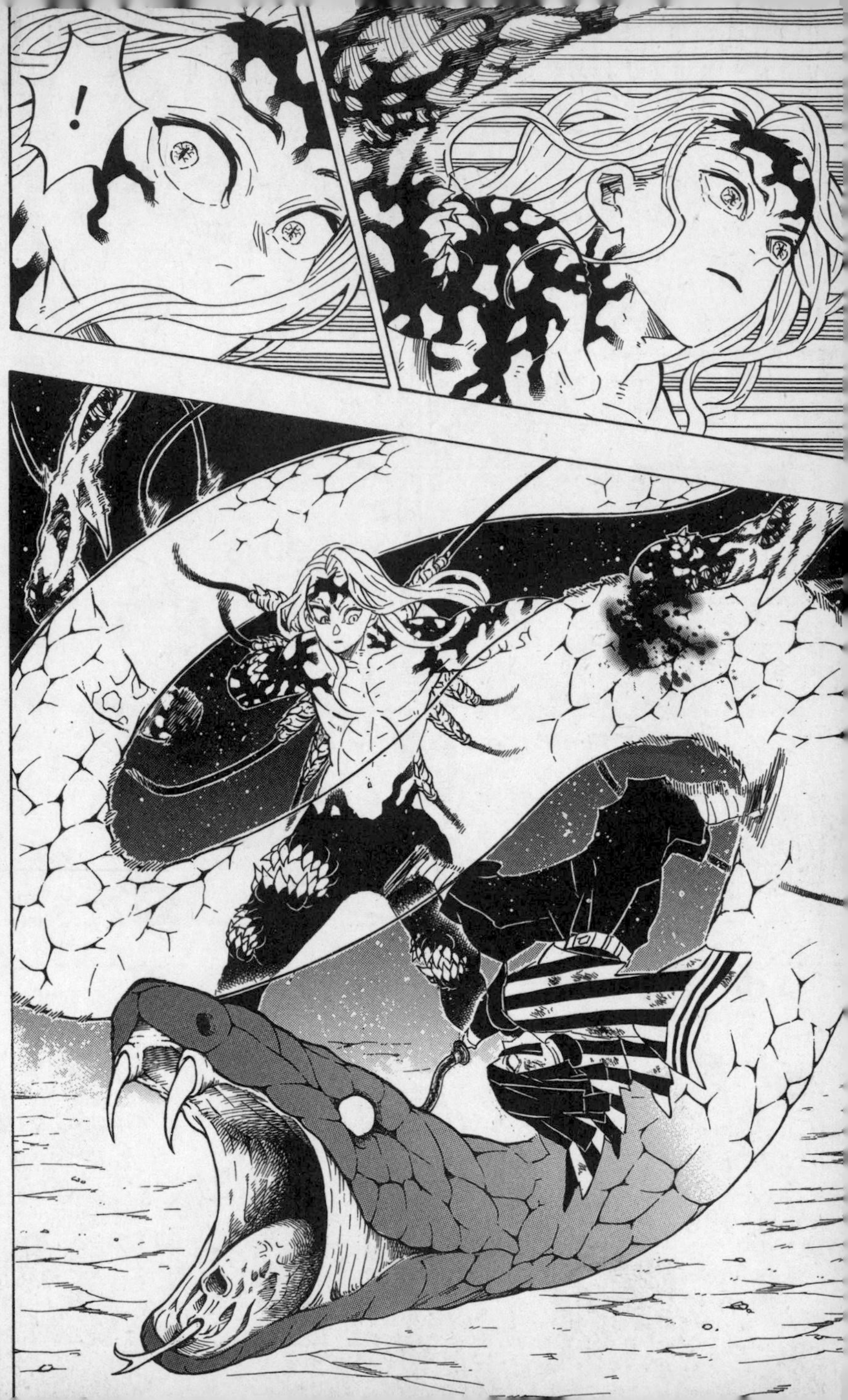
!

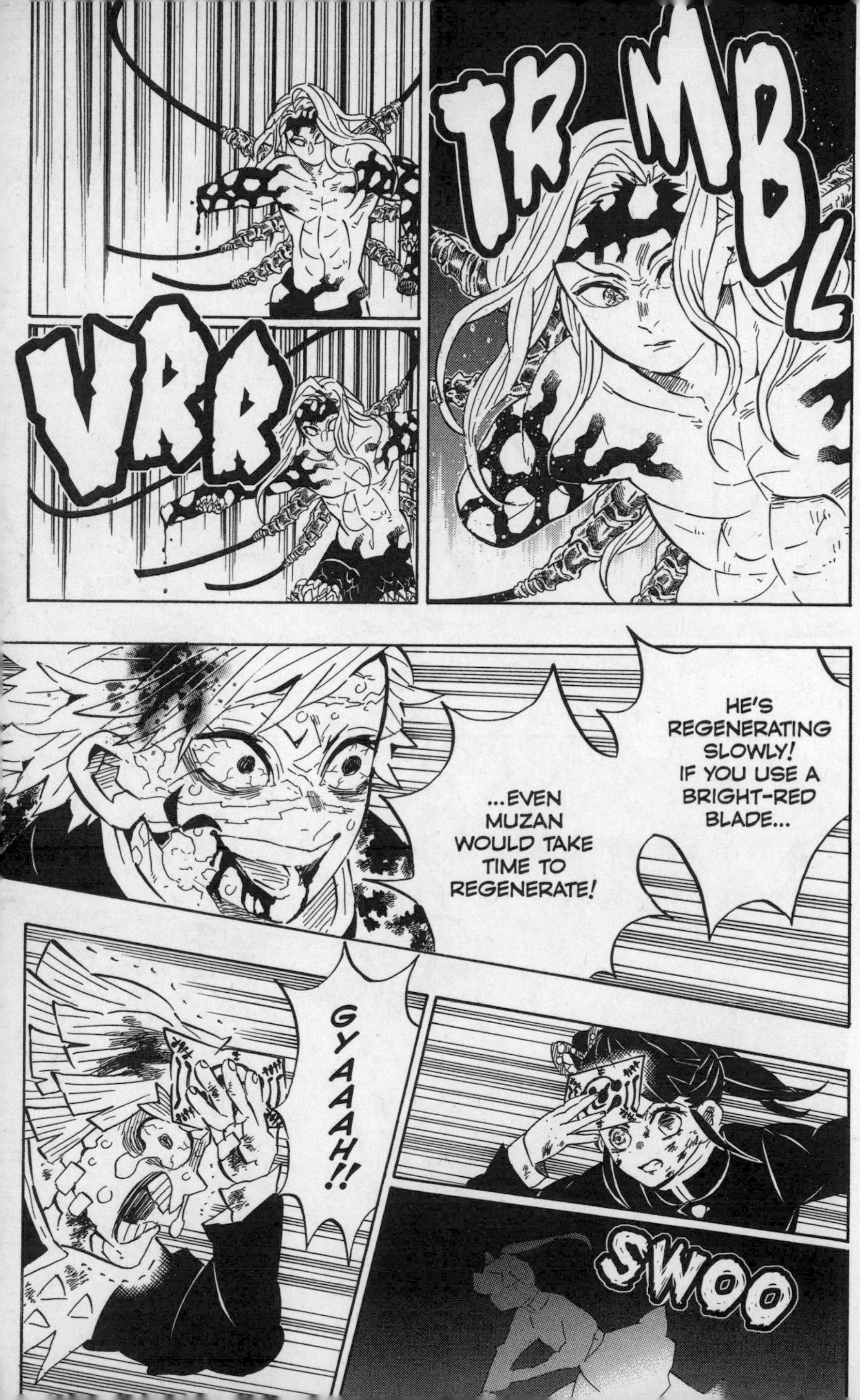
TR MBL
VRR
HE'S REGENERATING SLOWLY! IF YOU USE A BRIGHT-RED BLADE...
...EVEN MUZAN WOULD TAKE TIME TO REGENERATE!
SWOO
GYAAAAH!!

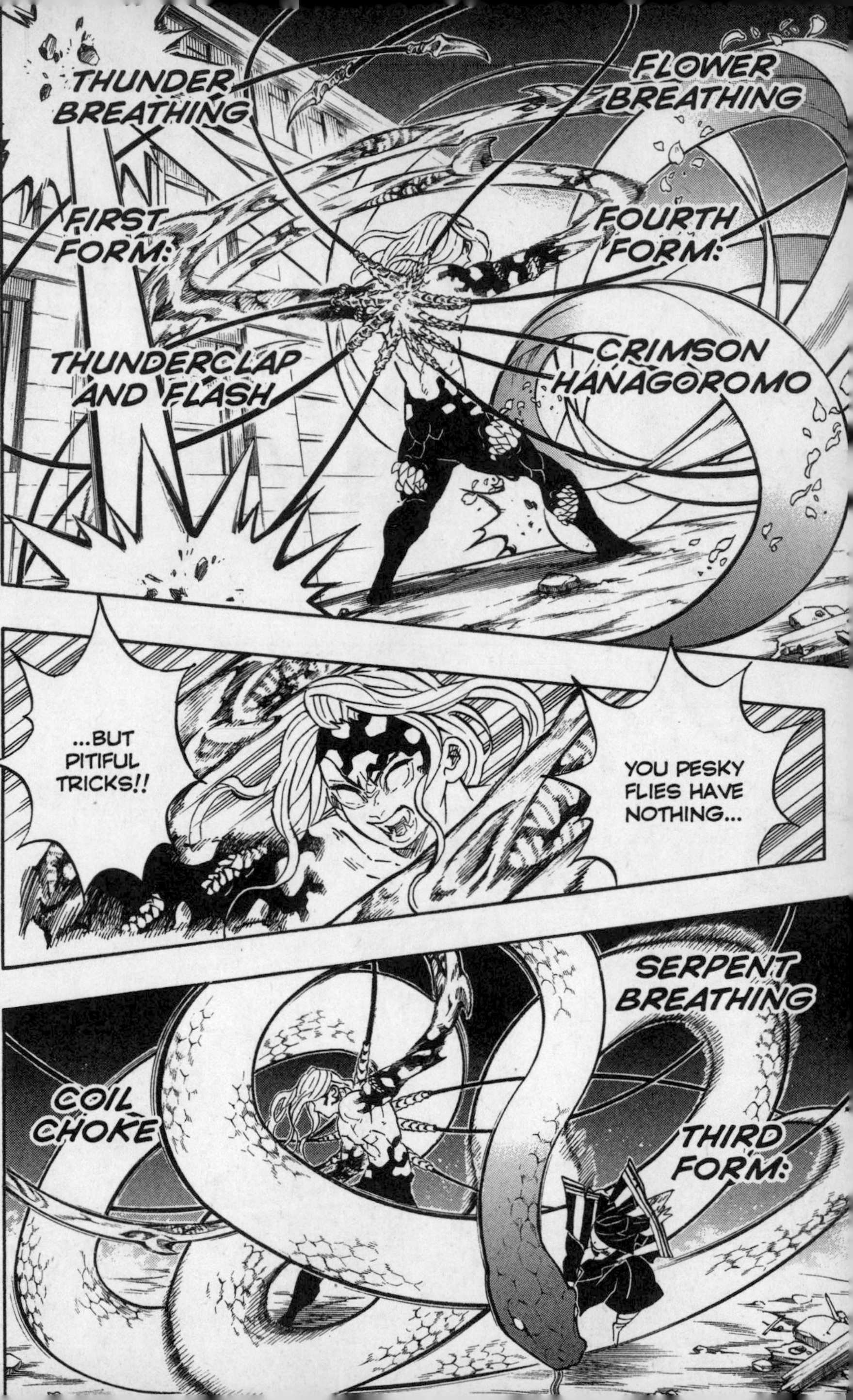
FLOWER BREATHING
FOURTH FORM:
CRIMSON HANAGOROMO
THUNDER BREATHING
FIRST FORM:
THUNDERCLAP AND FLASH
YOU PESKY FLIES HAVE NOTHING...
...BUT PITIFUL TRICKS!!
SERPENT BREATHING
THIRD FORM:
COIL CHOKE

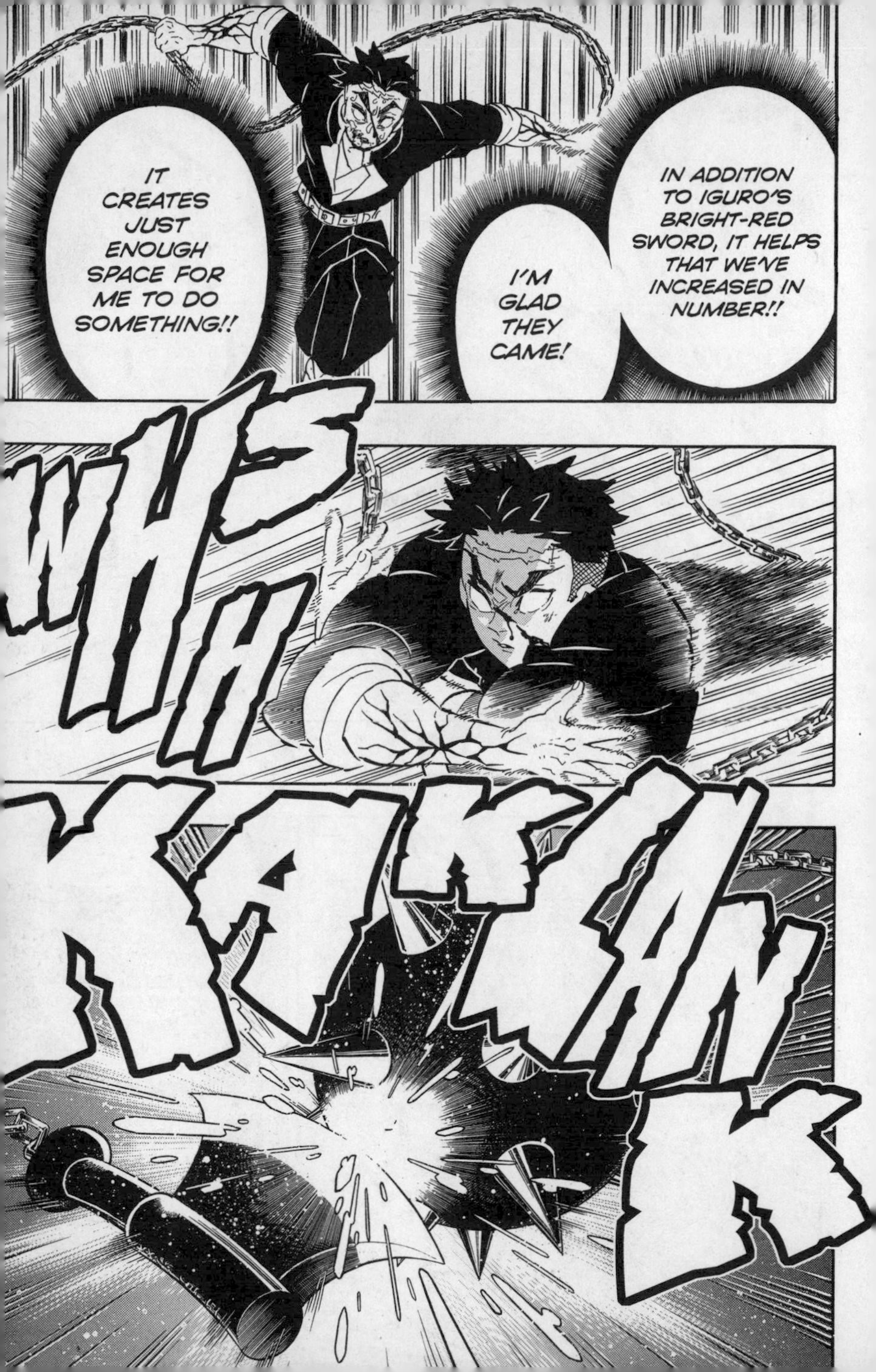
IN ADDITION TO IGURO'S BRIGHT-RED SWORD, IT HELPS THAT WE'VE INCREASED IN NUMBER!!
I'M GLAD THEY CAME!
IT CREATES JUST ENOUGH SPACE FOR ME TO DO SOMETHING!!
WHAM
KAKANK

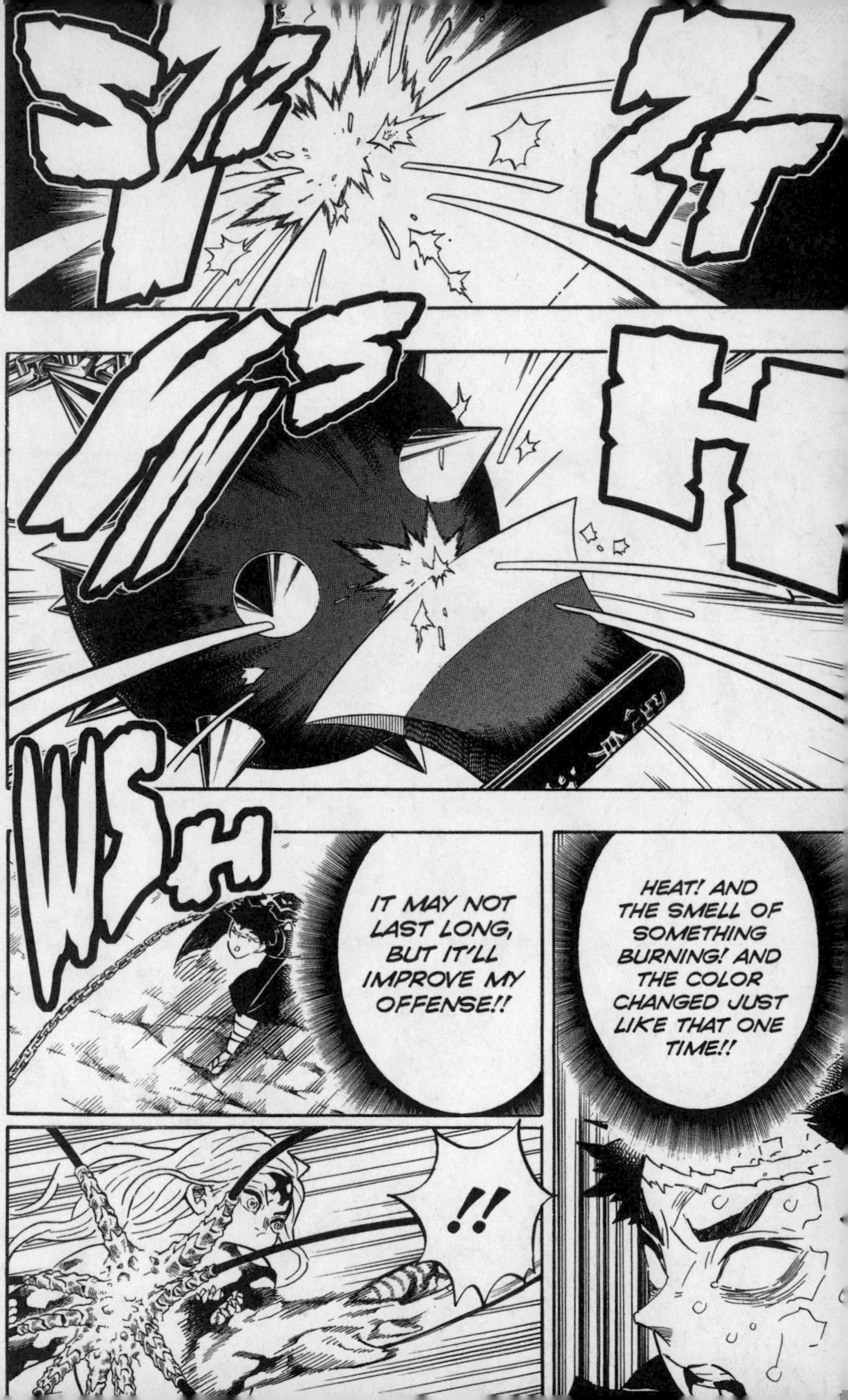
HEAT! AND THE SMELL OF SOMETHING BURNING! AND THE COLOR CHANGED JUST LIKE THAT ONE TIME!!
IT MAY NOT LAST LONG, BUT IT'LL IMPROVE MY OFFENSE!!
!!

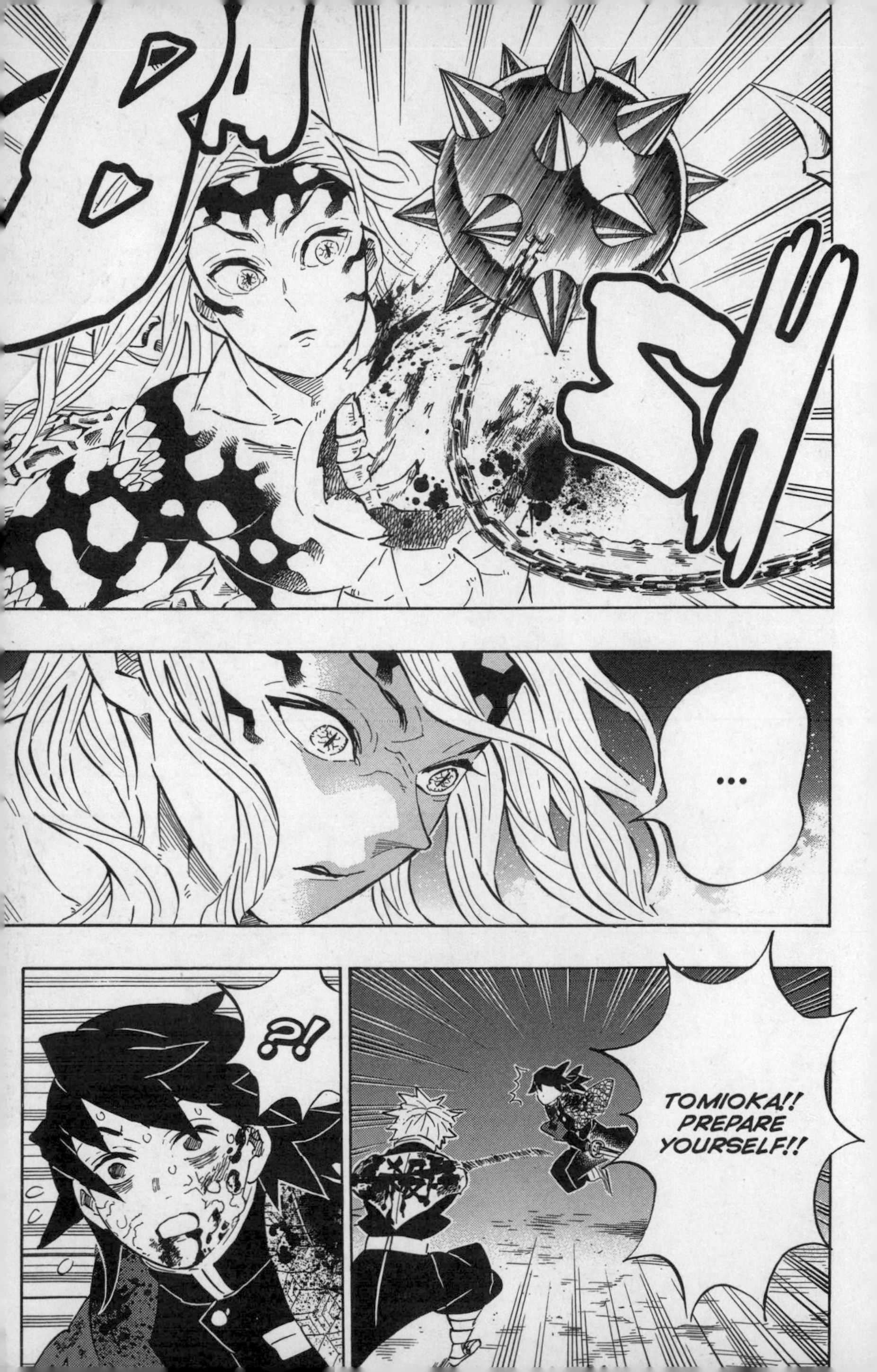
...
TOMIOKA!! PREPARE YOURSELF!!
?!

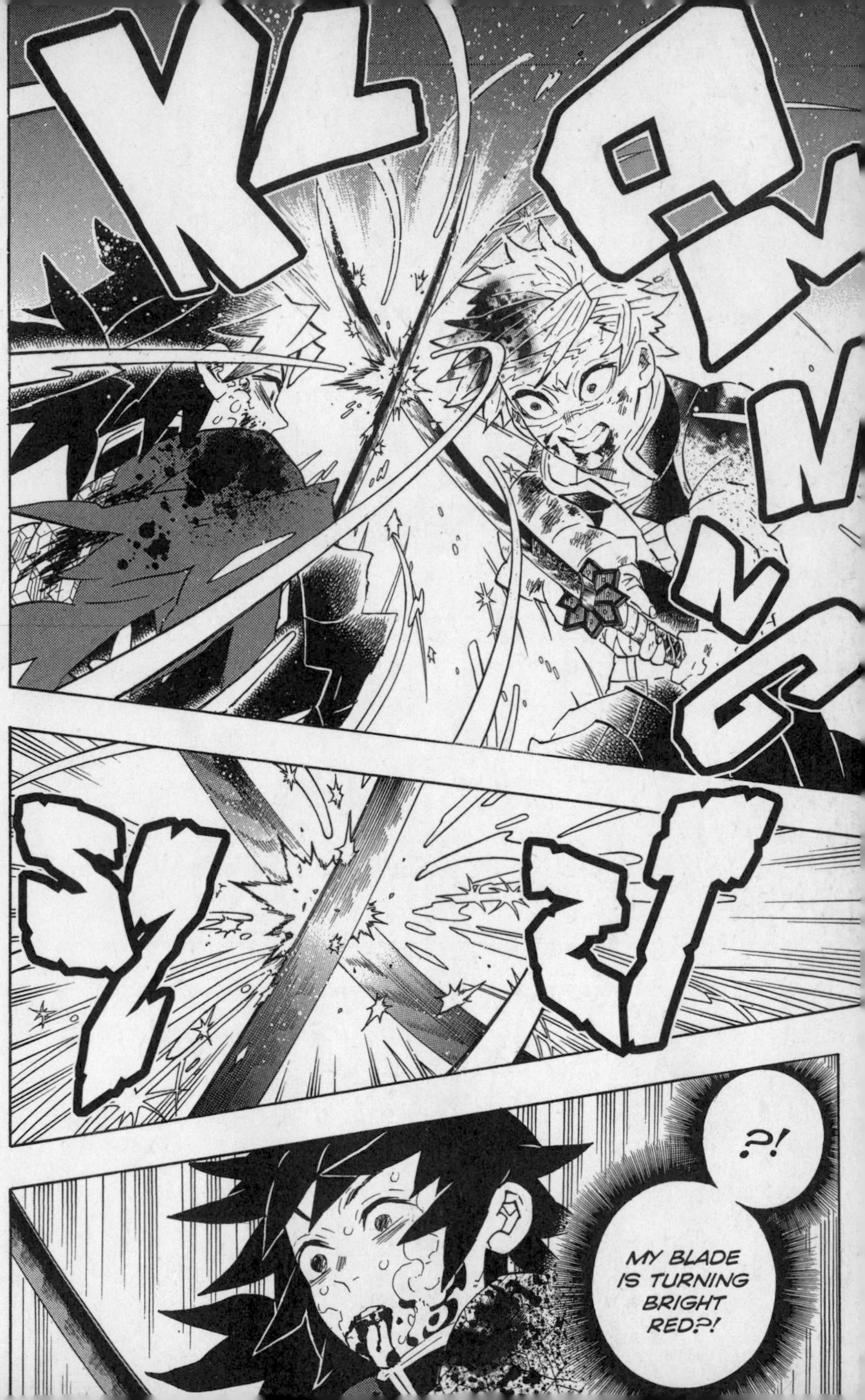
?!
MY BLADE IS TURNING BRIGHT RED?!

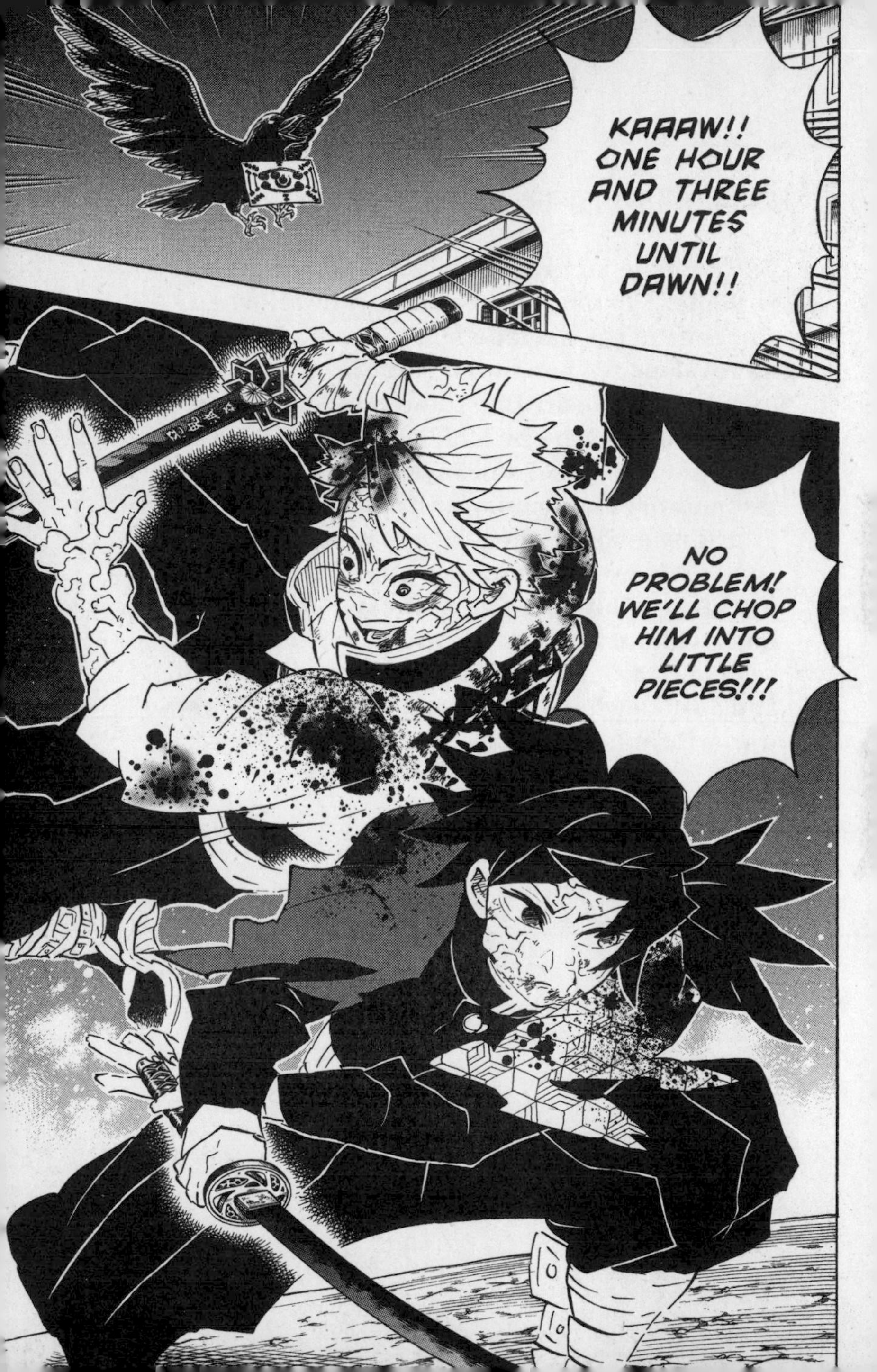
KAAAW!! ONE HOUR AND THREE MINUTES UNTIL DAWN!!
NO PROBLEM! WE'LL CHOP HIM INTO LITTLE PIECES!!!

SENGOKU WHISPERS

The Kamado family lives where Yoriichi lived with Uta. The house was an empty hovel when someone in the Kamado family came and took up residence. When the Demon Slayer Corps was in pursuit of Yoriichi, he came wandering back to the house where he had lived with Uta. There he found Sumiyoshi and Suyako, who was in her last month of pregnancy, and saved them from an attacking demon. Later, Suyako went into labor, so Yoriichi went to summon a midwife and came back incredibly fast. The next day, Sumire was born without any complications. Yoriichi felt redeemed to have been able to do for Sumiyoshi and Suyako what he had been unable to do for his own wife and child.

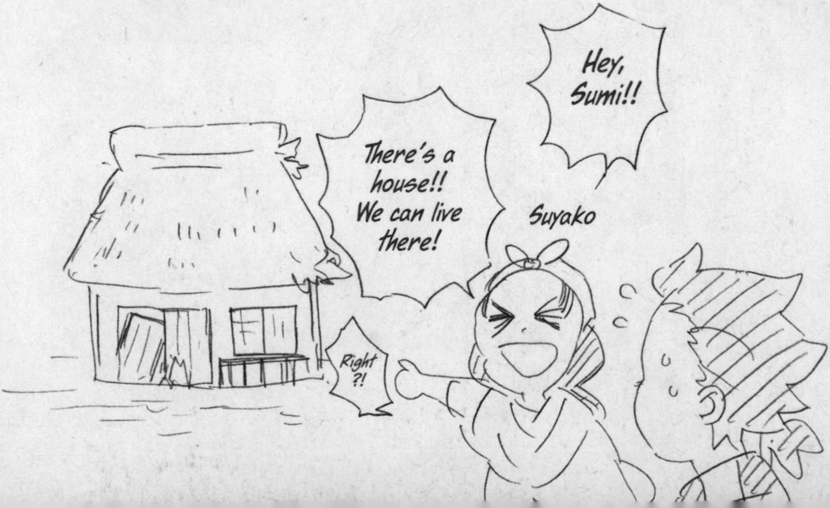
Hey, Sumi!!
There's a house!! We can live there!
Suyako
Right?!

CHAPTER 191:
WHICH ONE OF US IS THE DEMON?

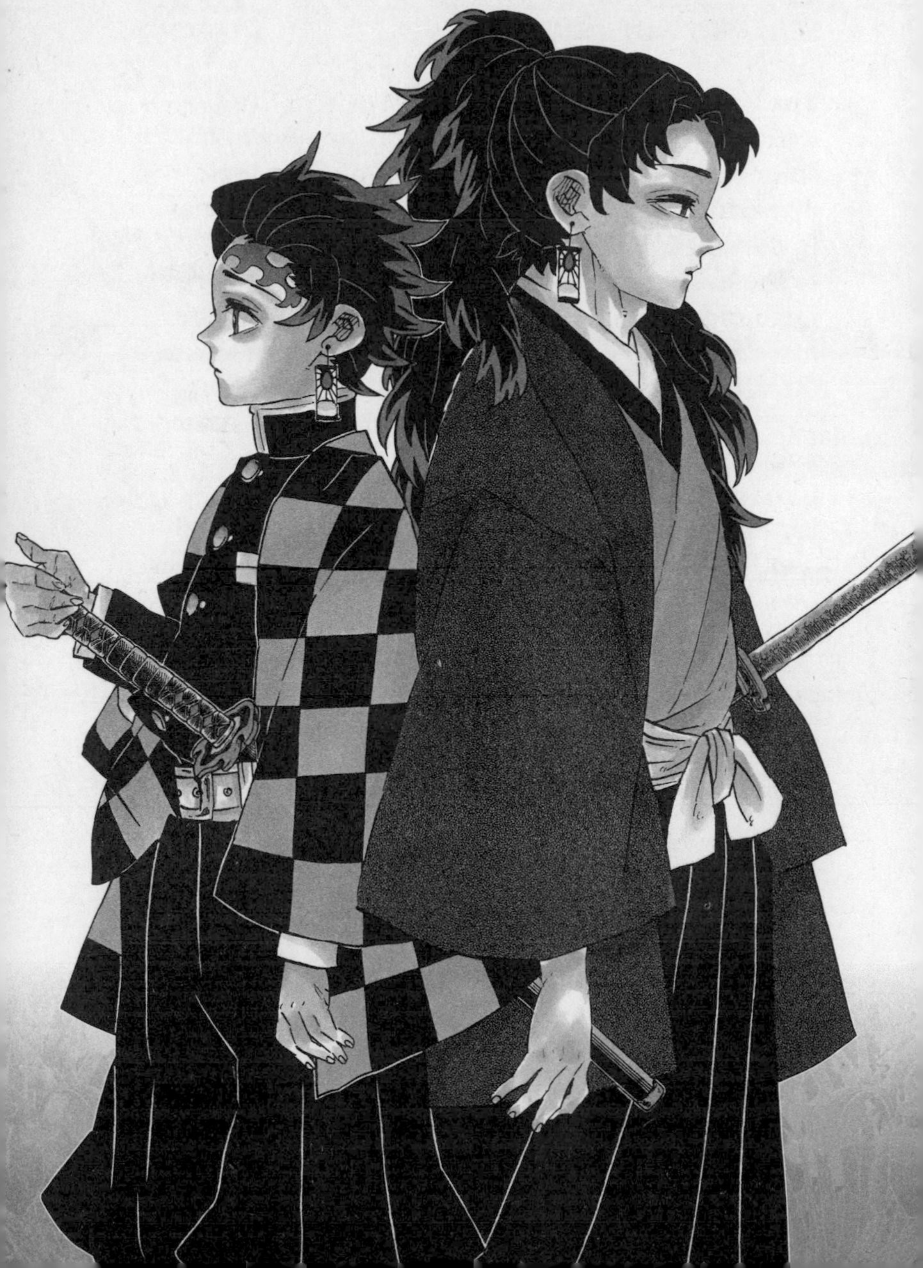

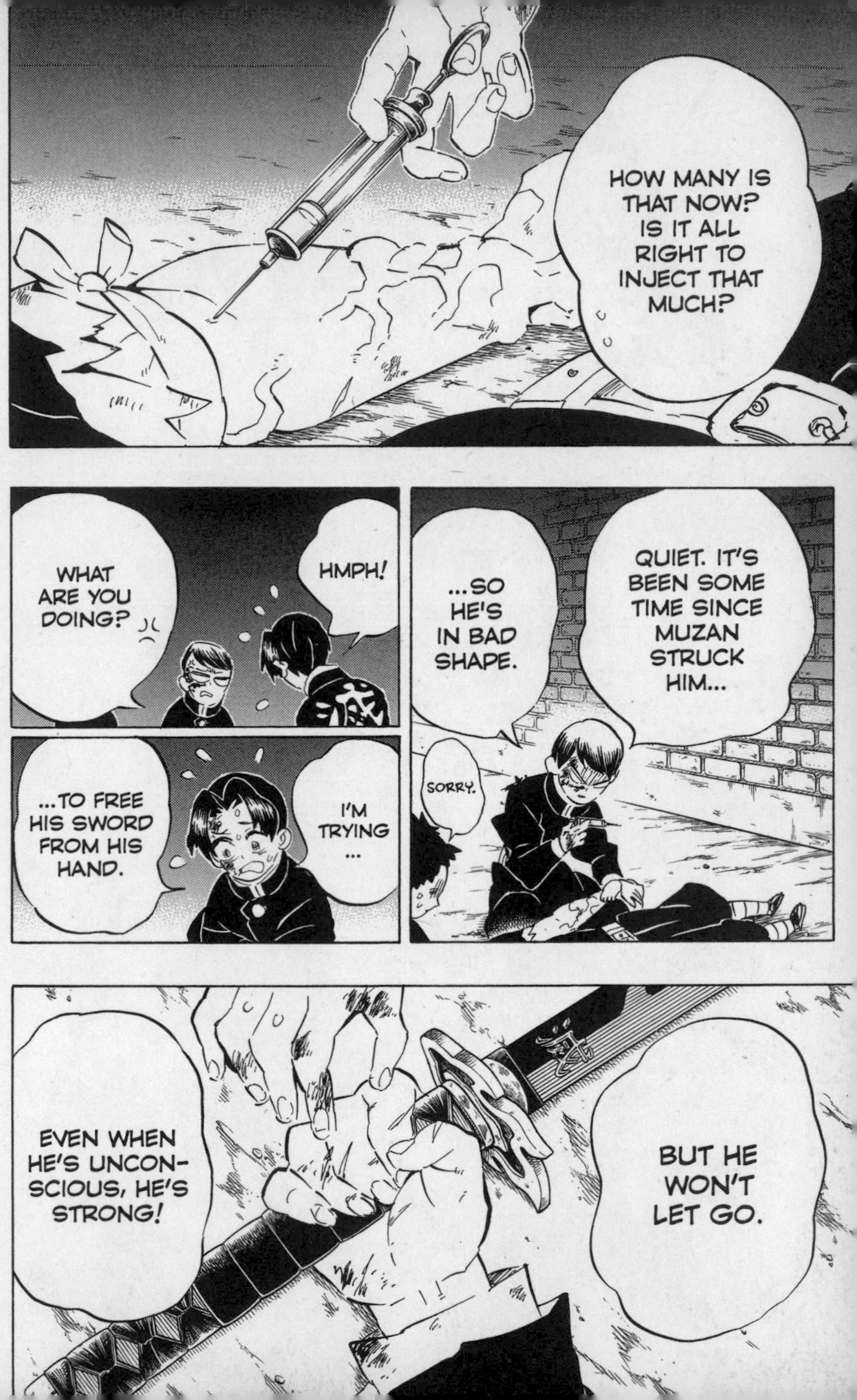
HOW MANY IS THAT NOW? IS IT ALL RIGHT TO INJECT THAT MUCH?
QUIET. IT'S BEEN SOME TIME SINCE MUZAN STRUCK HIM...
...SO HE'S IN BAD SHAPE.
SORRY.
HMPH!
WHAT ARE YOU DOING?
I'M TRYING...
...TO FREE HIS SWORD FROM HIS HAND.
BUT HE WON'T LET GO.
EVEN WHEN HE'S UNCONSCIOUS, HE'S STRONG!

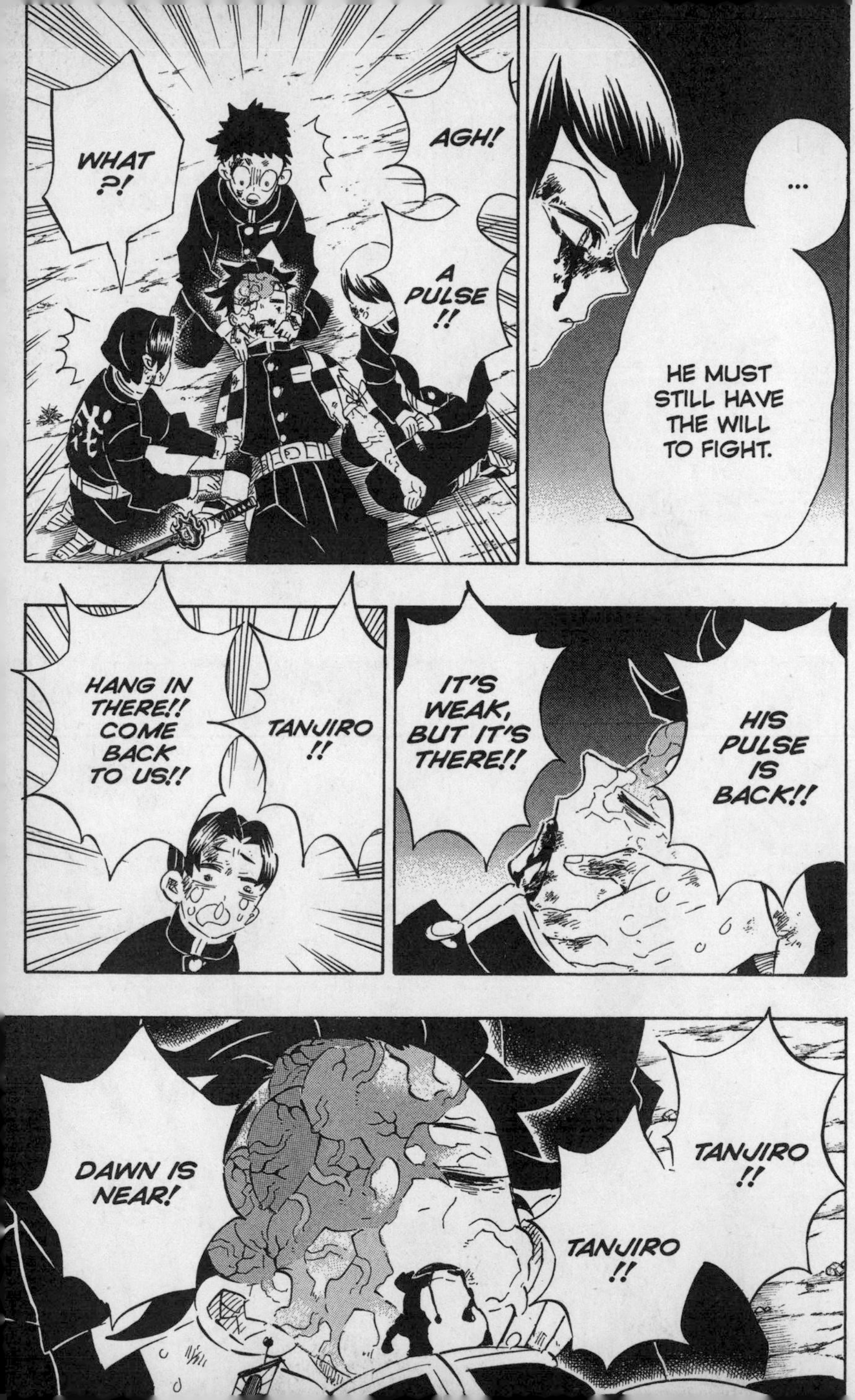
...
HE MUST STILL HAVE THE WILL TO FIGHT.
AGH!
A PULSE !!
WHAT ?!
HIS PULSE IS BACK!!
IT'S WEAK, BUT IT'S THERE!!
TANJIRO !!
HANG IN THERE!! COME BACK TO US!!
TANJIRO !!
TANJIRO !!
DAWN IS NEAR!

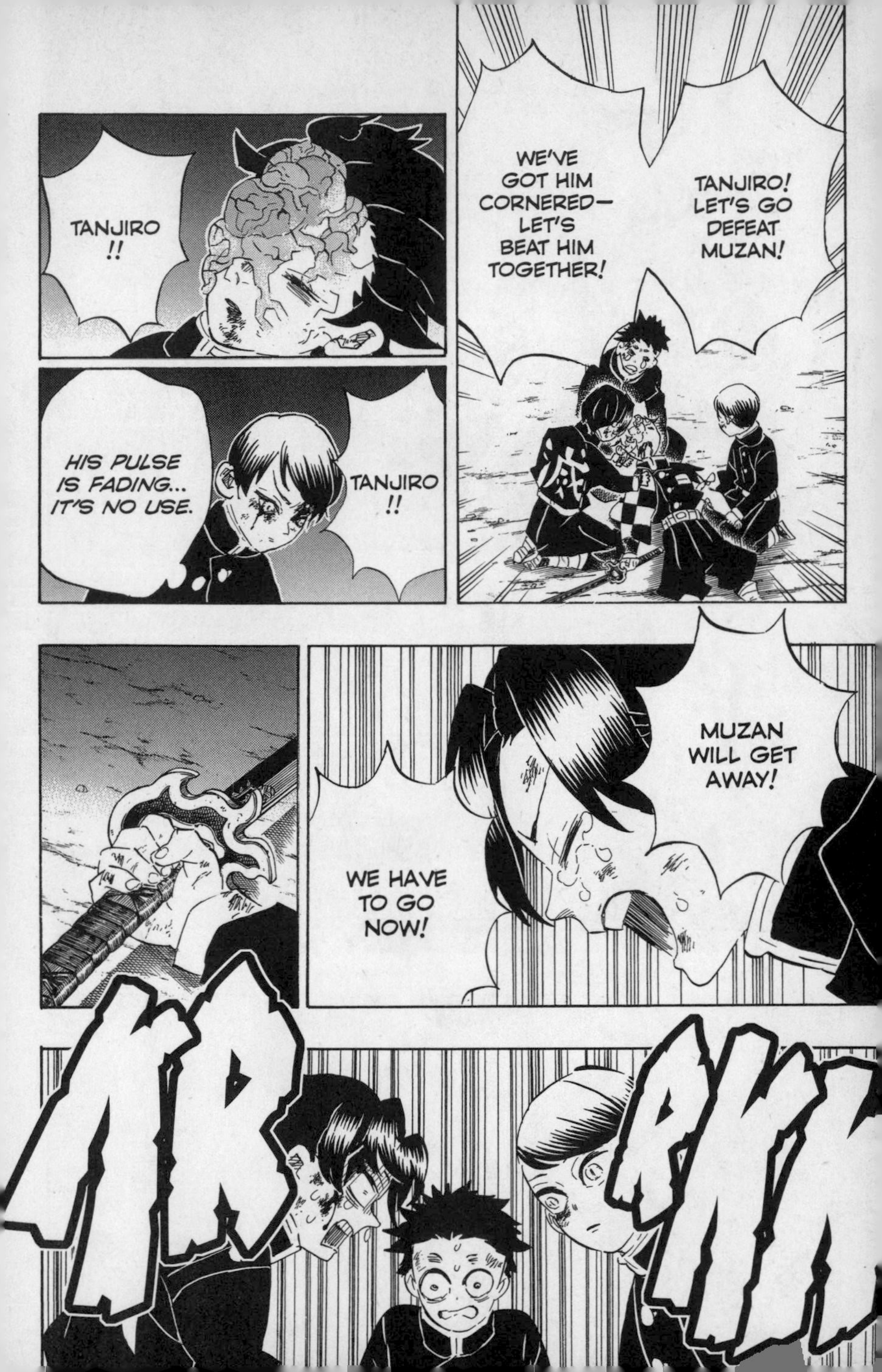
TANJIRO! LET'S GO DEFEAT MUZAN!
WE'VE GOT HIM CORNERED—LET'S BEAT HIM TOGETHER!
TANJIRO !!
TANJIRO !!
HIS PULSE IS FADING... IT'S NO USE.
MUZAN WILL GET AWAY!
WE HAVE TO GO NOW!

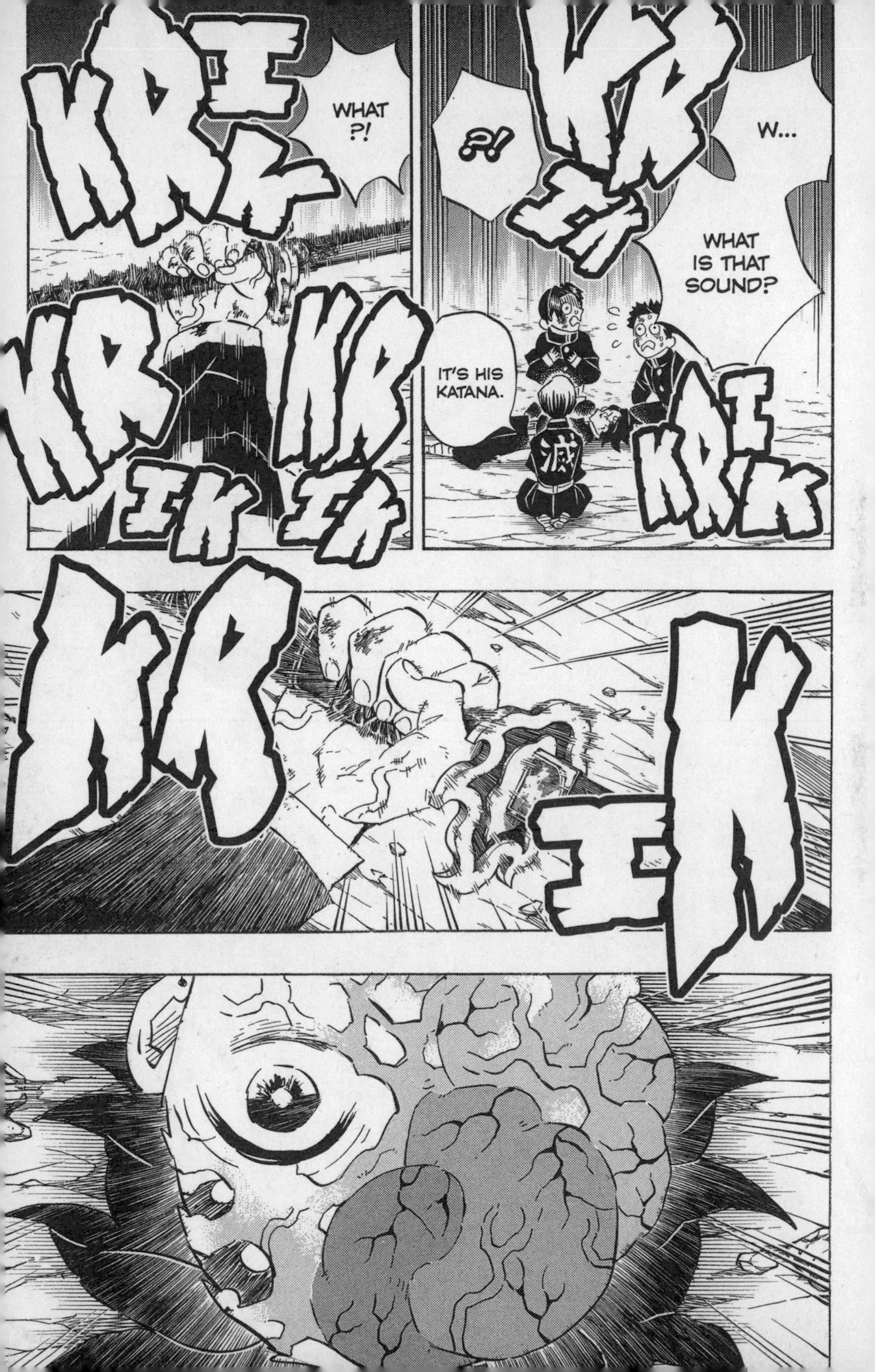
W...
WHAT IS THAT SOUND?
?!
IT'S HIS KATANA.
WHAT ?!

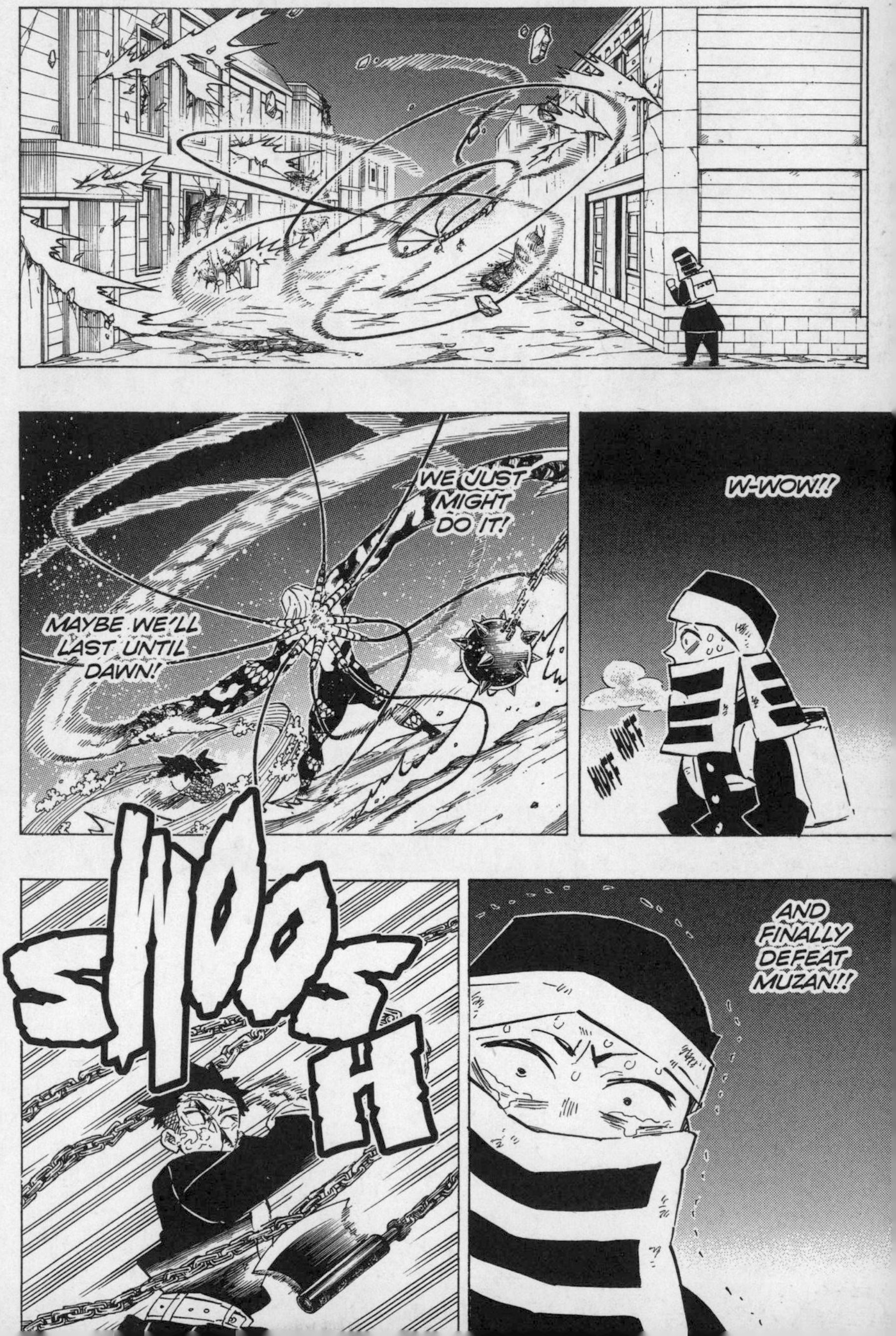
W-WOW!!
HUFF HUFF
WE JUST MIGHT DO IT!
MAYBE WE'LL LAST UNTIL DAWN!
AND FINALLY DEFEAT MUZAN!!
SWOOSH

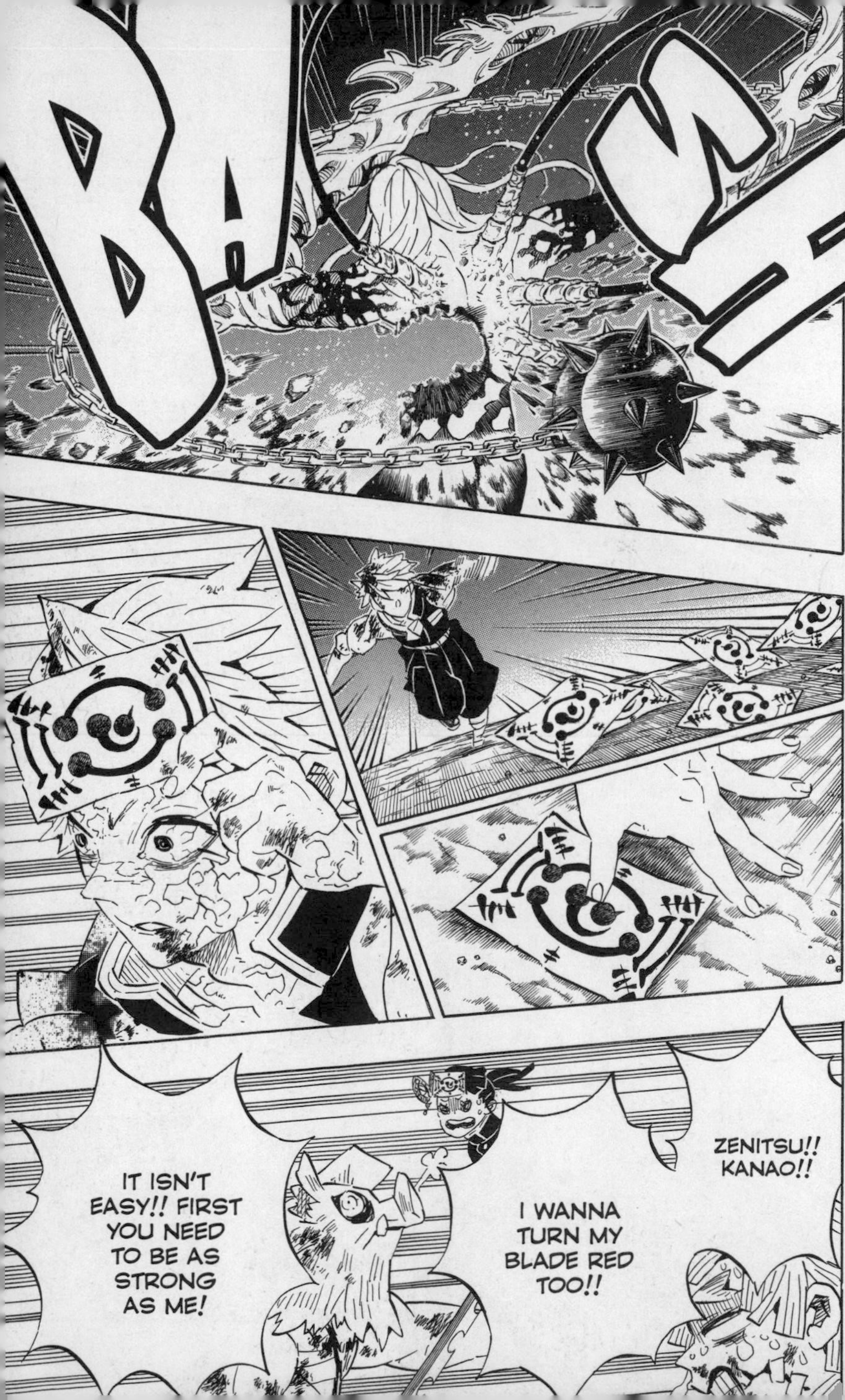
ZENITSU!! KANAO!!
I WANNA TURN MY BLADE RED TOO!!
IT ISN'T EASY!! FIRST YOU NEED TO BE AS STRONG AS ME!

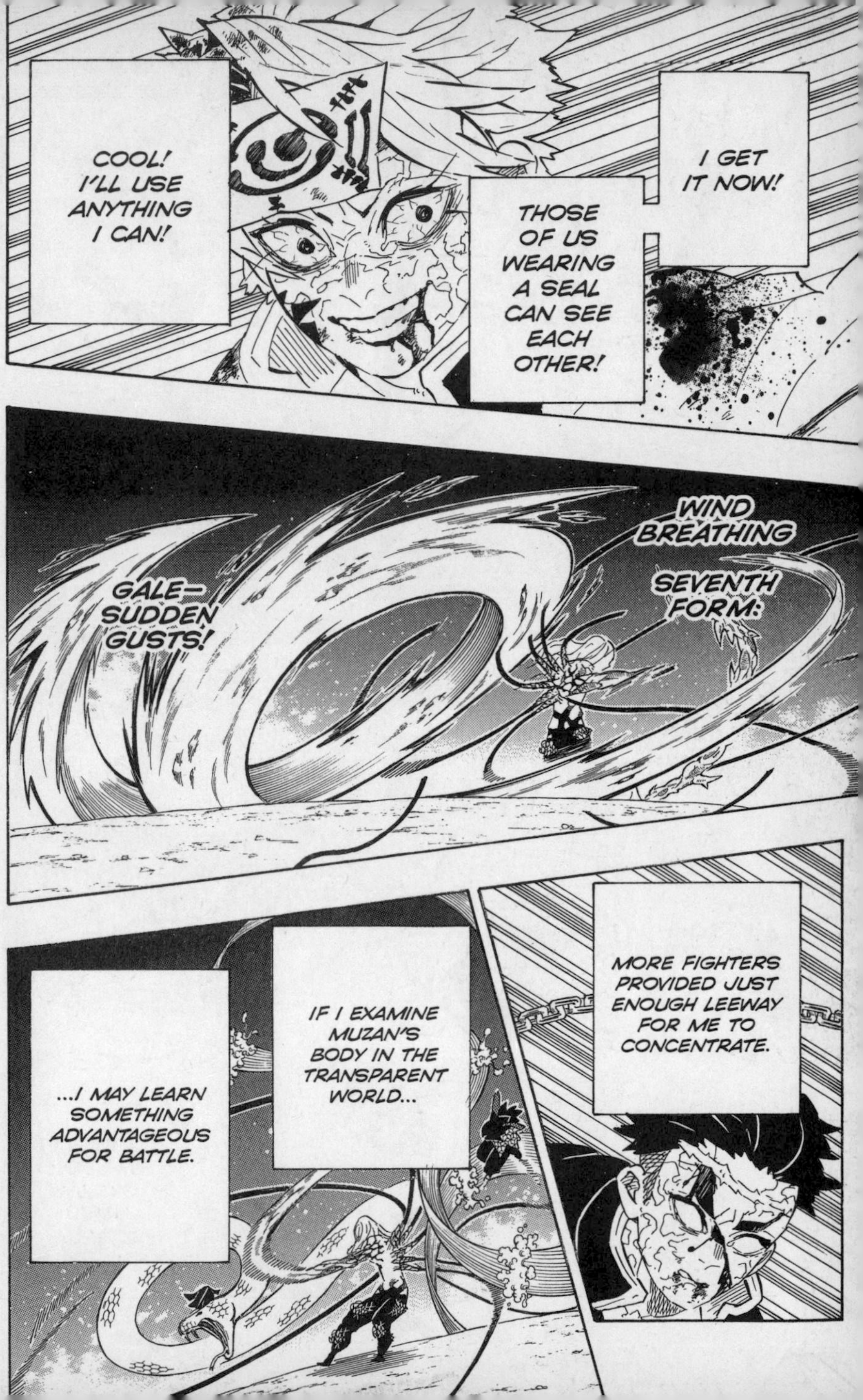
I GET IT NOW!
THOSE OF US WEARING A SEAL CAN SEE EACH OTHER!
COOL! I'LL USE ANYTHING I CAN!
WIND BREATHING
SEVENTH FORM:
GALE—SUDDEN GUSTS!
MORE FIGHTERS PROVIDED JUST ENOUGH LEEWAY FOR ME TO CONCENTRATE.
IF I EXAMINE MUZAN'S BODY IN THE TRANSPARENT WORLD...
...I MAY LEARN SOMETHING ADVANTAGEOUS FOR BATTLE.

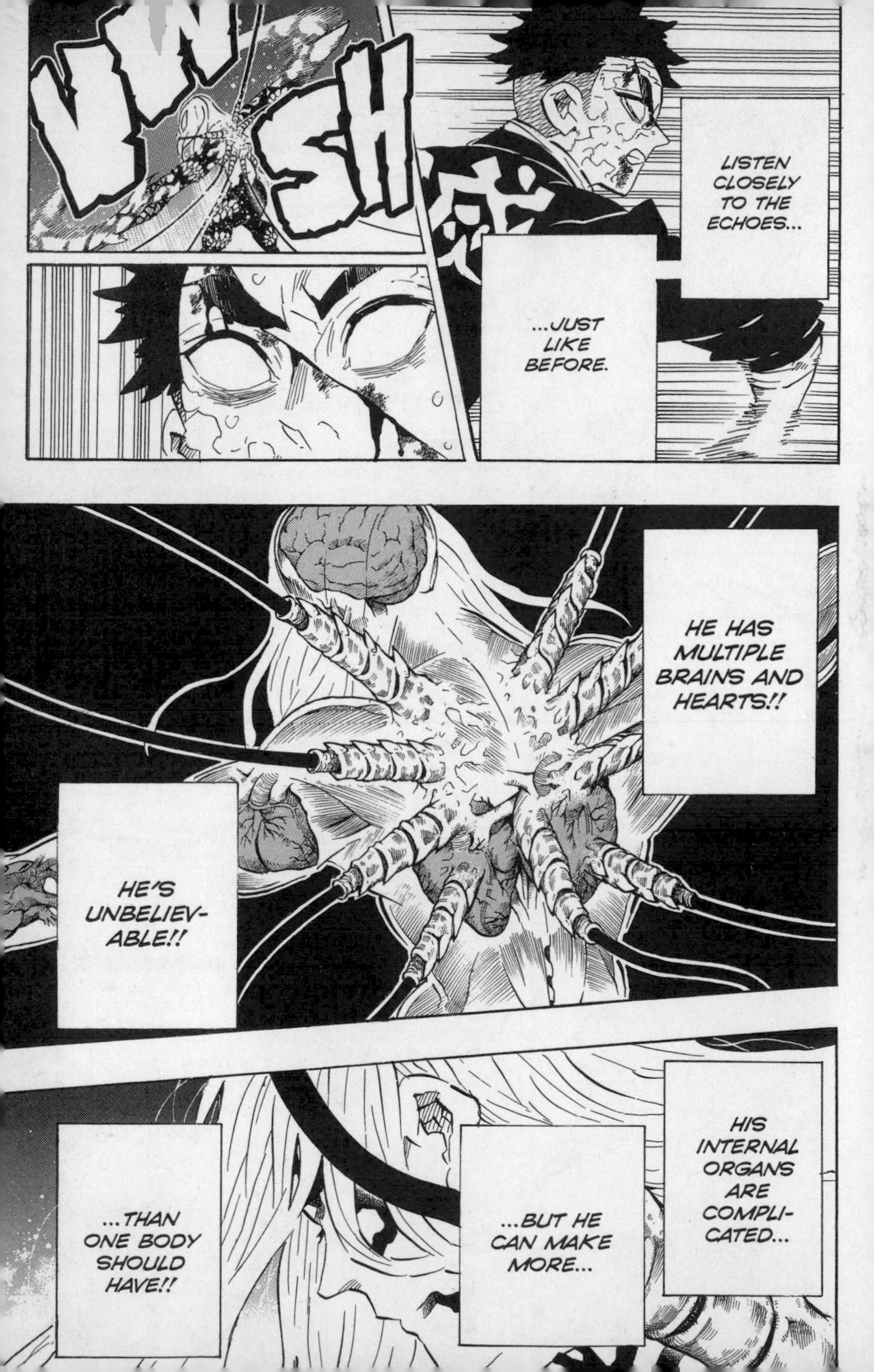
LISTEN CLOSELY TO THE ECHOES...
...JUST LIKE BEFORE.
WSH
HE HAS MULTIPLE BRAINS AND HEARTS!!
HE'S UNBELIEV-ABLE!!
HIS INTERNAL ORGANS ARE COMPLI-CATED...
...BUT HE CAN MAKE MORE...
...THAN ONE BODY SHOULD HAVE!!

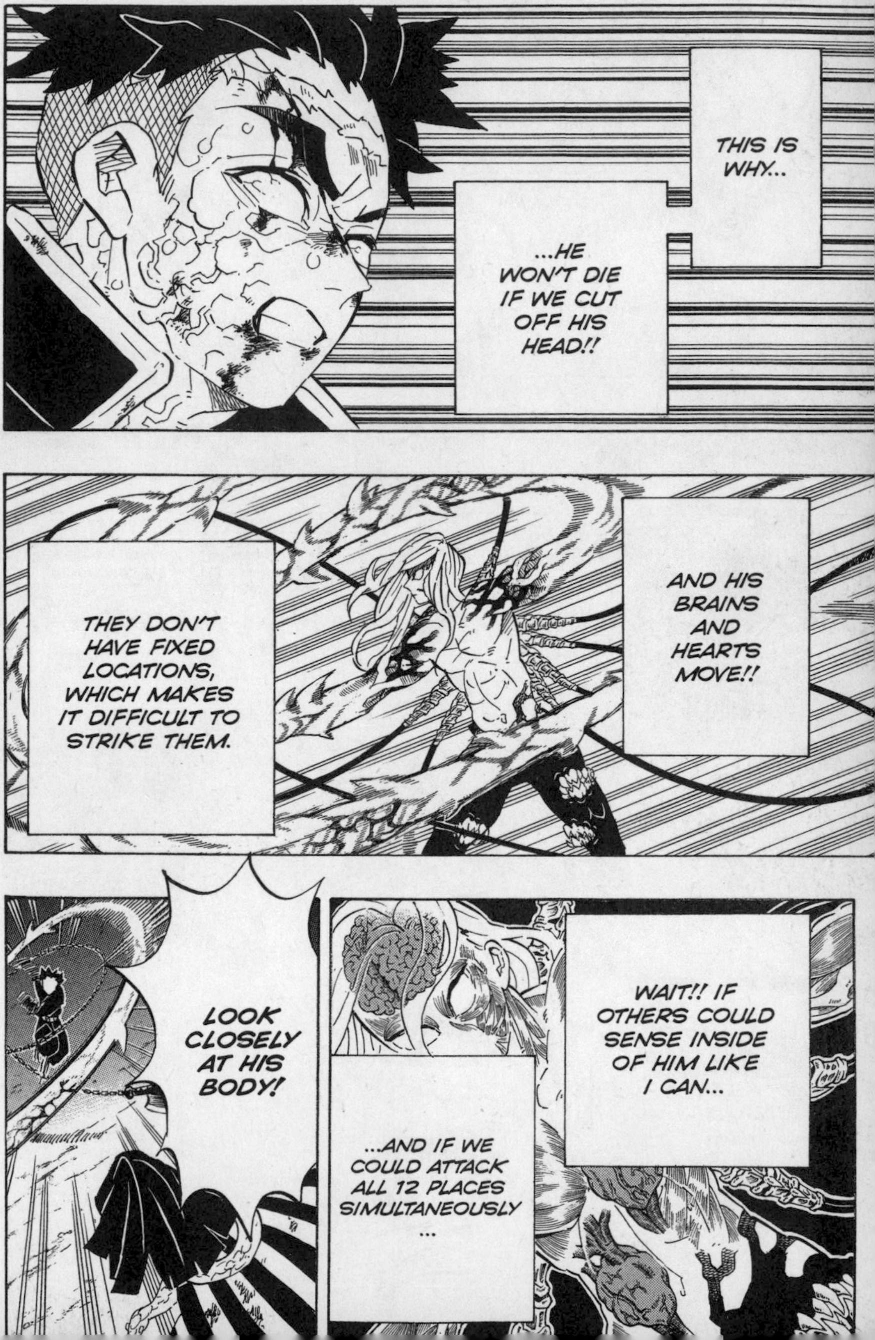
THIS IS WHY...
...HE WON'T DIE IF WE CUT OFF HIS HEAD!!
AND HIS BRAINS AND HEARTS MOVE!!
THEY DON'T HAVE FIXED LOCATIONS, WHICH MAKES IT DIFFICULT TO STRIKE THEM.
WAIT!! IF OTHERS COULD SENSE INSIDE OF HIM LIKE I CAN...
...AND IF WE COULD ATTACK ALL 12 PLACES SIMULTANEOUSLY...
LOOK CLOSELY AT HIS BODY!

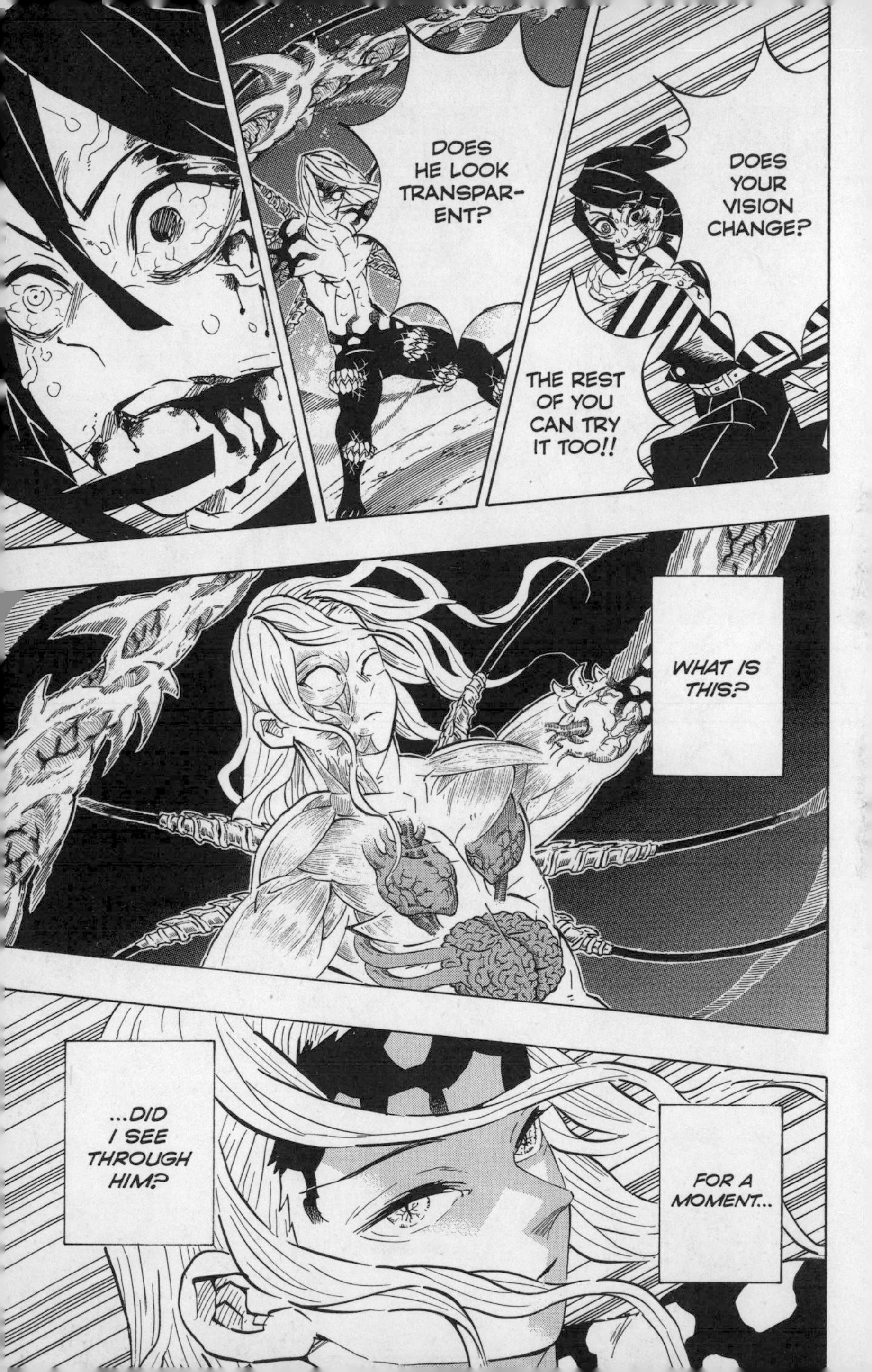
DOES YOUR VISION CHANGE?
THE REST OF YOU CAN TRY IT TOO!!
DOES HE LOOK TRANSPAR-ENT?
WHAT IS THIS?
FOR A MOMENT...
...DID I SEE THROUGH HIM?

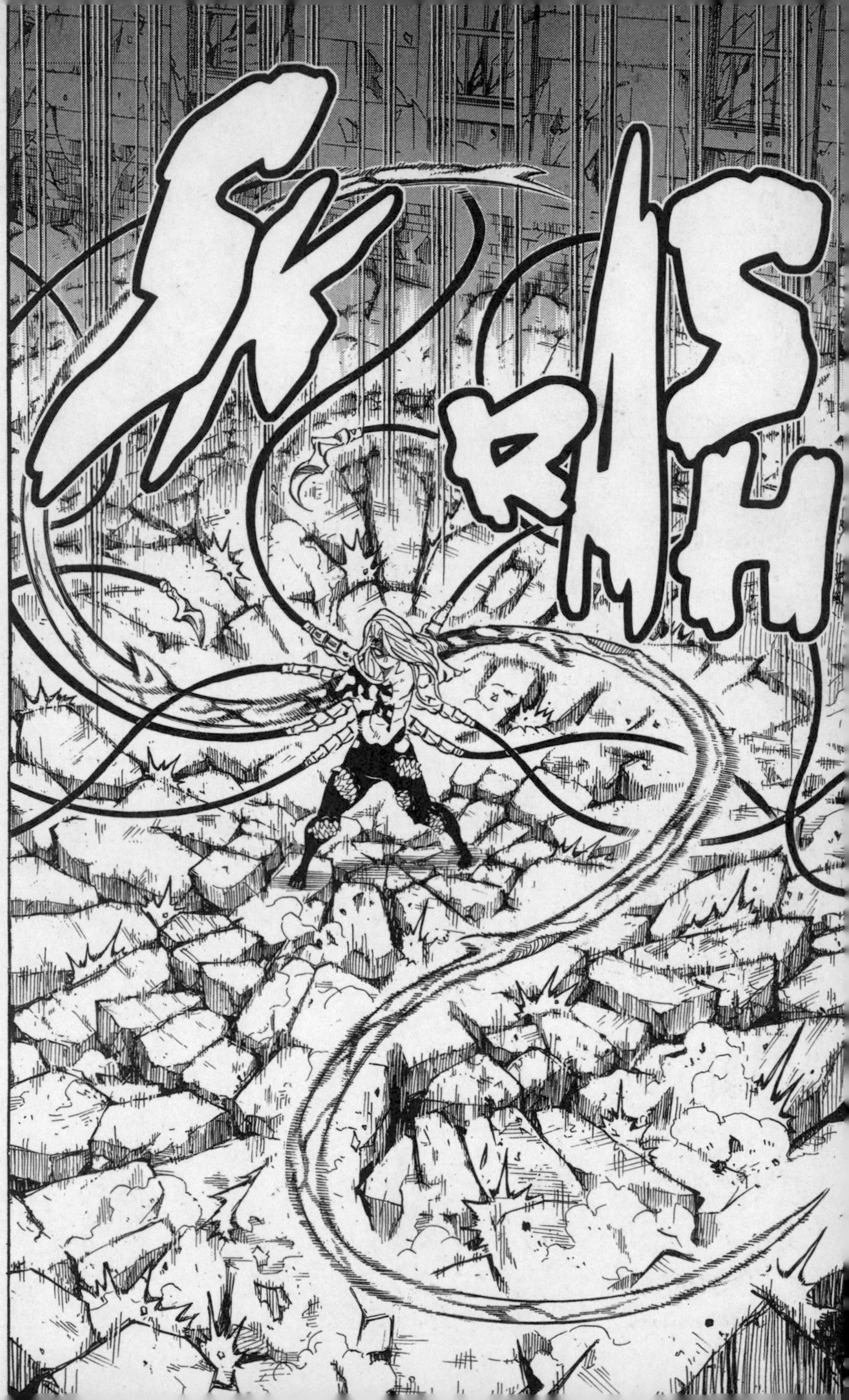
SKRASH

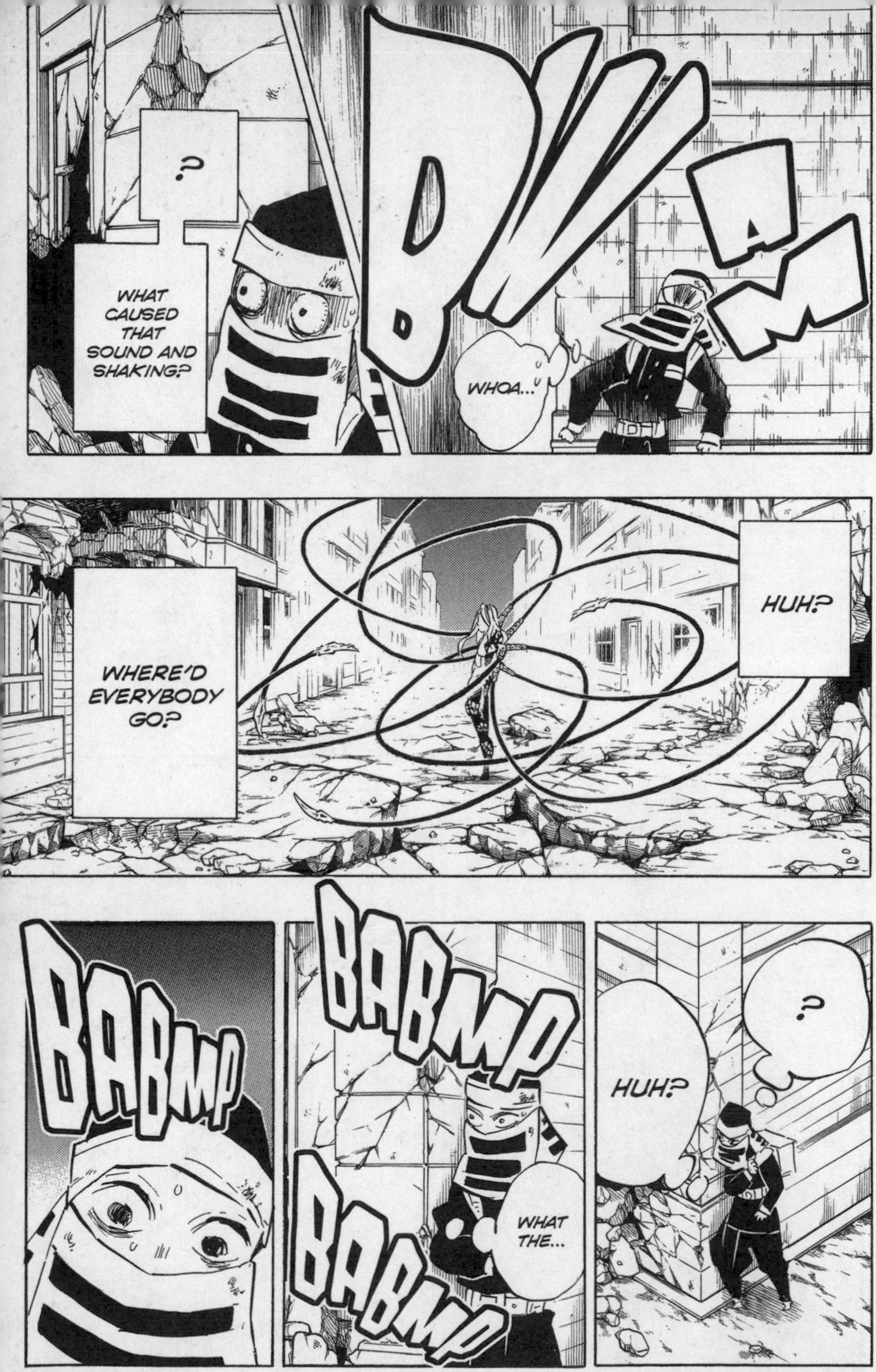
BWAM
WHOA...
?
WHAT CAUSED THAT SOUND AND SHAKING?
HUH?
WHERE'D EVERYBODY GO?
?
HUH?
BABMP
WHAT THE...
BABMP
BABMP

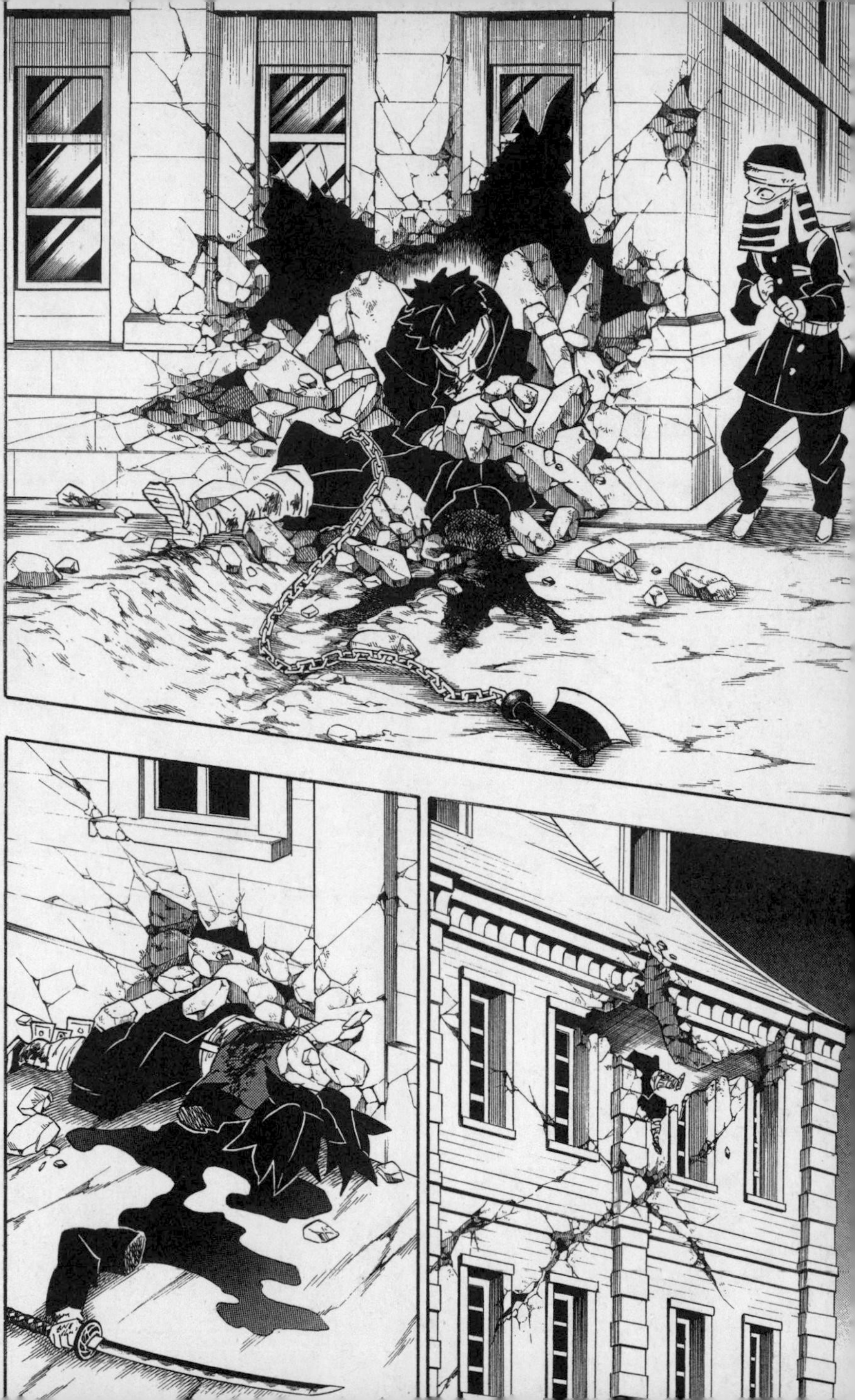

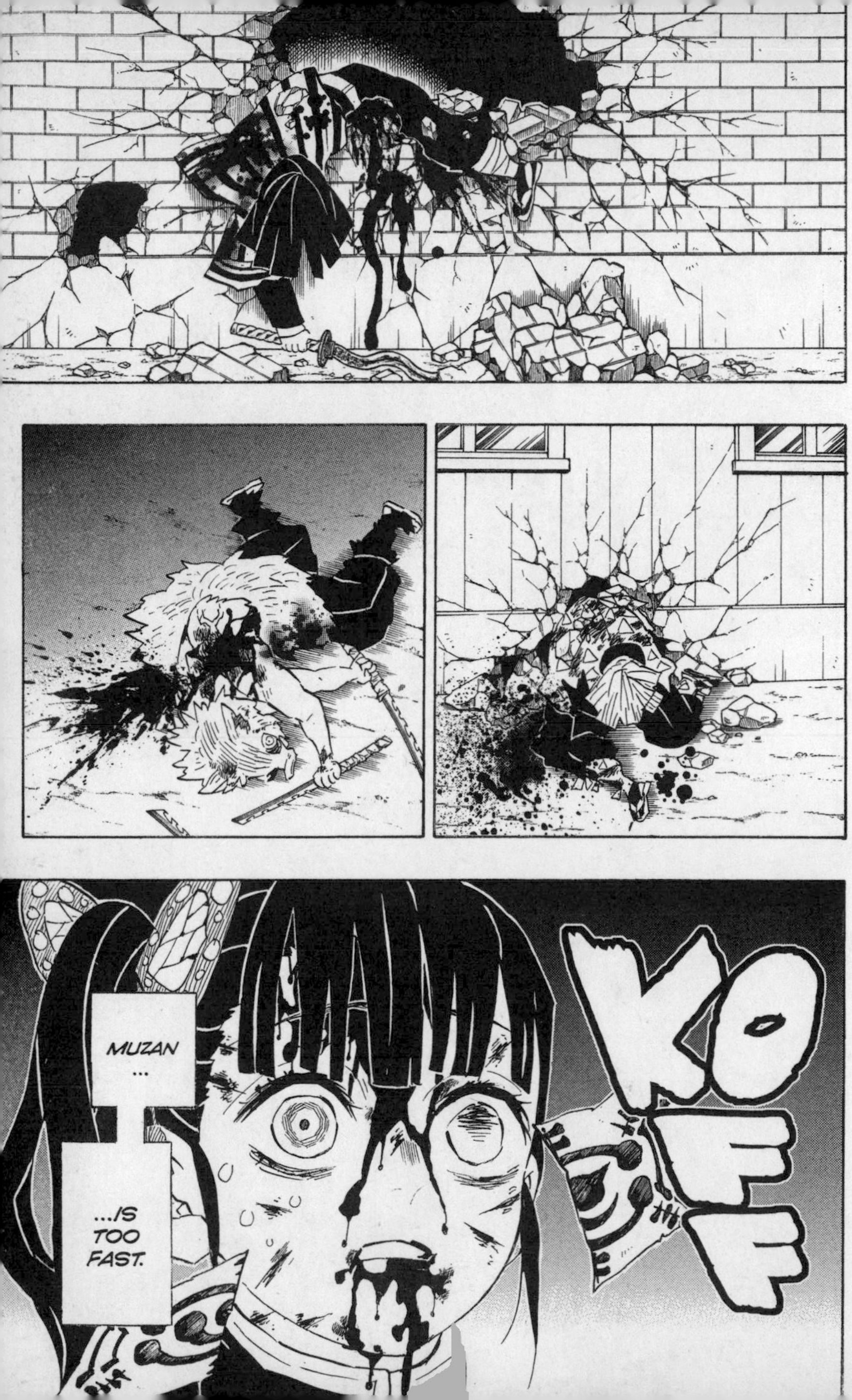
KOFF
MUZAN ...
...IS TOO FAST.

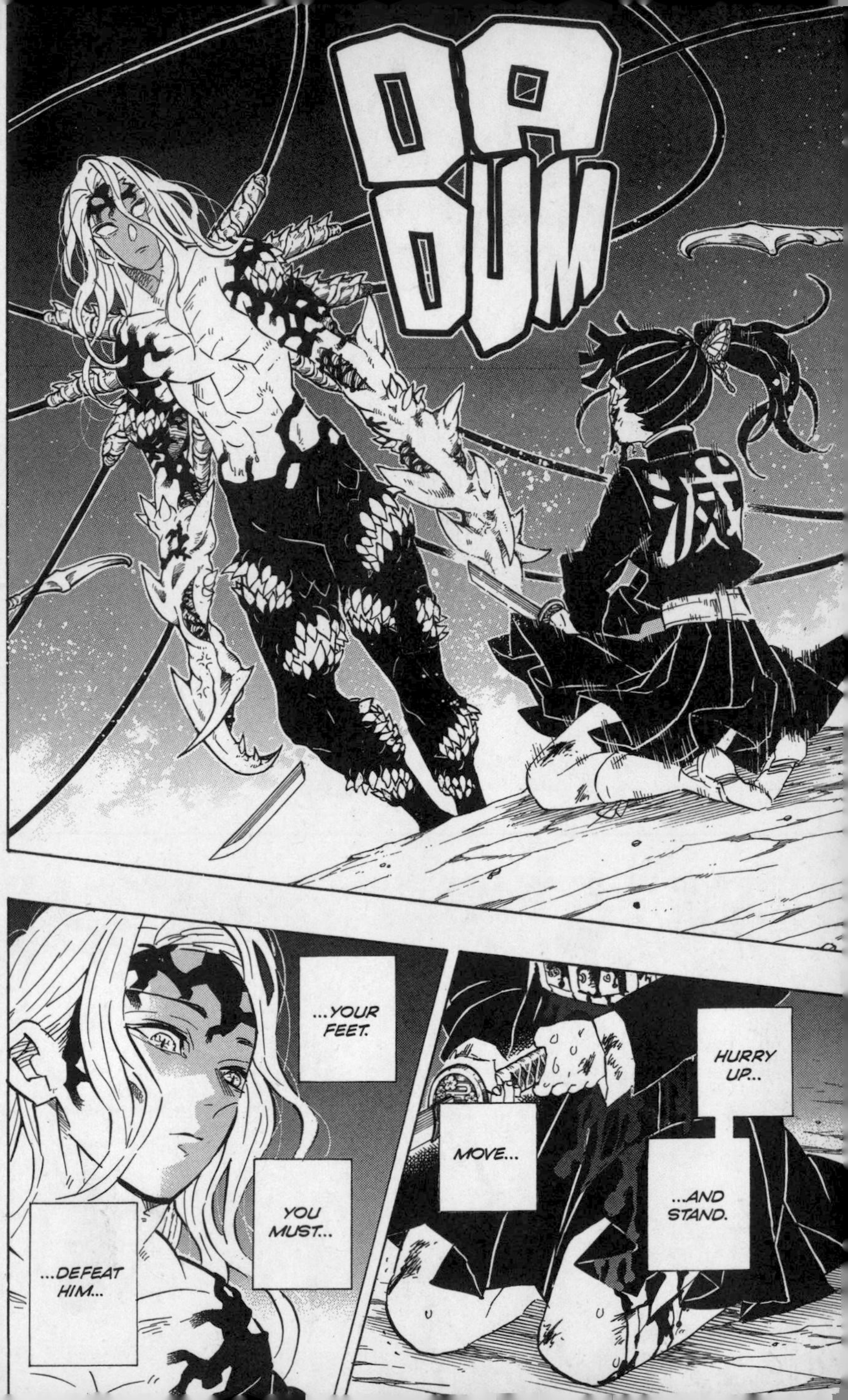
DA
DUM
HURRY UP...
MOVE...
...AND STAND.
...YOUR FEET.
YOU MUST...
...DEFEAT HIM...

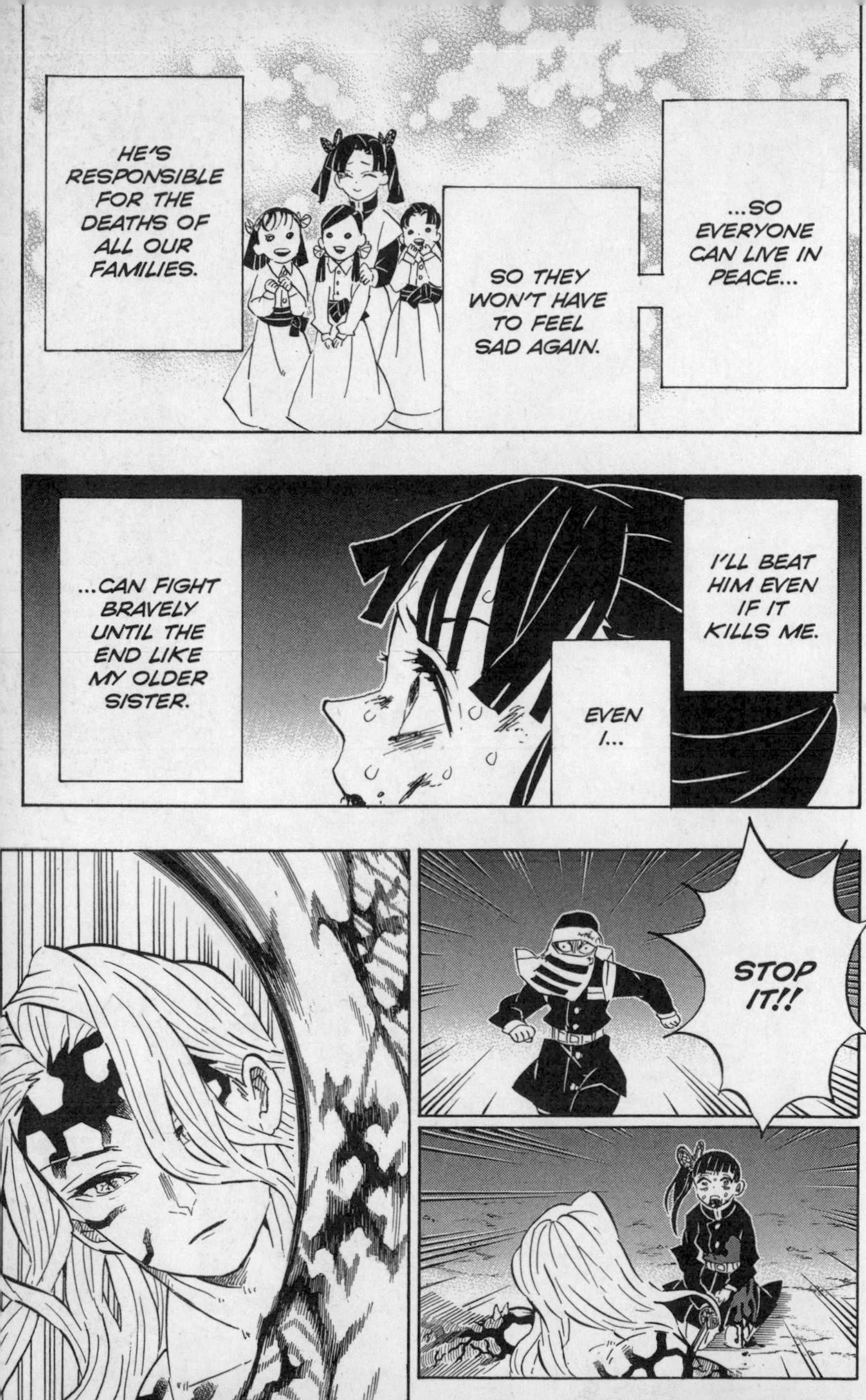
...SO EVERYONE CAN LIVE IN PEACE...
SO THEY WON'T HAVE TO FEEL SAD AGAIN.
HE'S RESPONSIBLE FOR THE DEATHS OF ALL OUR FAMILIES.
I'LL BEAT HIM EVEN IF IT KILLS ME.
EVEN I...
...CAN FIGHT BRAVELY UNTIL THE END LIKE MY OLDER SISTER.
STOP IT!!

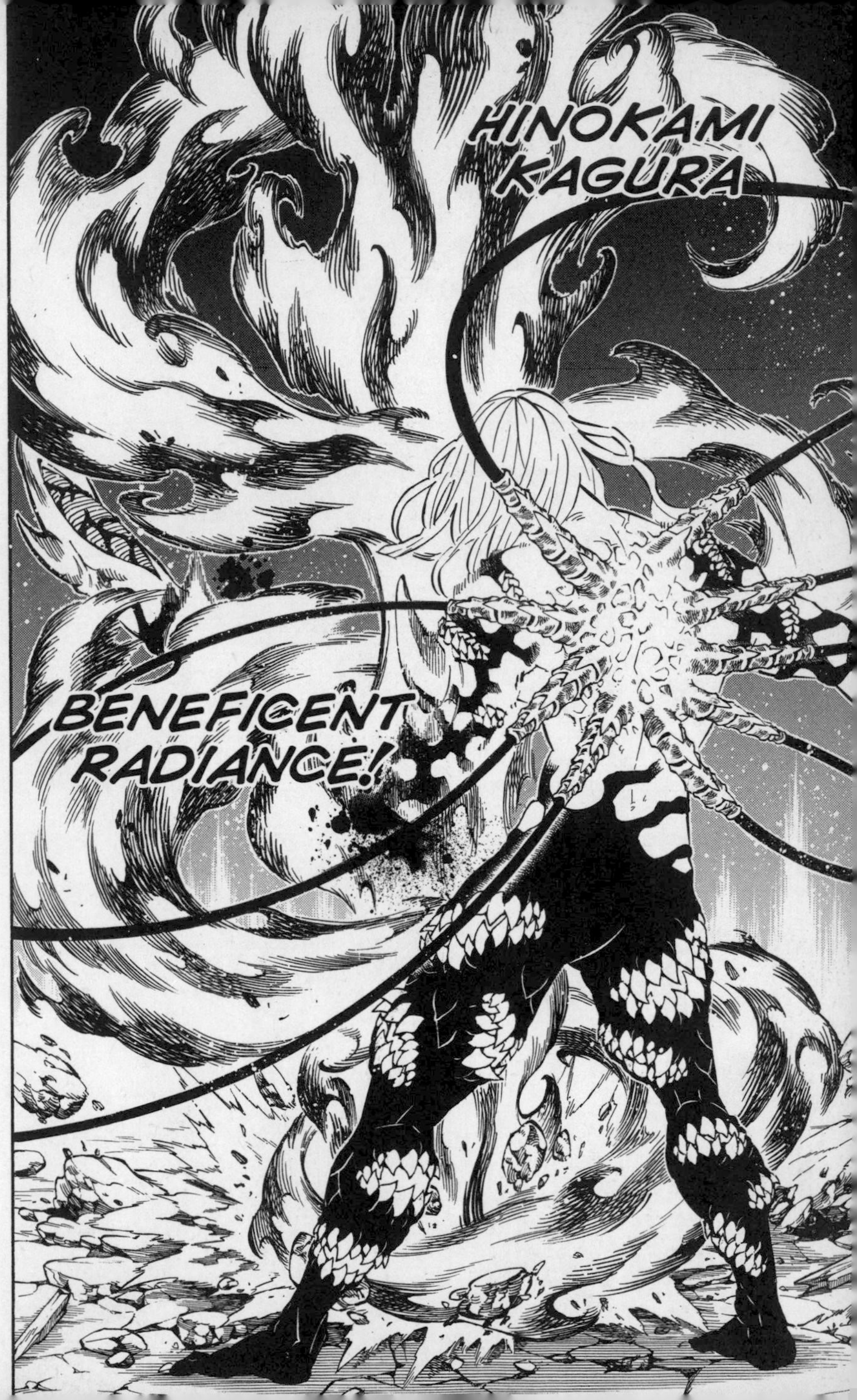
HINOKAMI KAGURA
BENEFICENT RADIANCE!

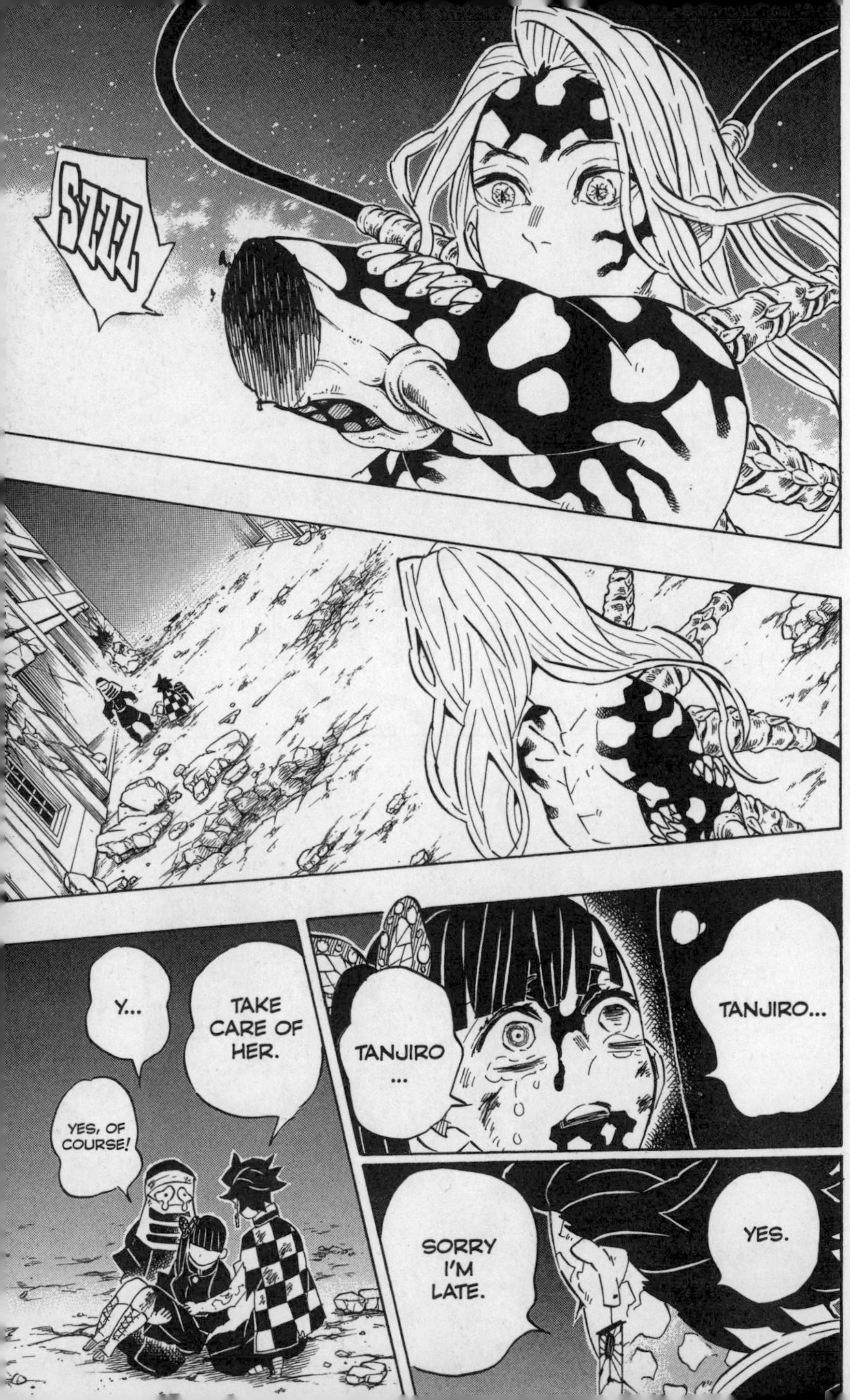
SZZZ
TANJIRO...
TANJIRO ...
YES.
SORRY I'M LATE.
TAKE CARE OF HER.
Y...
YES, OF COURSE!

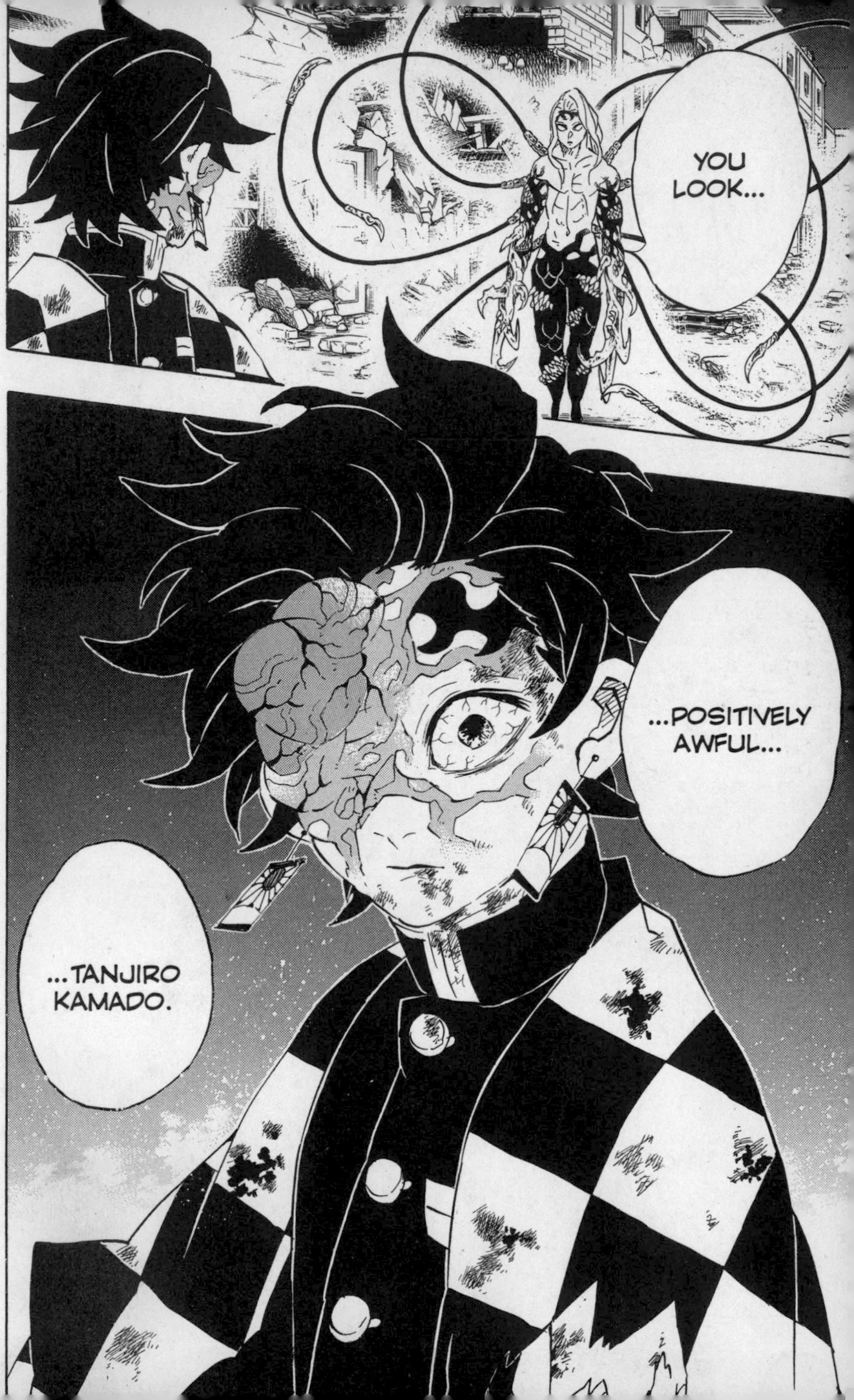
YOU LOOK...
...POSITIVELY AWFUL...
...TANJIRO KAMADO.

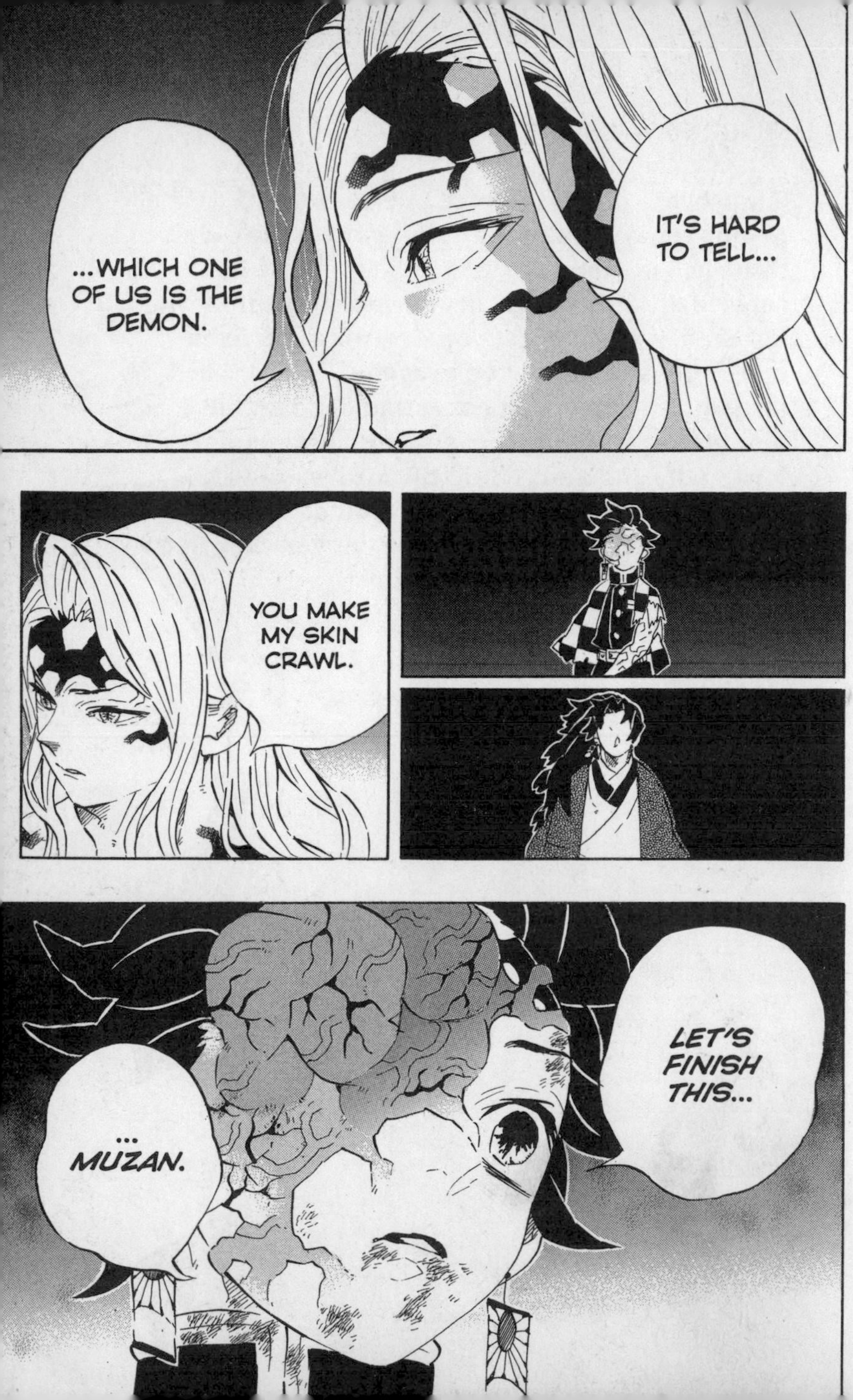
IT'S HARD TO TELL...
...WHICH ONE OF US IS THE DEMON.
YOU MAKE MY SKIN CRAWL.
LET'S FINISH THIS...
... MUZAN.

SENGOKU WHISPERS

Sumiyoshi's house is a nice one because of people repaying him for helping them. He didn't think he had done anything that great, so he refused offerings of gratitude, including money, but then a bunch of carpenters came and fixed up the house so it looked gorgeous. Sumiyoshi and Suyako helped a mother and child in the mountains, and they turned out to be a feudal lord's wife and heir. While the lord was away, a struggle broke out over who would be the successor. Finding their lives in danger, they fled but almost died in the mountains.

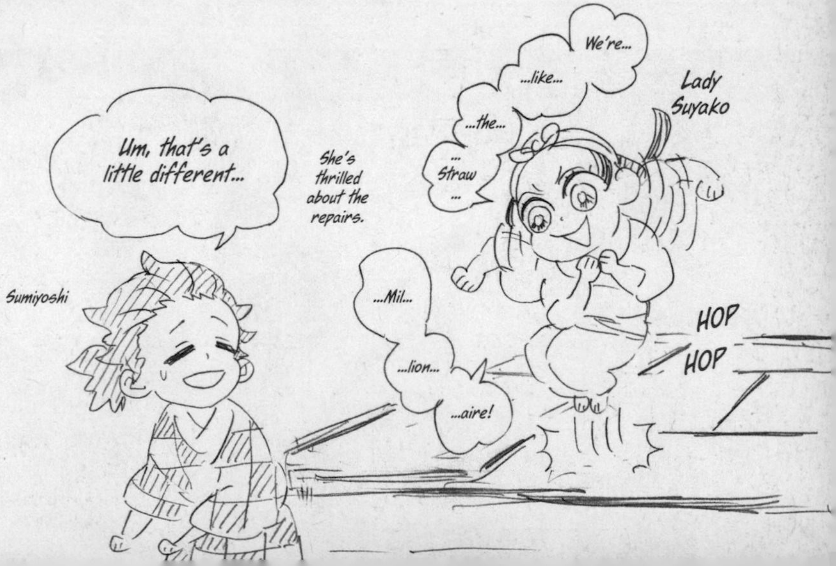
Lady Suyako
We're...
...like...
...the...
...Straw...
She's thrilled about the repairs.
Um, that's a little different...
HOP
HOP
...Mil...
...lion...
...aire!
Sumiyoshi

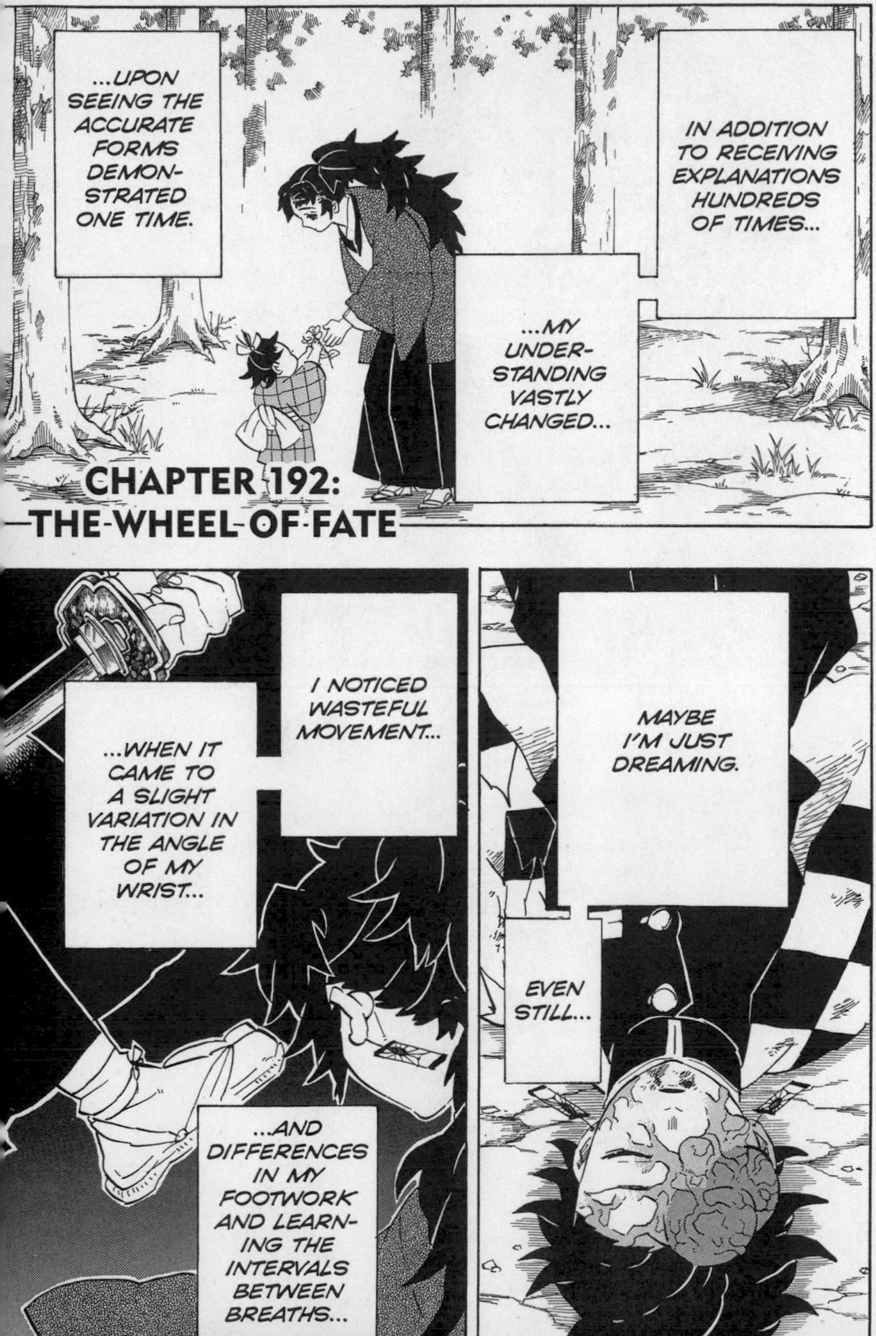
IN ADDITION TO RECEIVING EXPLANATIONS HUNDREDS OF TIMES...
...UPON SEEING THE ACCURATE FORMS DEMON-STRATED ONE TIME.
...MY UNDER-STANDING VASTLY CHANGED...
CHAPTER 192: THE WHEEL OF FATE
MAYBE I'M JUST DREAMING.
EVEN STILL...
I NOTICED WASTEFUL MOVEMENT...
...WHEN IT CAME TO A SLIGHT VARIATION IN THE ANGLE OF MY WRIST...
...AND DIFFERENCES IN MY FOOTWORK AND LEARN-ING THE INTERVALS BETWEEN BREATHS...

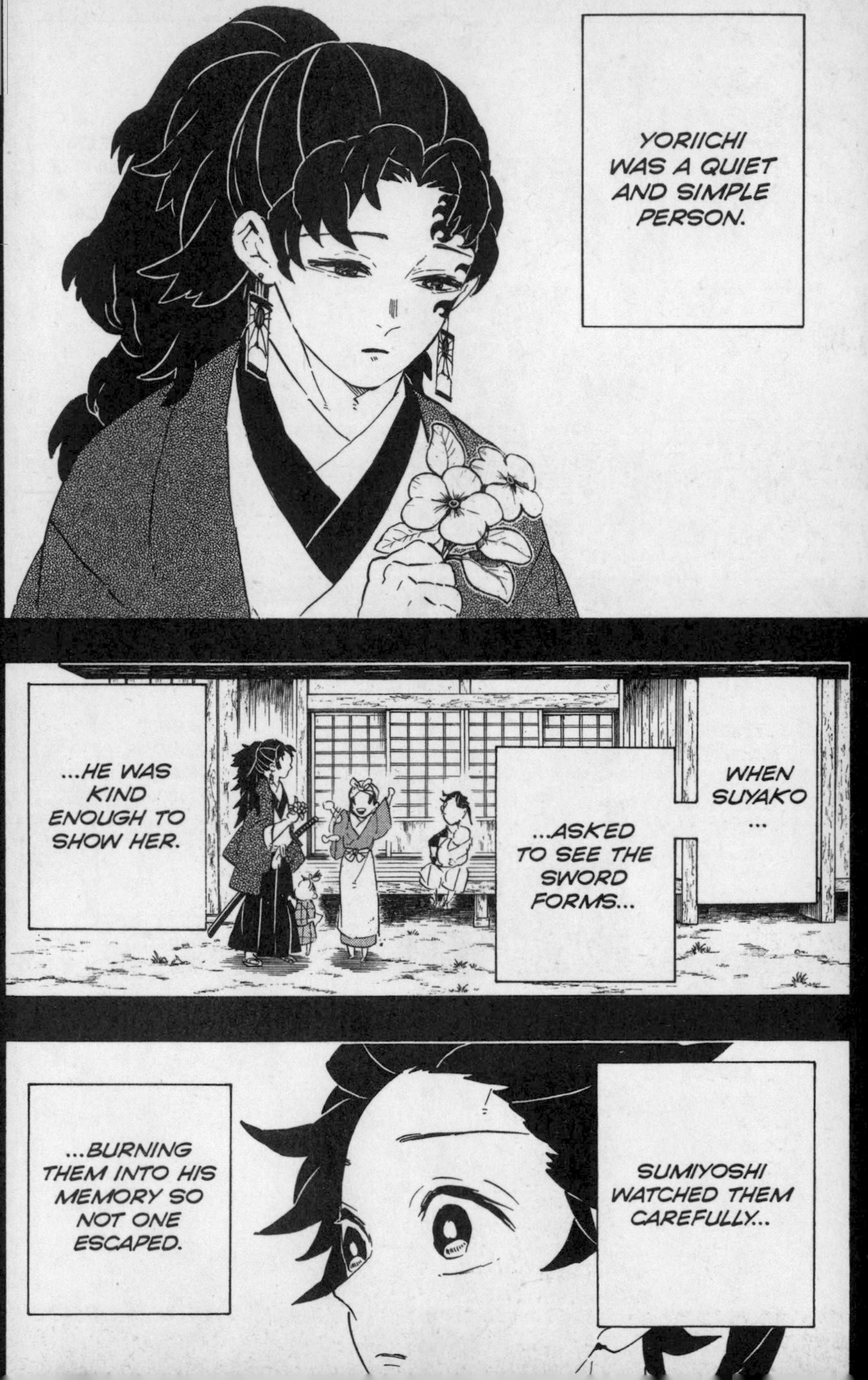
YORIICHI WAS A QUIET AND SIMPLE PERSON.
WHEN SUYAKO ...
...ASKED TO SEE THE SWORD FORMS...
...HE WAS KIND ENOUGH TO SHOW HER.
SUMIYOSHI WATCHED THEM CAREFULLY...
...BURNING THEM INTO HIS MEMORY SO NOT ONE ESCAPED.

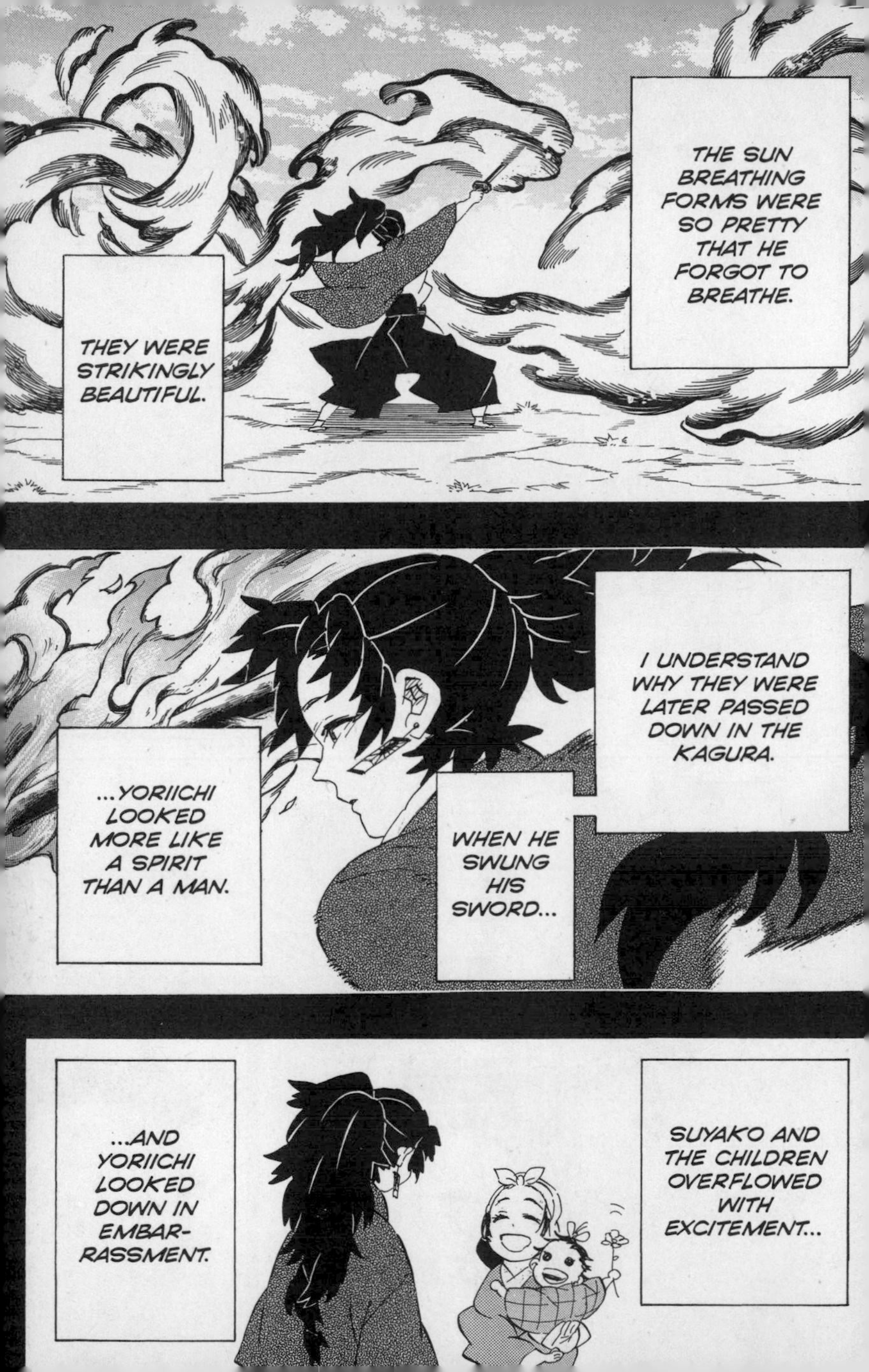
THE SUN BREATHING FORMS WERE SO PRETTY THAT HE FORGOT TO BREATHE.
THEY WERE STRIKINGLY BEAUTIFUL.
I UNDERSTAND WHY THEY WERE LATER PASSED DOWN IN THE KAGURA.
WHEN HE SWUNG HIS SWORD...
...YORIICHI LOOKED MORE LIKE A SPIRIT THAN A MAN.
SUYAKO AND THE CHILDREN OVERFLOWED WITH EXCITEMENT...
...AND YORIICHI LOOKED DOWN IN EMBAR-RASSMENT.

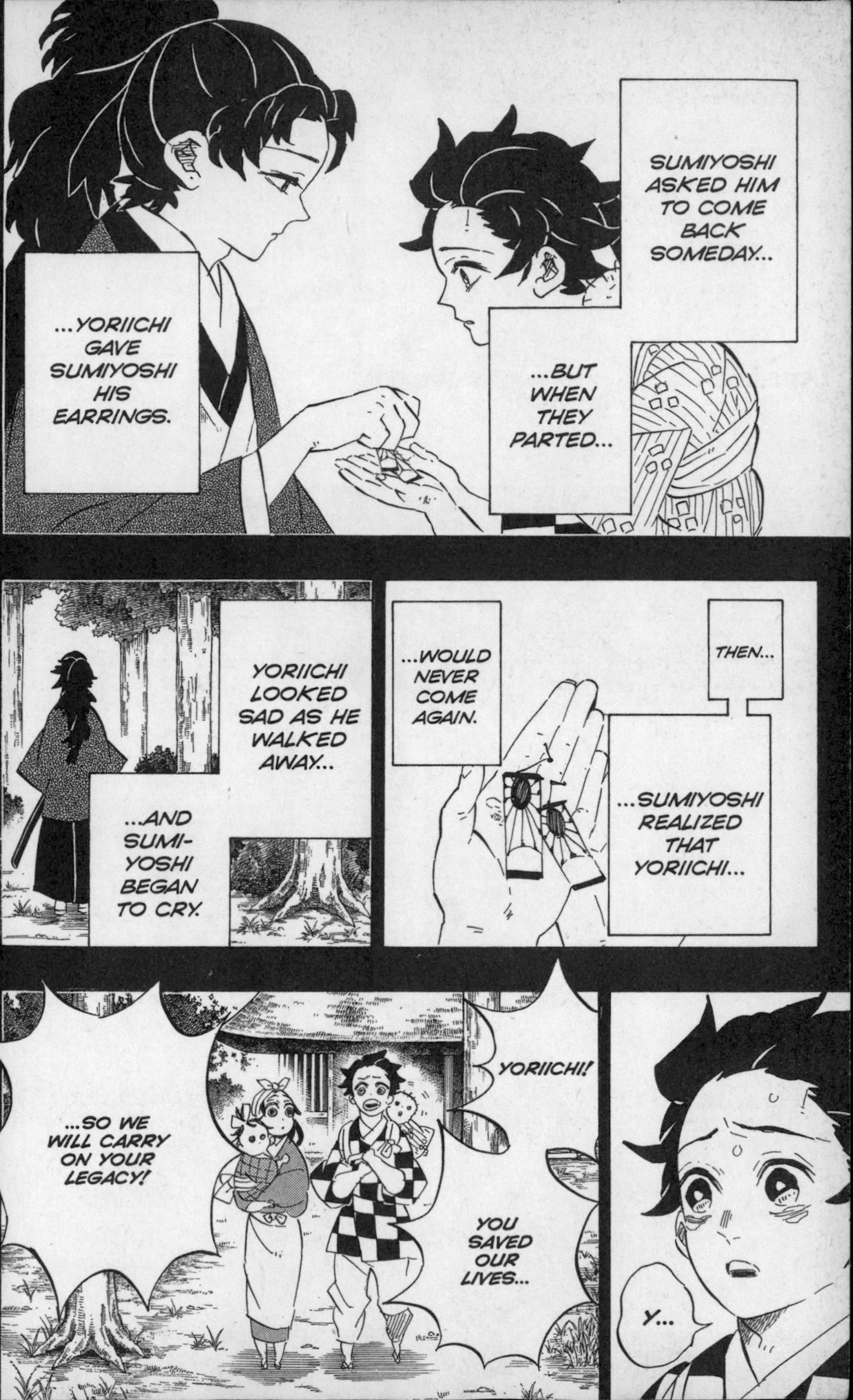
SUMIYOSHI ASKED HIM TO COME BACK SOMEDAY...
...BUT WHEN THEY PARTED...
...YORIICHI GAVE SUMIYOSHI HIS EARRINGS.
THEN...
...SUMIYOSHI REALIZED THAT YORIICHI...
...WOULD NEVER COME AGAIN.
YORIICHI LOOKED SAD AS HE WALKED AWAY...
...AND SUMI-YOSHI BEGAN TO CRY.
Y...
YORIICHI!
YOU SAVED OUR LIVES...
...SO WE WILL CARRY ON YOUR LEGACY!

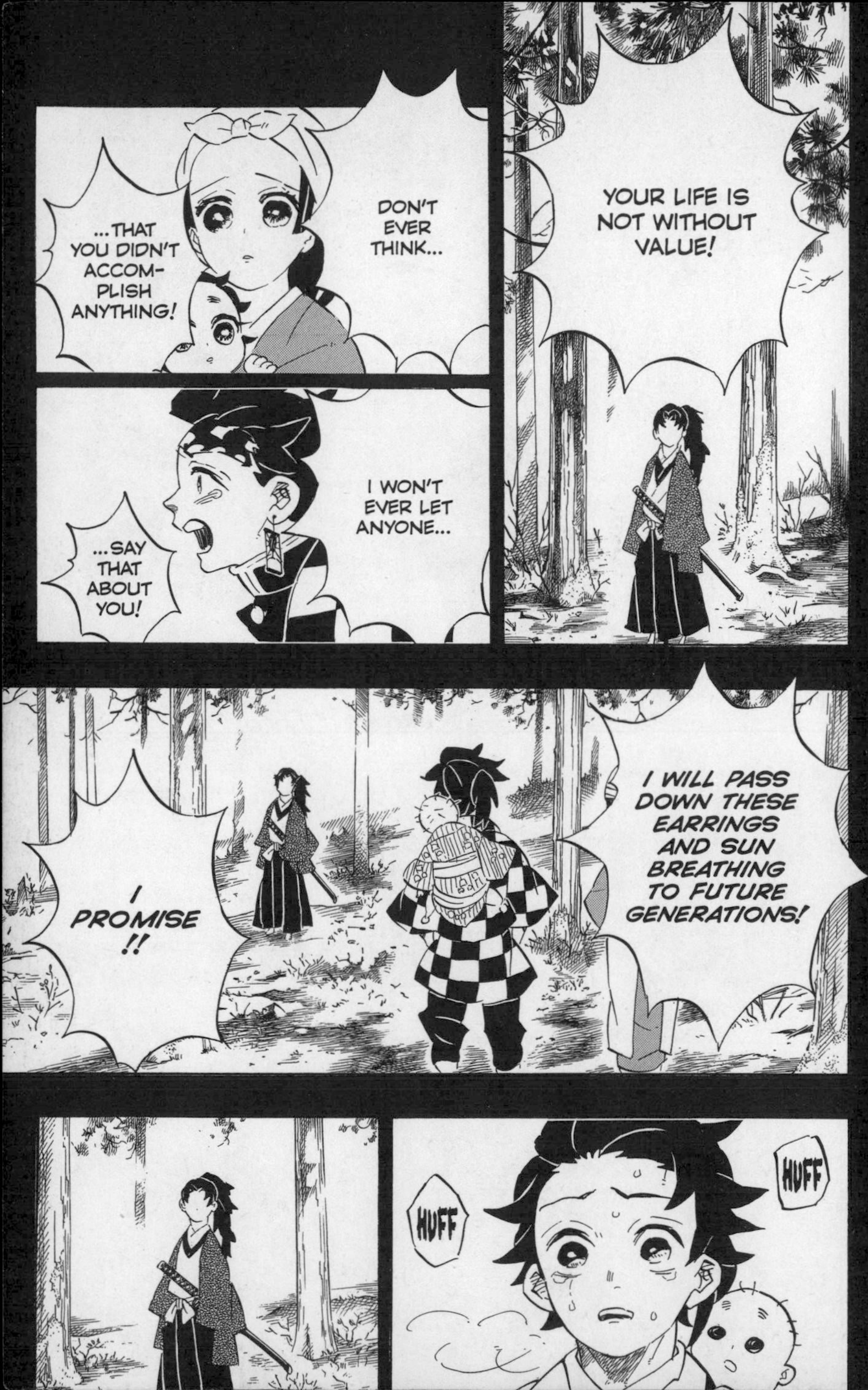
YOUR LIFE IS NOT WITHOUT VALUE!
DON'T EVER THINK...
...THAT YOU DIDN'T ACCOM-PLISH ANYTHING!
I WON'T EVER LET ANYONE...
...SAY THAT ABOUT YOU!
I WILL PASS DOWN THESE EARRINGS AND SUN BREATHING TO FUTURE GENERATIONS!
I PROMISE!!
HUFF
HUFF

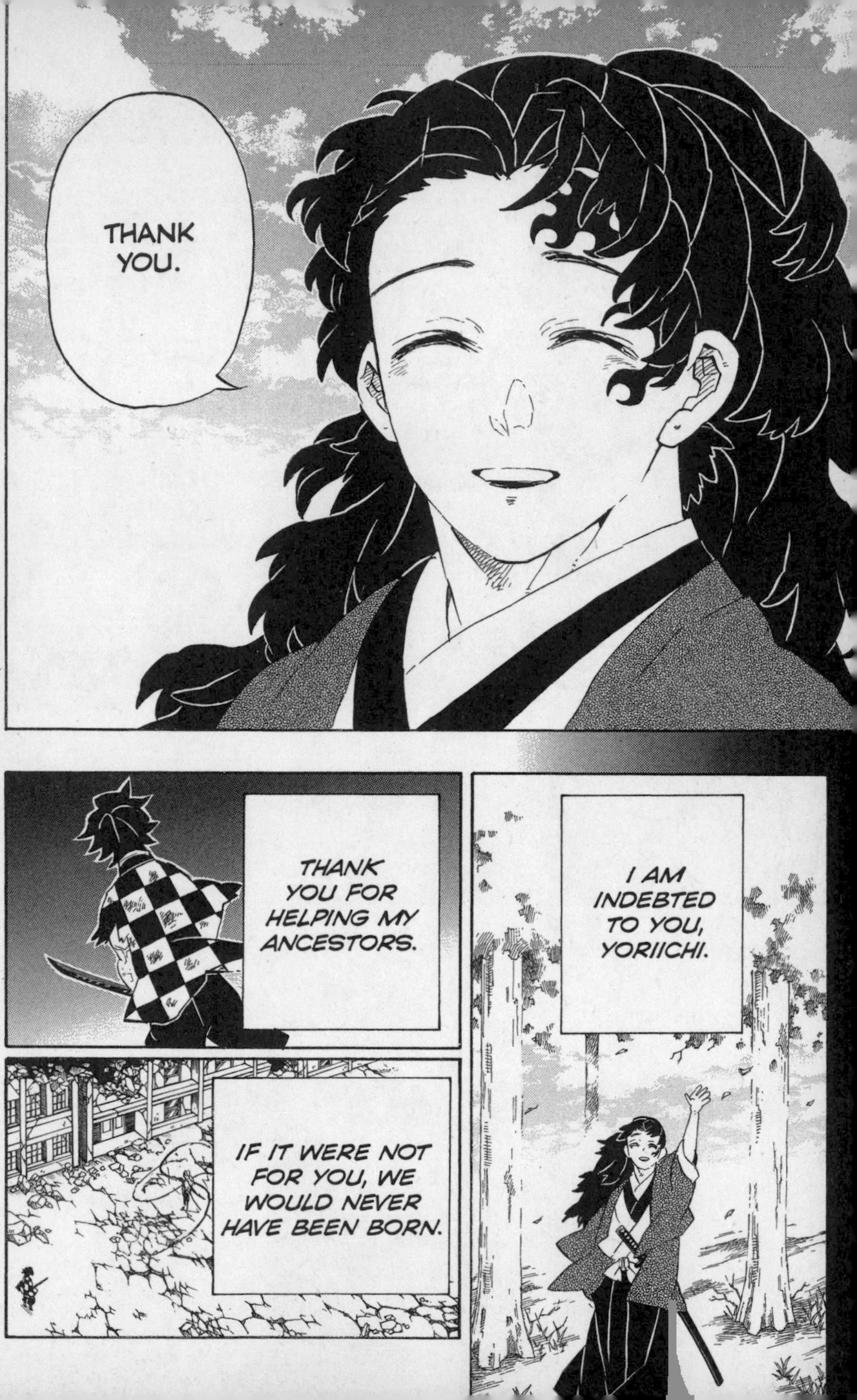
THANK YOU.
I AM INDEBTED TO YOU, YORIICHI.
THANK YOU FOR HELPING MY ANCESTORS.
IF IT WERE NOT FOR YOU, WE WOULD NEVER HAVE BEEN BORN.

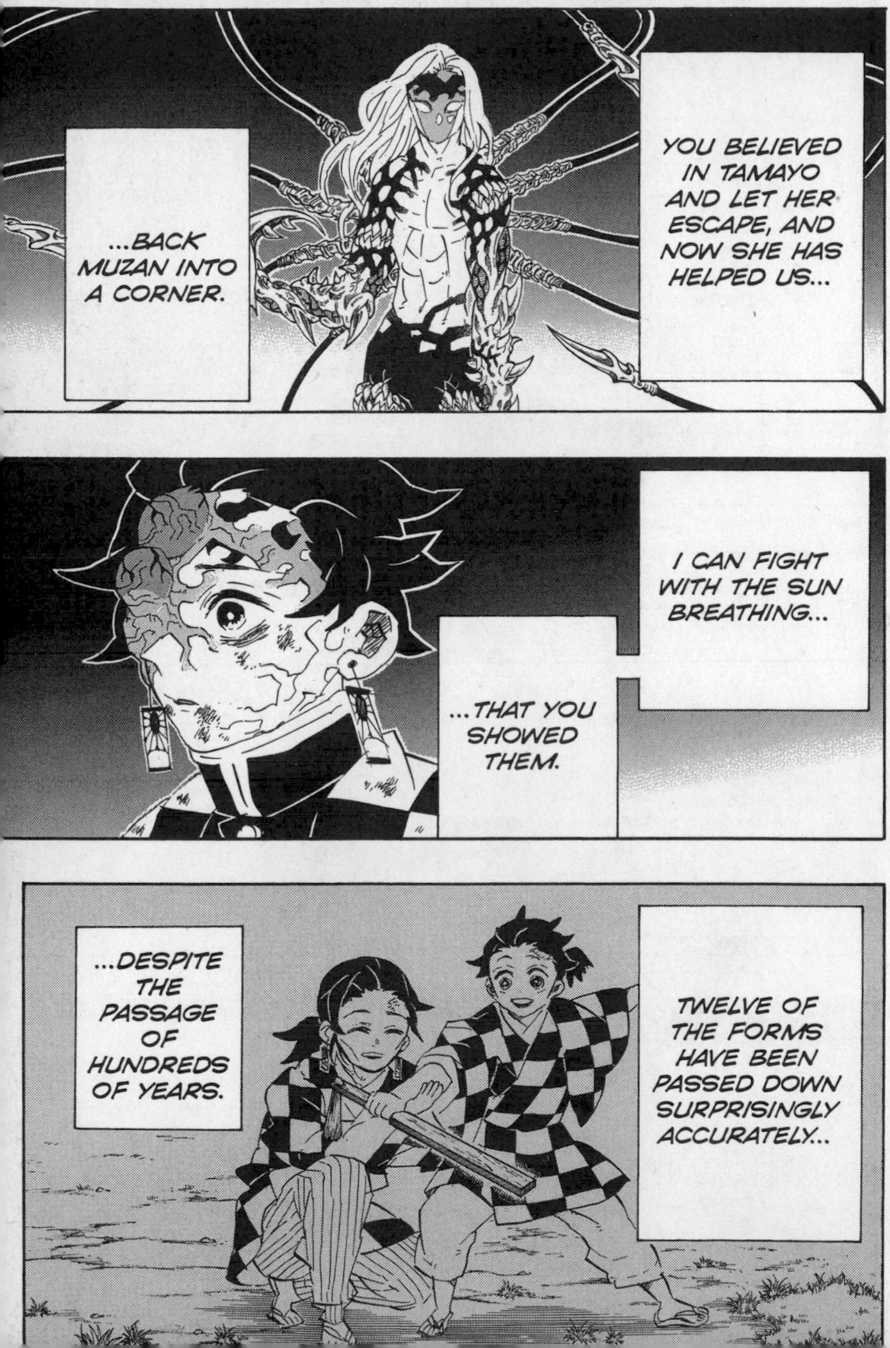
YOU BELIEVED IN TAMAYO AND LET HER ESCAPE, AND NOW SHE HAS HELPED US...
...BACK MUZAN INTO A CORNER.
I CAN FIGHT WITH THE SUN BREATHING...
...THAT YOU SHOWED THEM.
TWELVE OF THE FORMS HAVE BEEN PASSED DOWN SURPRISINGLY ACCURATELY...
...DESPITE THE PASSAGE OF HUNDREDS OF YEARS.

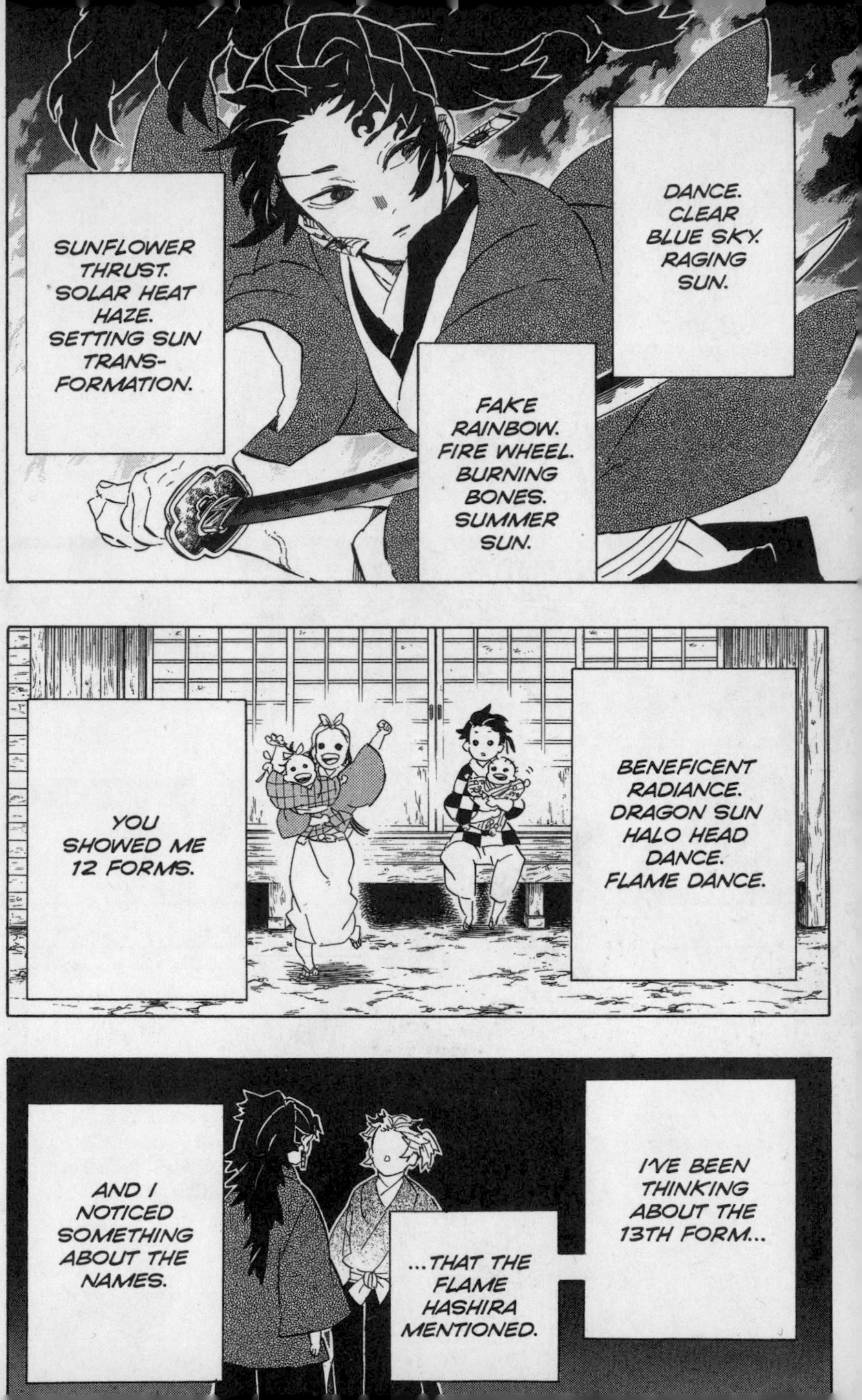
DANCE. CLEAR BLUE SKY. RAGING SUN.
FAKE RAINBOW. FIRE WHEEL. BURNING BONES. SUMMER SUN.
SUNFLOWER THRUST. SOLAR HEAT HAZE. SETTING SUN TRANS-FORMATION.
BENEFICENT RADIANCE. DRAGON SUN HALO HEAD DANCE. FLAME DANCE.
YOU SHOWED ME 12 FORMS.
I'VE BEEN THINKING ABOUT THE 13TH FORM...
...THAT THE FLAME HASHIRA MENTIONED.
AND I NOTICED SOMETHING ABOUT THE NAMES.

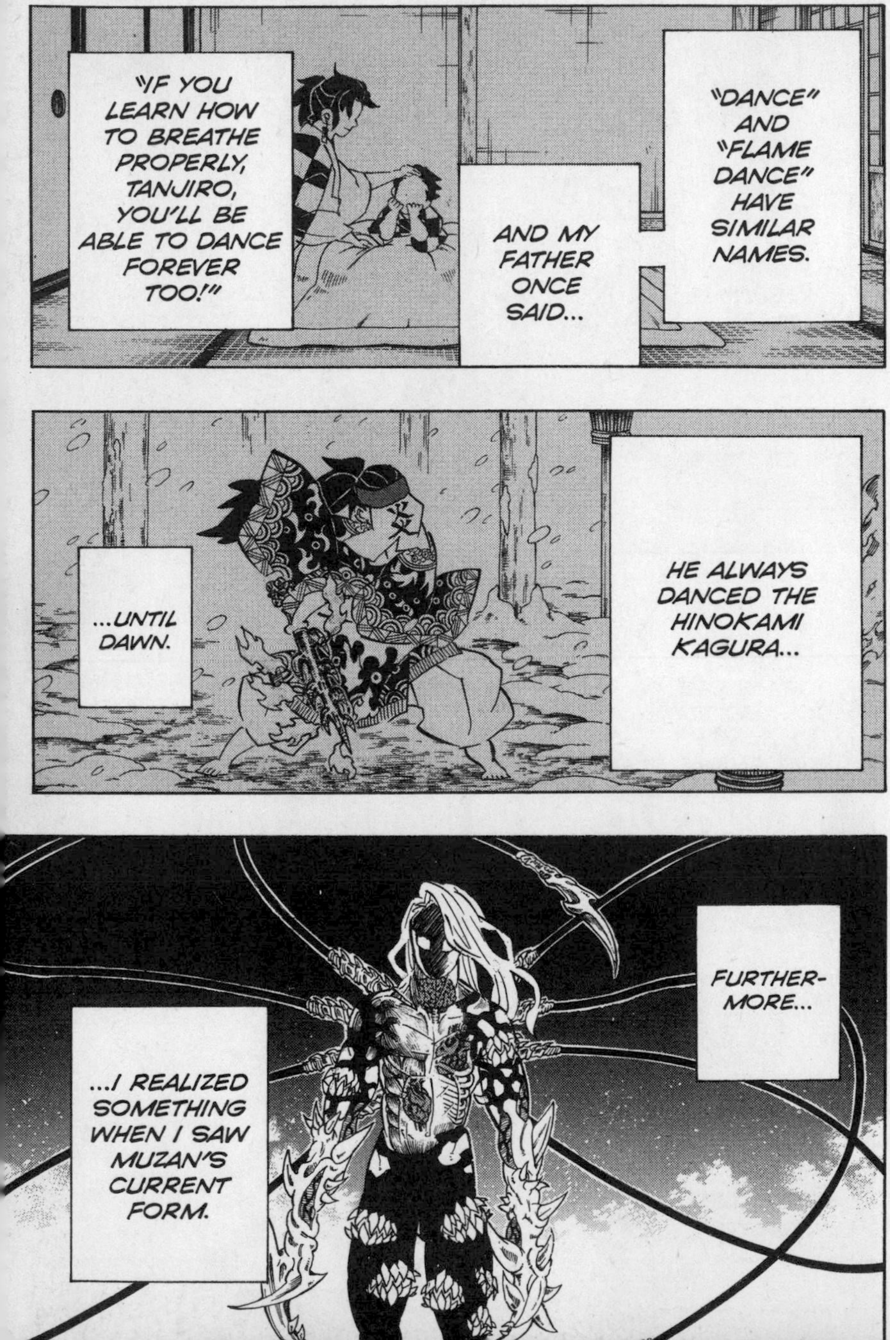
"DANCE" AND "FLAME DANCE" HAVE SIMILAR NAMES.
AND MY FATHER ONCE SAID...
"IF YOU LEARN HOW TO BREATHE PROPERLY, TANJIRO, YOU'LL BE ABLE TO DANCE FOREVER TOO!"
HE ALWAYS DANCED THE HINOKAMI KAGURA...
...UNTIL DAWN.
FURTHER-MORE...
...I REALIZED SOMETHING WHEN I SAW MUZAN'S CURRENT FORM.

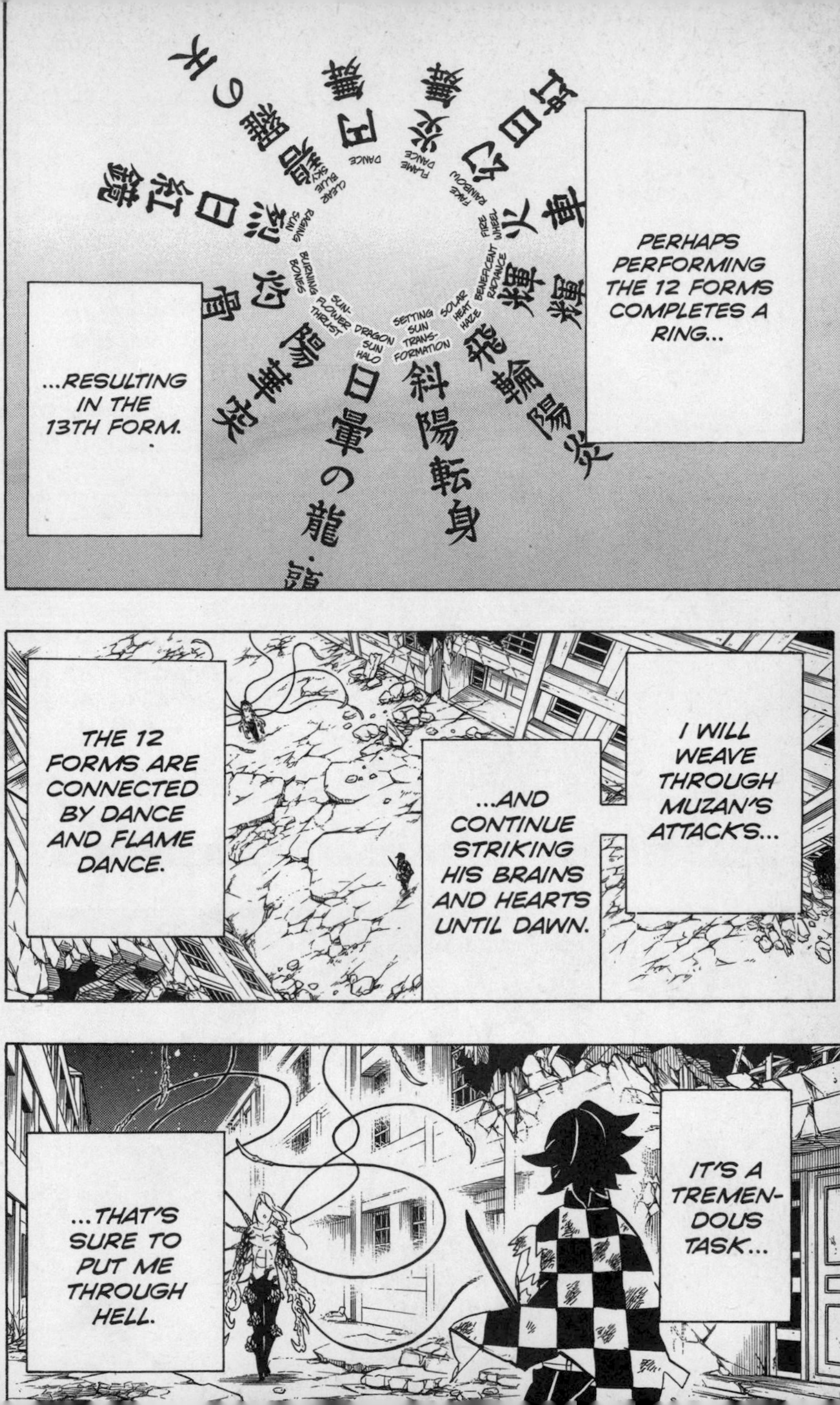
PERHAPS PERFORMING THE 12 FORMS COMPLETES A RING...
DANCE
CLEAR BLUE SKY
RAGING SUN
BURNING BONES
SUN-FLOWER THRUST
DRAGON SUN HALO
SETTING SUN TRANS-FORMATION
SOLAR HEAT HAZE
BENEFICENT RADIANCE
FIRE WHEEL
FAKE RAINBOW
FLAME DANCE
...RESULTING IN THE 13TH FORM.
I WILL WEAVE THROUGH MUZAN'S ATTACKS...
...AND CONTINUE STRIKING HIS BRAINS AND HEARTS UNTIL DAWN.
THE 12 FORMS ARE CONNECTED BY DANCE AND FLAME DANCE.
IT'S A TREMEN-DOUS TASK...
...THAT'S SURE TO PUT ME THROUGH HELL.

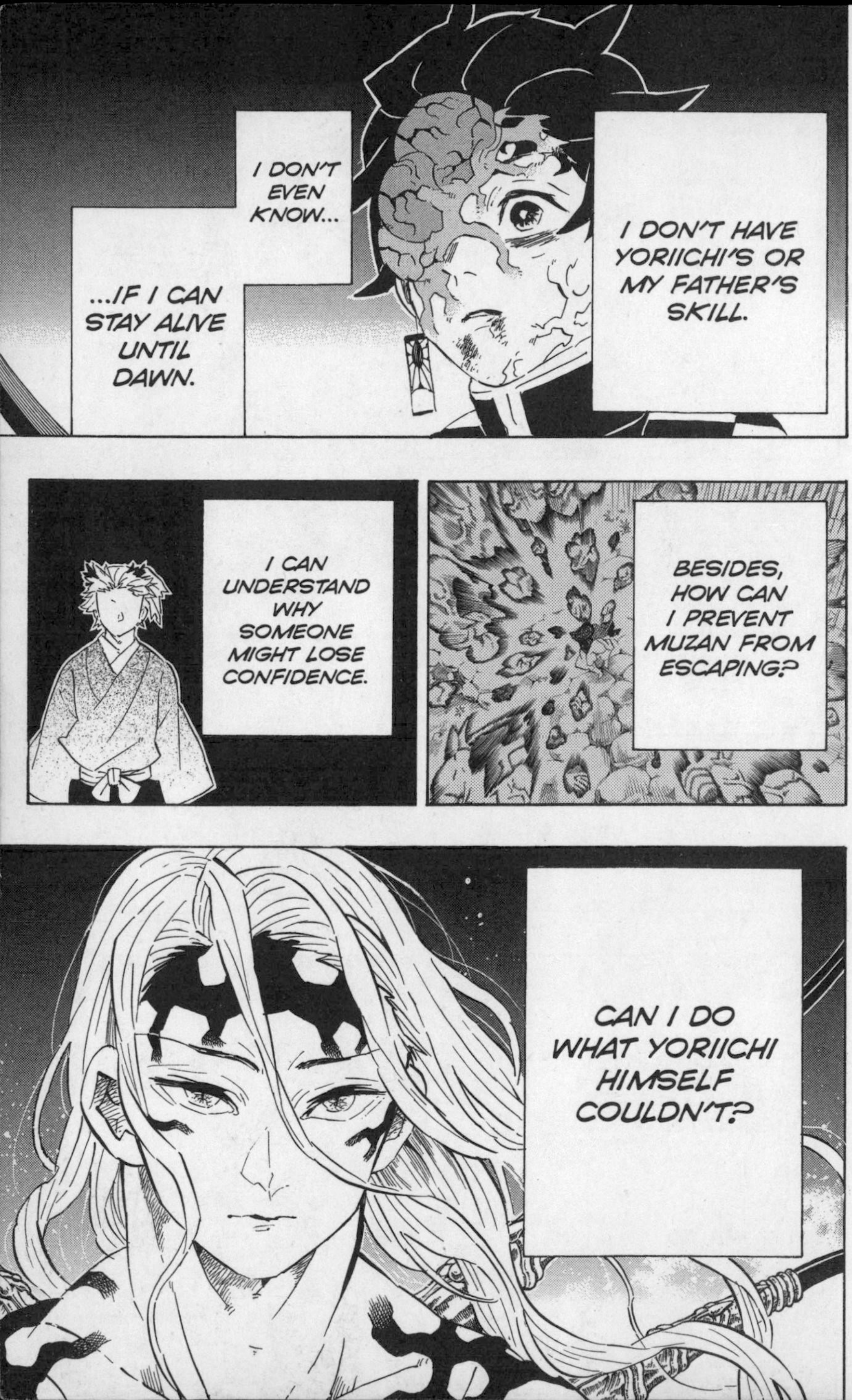
I DON'T HAVE YORIICHI'S OR MY FATHER'S SKILL.
I DON'T EVEN KNOW...
...IF I CAN STAY ALIVE UNTIL DAWN.
BESIDES, HOW CAN I PREVENT MUZAN FROM ESCAPING?
I CAN UNDERSTAND WHY SOMEONE MIGHT LOSE CONFIDENCE.
CAN I DO WHAT YORIICHI HIMSELF COULDN'T?

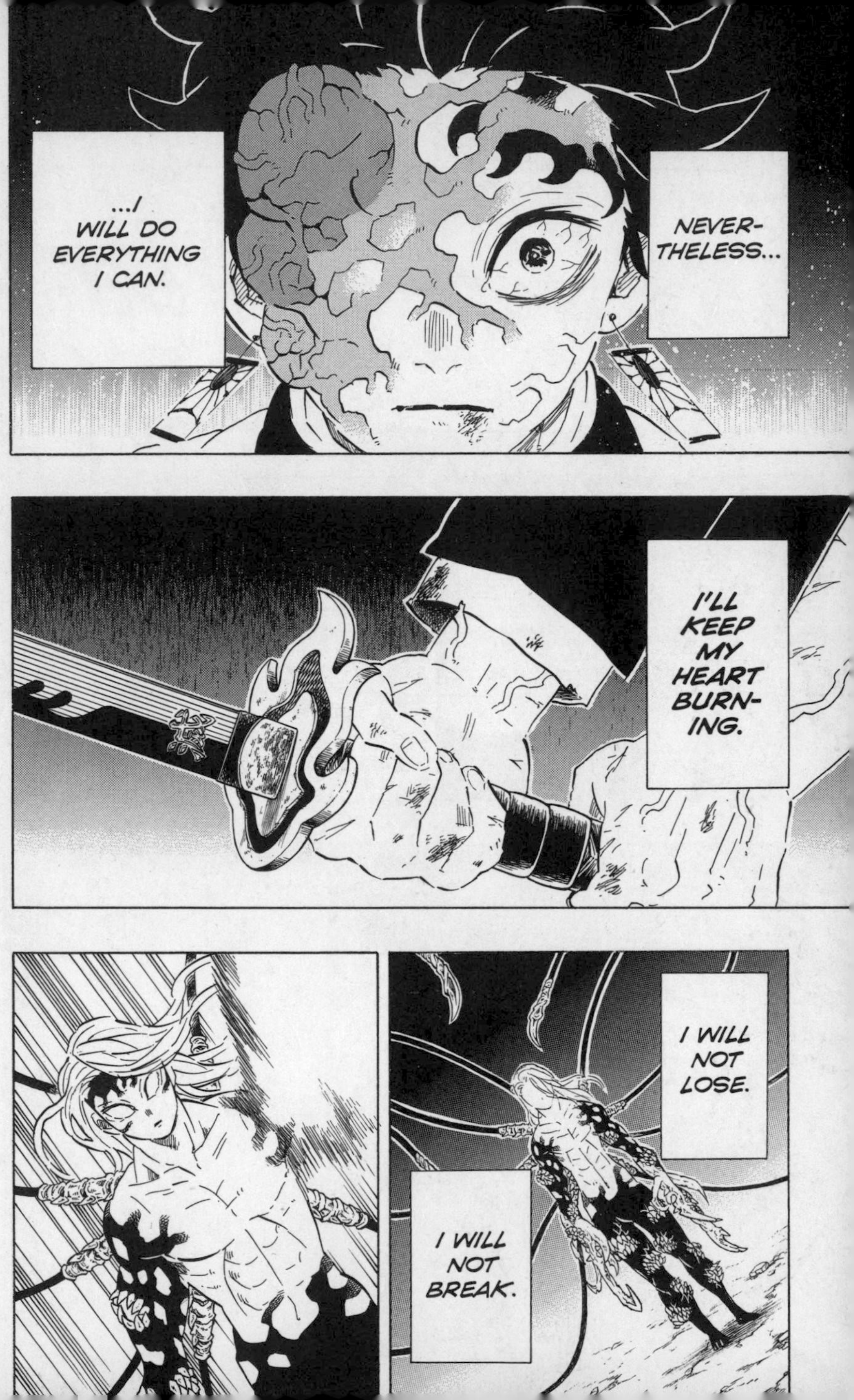
NEVER-THELESS...
...I WILL DO EVERYTHING I CAN.
I'LL KEEP MY HEART BURNING.
I WILL NOT LOSE.
I WILL NOT BREAK.

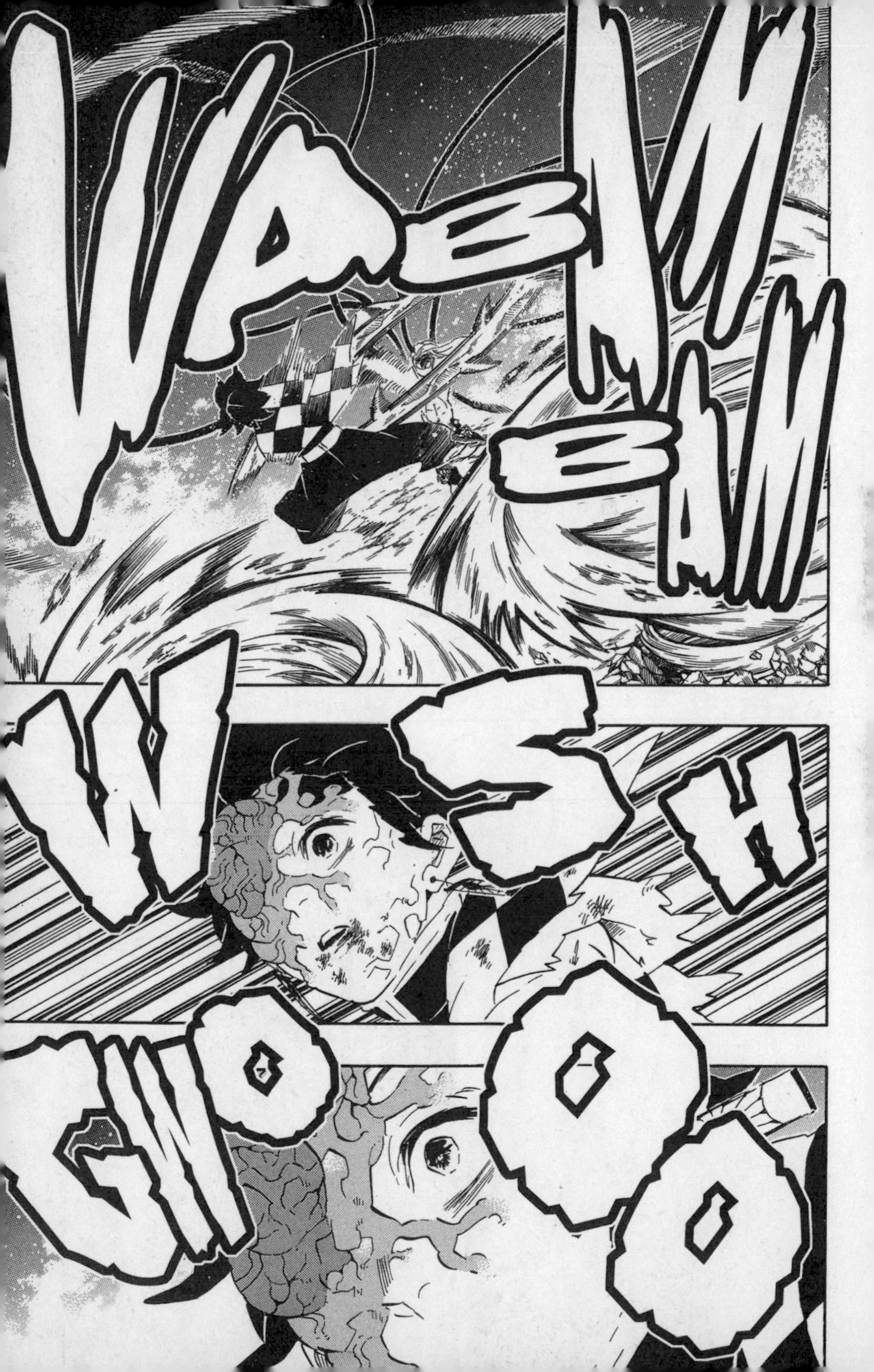

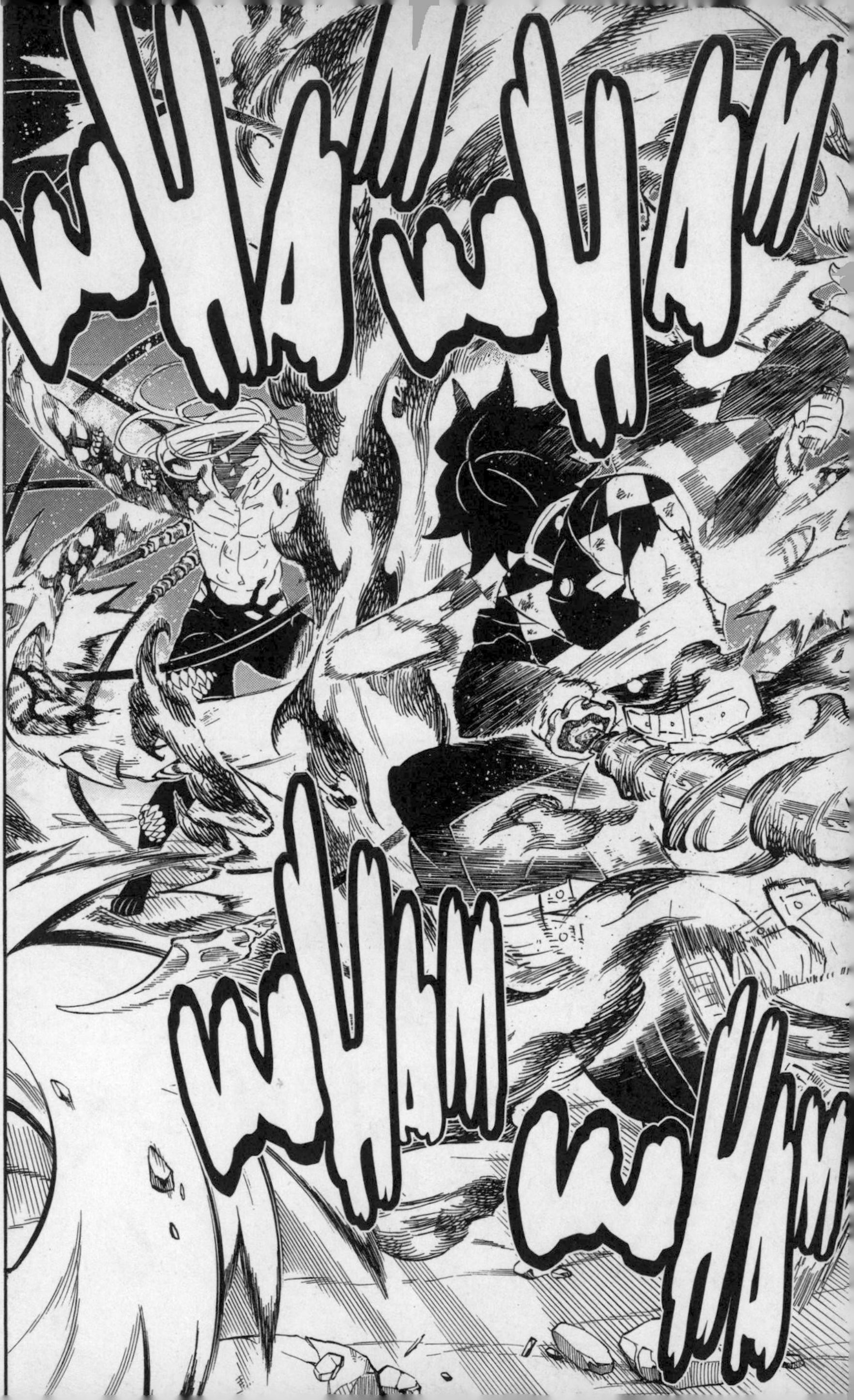
WHAM
WHAM
WHAM
WHAM

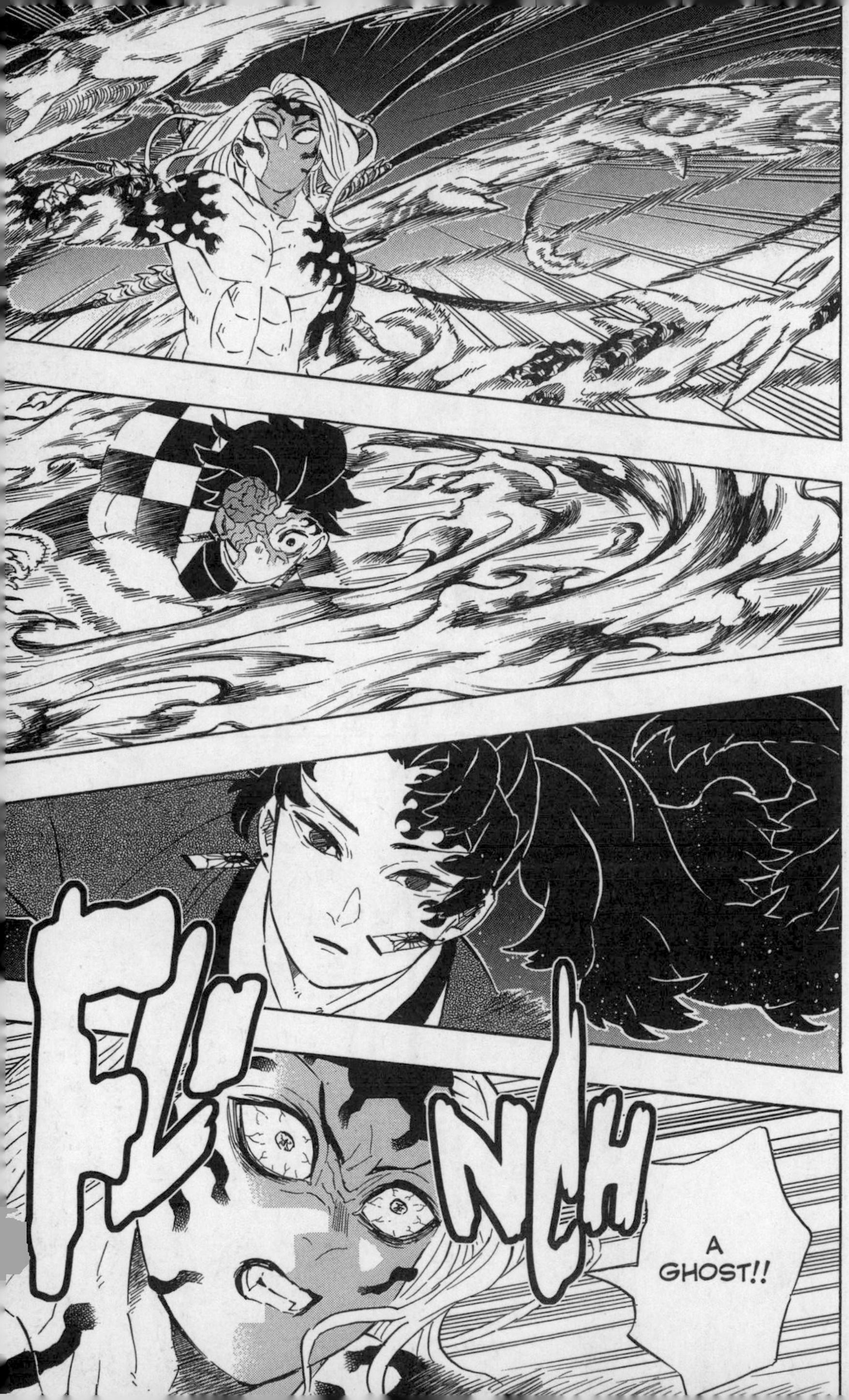
FLINCH
A GHOST!!

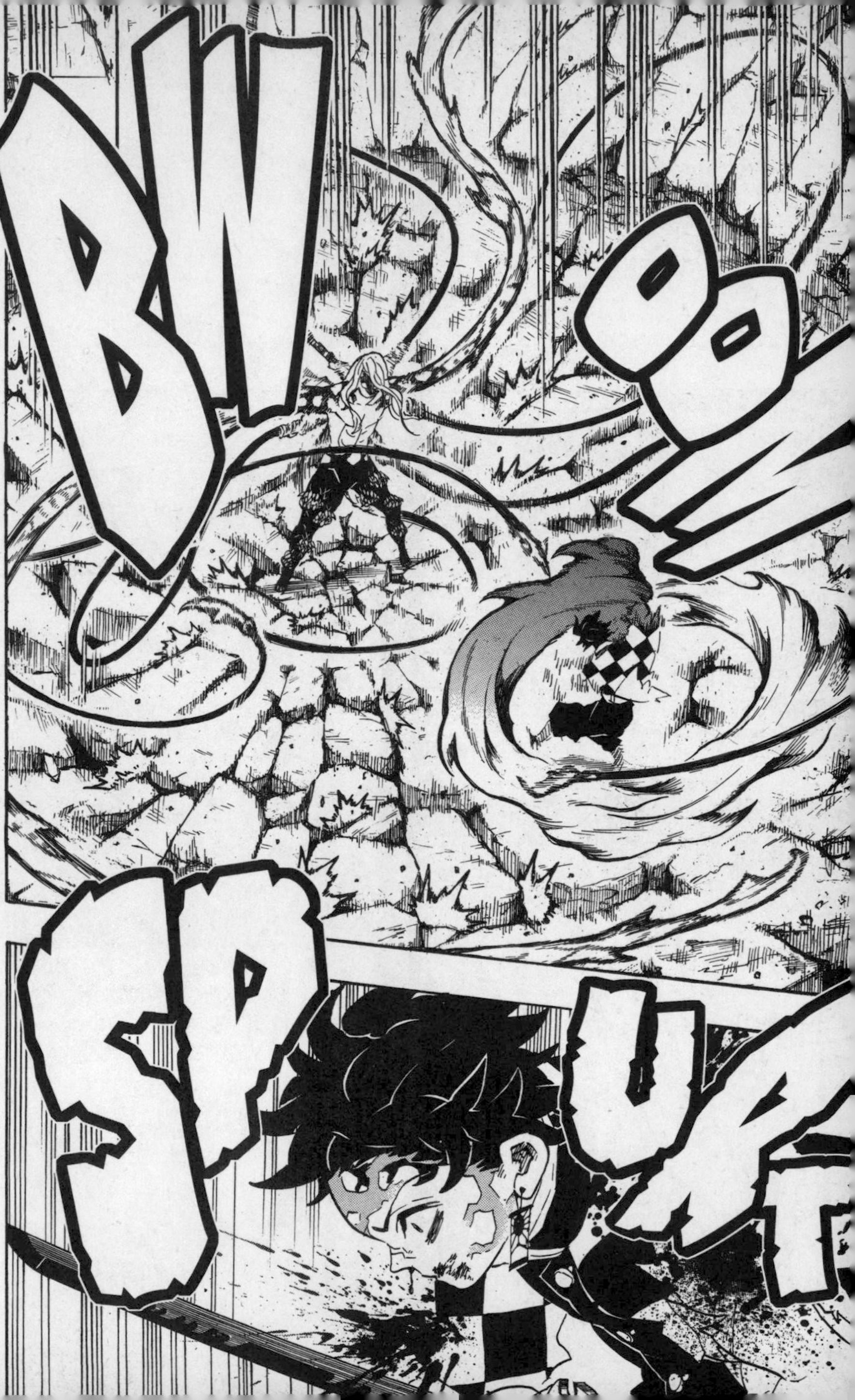
BWOOM
SPURT

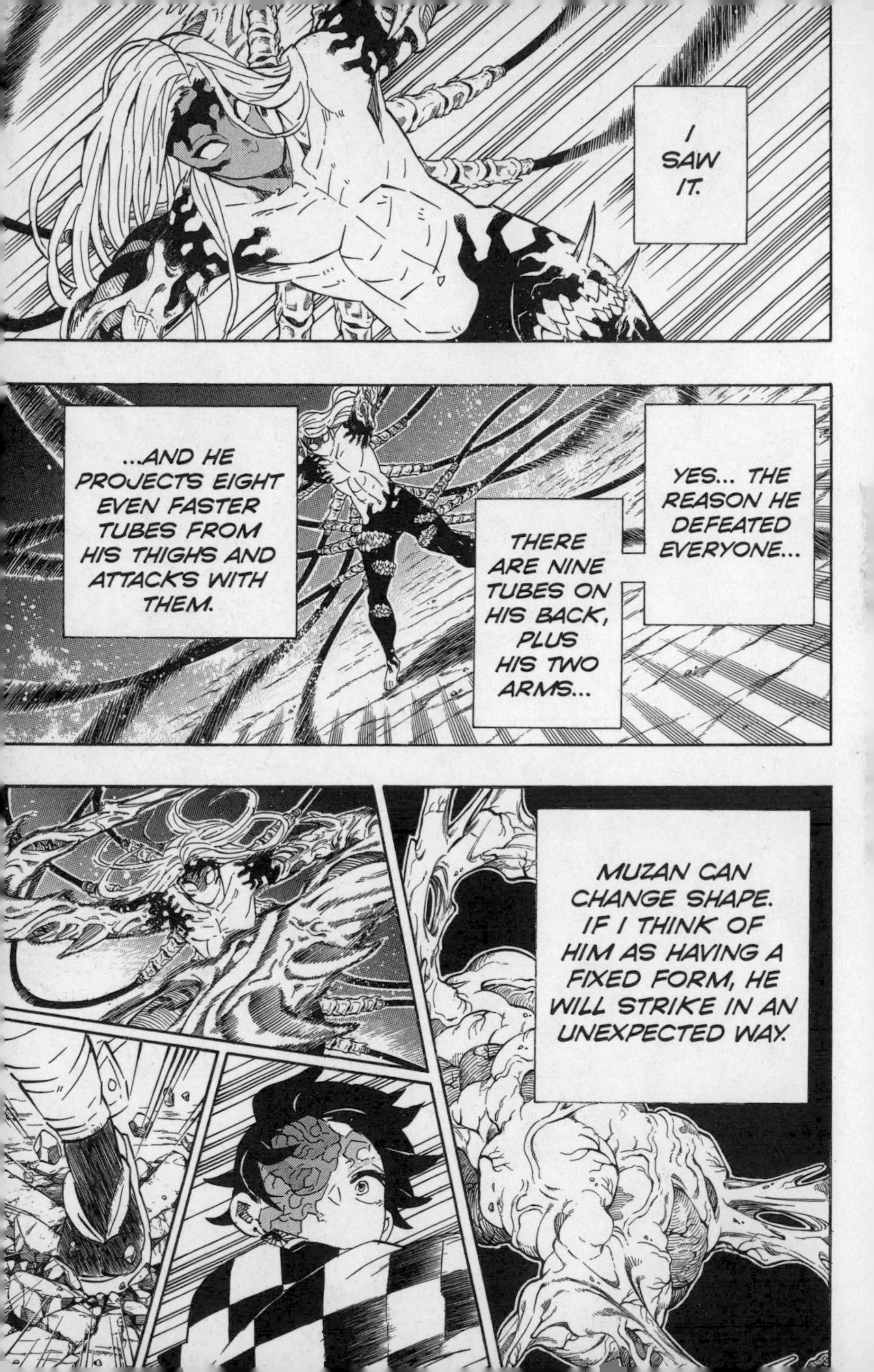
I SAW IT.
YES... THE REASON HE DEFEATED EVERYONE...
THERE ARE NINE TUBES ON HIS BACK, PLUS HIS TWO ARMS...
...AND HE PROJECTS EIGHT EVEN FASTER TUBES FROM HIS THIGHS AND ATTACKS WITH THEM.
MUZAN CAN CHANGE SHAPE. IF I THINK OF HIM AS HAVING A FIXED FORM, HE WILL STRIKE IN AN UNEXPECTED WAY.

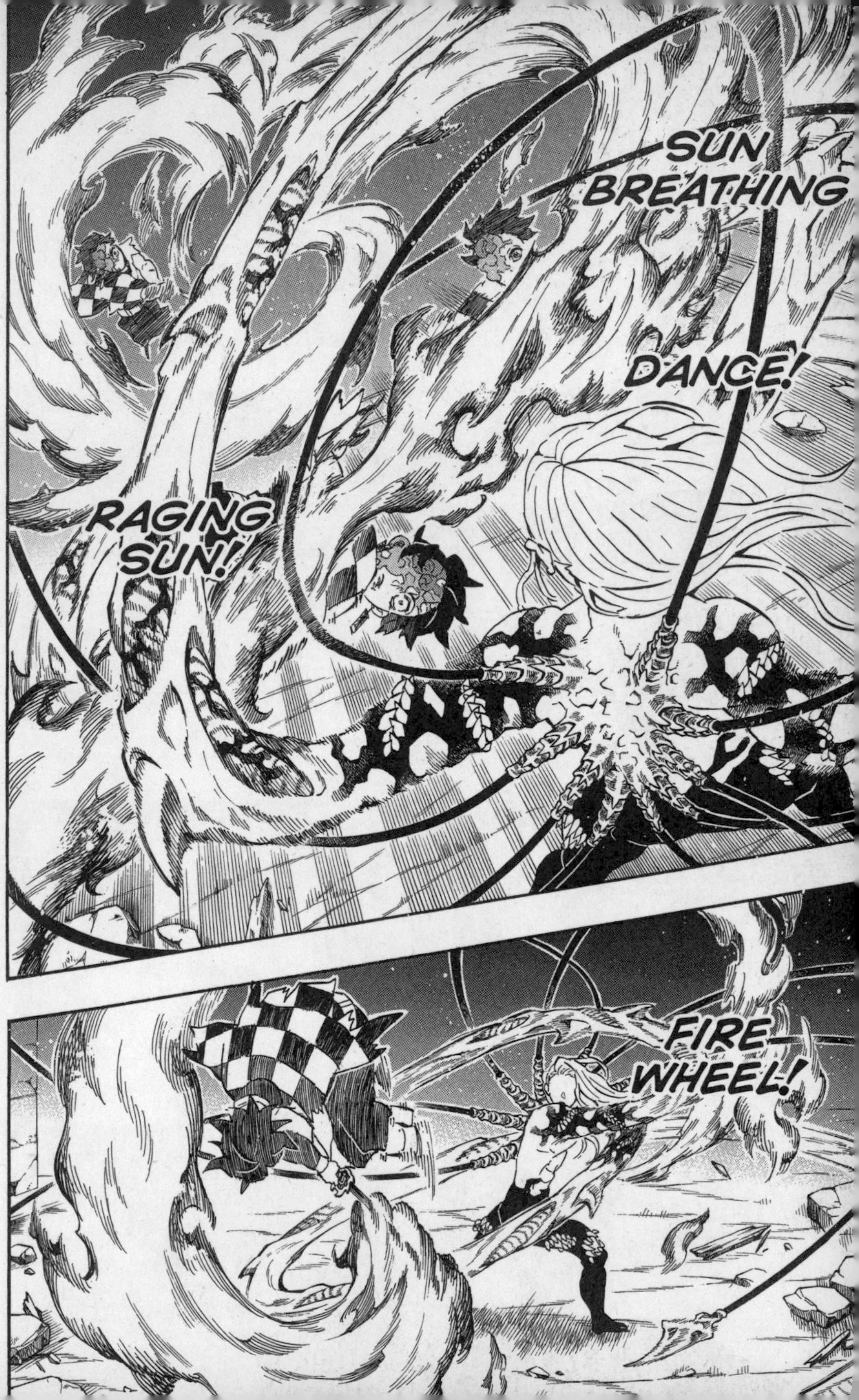
SUN BREATHING
DANCE!
RAGING SUN!
FIRE WHEEL!

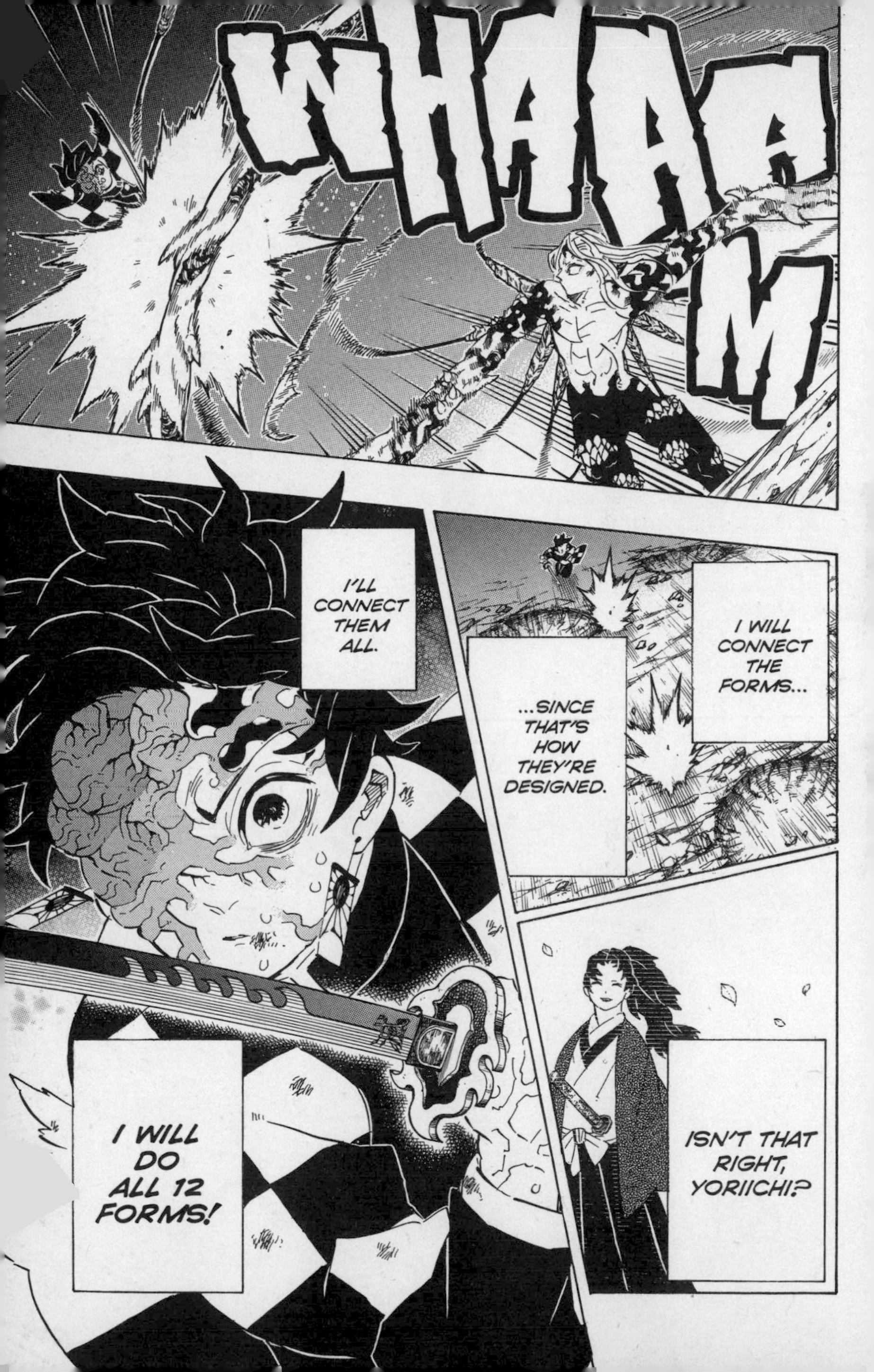
WHAAM
I WILL CONNECT THE FORMS...
...SINCE THAT'S HOW THEY'RE DESIGNED.
ISN'T THAT RIGHT, YORIICHI?
I'LL CONNECT THEM ALL.
I WILL DO ALL 12 FORMS!

The meanings of the flowers
that Sumire gave Yoriichi:

● White periwinkle—
  Lifelong friendship

● Pale pink periwinkle—
  Fond memories

Yep!

I gave 'em
to him!!

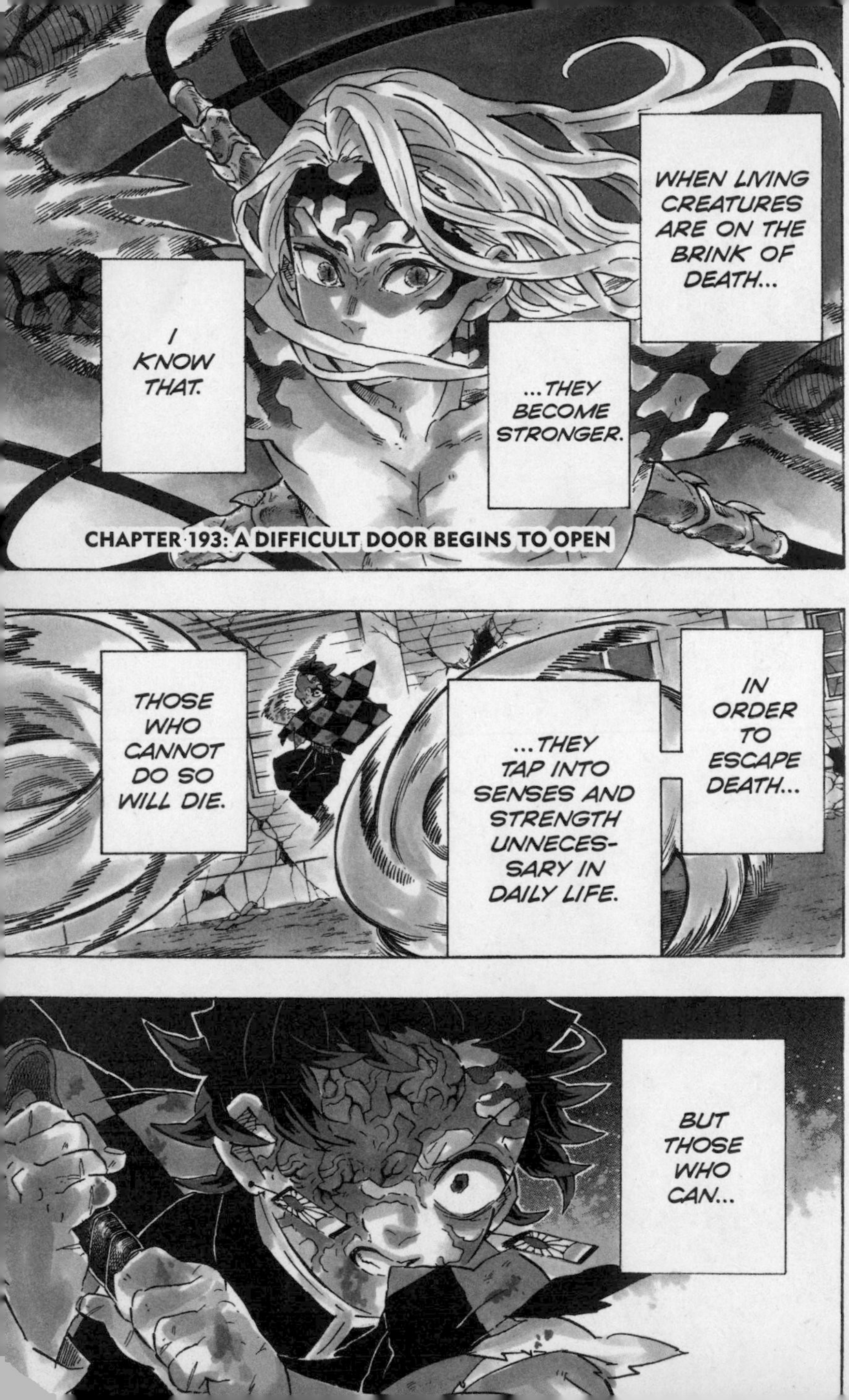
WHEN LIVING CREATURES ARE ON THE BRINK OF DEATH...
...THEY BECOME STRONGER.
I KNOW THAT.
CHAPTER 193: A DIFFICULT DOOR BEGINS TO OPEN
IN ORDER TO ESCAPE DEATH...
...THEY TAP INTO SENSES AND STRENGTH UNNECES-SARY IN DAILY LIFE.
THOSE WHO CANNOT DO SO WILL DIE.
BUT THOSE WHO CAN...

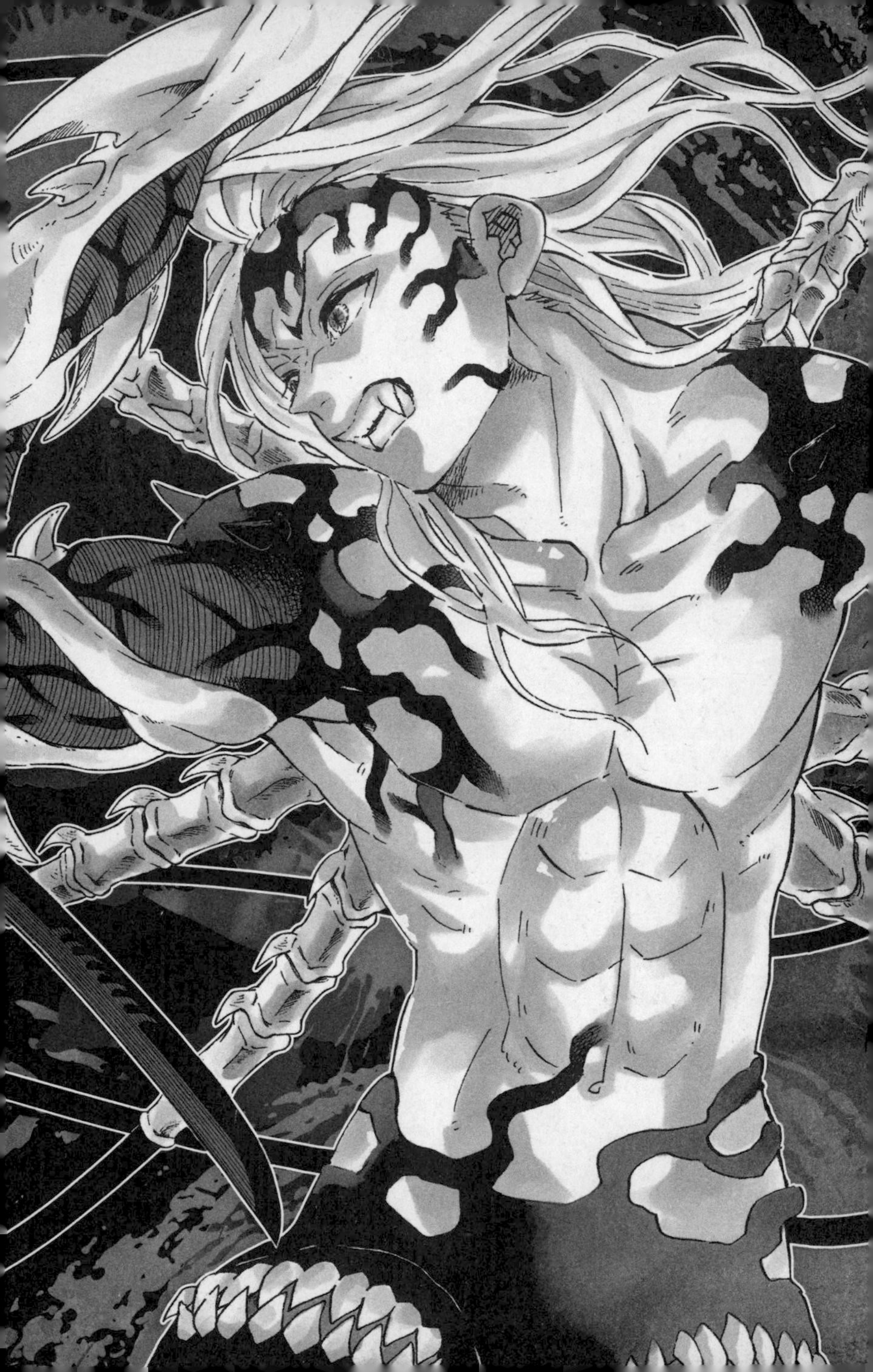

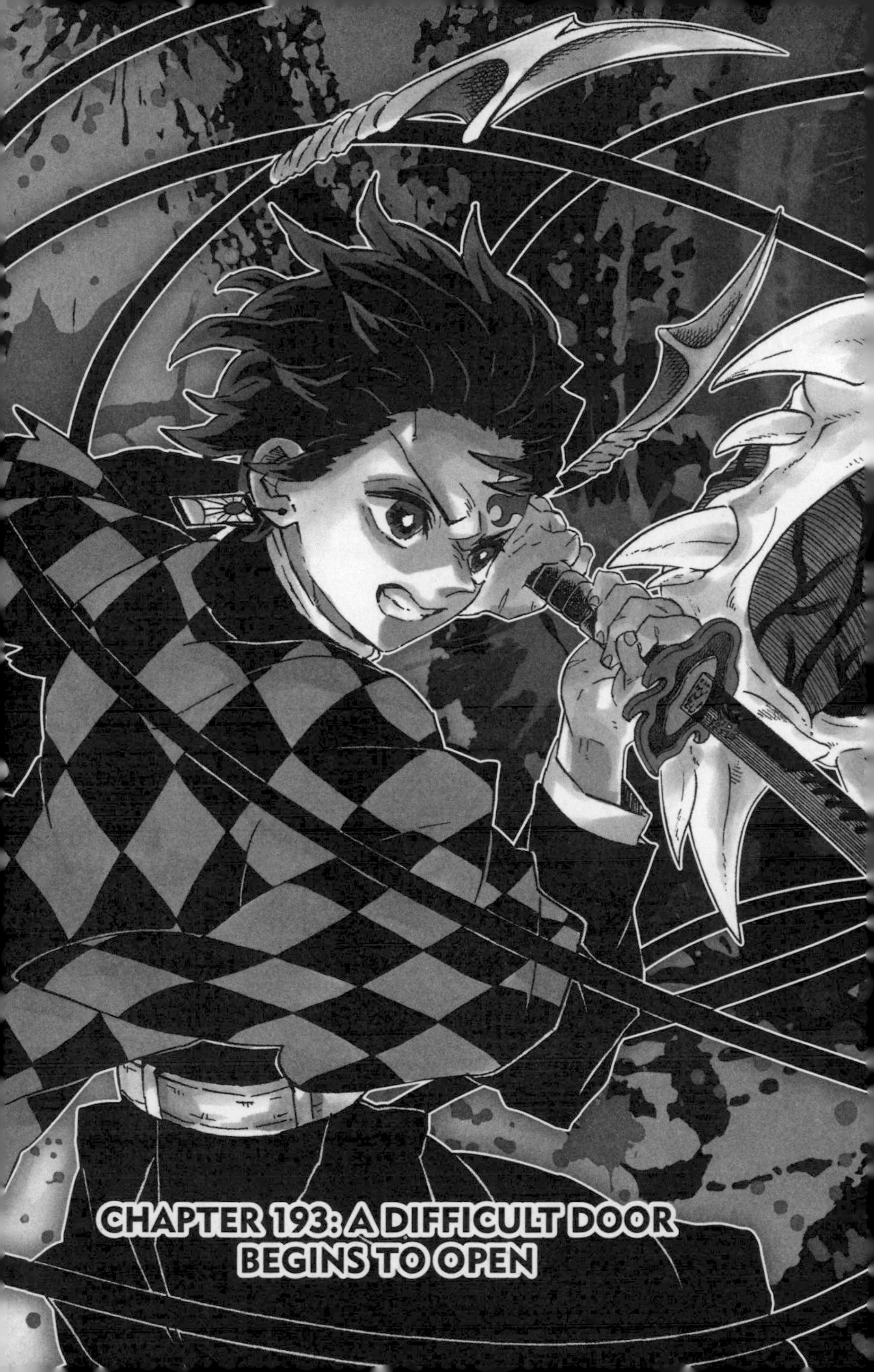
CHAPTER 193: A DIFFICULT DOOR BEGINS TO OPEN

Being capable, competent, and proficient are all different things. Being capable means practicing over and over to become able to perform a certain technique. Being competent means learning how to do it reliably from any position and under any circumstances. Being proficient means developing it to the point of always being able to deploy it at maximum effectiveness, better and faster than anybody else.

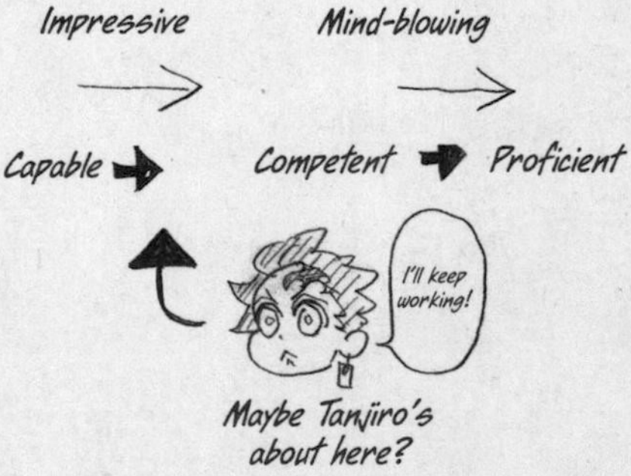

Impressive
Mind-blowing
Capable
Competent
Proficient
I'll keep working!
Maybe Tanjiro's about here?

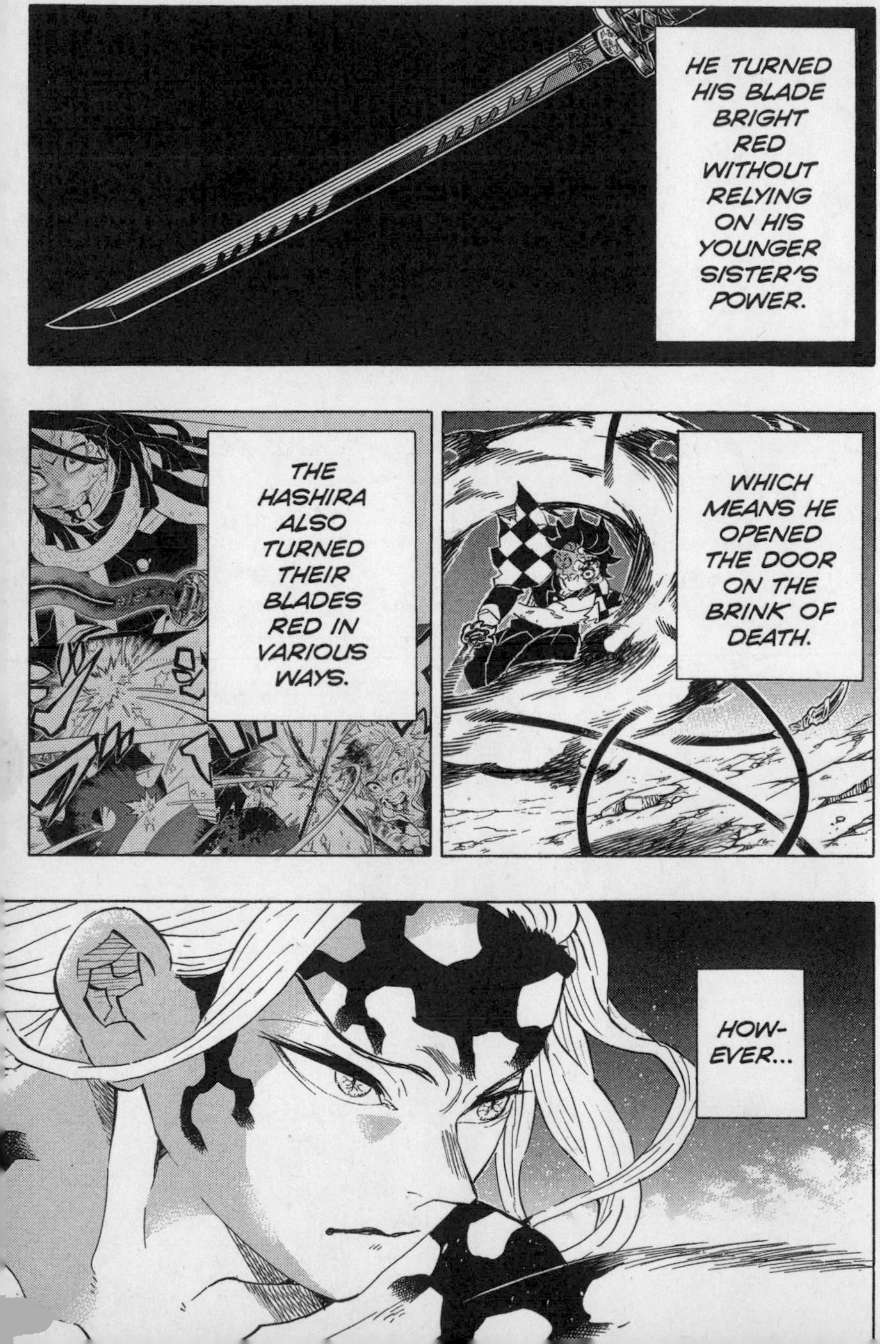
HE TURNED HIS BLADE BRIGHT RED WITHOUT RELYING ON HIS YOUNGER SISTER'S POWER.
WHICH MEANS HE OPENED THE DOOR ON THE BRINK OF DEATH.
THE HASHIRA ALSO TURNED THEIR BLADES RED IN VARIOUS WAYS.
HOW-EVER...

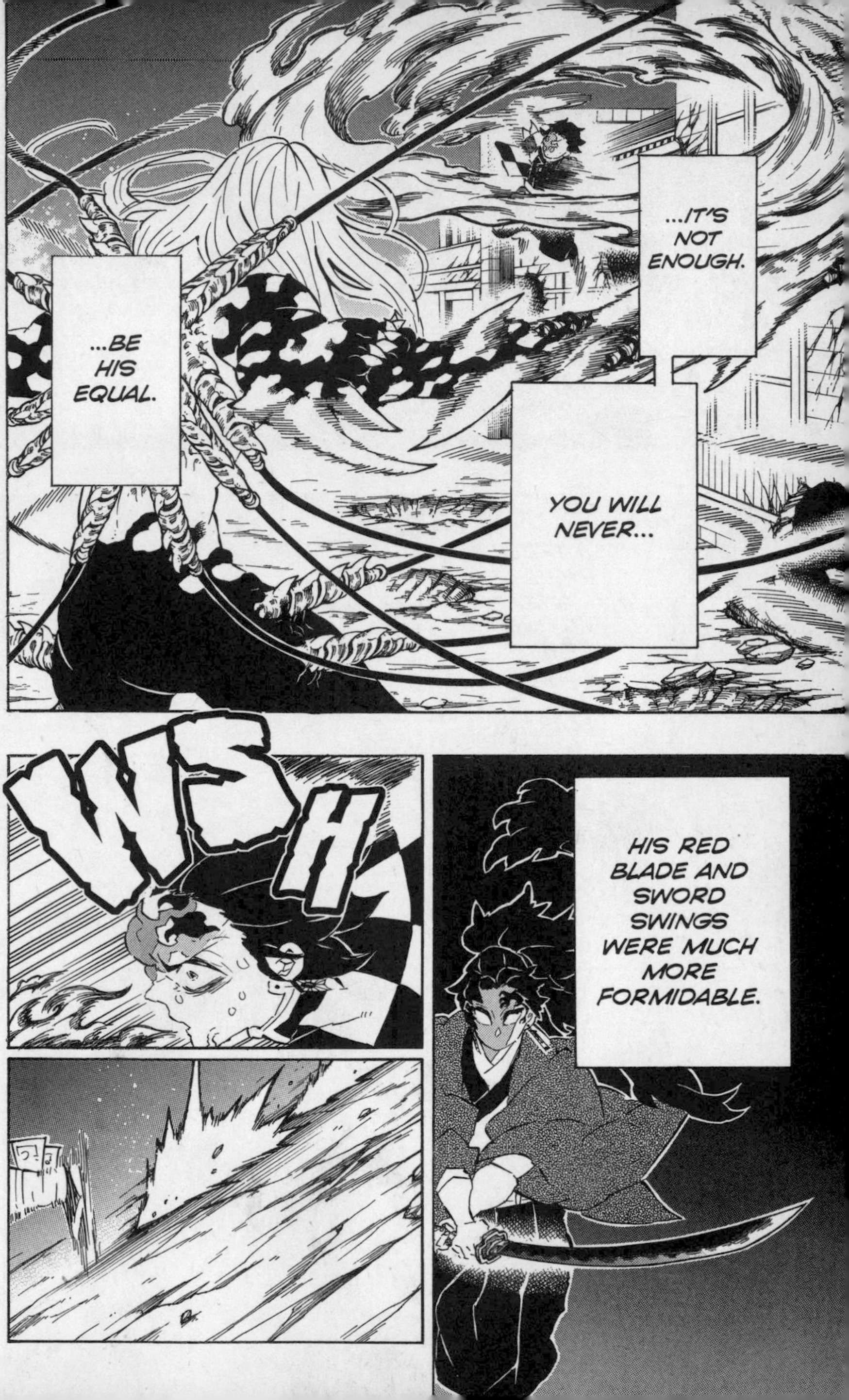
...IT'S NOT ENOUGH.
YOU WILL NEVER...
...BE HIS EQUAL.
HIS RED BLADE AND SWORD SWINGS WERE MUCH MORE FORMIDABLE.
WSH

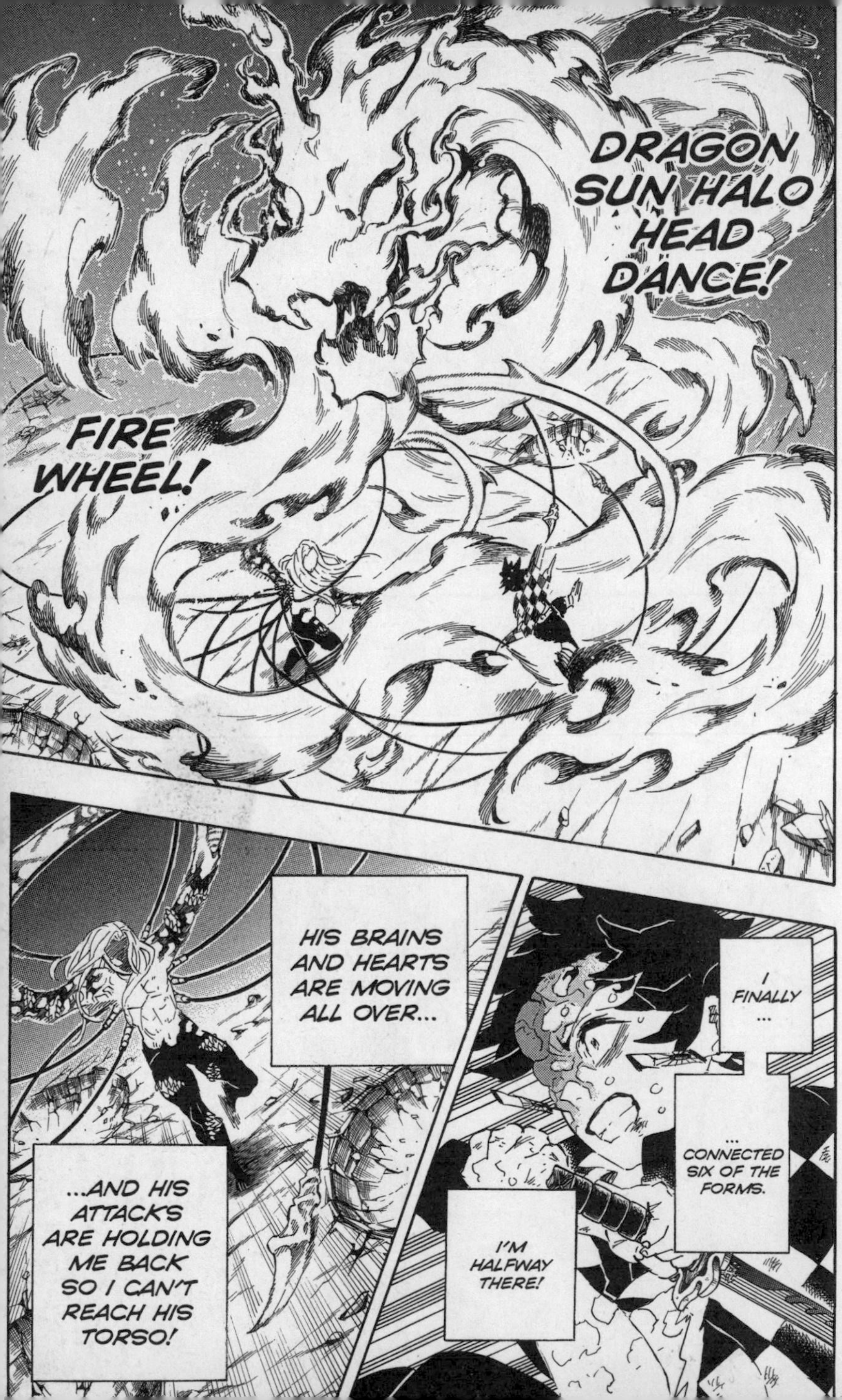
DRAGON SUN HALO HEAD DANCE!
FIRE WHEEL!
I FINALLY ...
... CONNECTED SIX OF THE FORMS.
I'M HALFWAY THERE!
HIS BRAINS AND HEARTS ARE MOVING ALL OVER...
...AND HIS ATTACKS ARE HOLDING ME BACK SO I CAN'T REACH HIS TORSO!

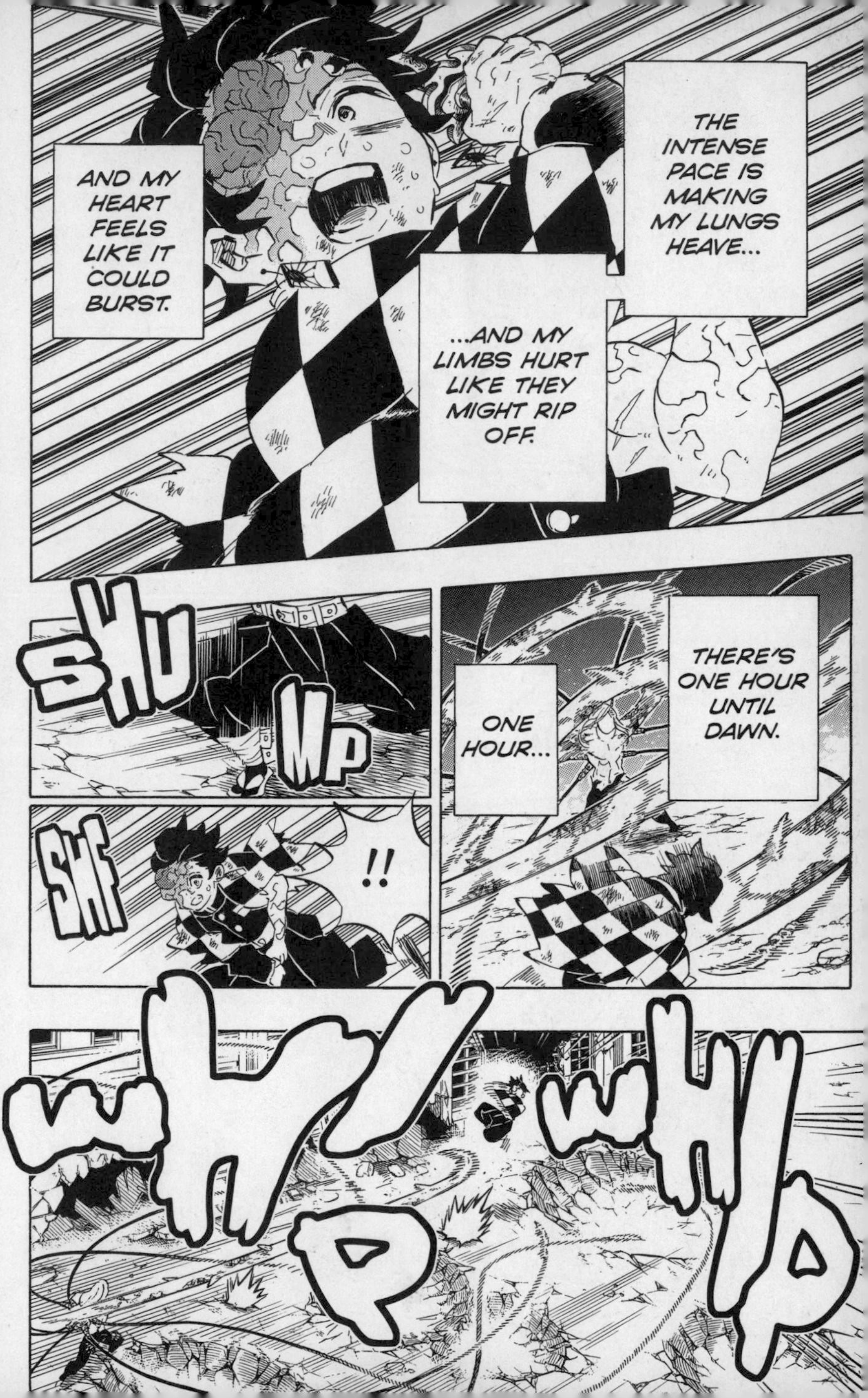
THE INTENSE PACE IS MAKING MY LUNGS HEAVE...
...AND MY LIMBS HURT LIKE THEY MIGHT RIP OFF.
AND MY HEART FEELS LIKE IT COULD BURST.
THERE'S ONE HOUR UNTIL DAWN.
ONE HOUR...
SHUMP
SHF
!!
WHIP
WHIP

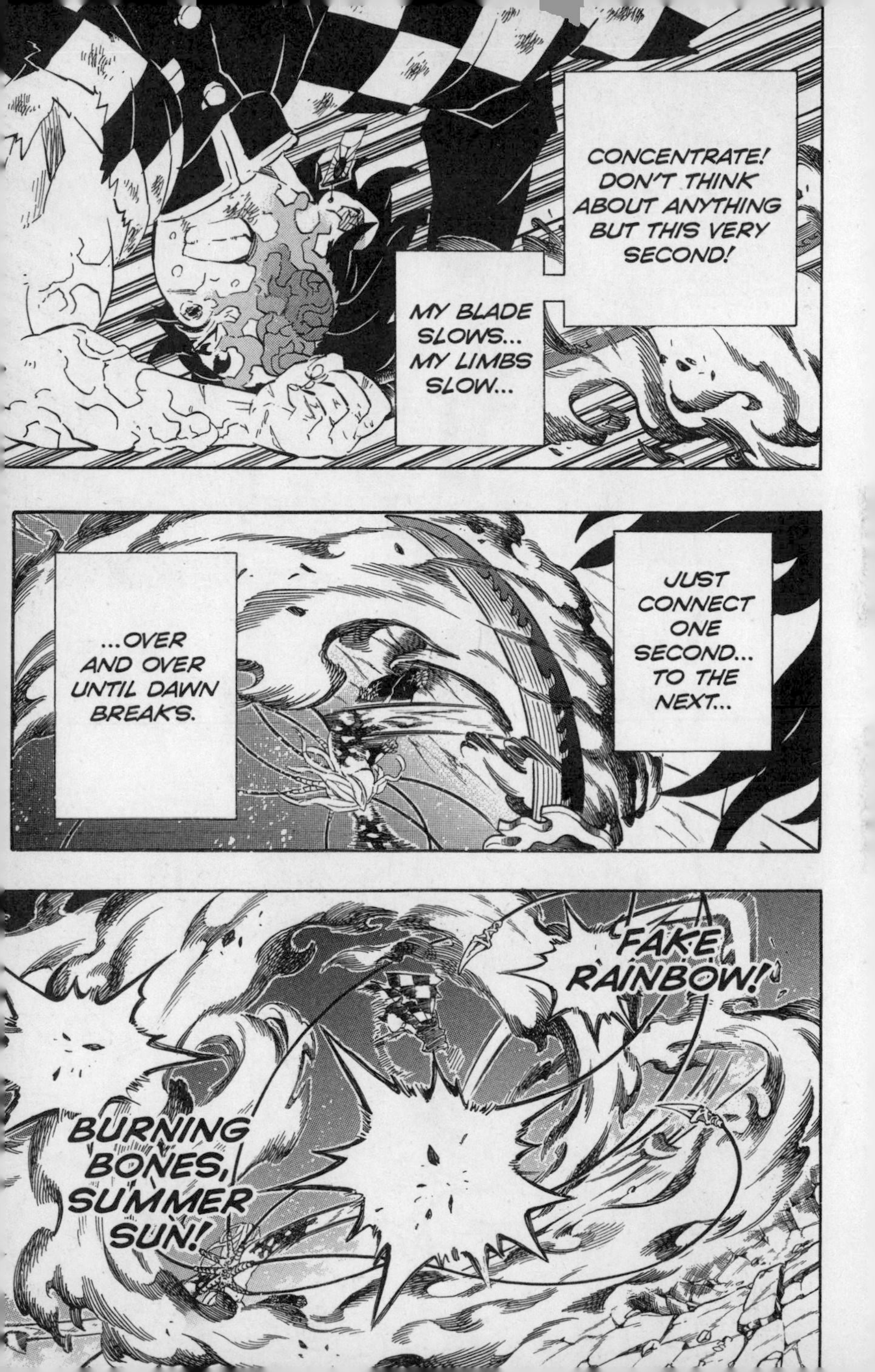
CONCENTRATE! DON'T THINK ABOUT ANYTHING BUT THIS VERY SECOND!
MY BLADE SLOWS... MY LIMBS SLOW...
JUST CONNECT ONE SECOND... TO THE NEXT...
...OVER AND OVER UNTIL DAWN BREAKS.
FAKE RAINBOW!
BURNING BONES, SUMMER SUN!

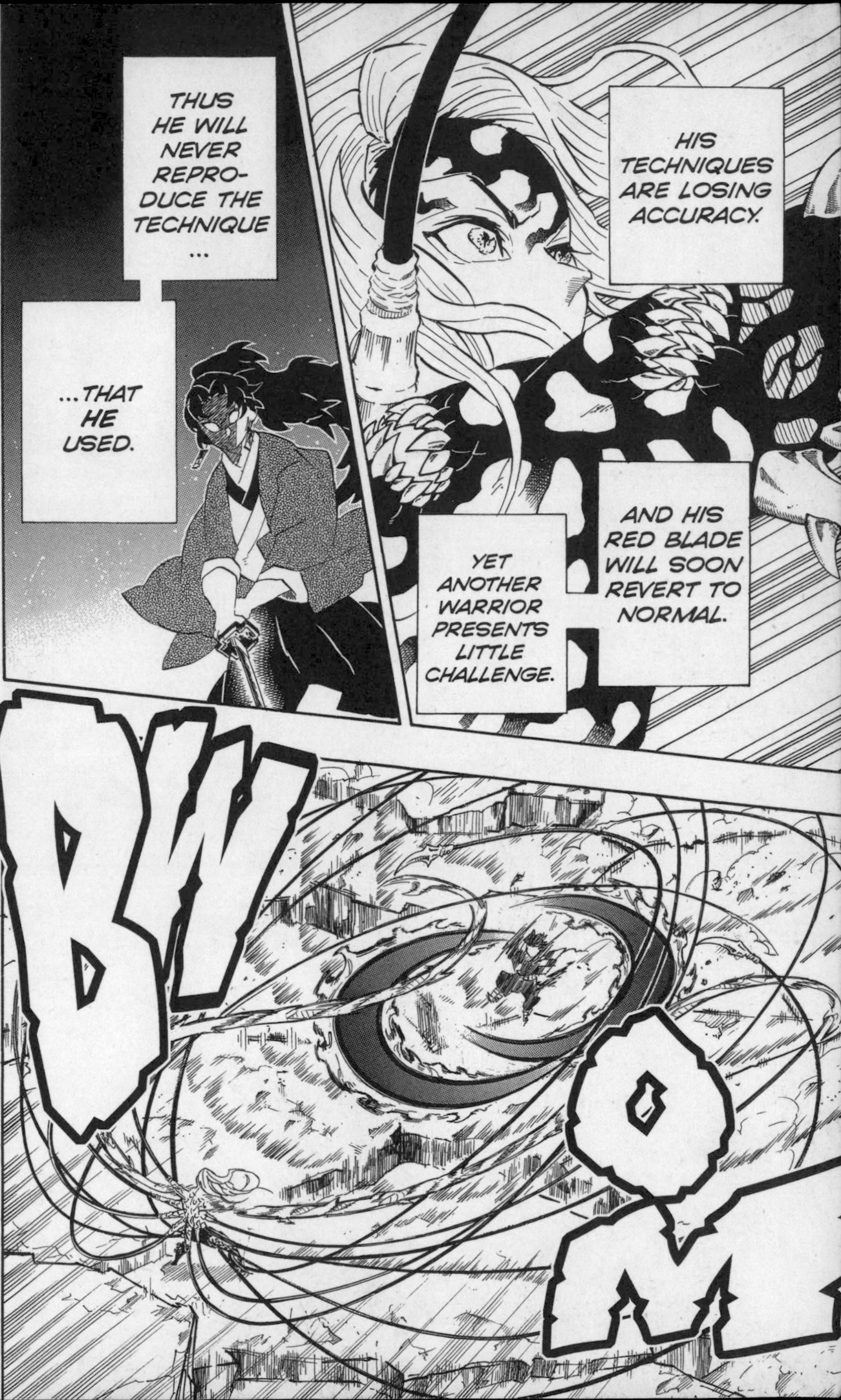
HIS TECHNIQUES ARE LOSING ACCURACY.
AND HIS RED BLADE WILL SOON REVERT TO NORMAL.
YET ANOTHER WARRIOR PRESENTS LITTLE CHALLENGE.
THUS HE WILL NEVER REPRODUCE THE TECHNIQUE ...
...THAT HE USED.
BWOM

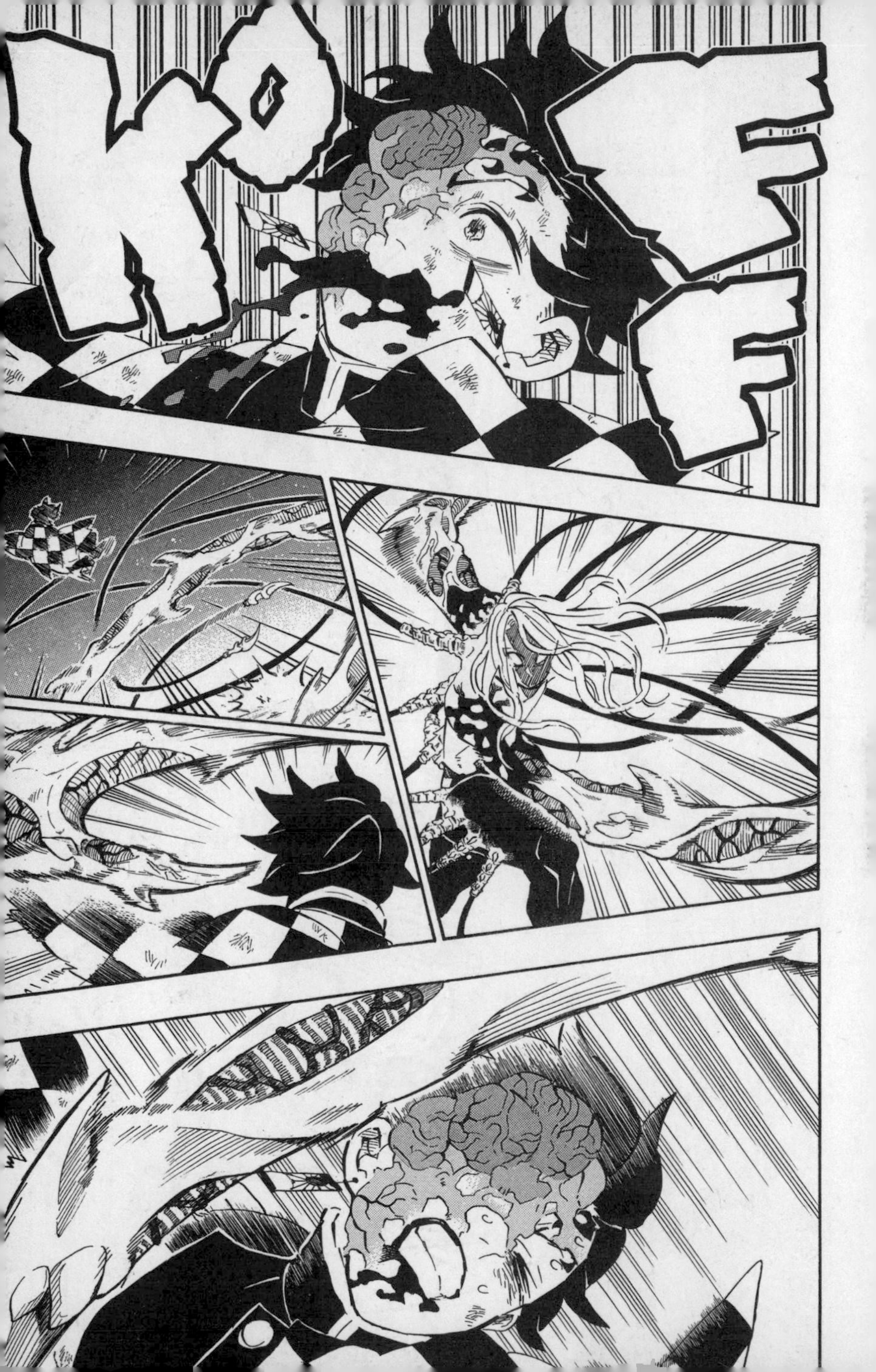
KOFF

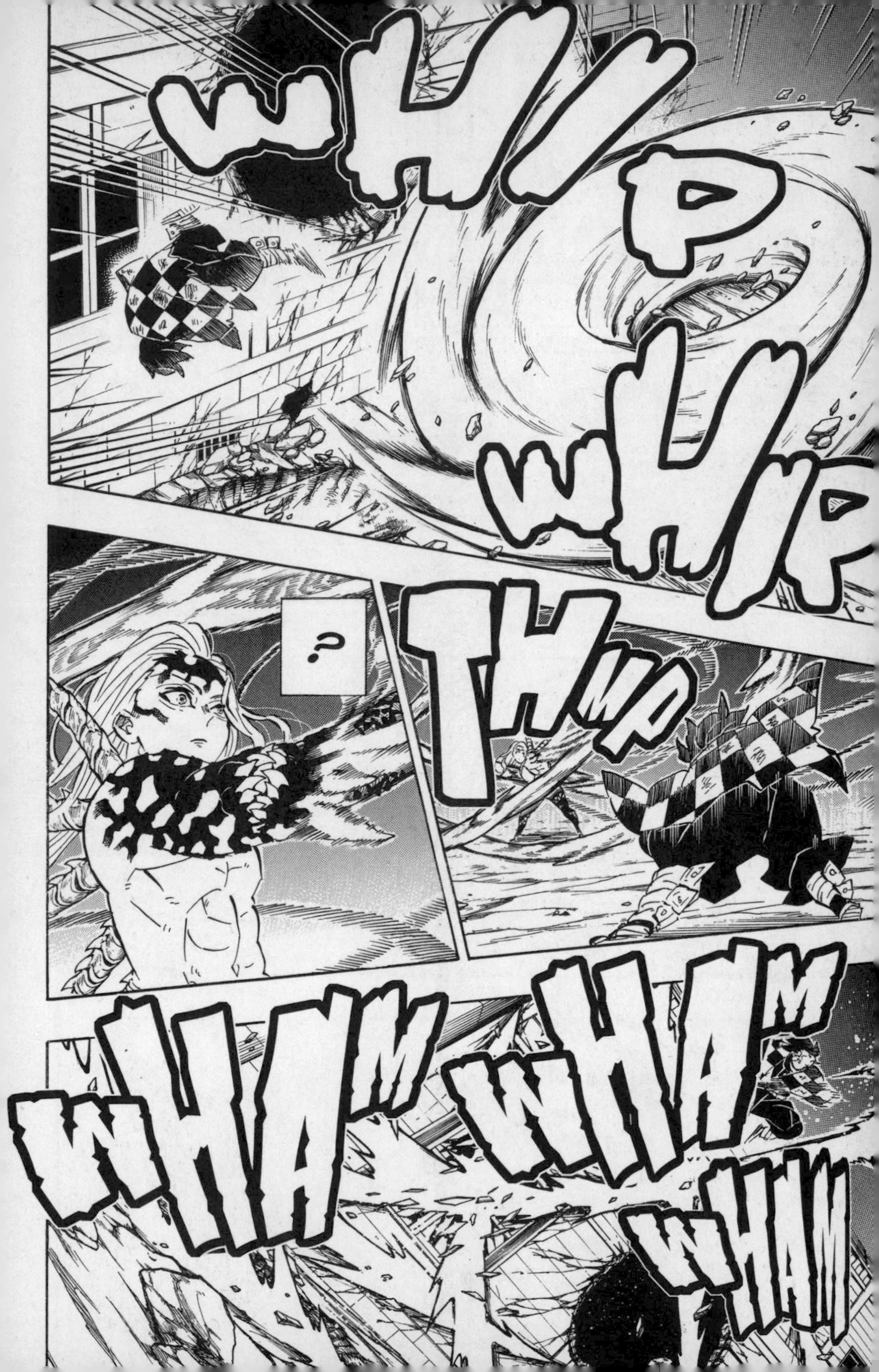
WHIP
WHIP
THUMP
?
WHAM
WHAM
WHAM

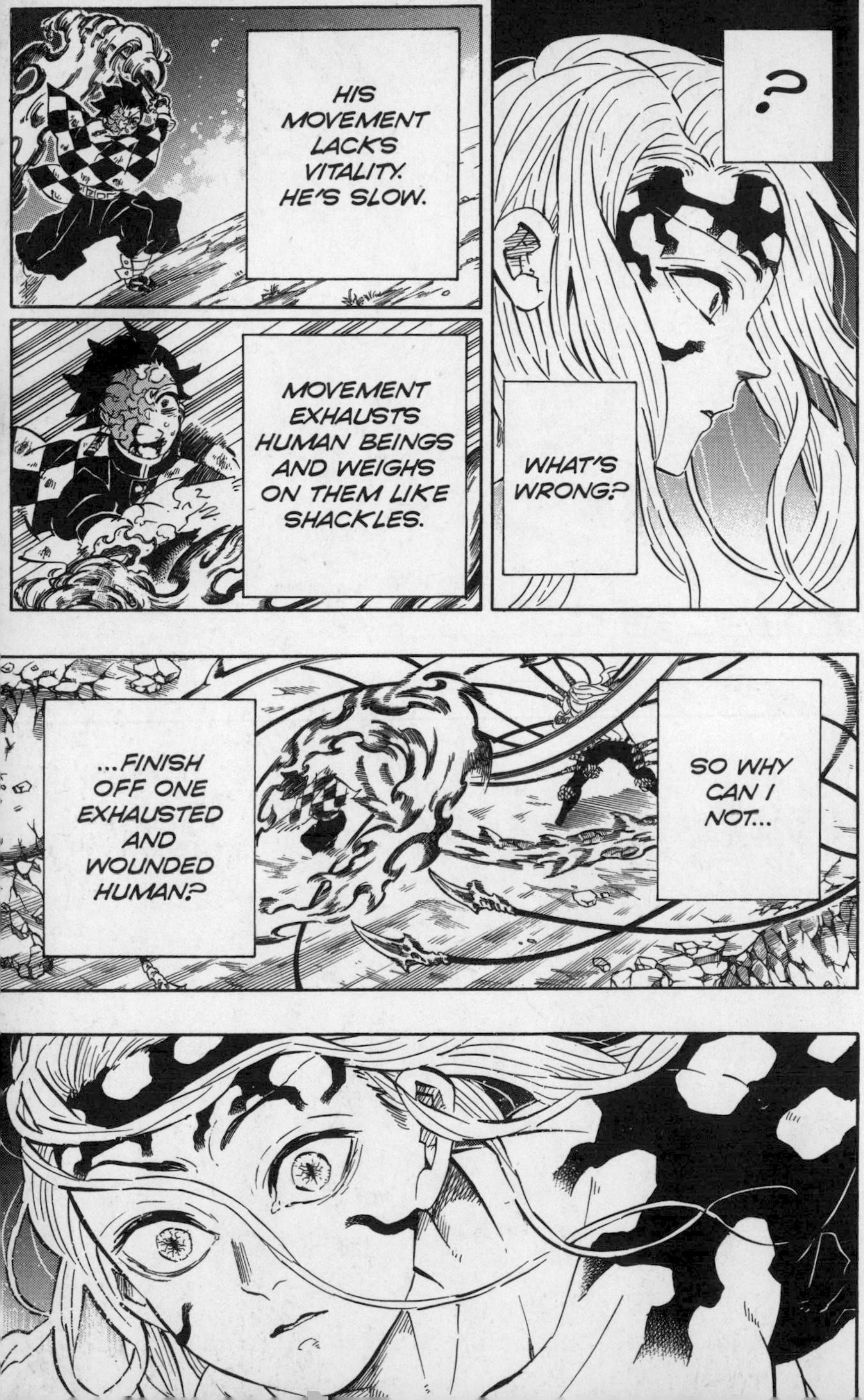
?
WHAT'S WRONG?
HIS MOVEMENT LACKS VITALITY. HE'S SLOW.
MOVEMENT EXHAUSTS HUMAN BEINGS AND WEIGHS ON THEM LIKE SHACKLES.
SO WHY CAN I NOT...
...FINISH OFF ONE EXHAUSTED AND WOUNDED HUMAN?

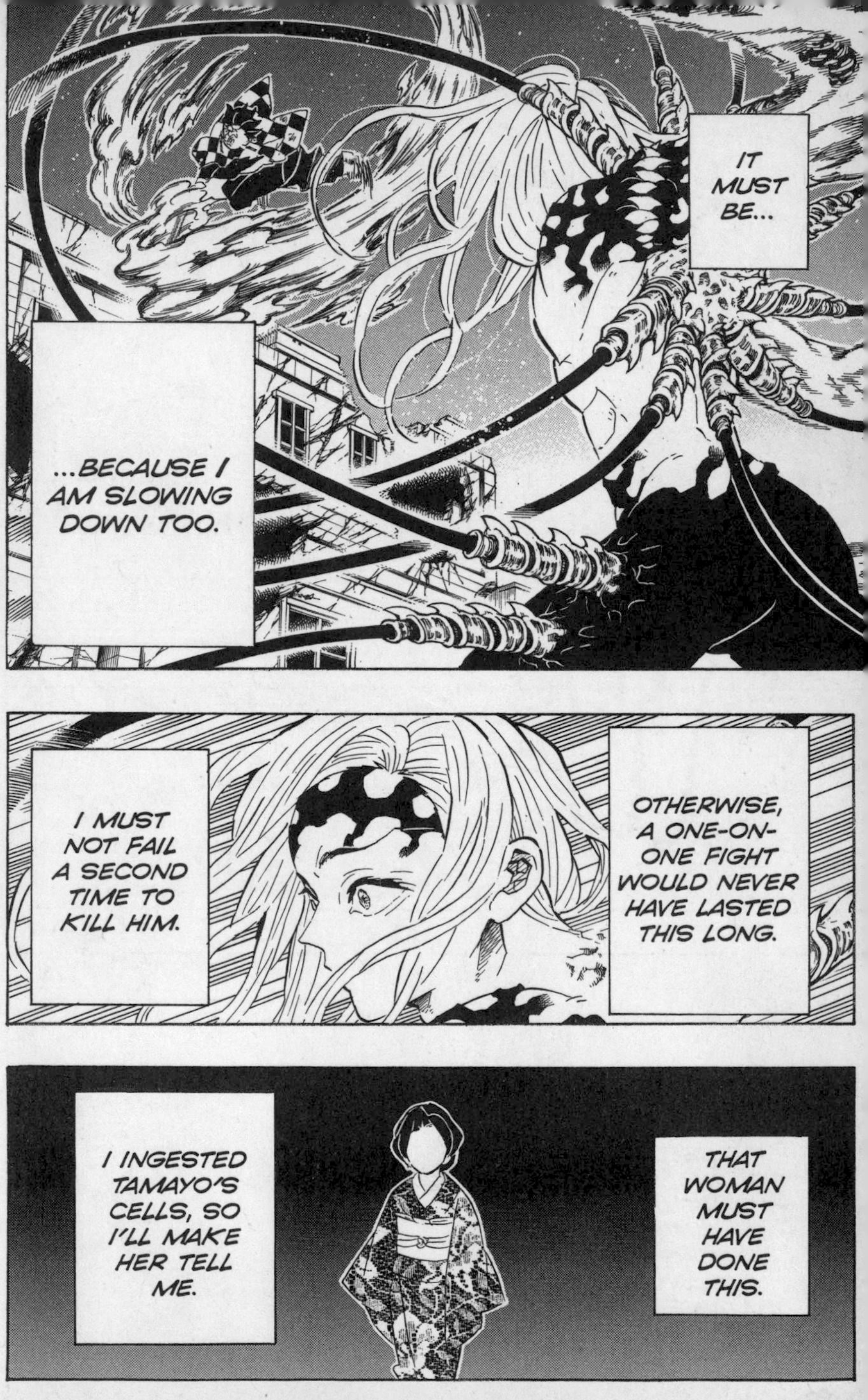
IT MUST BE...
...BECAUSE I AM SLOWING DOWN TOO.
OTHERWISE, A ONE-ON-ONE FIGHT WOULD NEVER HAVE LASTED THIS LONG.
I MUST NOT FAIL A SECOND TIME TO KILL HIM.
THAT WOMAN MUST HAVE DONE THIS.
I INGESTED TAMAYO'S CELLS, SO I'LL MAKE HER TELL ME.

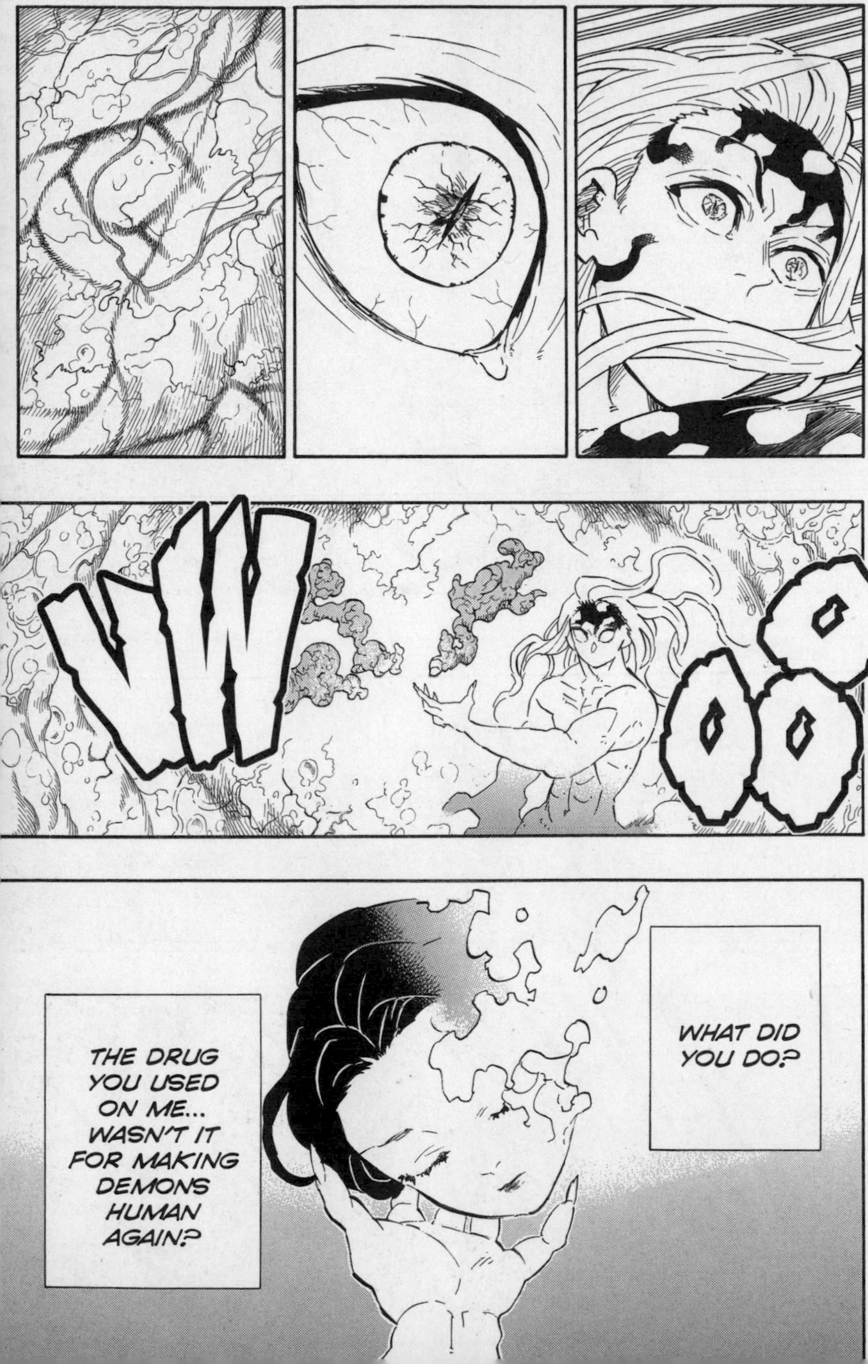
VWOOO
WHAT DID YOU DO?
THE DRUG YOU USED ON ME... WASN'T IT FOR MAKING DEMONS HUMAN AGAIN?

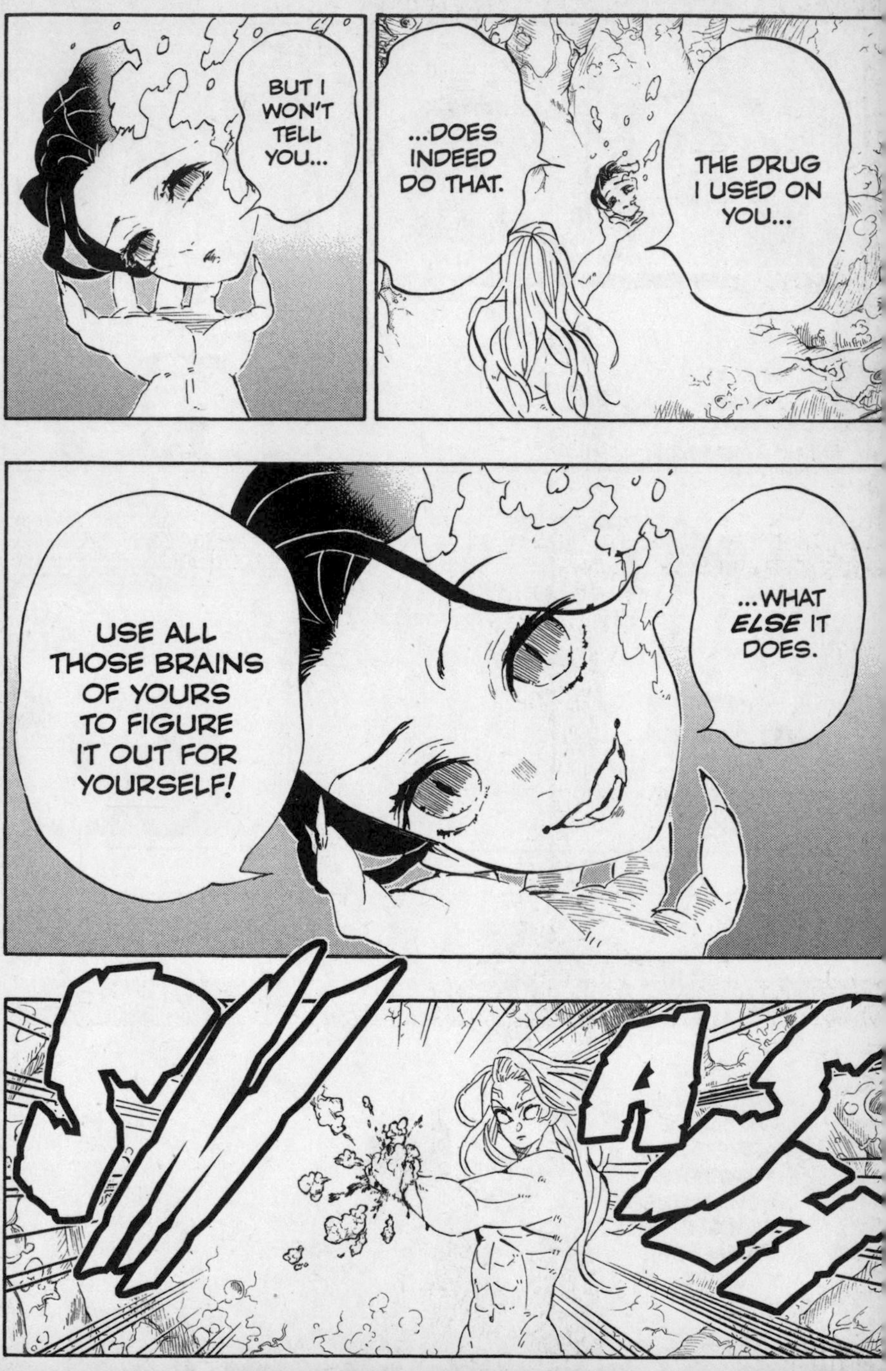
THE DRUG I USED ON YOU...
...DOES INDEED DO THAT.
BUT I WON'T TELL YOU...
...WHAT *ELSE* IT DOES.
USE ALL THOSE BRAINS OF YOURS TO FIGURE IT OUT FOR YOURSELF!

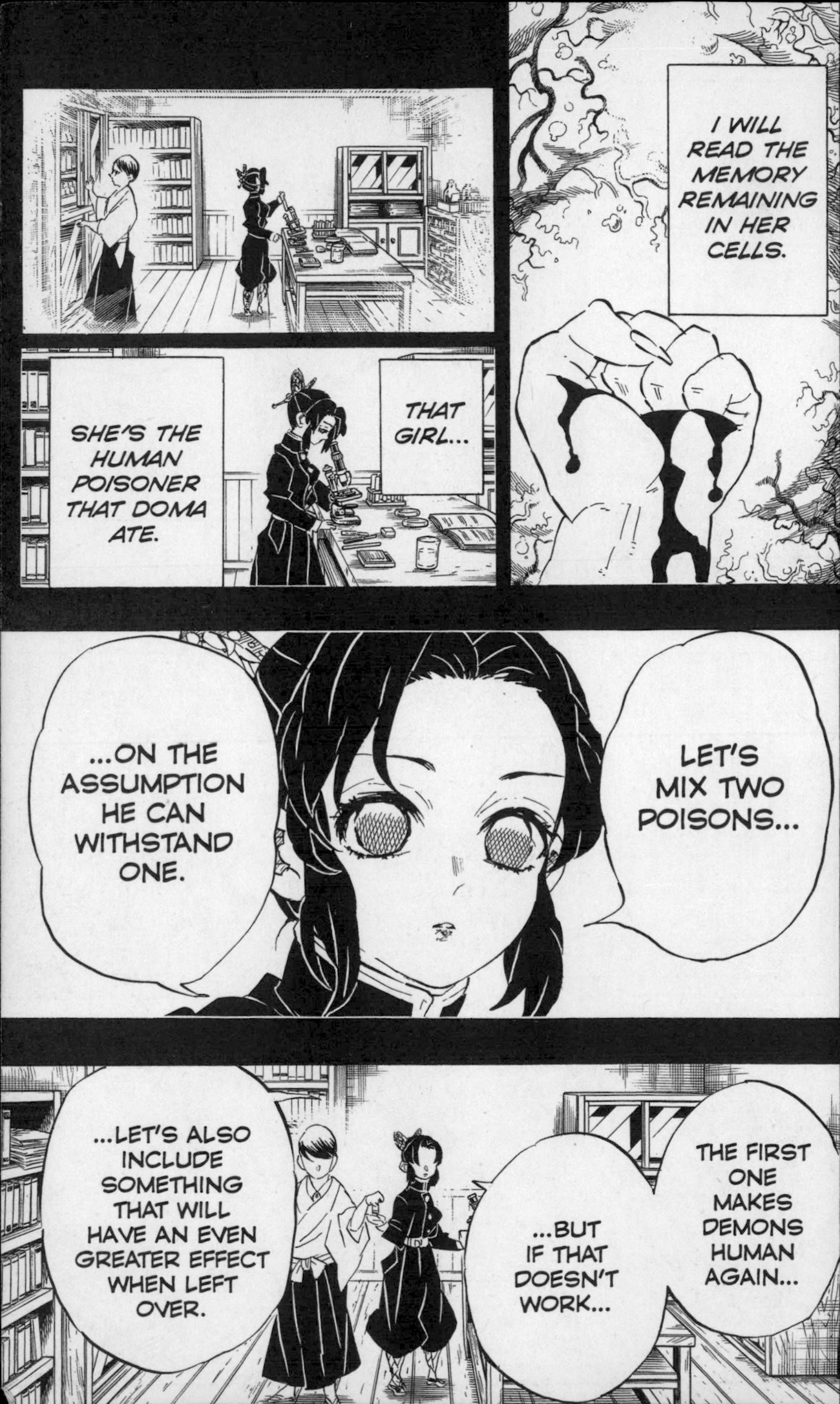
I WILL READ THE MEMORY REMAINING IN HER CELLS.
THAT GIRL...
SHE'S THE HUMAN POISONER THAT DOMA ATE.
LET'S MIX TWO POISONS...
...ON THE ASSUMPTION HE CAN WITHSTAND ONE.
THE FIRST ONE MAKES DEMONS HUMAN AGAIN...
...BUT IF THAT DOESN'T WORK...
...LET'S ALSO INCLUDE SOMETHING THAT WILL HAVE AN EVEN GREATER EFFECT WHEN LEFT OVER.

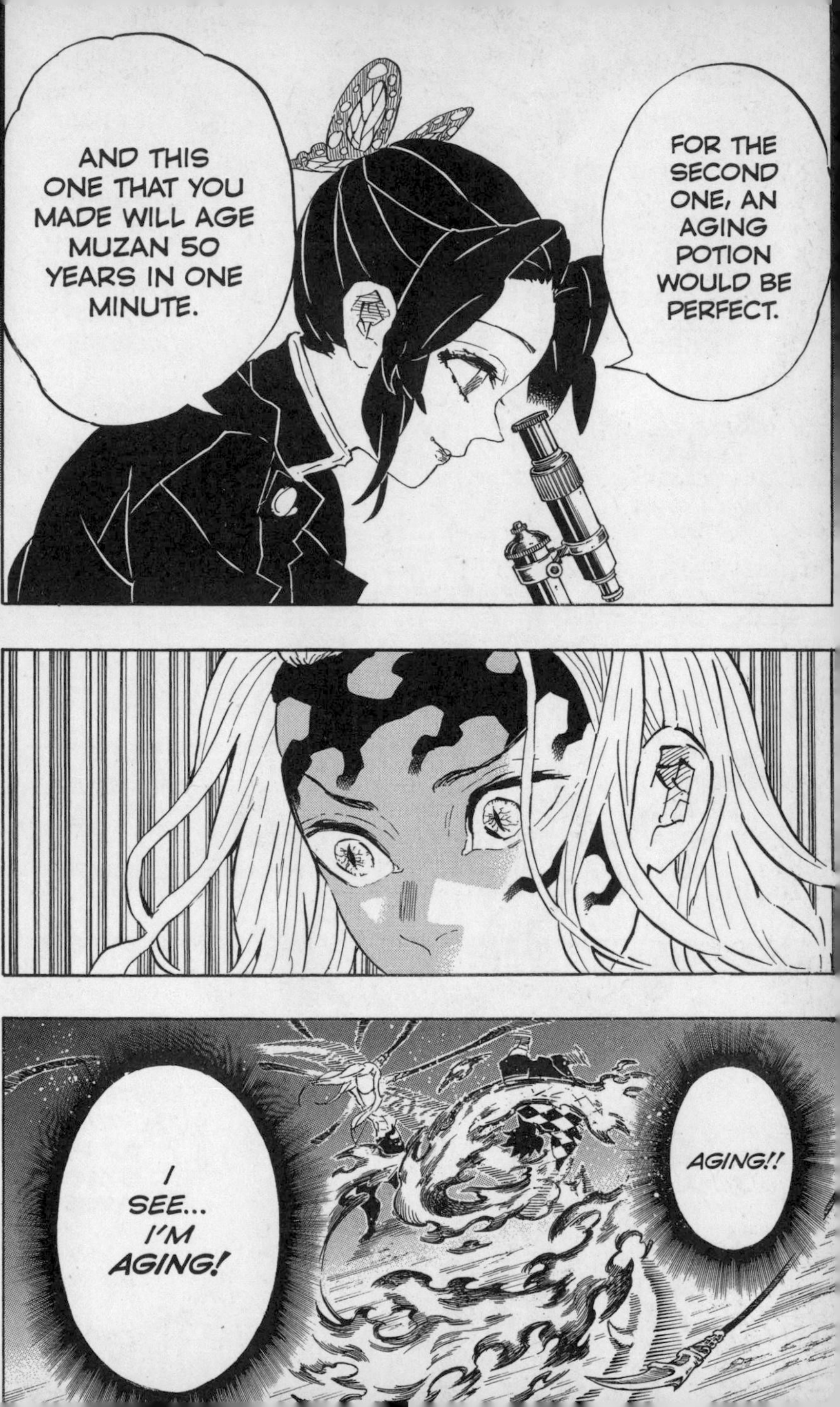
FOR THE SECOND ONE, AN AGING POTION WOULD BE PERFECT.
AND THIS ONE THAT YOU MADE WILL AGE MUZAN 50 YEARS IN ONE MINUTE.
AGING!!
I SEE... I'M AGING!

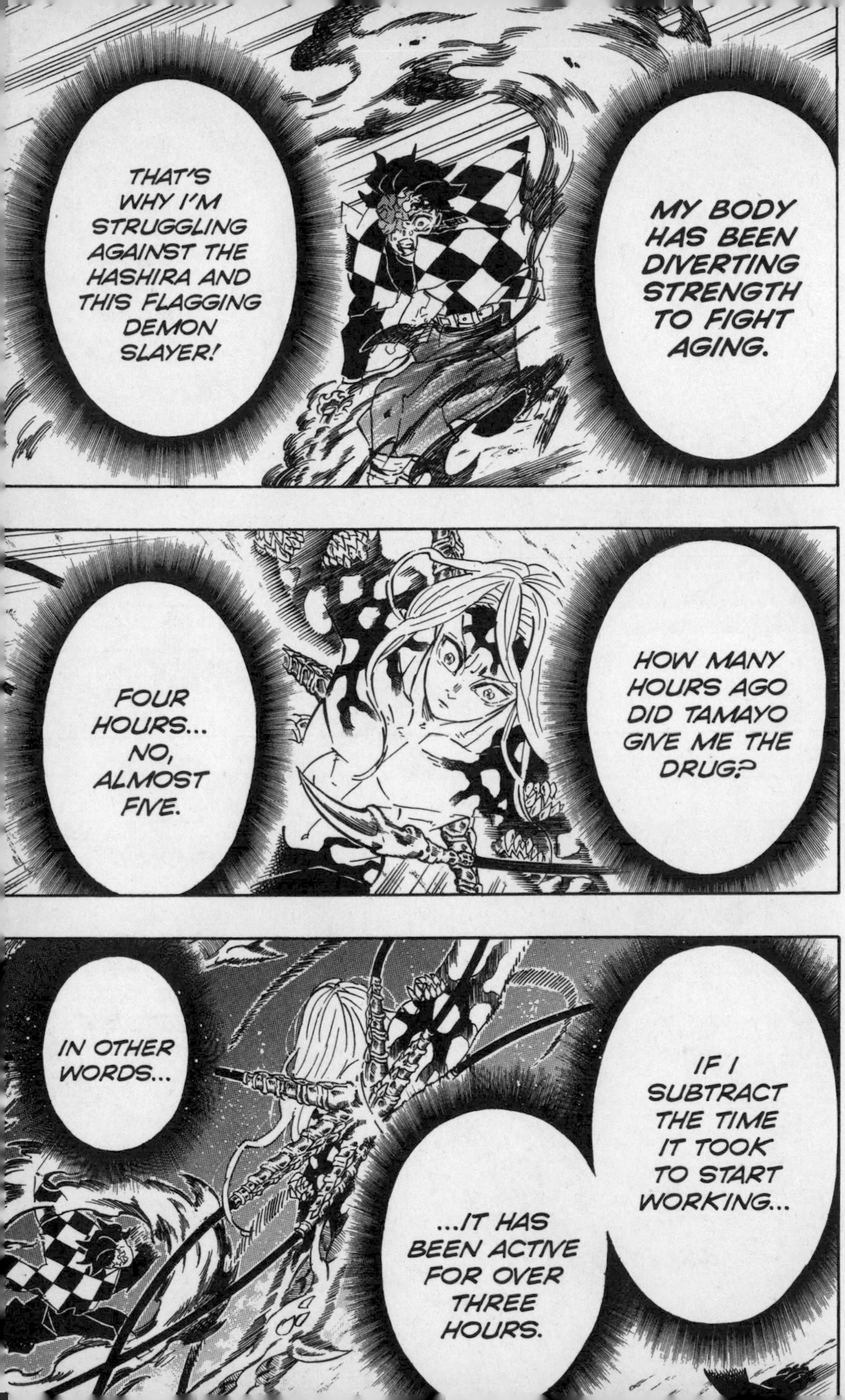
MY BODY HAS BEEN DIVERTING STRENGTH TO FIGHT AGING.
THAT'S WHY I'M STRUGGLING AGAINST THE HASHIRA AND THIS FLAGGING DEMON SLAYER!
HOW MANY HOURS AGO DID TAMAYO GIVE ME THE DRUG?
FOUR HOURS... NO, ALMOST FIVE.
IN OTHER WORDS...
IF I SUBTRACT THE TIME IT TOOK TO START WORKING...
...IT HAS BEEN ACTIVE FOR OVER THREE HOURS.

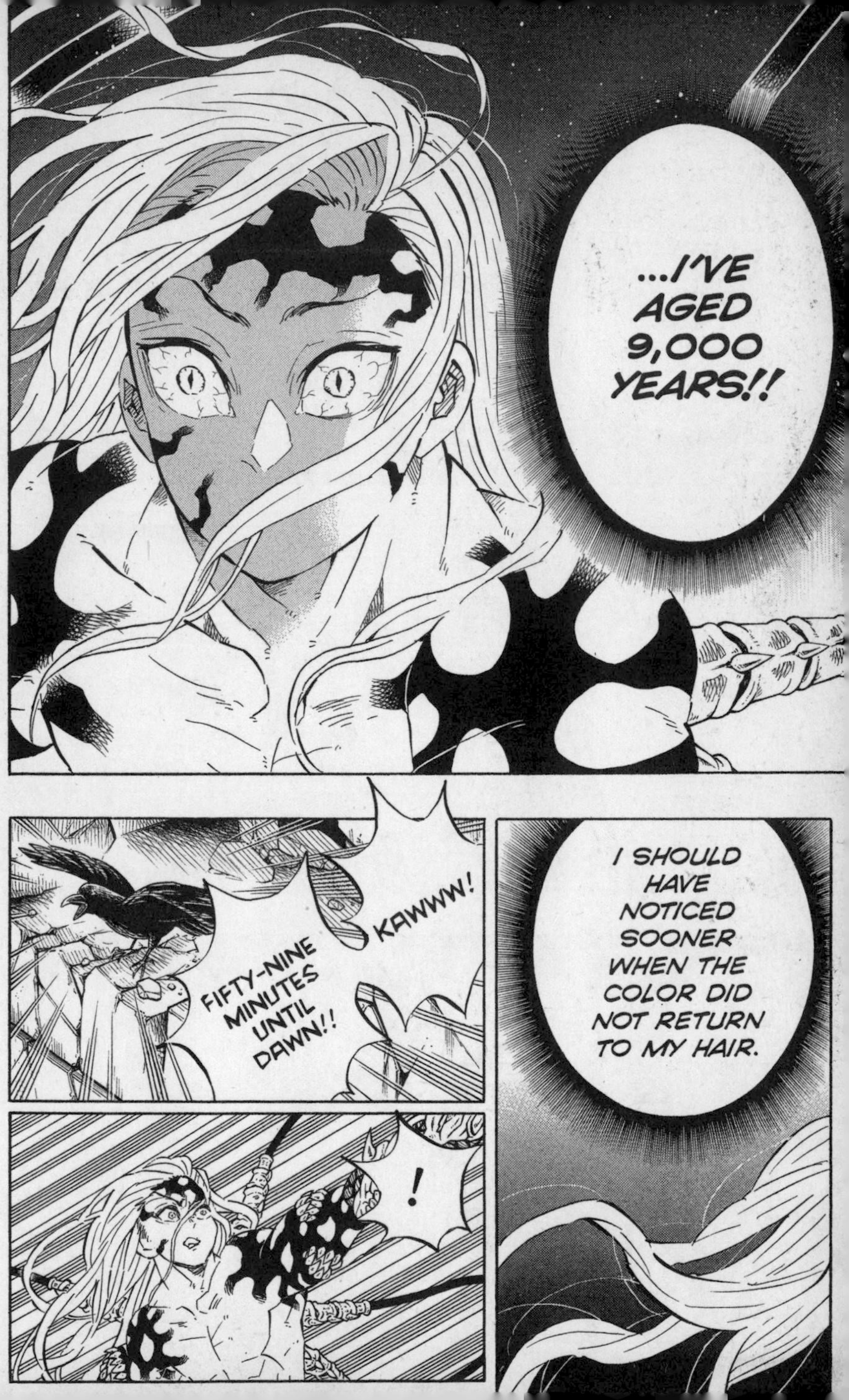
...I'VE AGED 9,000 YEARS!!
I SHOULD HAVE NOTICED SOONER WHEN THE COLOR DID NOT RETURN TO MY HAIR.
KAWWW!
FIFTY-NINE MINUTES UNTIL DAWN!!
!

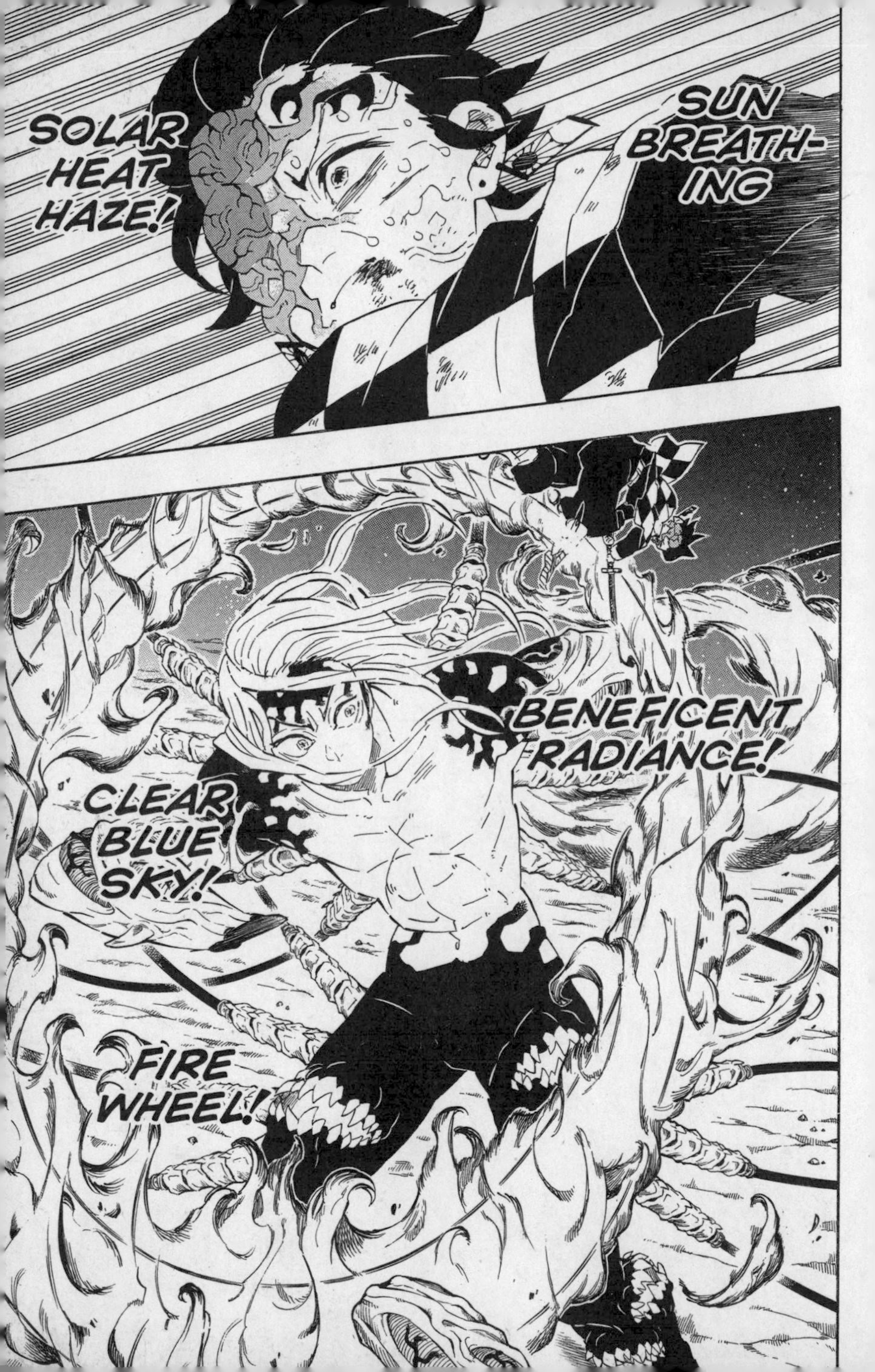
SUN BREATHING
SOLAR HEAT HAZE!
BENEFICENT RADIANCE!
CLEAR BLUE SKY!
FIRE WHEEL!

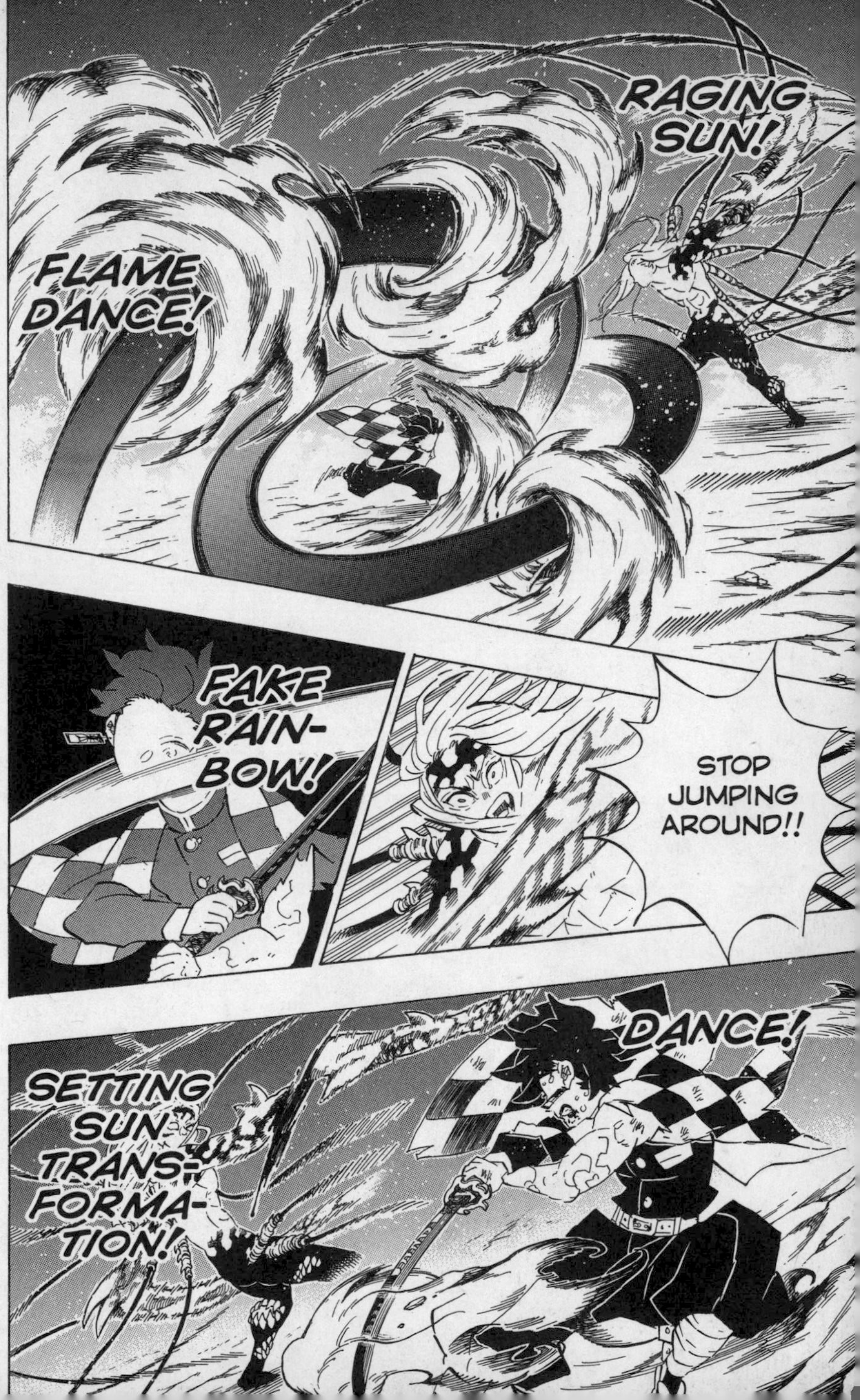
RAGING SUN!
FLAME DANCE!
STOP JUMPING AROUND!!
FAKE RAIN-BOW!
DANCE!
SETTING SUN TRANS-FORMA-TION!

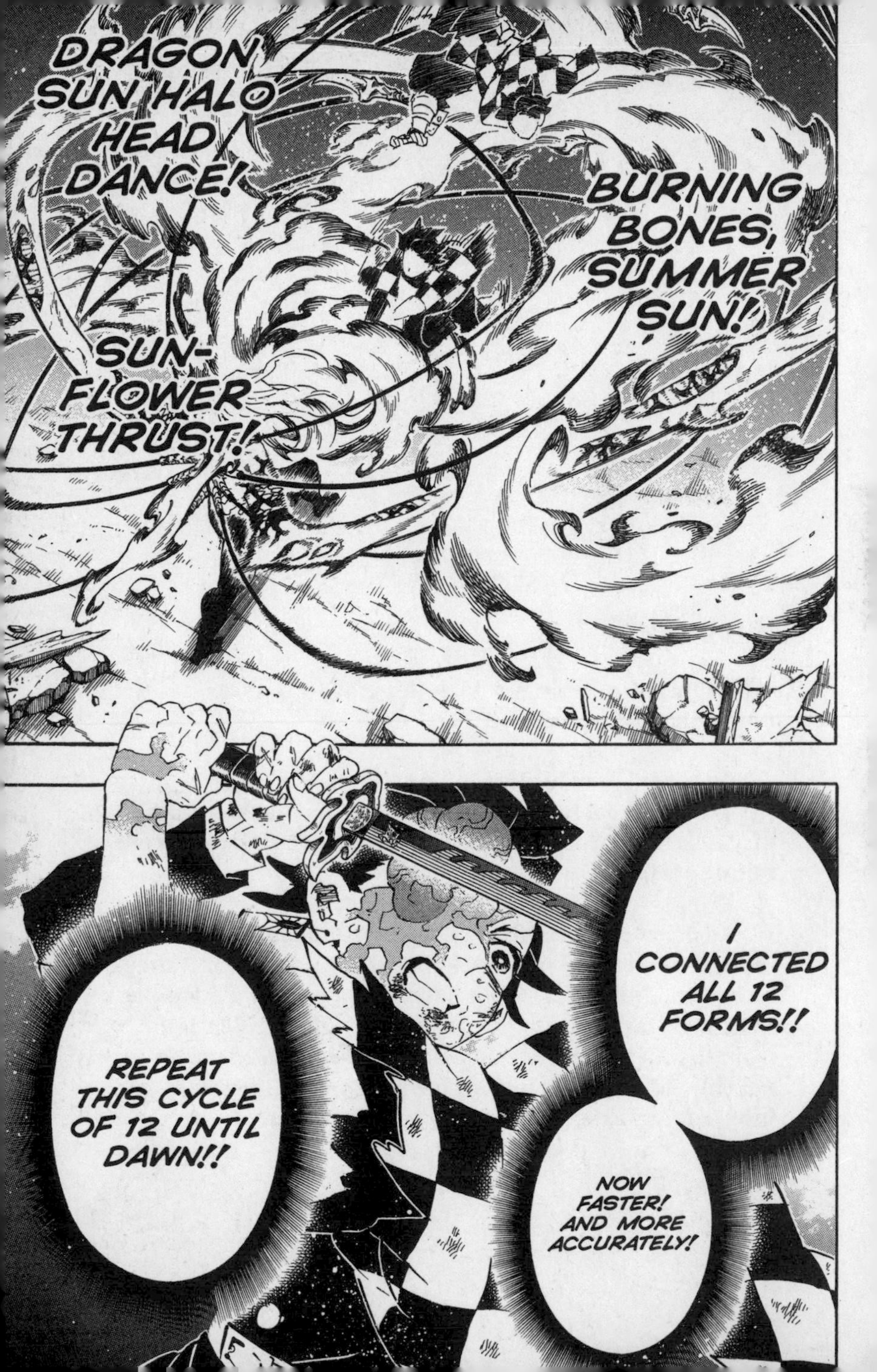
BURNING BONES, SUMMER SUN!
DRAGON SUN HALO HEAD DANCE!
SUN-FLOWER THRUST!
I CONNECTED ALL 12 FORMS!!
NOW FASTER! AND MORE ACCURATELY!
REPEAT THIS CYCLE OF 12 UNTIL DAWN!!

MUZAN'S ABILITIES

• Thin tubes: nine on his back (length: 4 m), fast, unpredictable movement

• Thin tubes: four in each thigh for a total of eight (length: 7 m), faster than the tubes on his back. Unlike his back tubes, they extend and retract. They attack from blind spots.

• Both arms can drastically lengthen and shorten (approx. 90 cm–10 m). Since they don't have a fixed shape or length, their attacks are hard to read. They also make it difficult for attackers to get in close. The inhalations from the many irregularly positioned mouths draw in nearby objects, clearing out a wide space. The size of the inhalations varies from moment to moment.

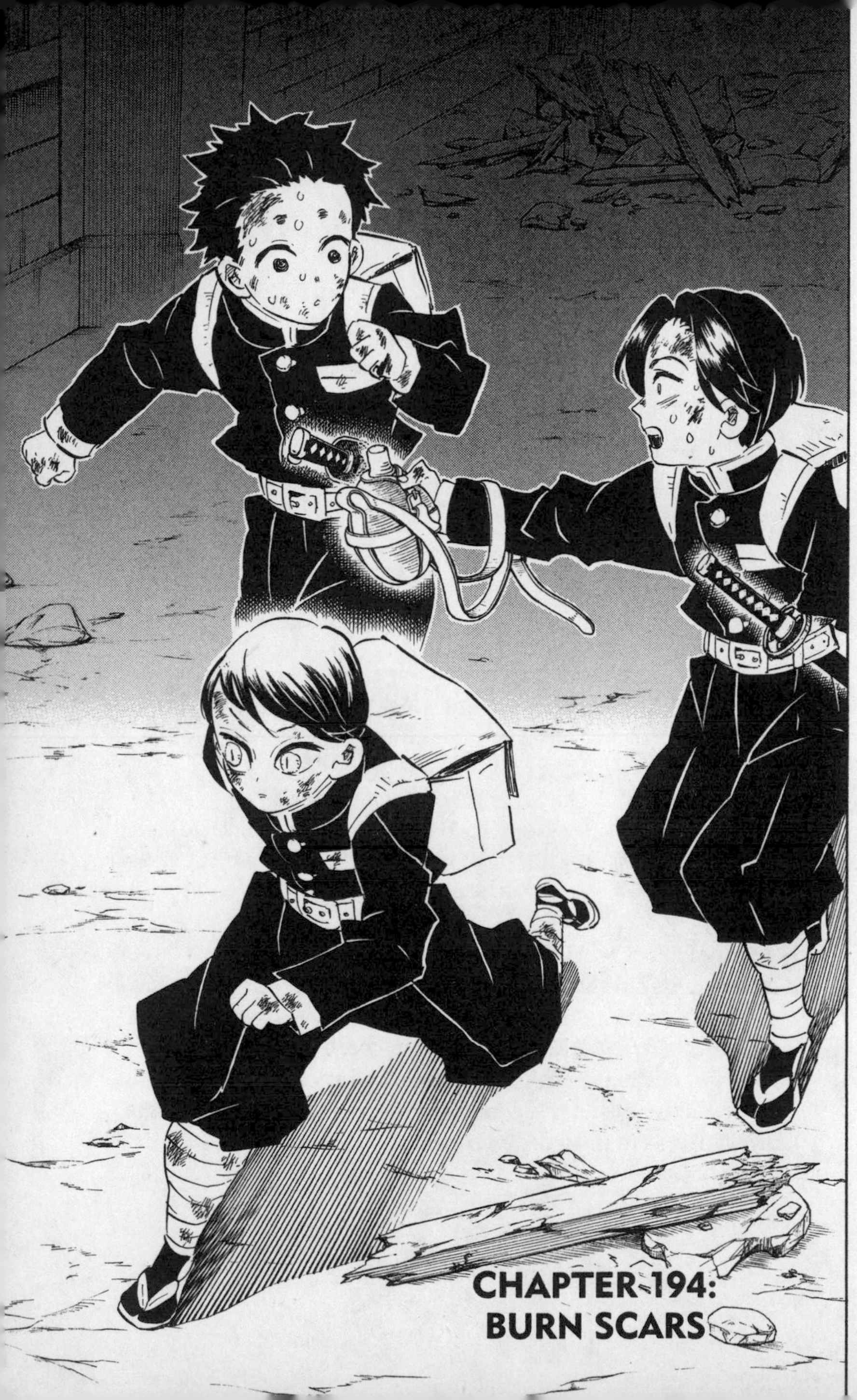
CHAPTER 194:
BURN SCARS

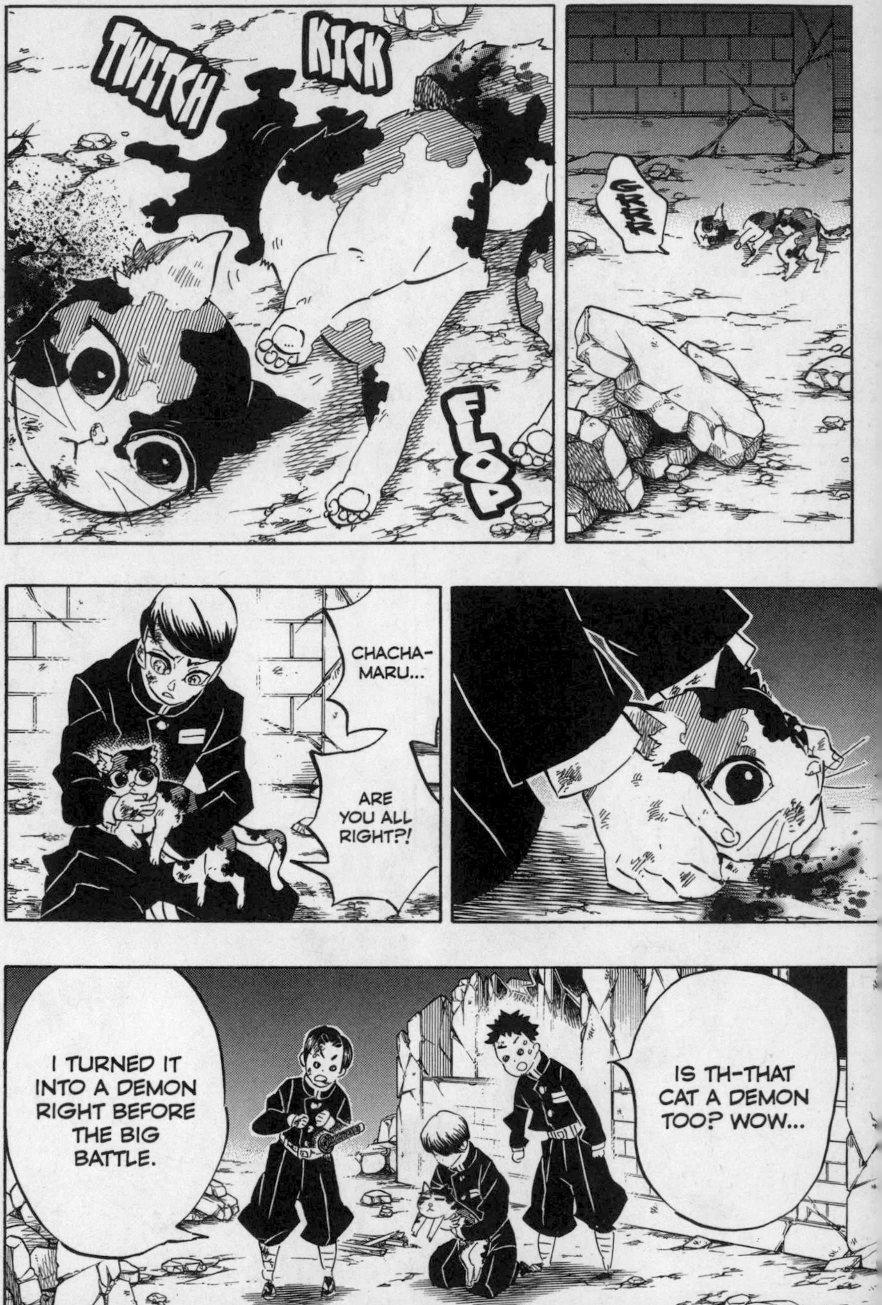
GRRRR
KICK
TWITCH
FLOP
CHACHA-MARU...
ARE YOU ALL RIGHT?!
IS TH-THAT CAT A DEMON TOO? WOW...
I TURNED IT INTO A DEMON RIGHT BEFORE THE BIG BATTLE.

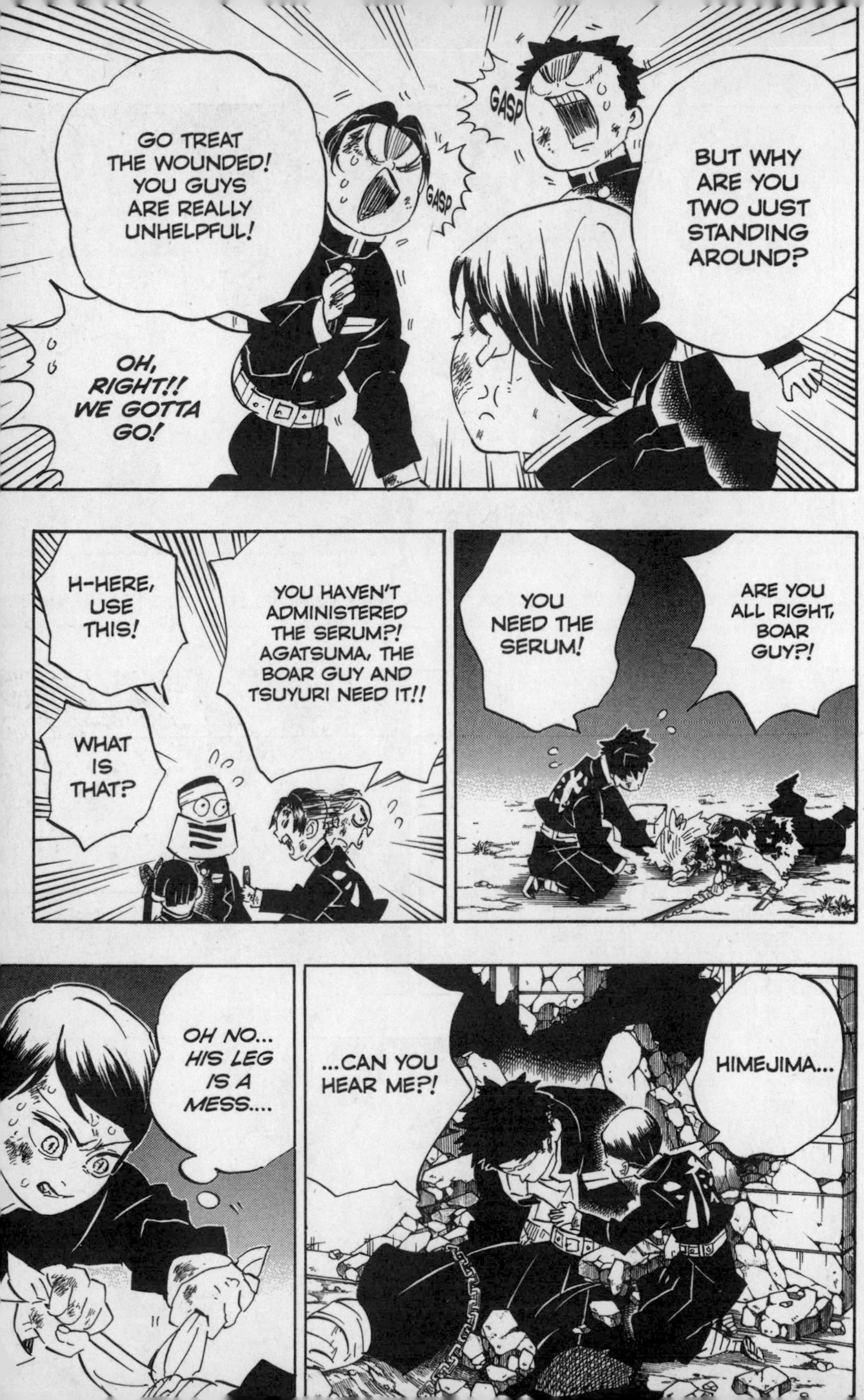
BUT WHY ARE YOU TWO JUST STANDING AROUND?
GASP
GASP
GO TREAT THE WOUNDED! YOU GUYS ARE REALLY UNHELPFUL!
OH, RIGHT!! WE GOTTA GO!
ARE YOU ALL RIGHT, BOAR GUY?!
YOU NEED THE SERUM!
YOU HAVEN'T ADMINISTERED THE SERUM?! AGATSUMA, THE BOAR GUY AND TSUYURI NEED IT!!
H-HERE, USE THIS!
WHAT IS THAT?
HIMEJIMA...
...CAN YOU HEAR ME?!
OH NO... HIS LEG IS A MESS....

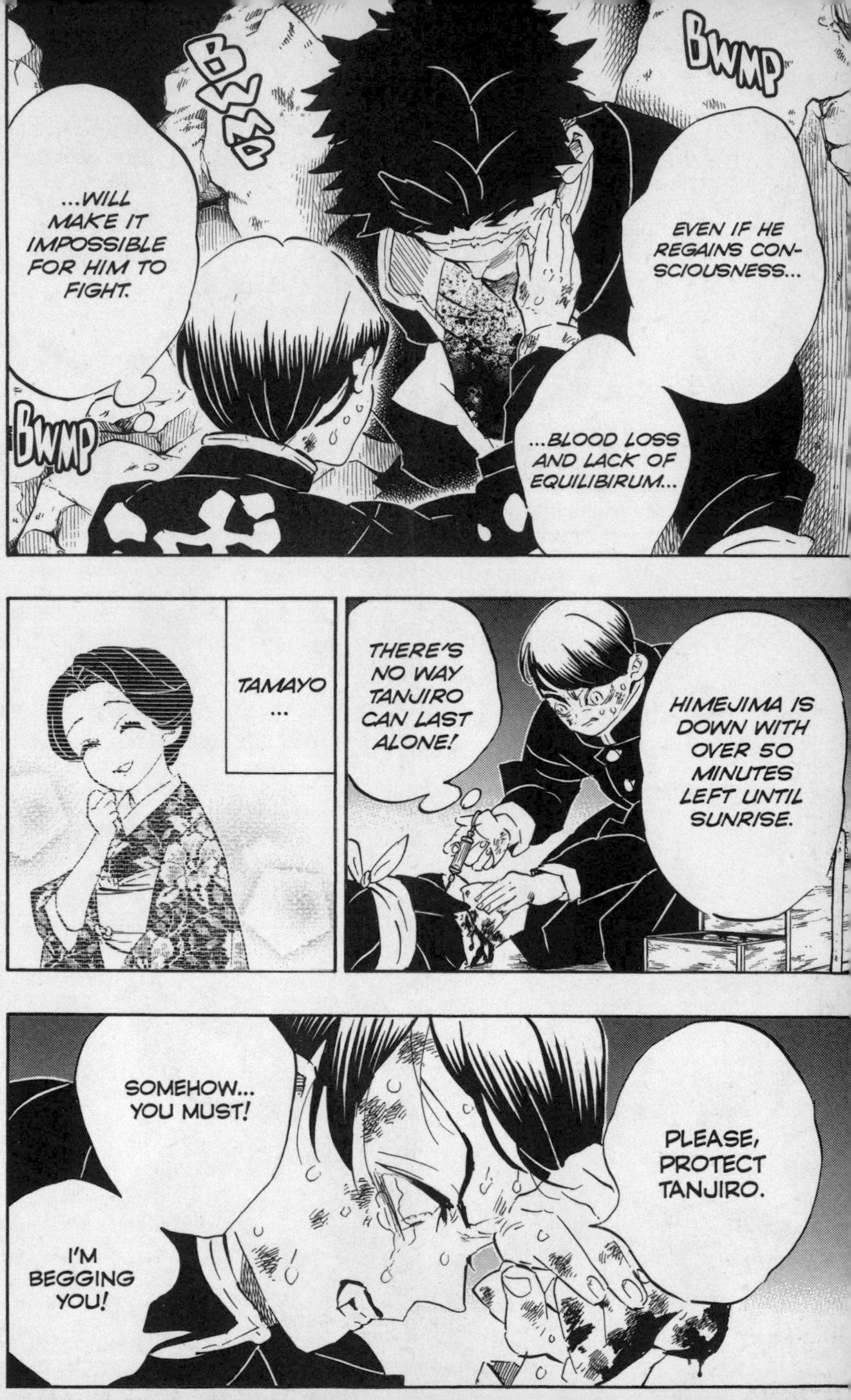
BWMP
EVEN IF HE REGAINS CONSCIOUSNESS...
...BLOOD LOSS AND LACK OF EQUILIBIRUM...
BWMP
...WILL MAKE IT IMPOSSIBLE FOR HIM TO FIGHT.
BWMP
HIMEJIMA IS DOWN WITH OVER 50 MINUTES LEFT UNTIL SUNRISE.
THERE'S NO WAY TANJIRO CAN LAST ALONE!
TAMAYO ...
PLEASE, PROTECT TANJIRO.
SOMEHOW... YOU MUST!
I'M BEGGING YOU!

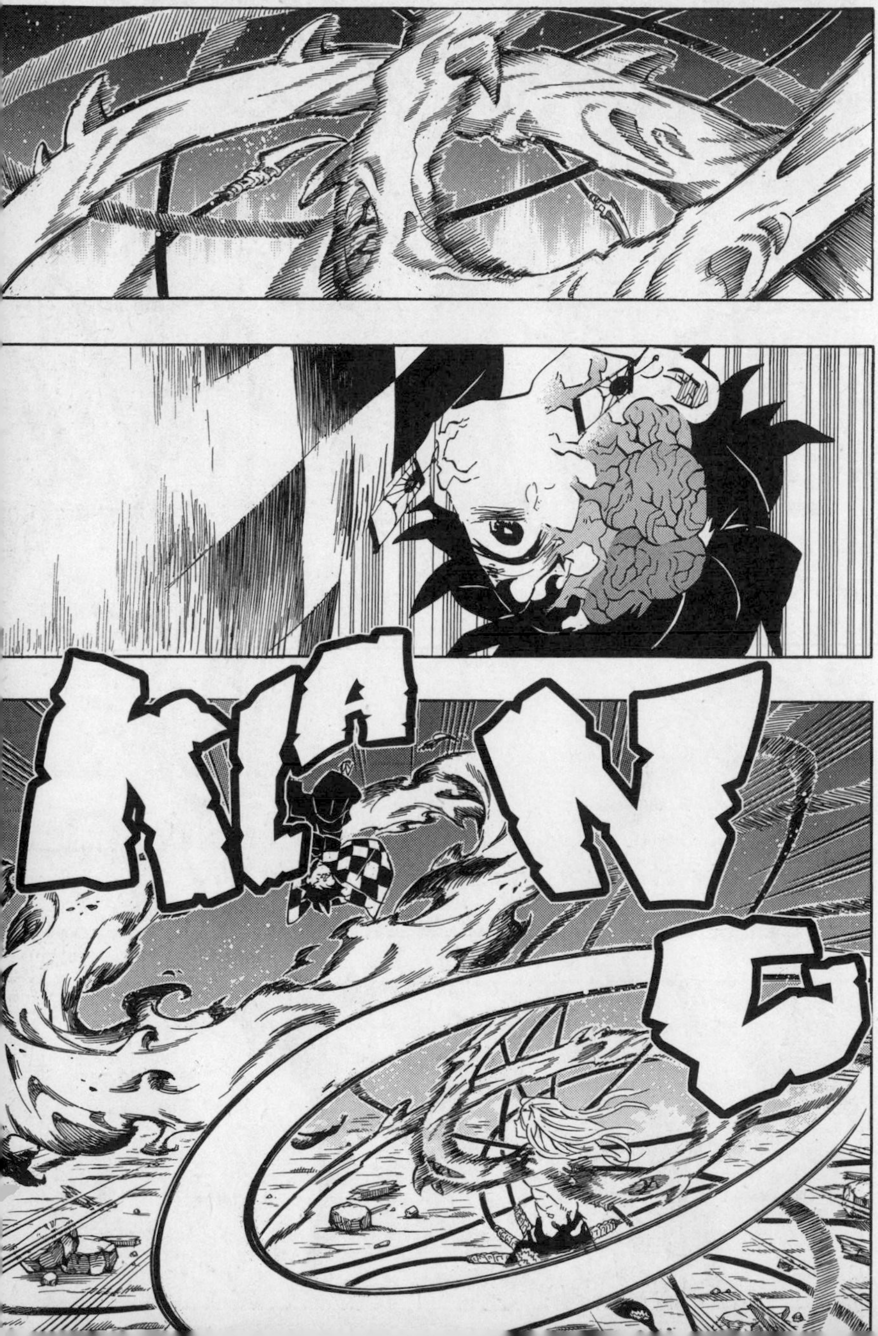
KLANG

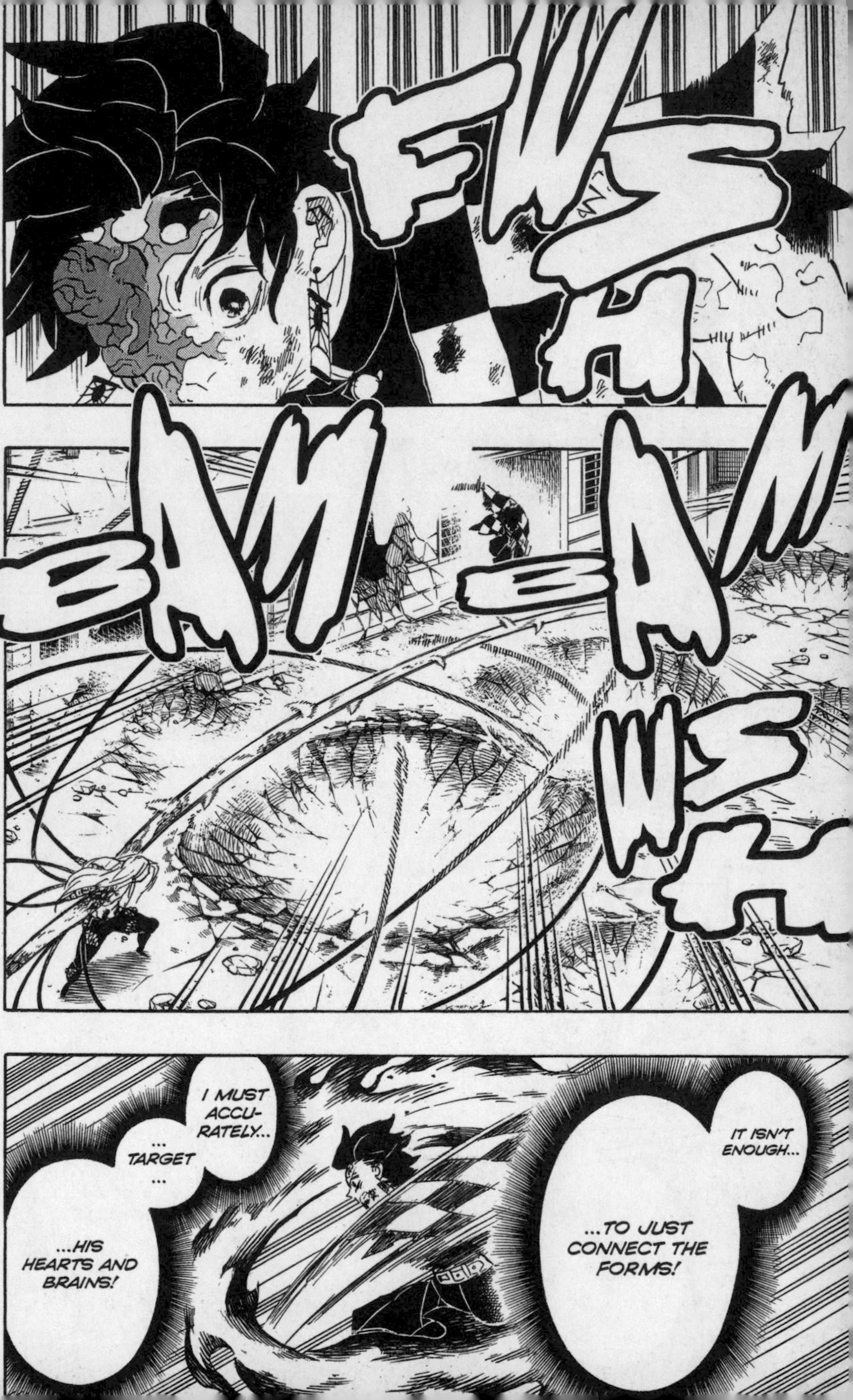
FWSH
BAM
BAM
WSH
IT ISN'T ENOUGH...
...TO JUST CONNECT THE FORMS!
I MUST ACCURATELY...
...TARGET...
...HIS HEARTS AND BRAINS!

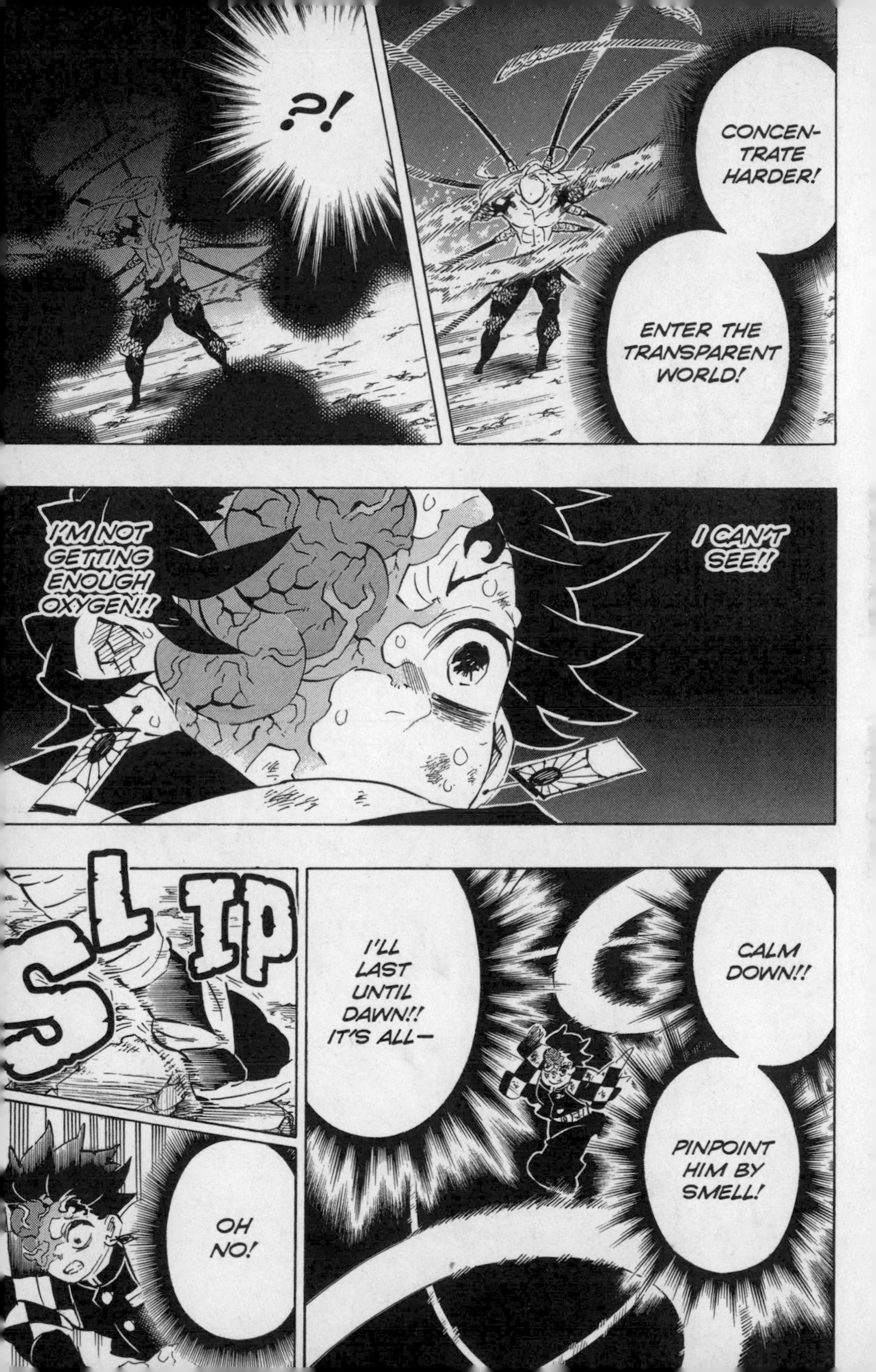
CONCEN-
TRATE
HARDER!
ENTER THE
TRANSPARENT
WORLD!
?!
I CAN'T
SEE!!
I'M NOT
GETTING
ENOUGH
OXYGEN!!
CALM
DOWN!!
PINPOINT
HIM BY
SMELL!
I'LL
LAST
UNTIL
DAWN!!
IT'S ALL—
SLIP
OH
NO!

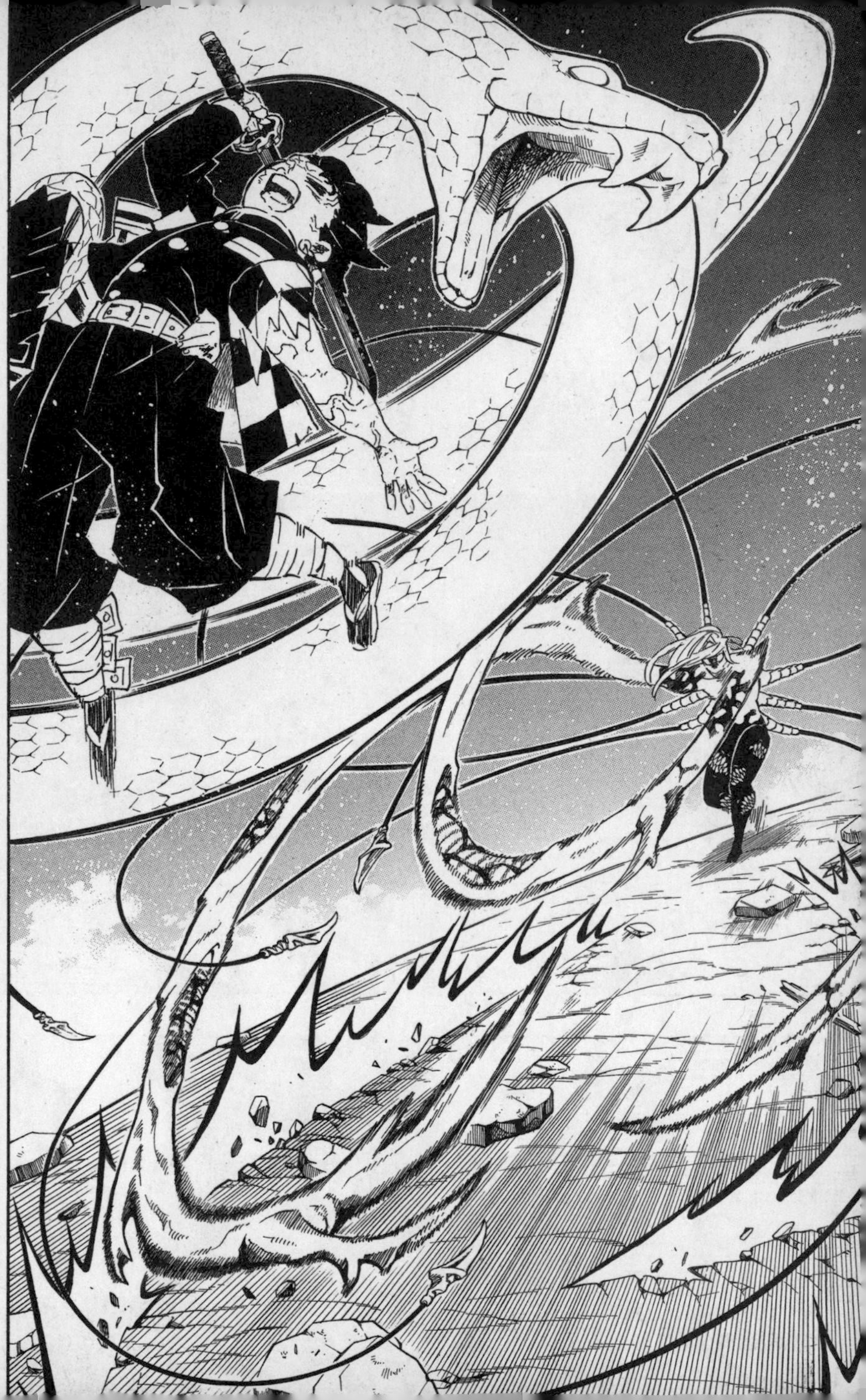

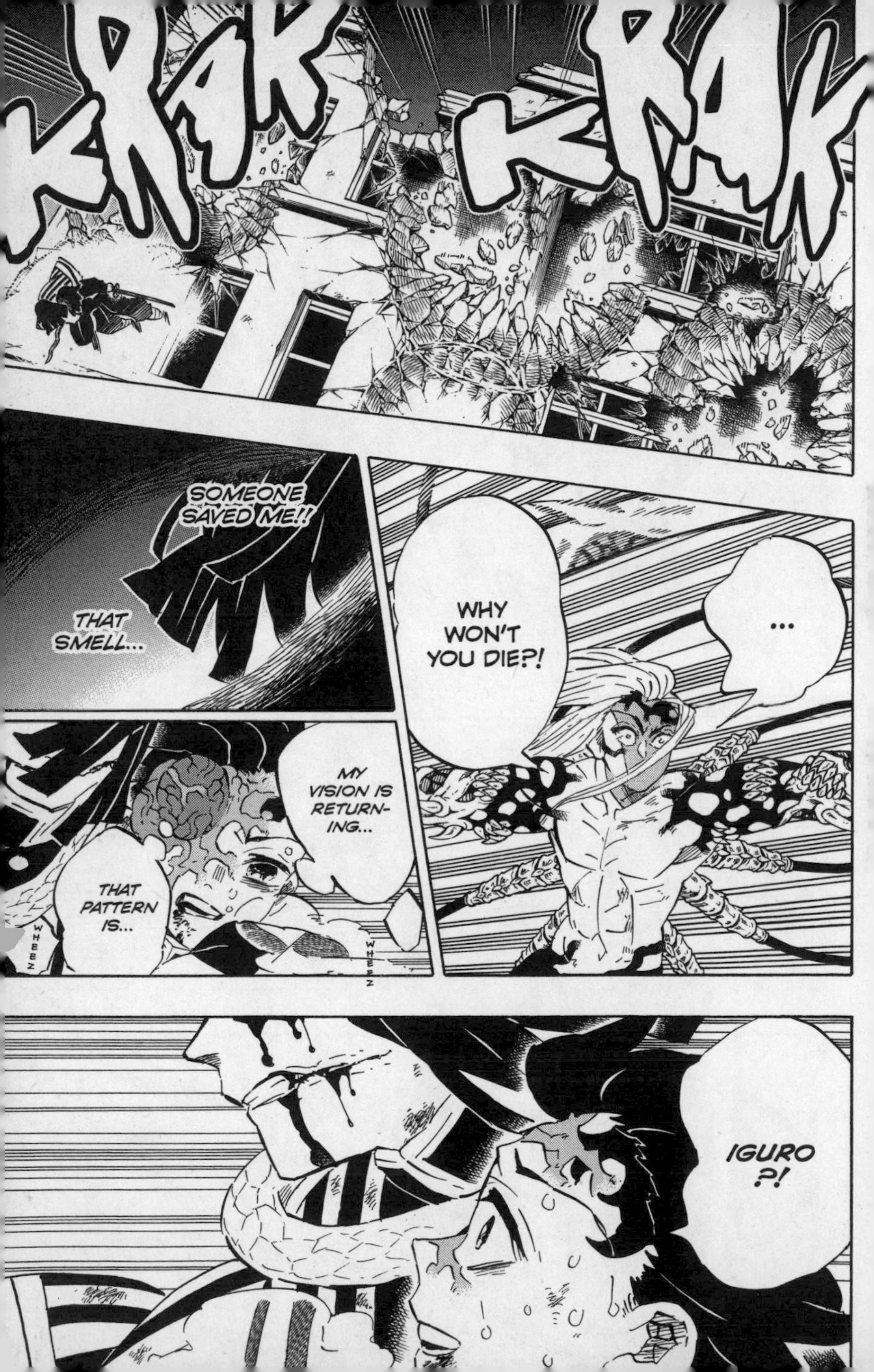
KRAK
KRAK
...
WHY WON'T YOU DIE?!
SOMEONE SAVED ME!!
THAT SMELL...
WHEEZ
MY VISION IS RETURNING...
THAT PATTERN IS...
WHEEZ
IGURO?!

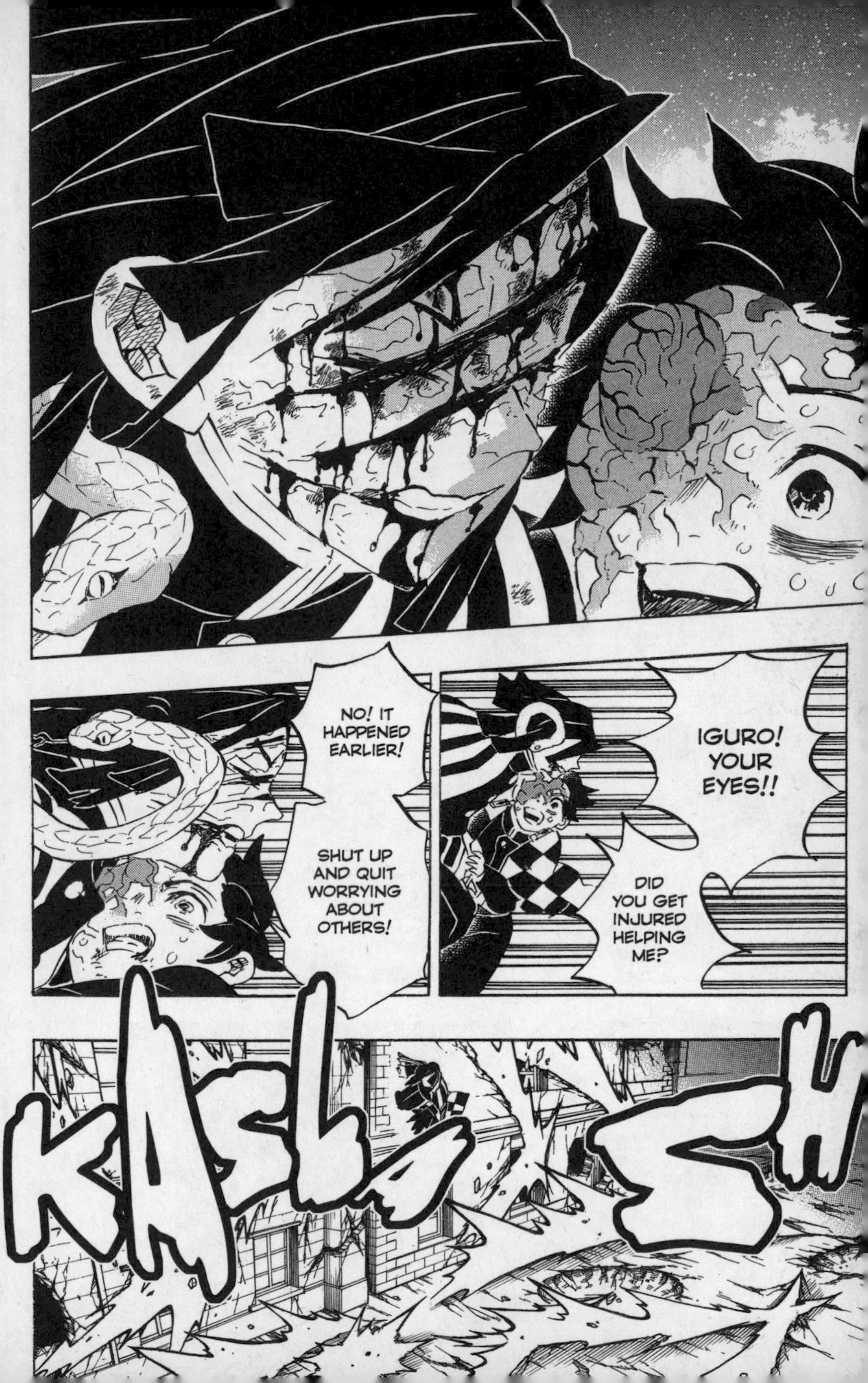
IGURO! YOUR EYES!!
DID YOU GET INJURED HELPING ME?
NO! IT HAPPENED EARLIER!
SHUT UP AND QUIT WORRYING ABOUT OTHERS!
KASLASH

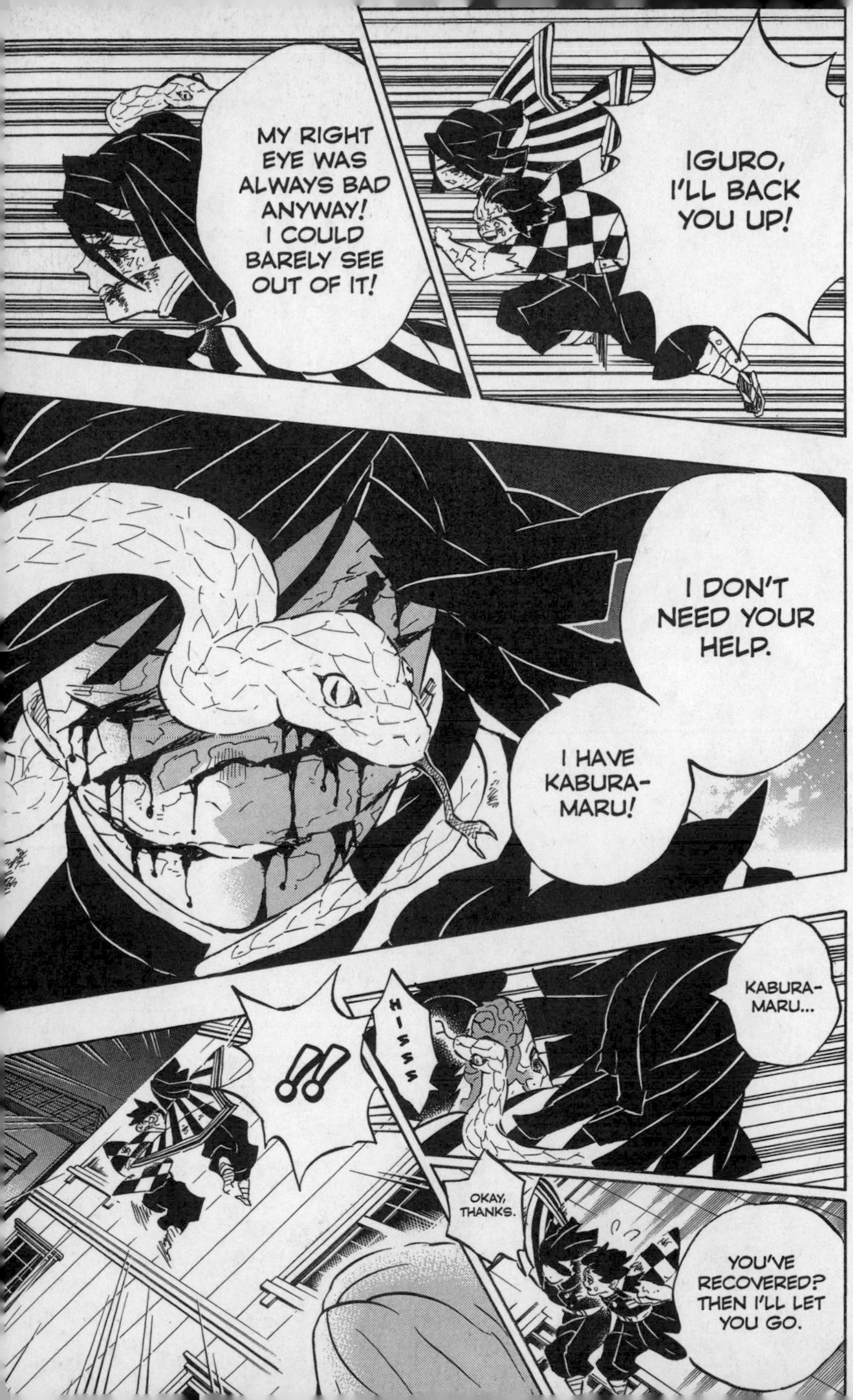
IGURO, I'LL BACK YOU UP!
MY RIGHT EYE WAS ALWAYS BAD ANYWAY! I COULD BARELY SEE OUT OF IT!
I DON'T NEED YOUR HELP.
I HAVE KABURA-MARU!
KABURA-MARU...
HISSS
!!
YOU'VE RECOVERED? THEN I'LL LET YOU GO.
OKAY, THANKS.

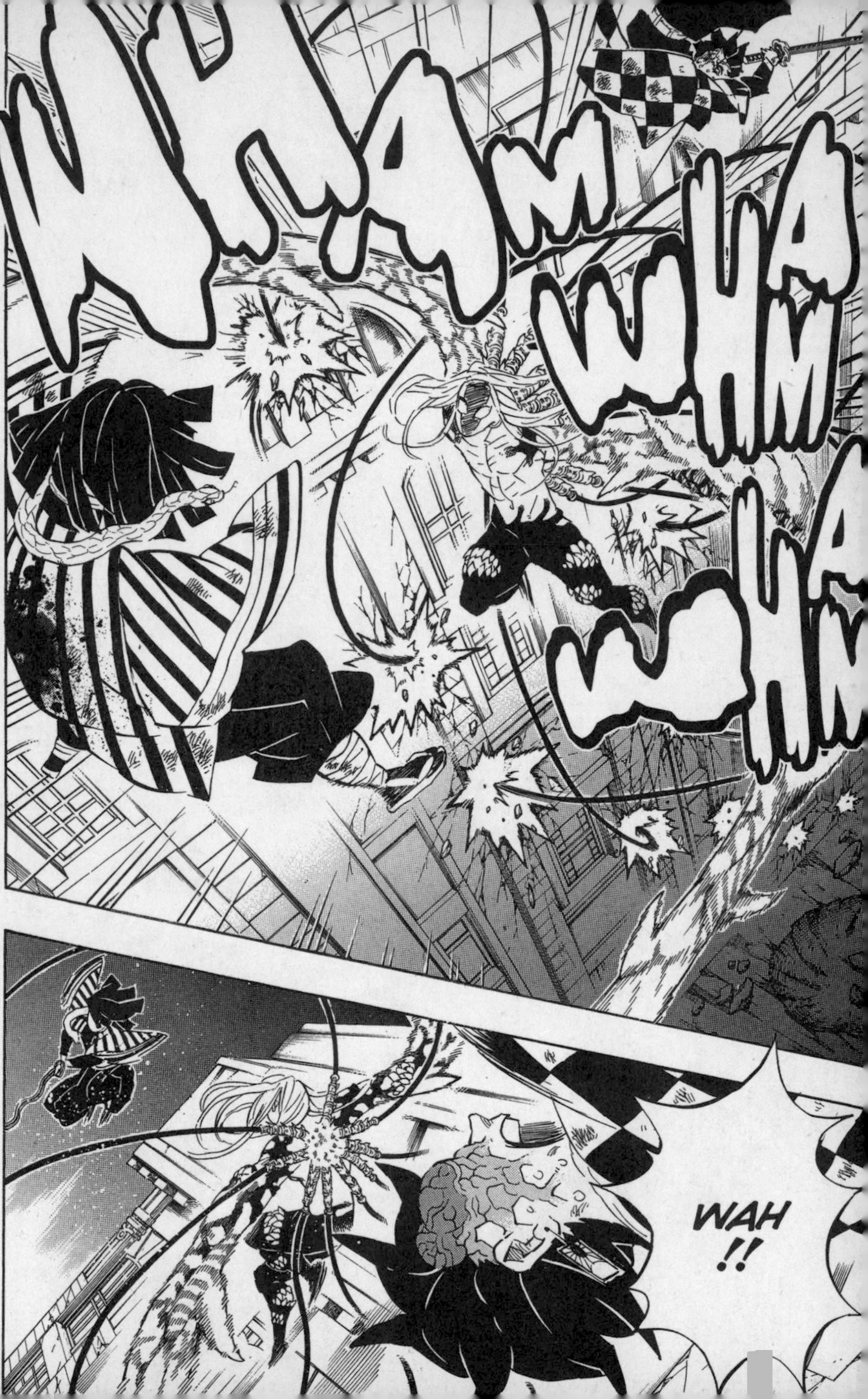
WHAM
WHAM
WHAM
WAH !!

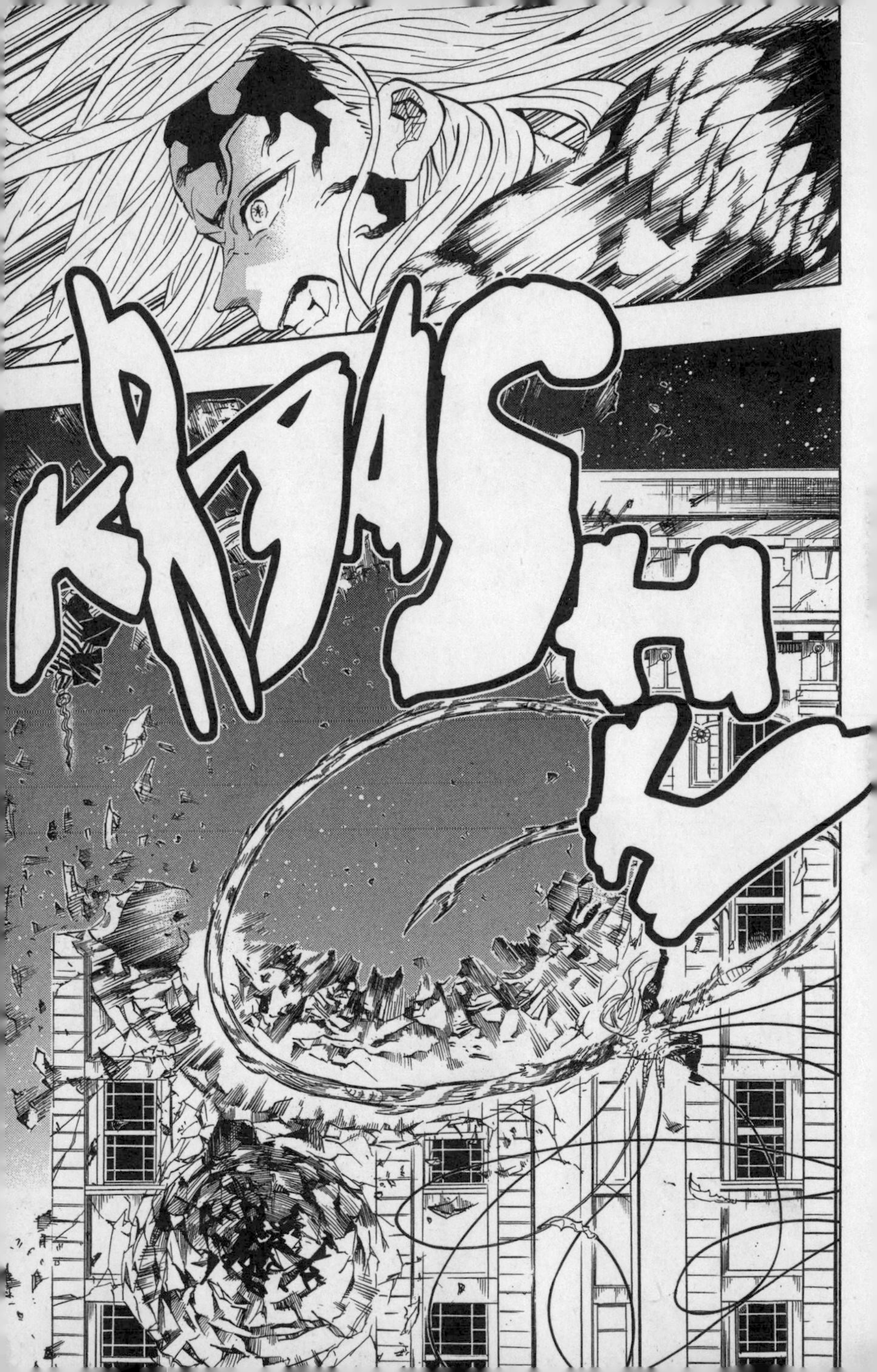
KRASH

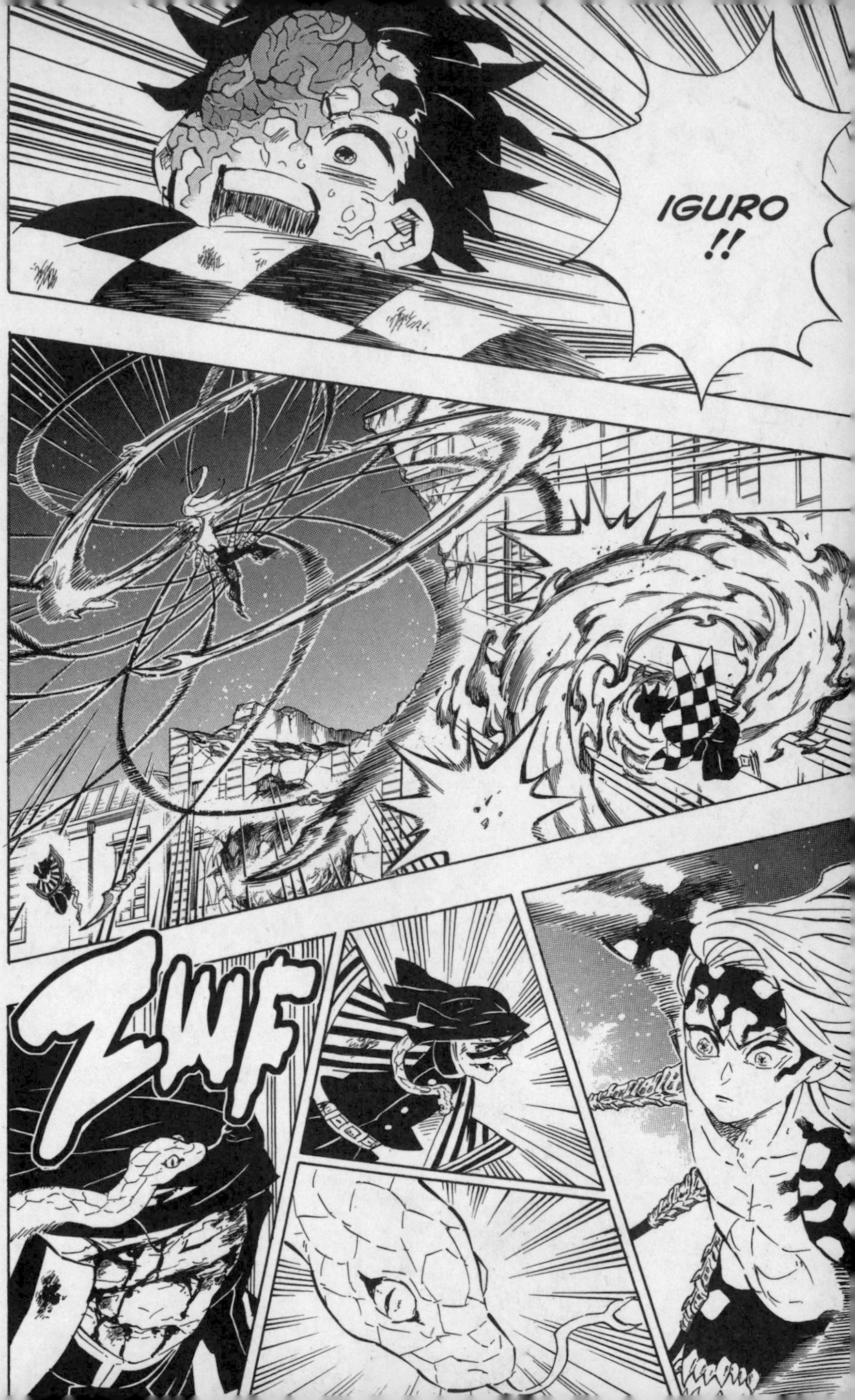
IGURO !!
ZUF

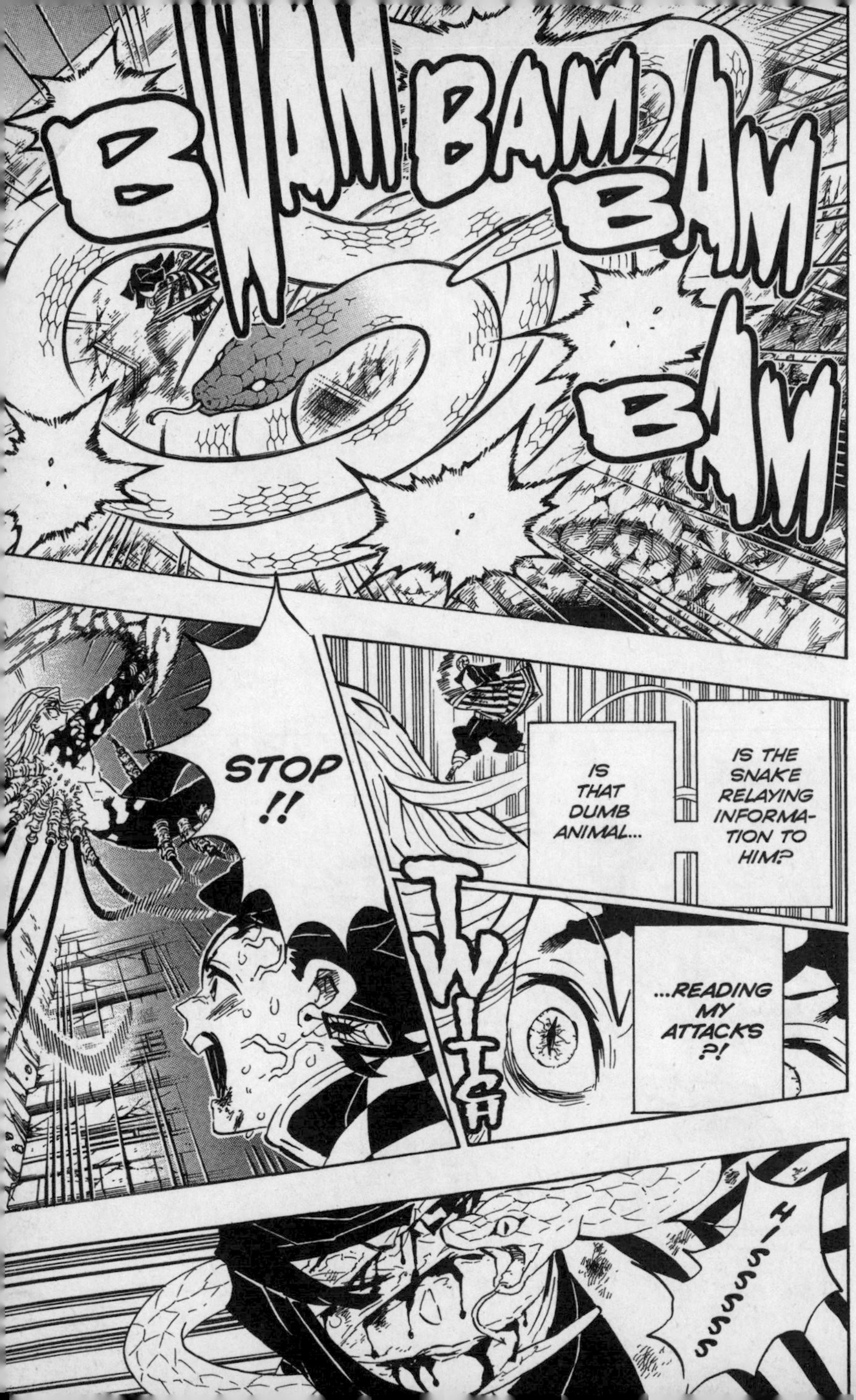
BAM
BAM
BAM
BAM
IS THE SNAKE RELAYING INFORMATION TO HIM?
IS THAT DUMB ANIMAL...
...READING MY ATTACKS?!
TWITCH
STOP!!
HISSSSSS

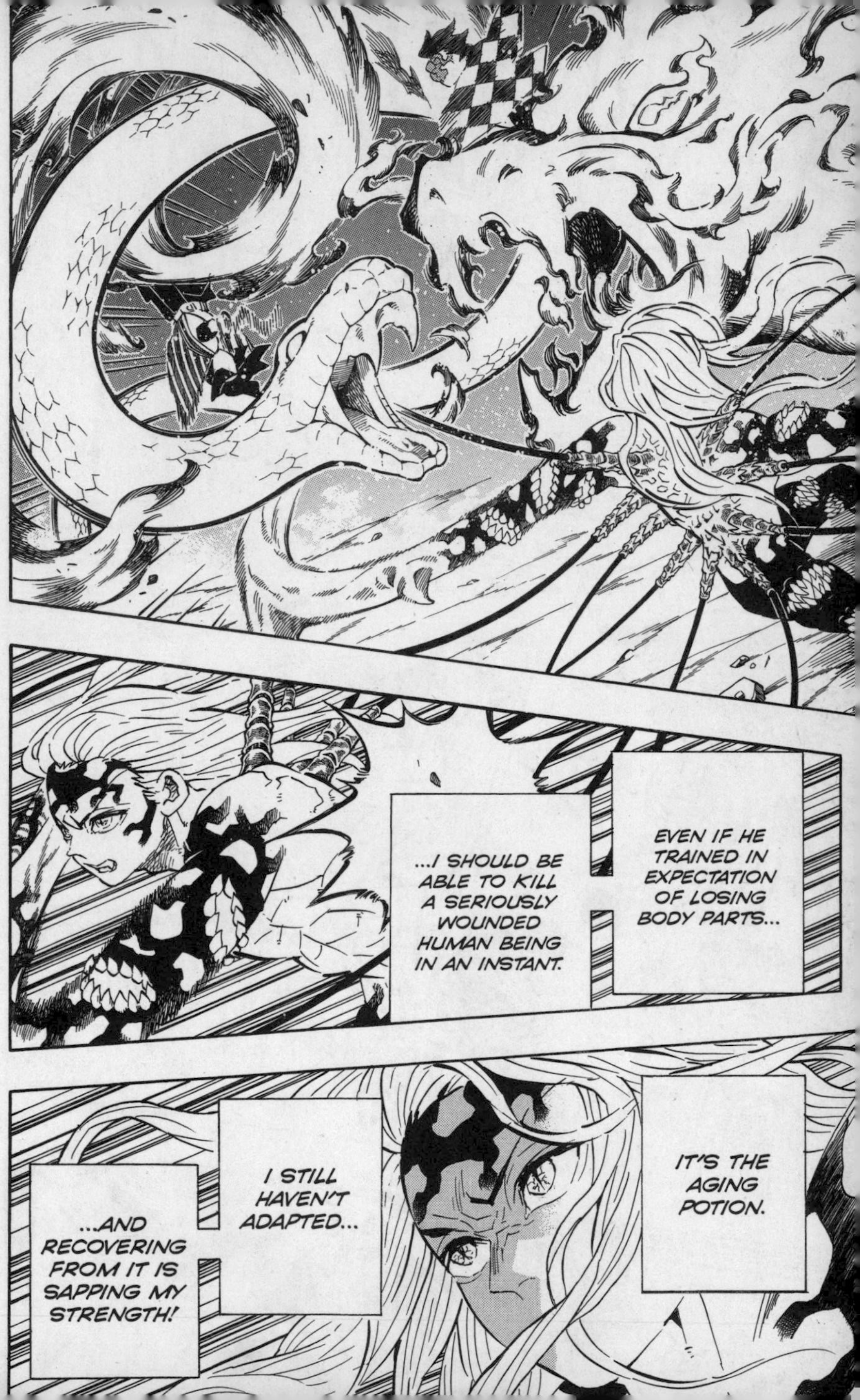
EVEN IF HE TRAINED IN EXPECTATION OF LOSING BODY PARTS...
...I SHOULD BE ABLE TO KILL A SERIOUSLY WOUNDED HUMAN BEING IN AN INSTANT.
IT'S THE AGING POTION.
I STILL HAVEN'T ADAPTED...
...AND RECOVERING FROM IT IS SAPPING MY STRENGTH!

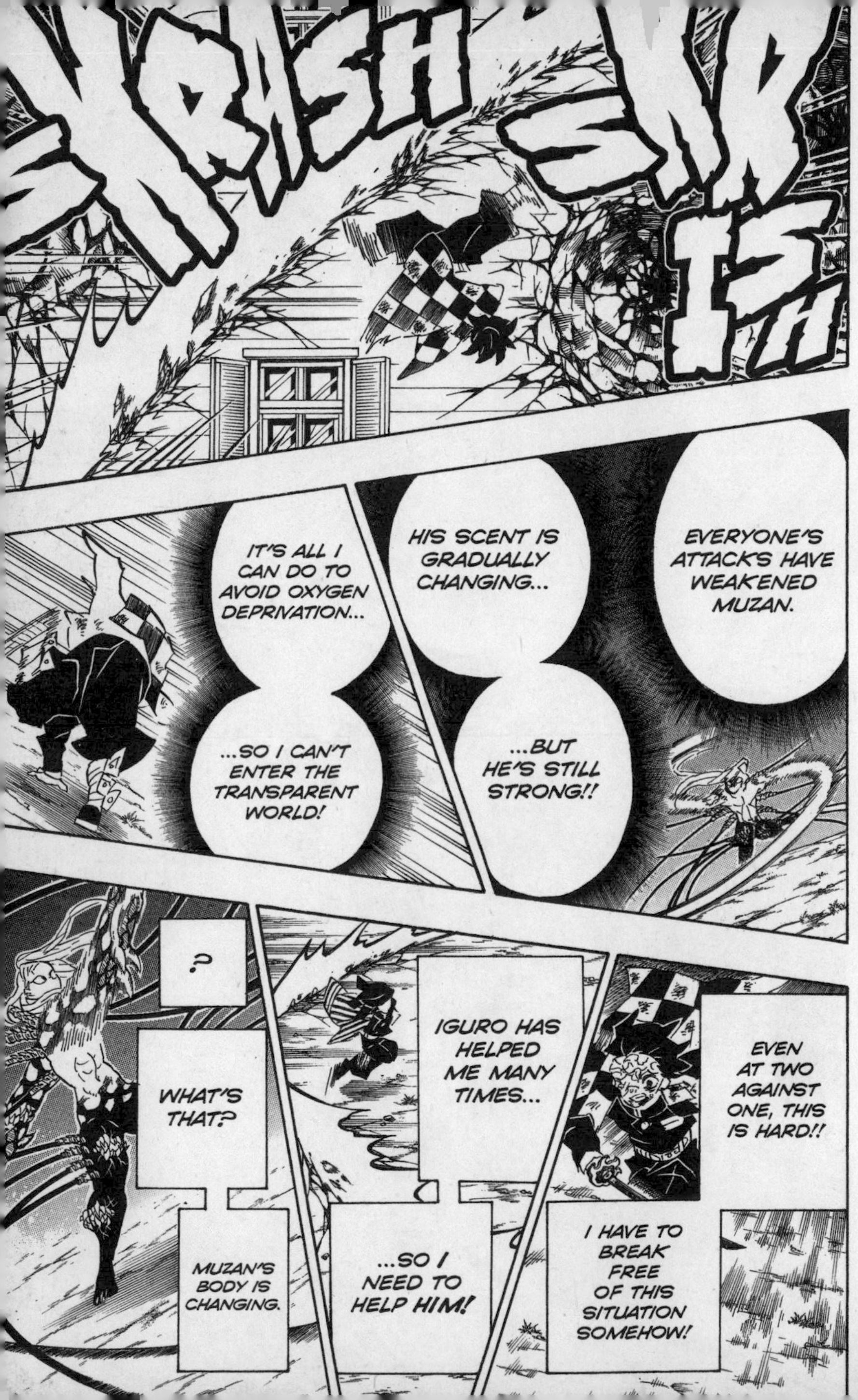
EVERYONE'S ATTACK'S HAVE WEAKENED MUZAN.
HIS SCENT IS GRADUALLY CHANGING...
...BUT HE'S STILL STRONG!!
IT'S ALL I CAN DO TO AVOID OXYGEN DEPRIVATION...
...SO I CAN'T ENTER THE TRANSPARENT WORLD!
EVEN AT TWO AGAINST ONE, THIS IS HARD!!
I HAVE TO BREAK FREE OF THIS SITUATION SOMEHOW!
IGURO HAS HELPED ME MANY TIMES...
...SO I NEED TO HELP HIM!
?
WHAT'S THAT?
MUZAN'S BODY IS CHANGING.

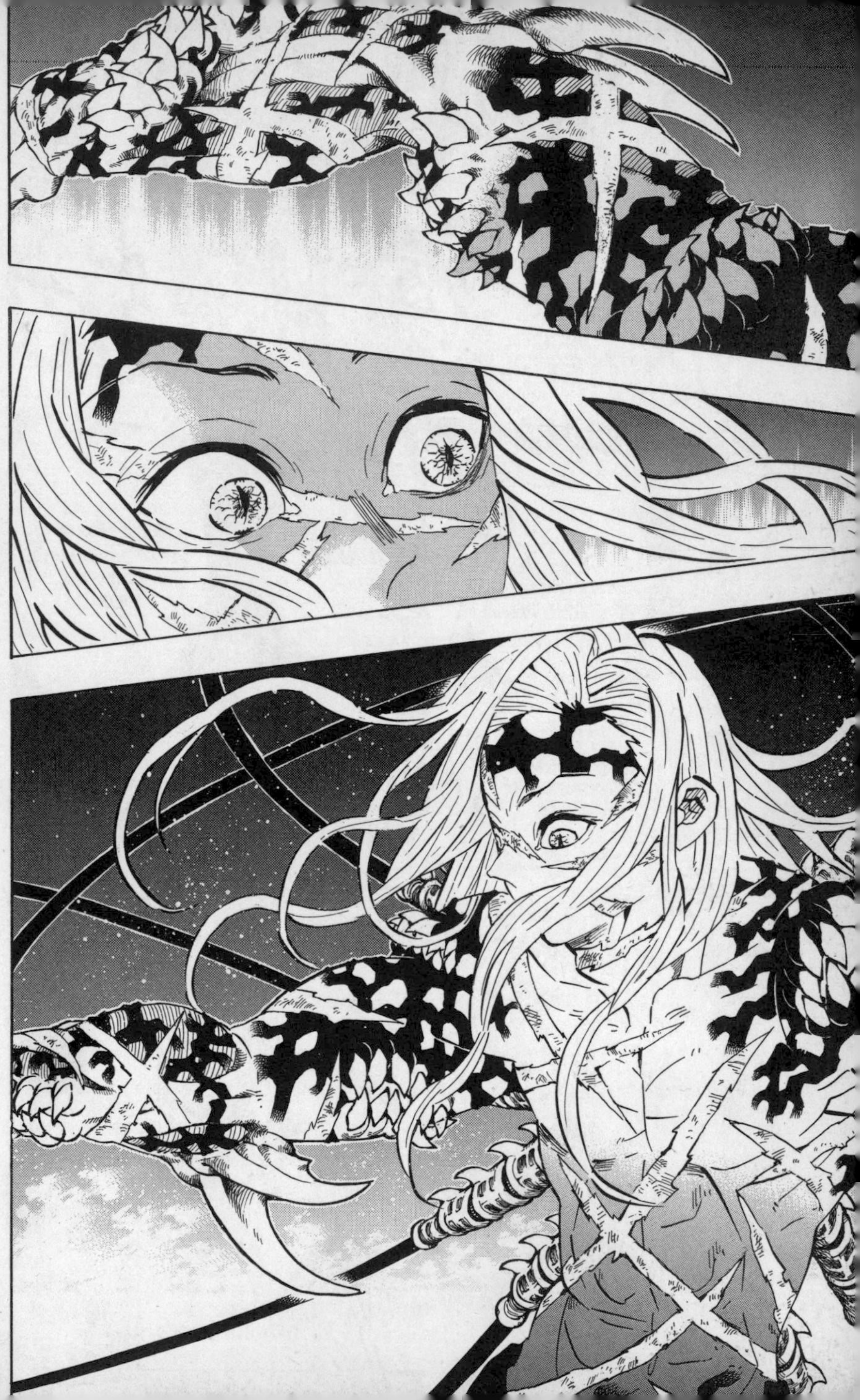

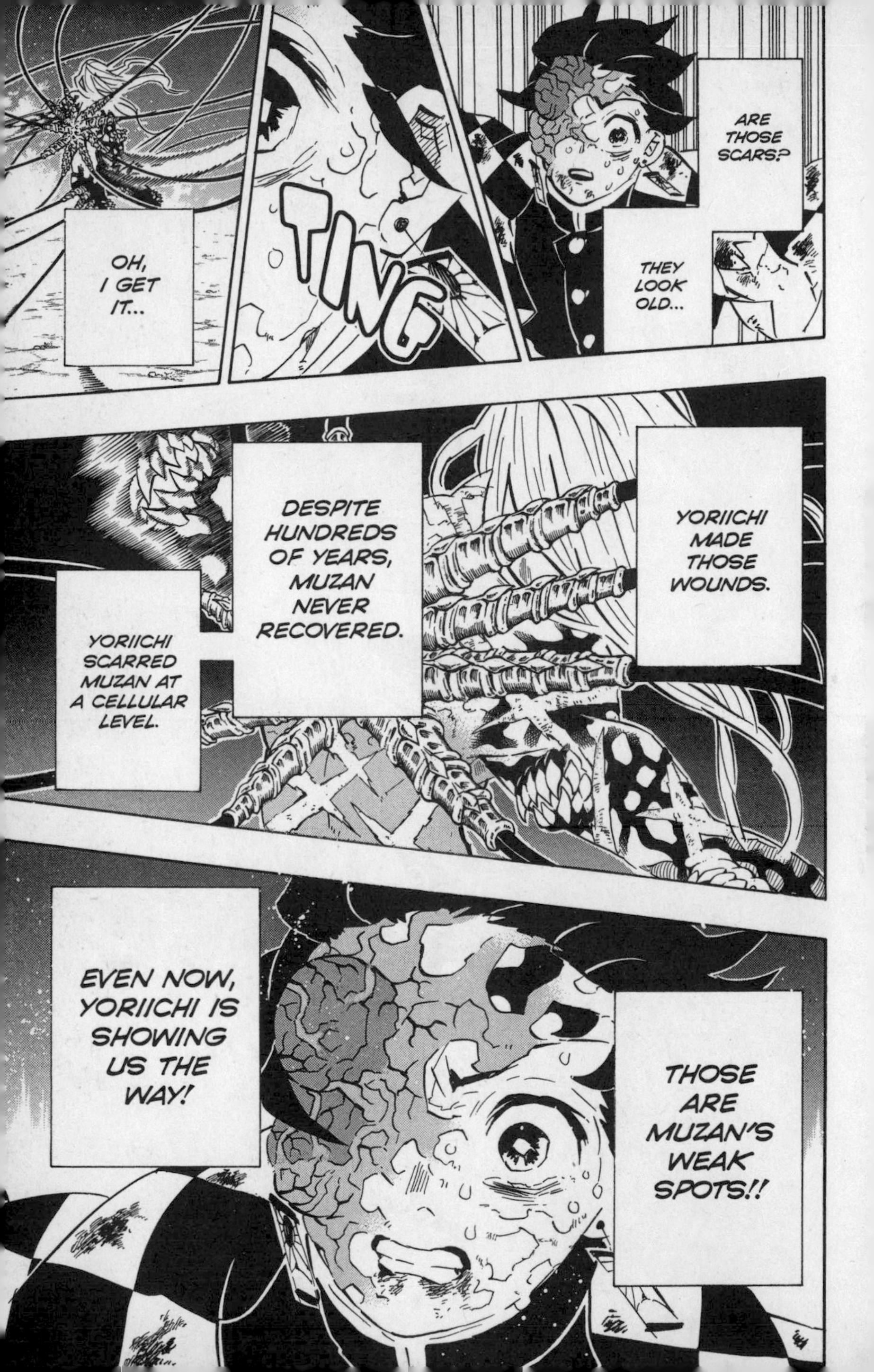
ARE THOSE SCARS?
THEY LOOK OLD...
TING
OH, I GET IT...
YORIICHI MADE THOSE WOUNDS.
DESPITE HUNDREDS OF YEARS, MUZAN NEVER RECOVERED.
YORIICHI SCARRED MUZAN AT A CELLULAR LEVEL.
THOSE ARE MUZAN'S WEAK SPOTS!!
EVEN NOW, YORIICHI IS SHOWING US THE WAY!

Taisho Whispers

Despite the lack of time while developing the drug, Tamayo managed to turn the cat Chachamaru into a demon. She felt sorry that Chachamaru couldn't choose to become a demon of its own free will, but this way Yushiro wouldn't be alone and feel as lonely.

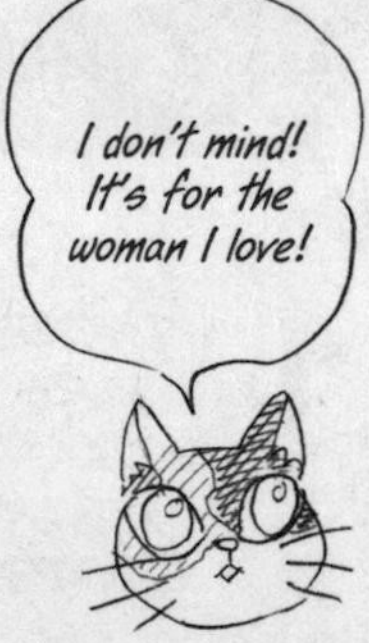
I don't mind! It's for the woman I love!

Handsome Cat

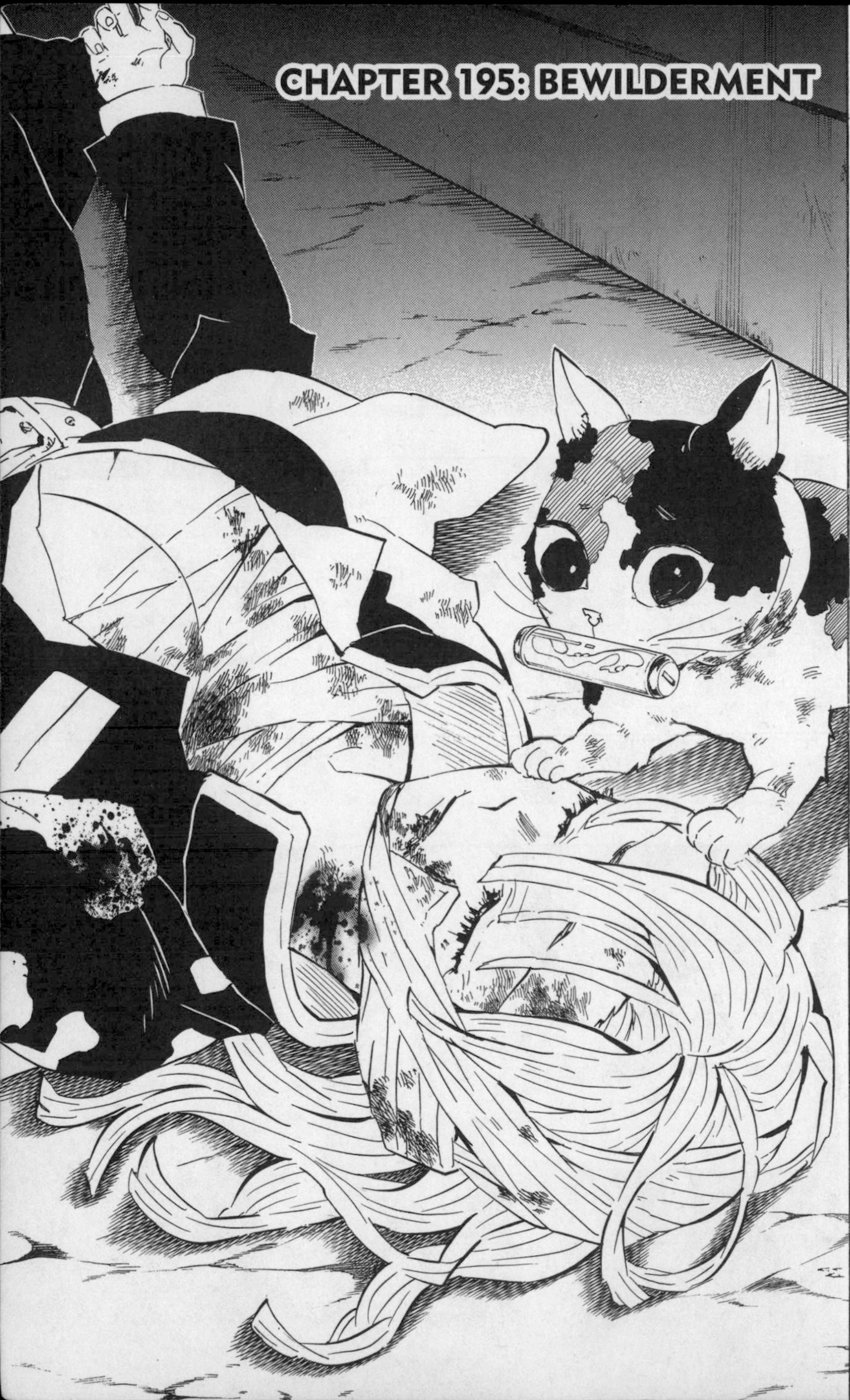
CHAPTER 195: BEWILDERMENT

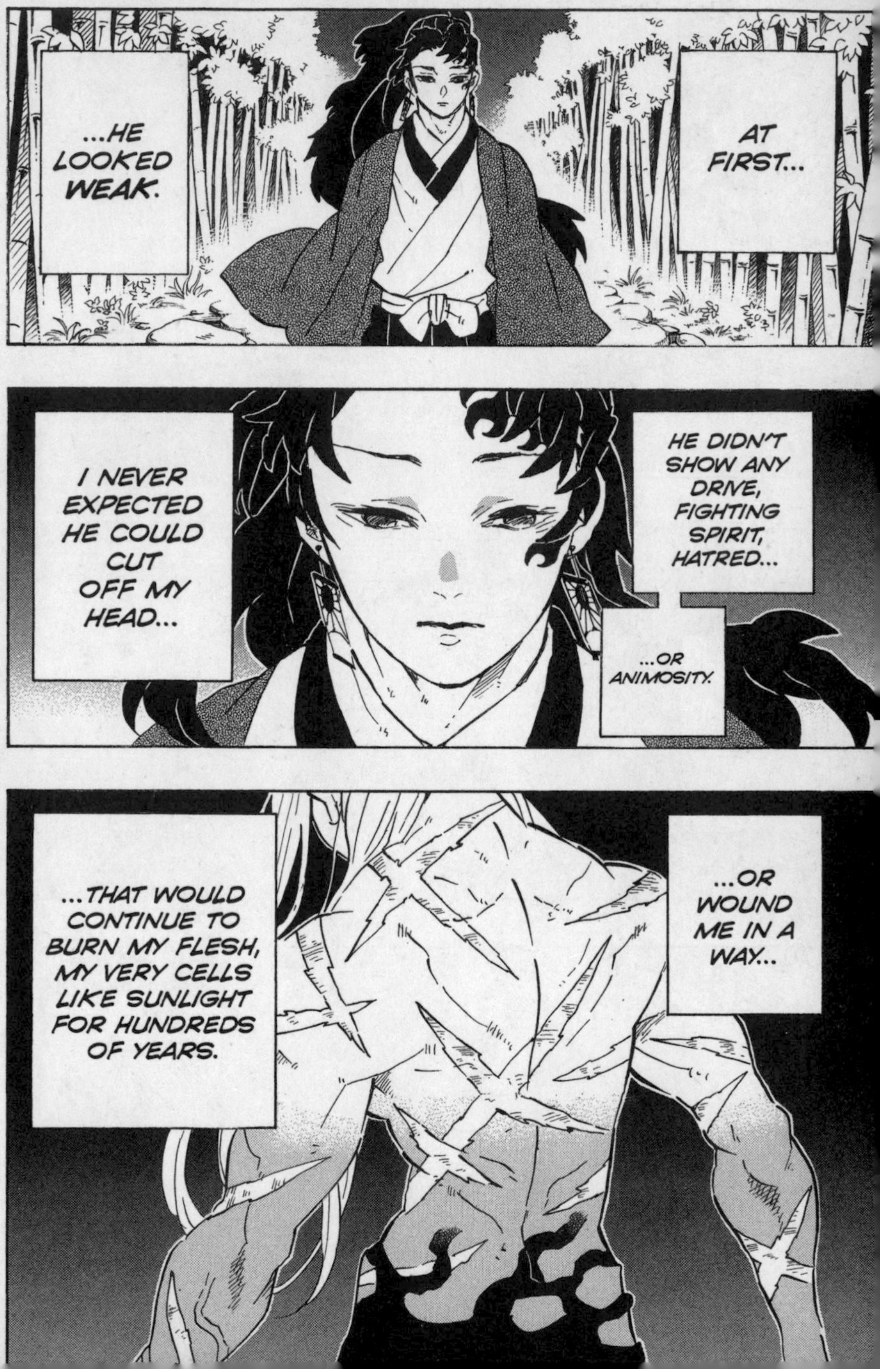
AT FIRST...
...HE LOOKED WEAK.
HE DIDN'T SHOW ANY DRIVE, FIGHTING SPIRIT, HATRED...
...OR ANIMOSITY.
I NEVER EXPECTED HE COULD CUT OFF MY HEAD...
...OR WOUND ME IN A WAY...
...THAT WOULD CONTINUE TO BURN MY FLESH, MY VERY CELLS LIKE SUNLIGHT FOR HUNDREDS OF YEARS.

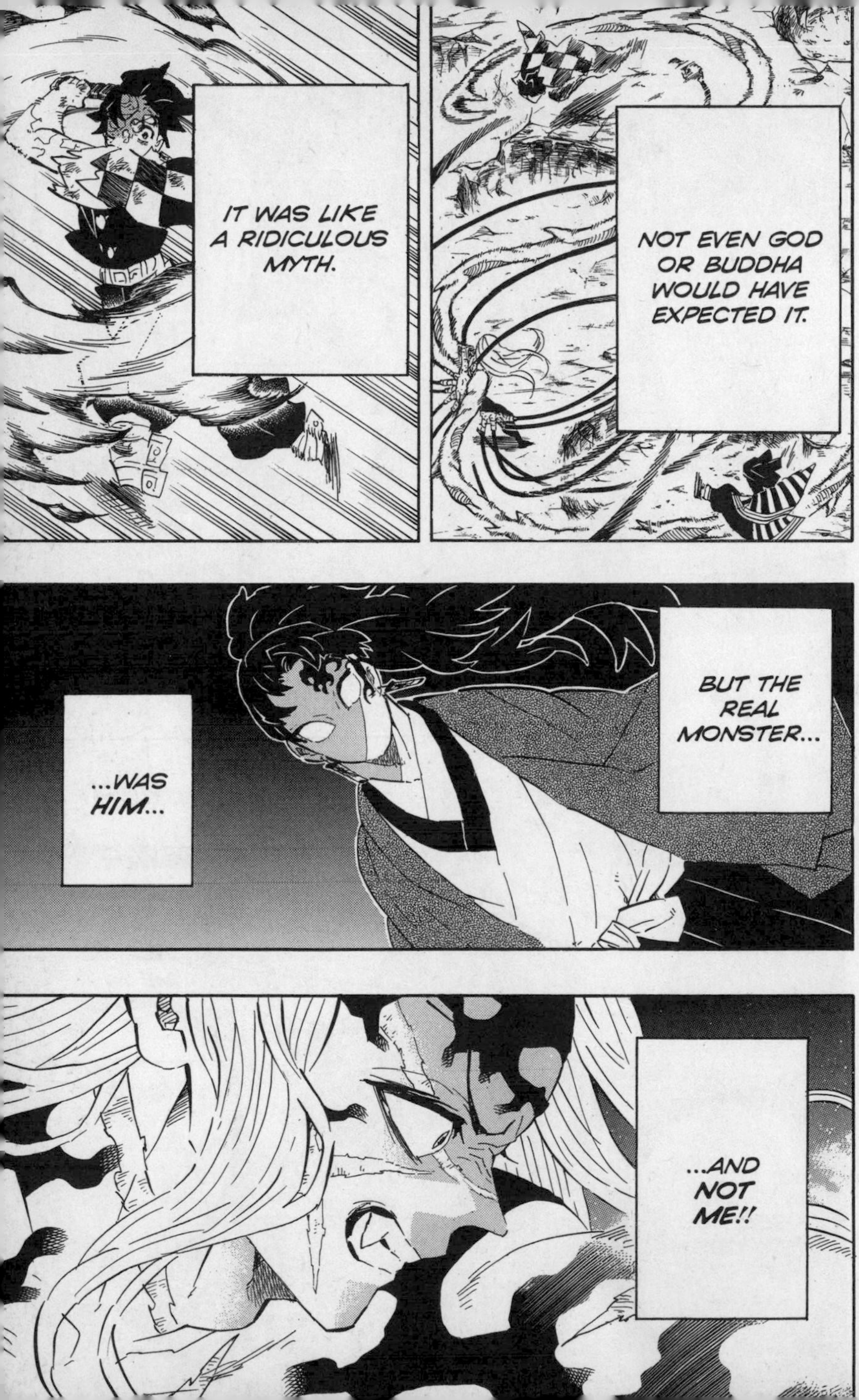
NOT EVEN GOD OR BUDDHA WOULD HAVE EXPECTED IT.
IT WAS LIKE A RIDICULOUS MYTH.
BUT THE REAL MONSTER...
...WAS HIM...
...AND NOT ME!!

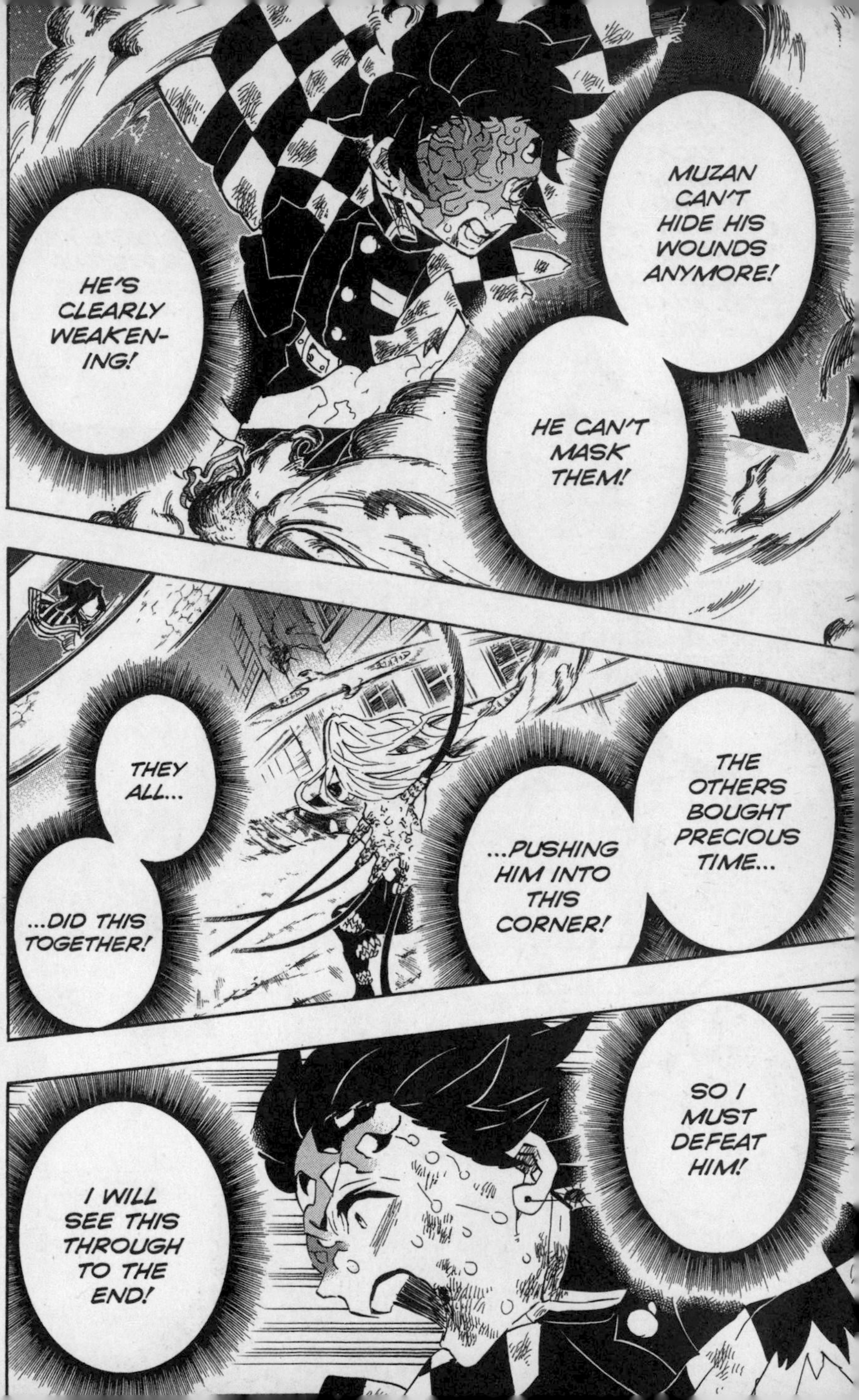
MUZAN CAN'T HIDE HIS WOUNDS ANYMORE!
HE CAN'T MASK THEM!
HE'S CLEARLY WEAKEN-ING!
THE OTHERS BOUGHT PRECIOUS TIME...
...PUSHING HIM INTO THIS CORNER!
THEY ALL...
...DID THIS TOGETHER!
SO I MUST DEFEAT HIM!
I WILL SEE THIS THROUGH TO THE END!

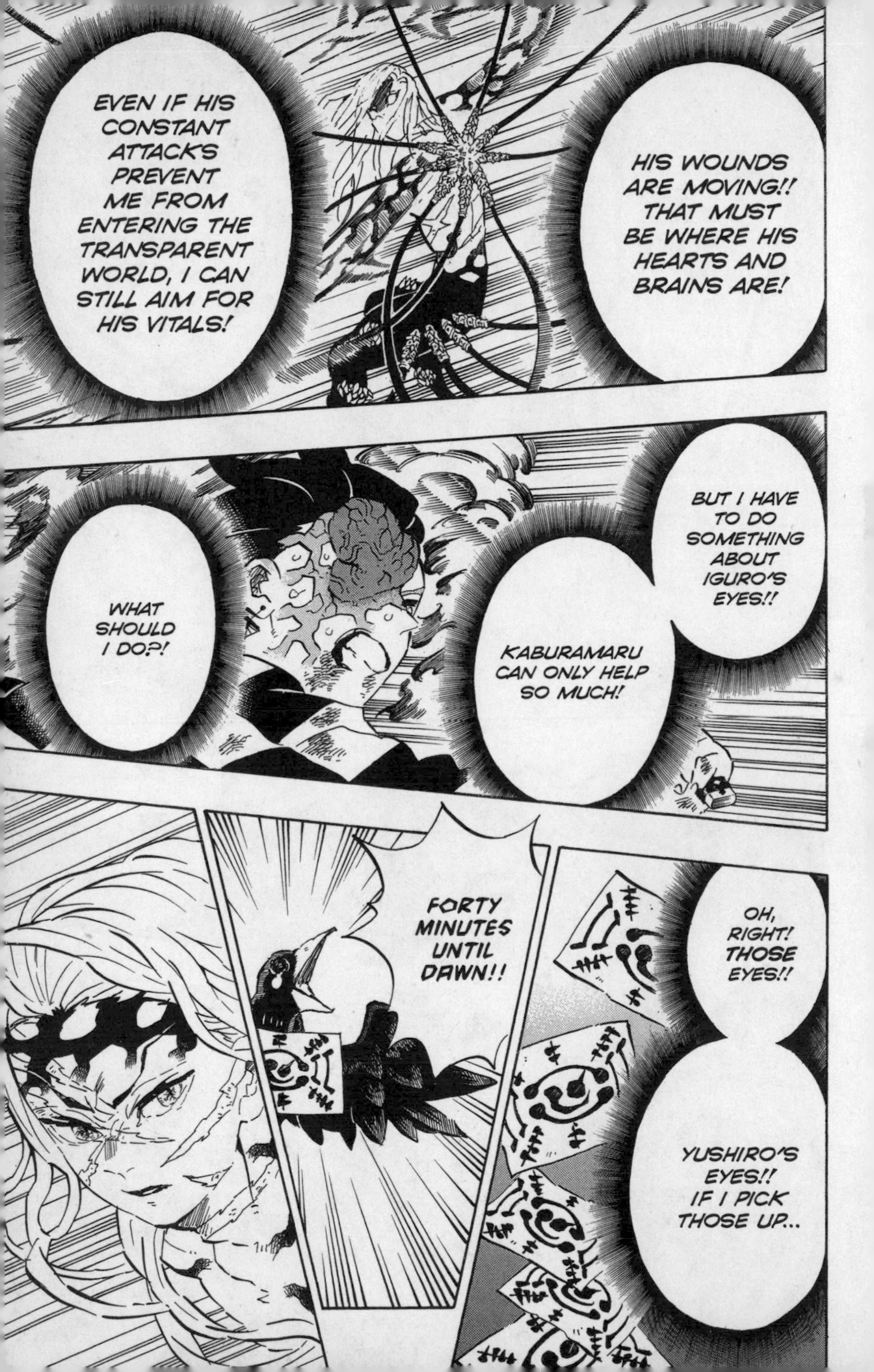
HIS WOUNDS ARE MOVING!! THAT MUST BE WHERE HIS HEARTS AND BRAINS ARE!
EVEN IF HIS CONSTANT ATTACK'S PREVENT ME FROM ENTERING THE TRANSPARENT WORLD, I CAN STILL AIM FOR HIS VITALS!
BUT I HAVE TO DO SOMETHING ABOUT IGURO'S EYES!!
KABURAMARU CAN ONLY HELP SO MUCH!
WHAT SHOULD I DO?!
OH, RIGHT! THOSE EYES!!
YUSHIRO'S EYES!! IF I PICK THOSE UP...
FORTY MINUTES UNTIL DAWN!!

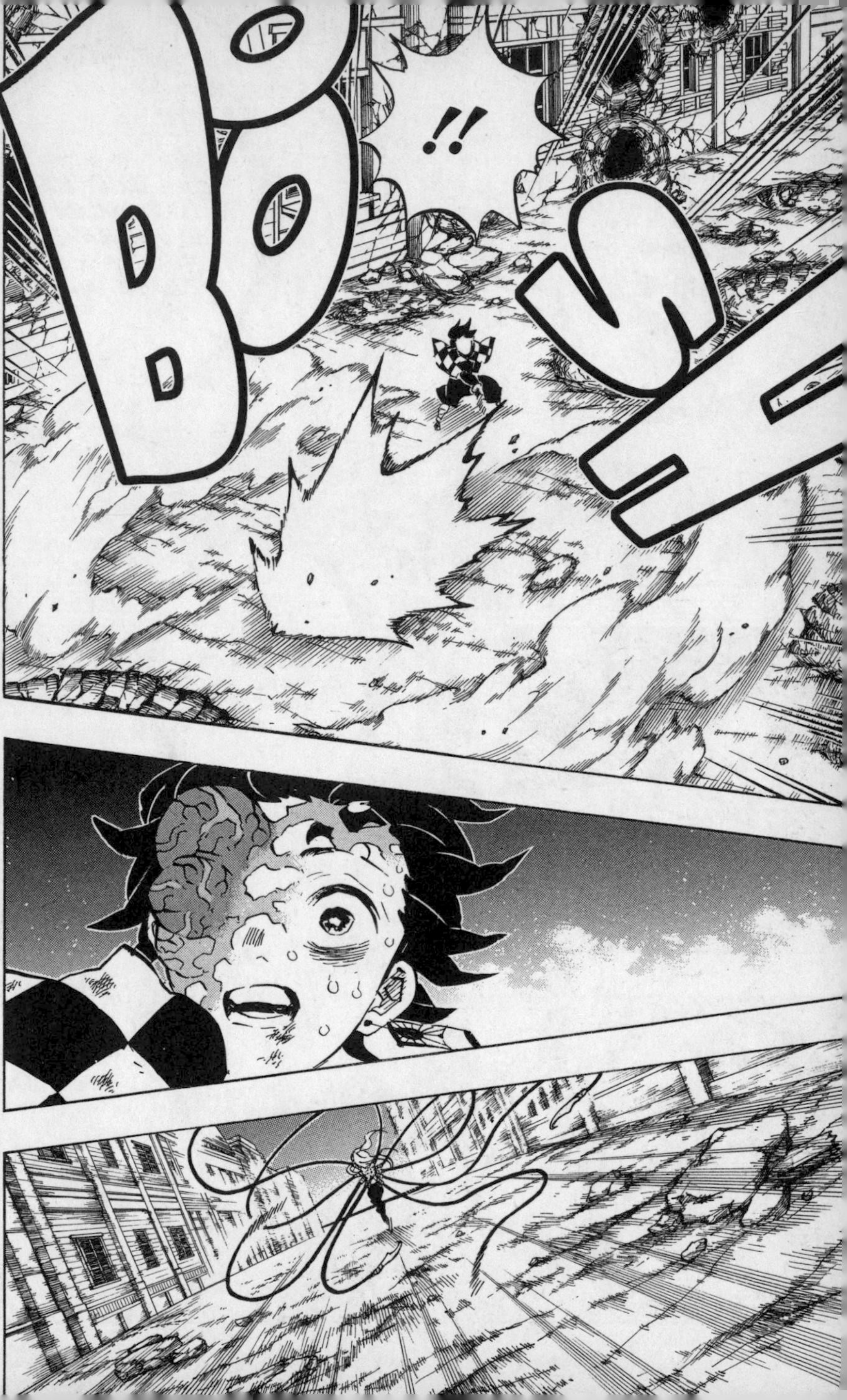
!!

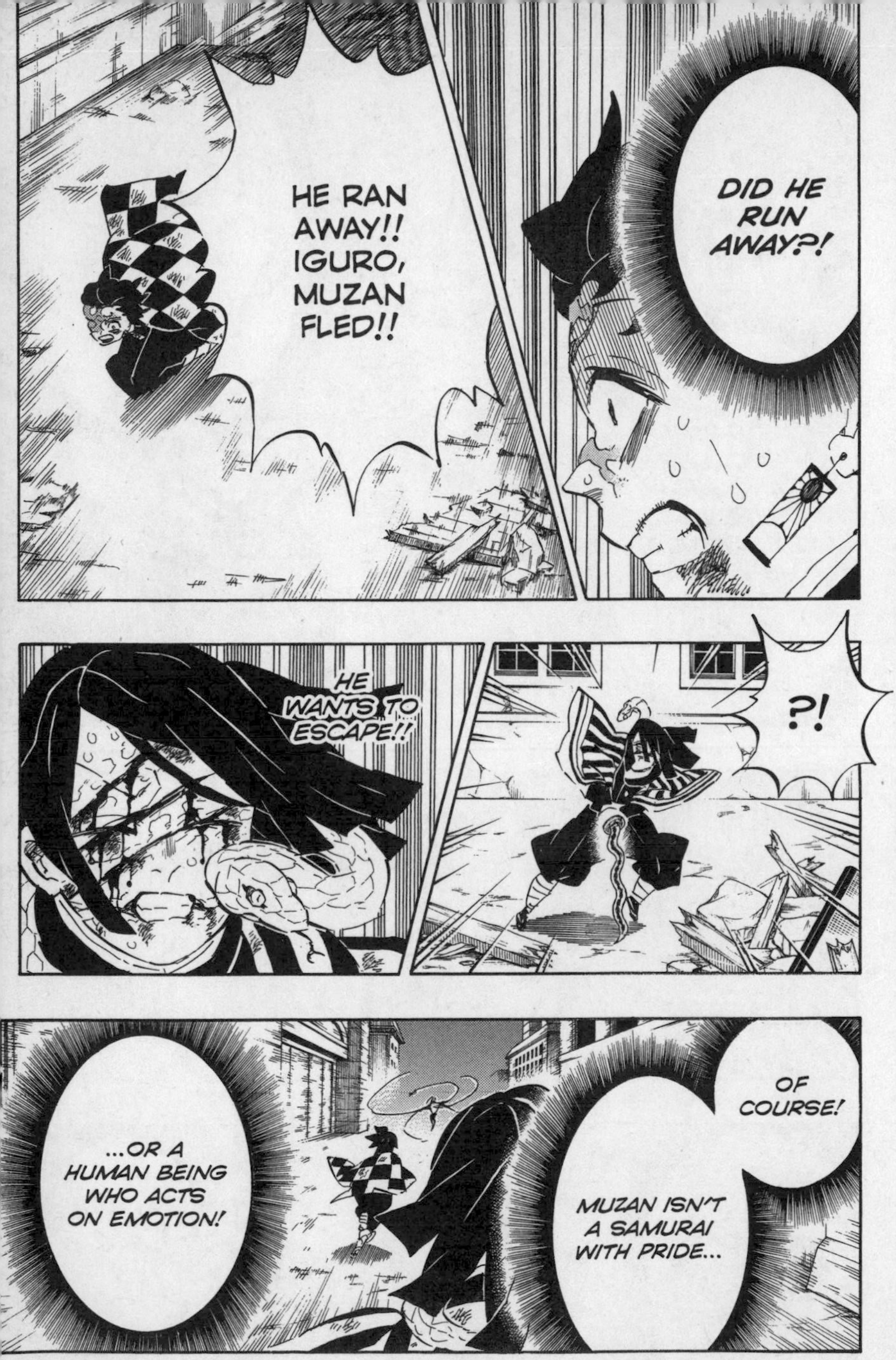
DID HE RUN AWAY?!
HE RAN AWAY!! IGURO, MUZAN FLED!!
?!
HE WANTS TO ESCAPE!!
OF COURSE!
MUZAN ISN'T A SAMURAI WITH PRIDE...
...OR A HUMAN BEING WHO ACTS ON EMOTION!

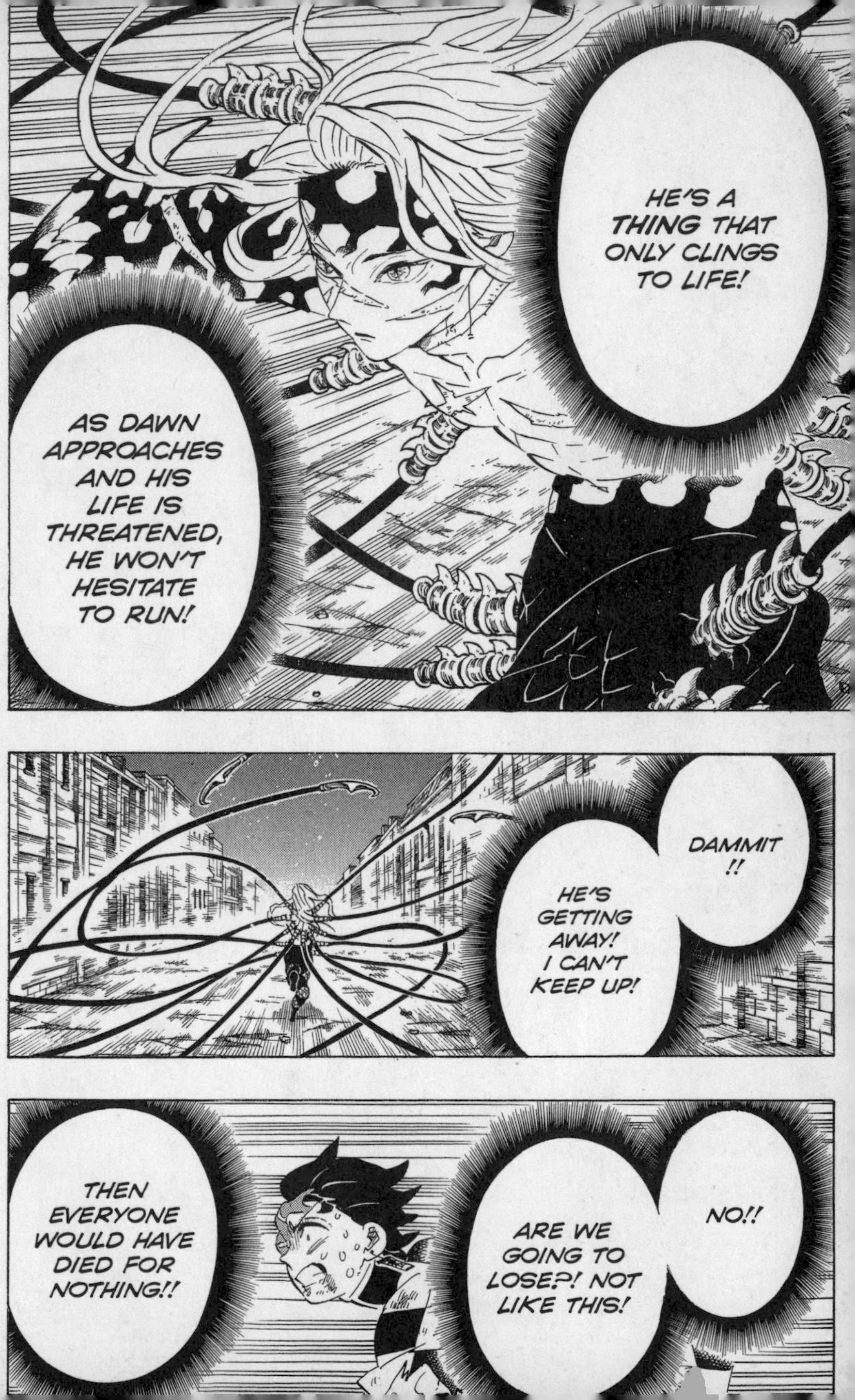
HE'S A THING THAT ONLY CLINGS TO LIFE!
AS DAWN APPROACHES AND HIS LIFE IS THREATENED, HE WON'T HESITATE TO RUN!
DAMMIT!!
HE'S GETTING AWAY! I CAN'T KEEP UP!
NO!!
ARE WE GOING TO LOSE?! NOT LIKE THIS!
THEN EVERYONE WOULD HAVE DIED FOR NOTHING!!

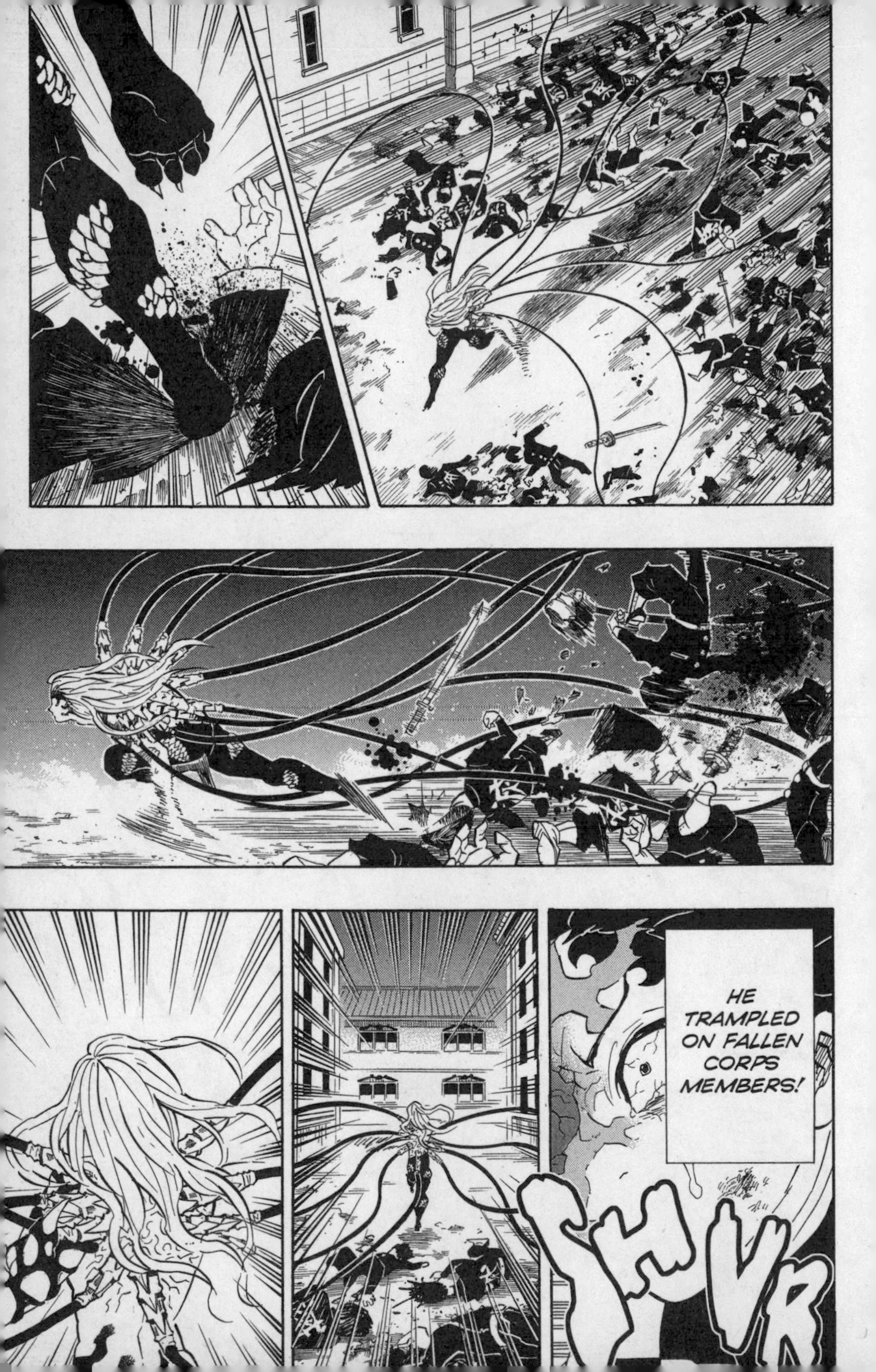
HE TRAMPLED ON FALLEN CORPS MEMBERS!
SHVR

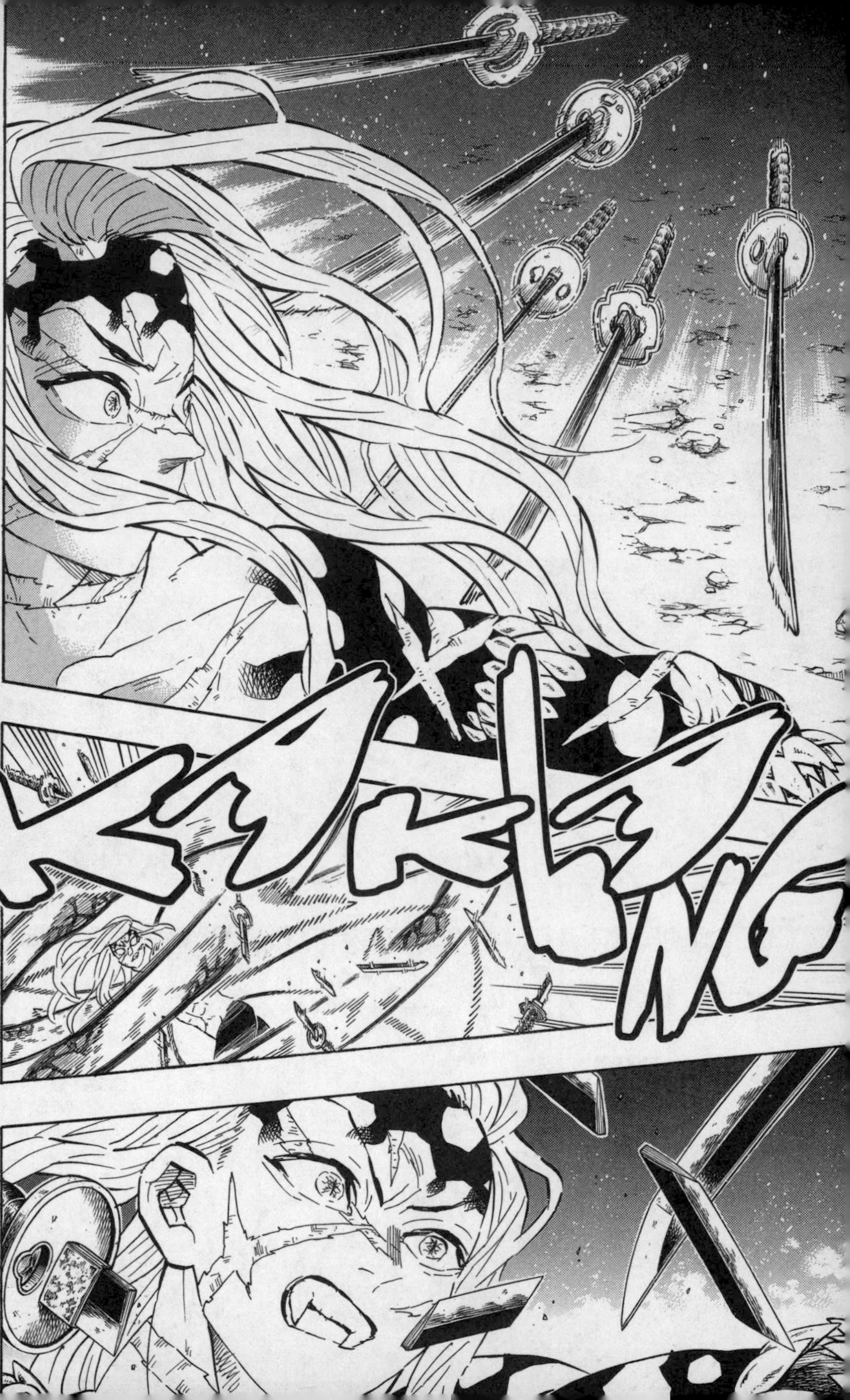

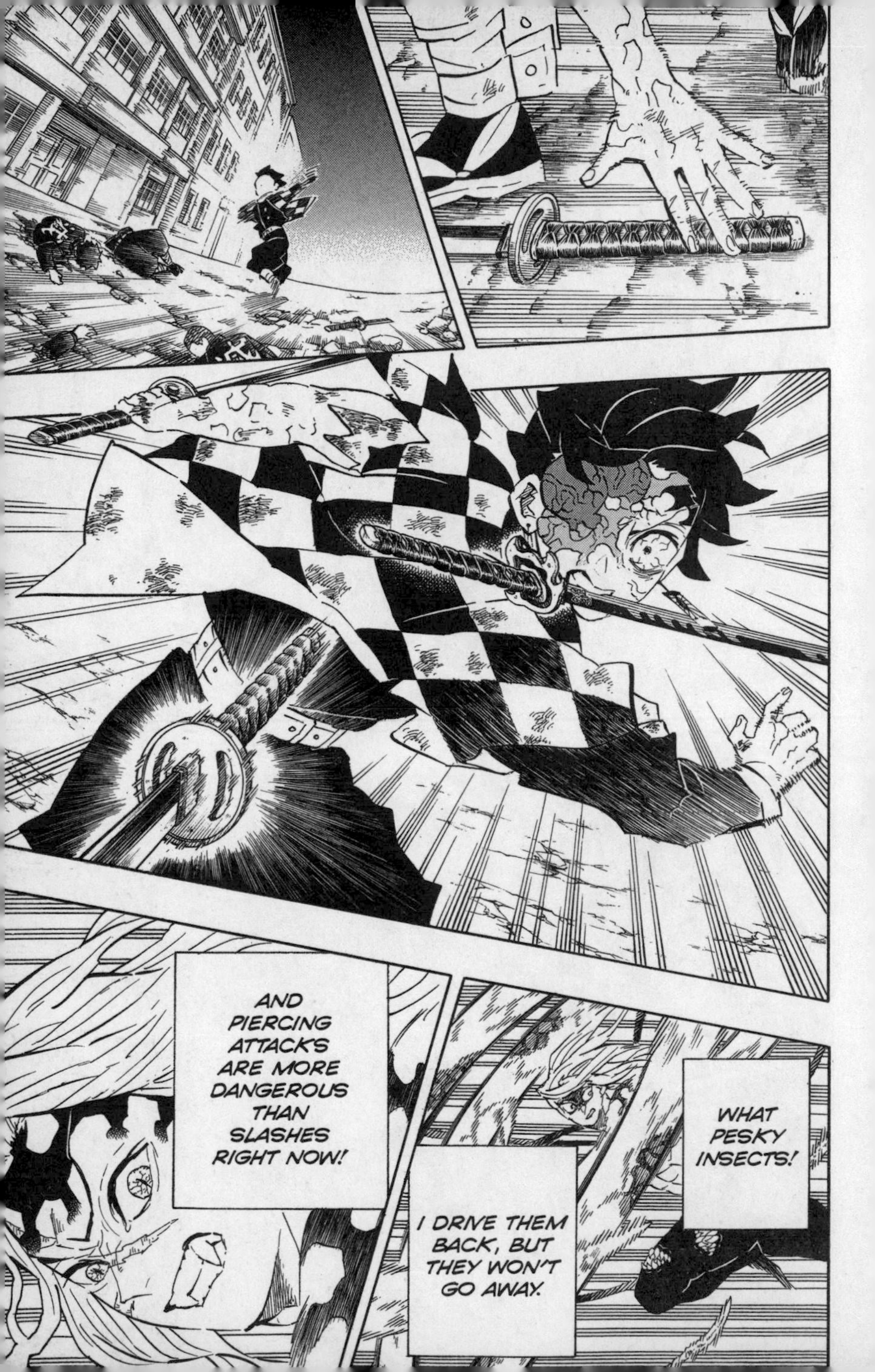
WHAT PESKY INSECTS!
I DRIVE THEM BACK, BUT THEY WON'T GO AWAY.
AND PIERCING ATTACKS ARE MORE DANGEROUS THAN SLASHES RIGHT NOW!

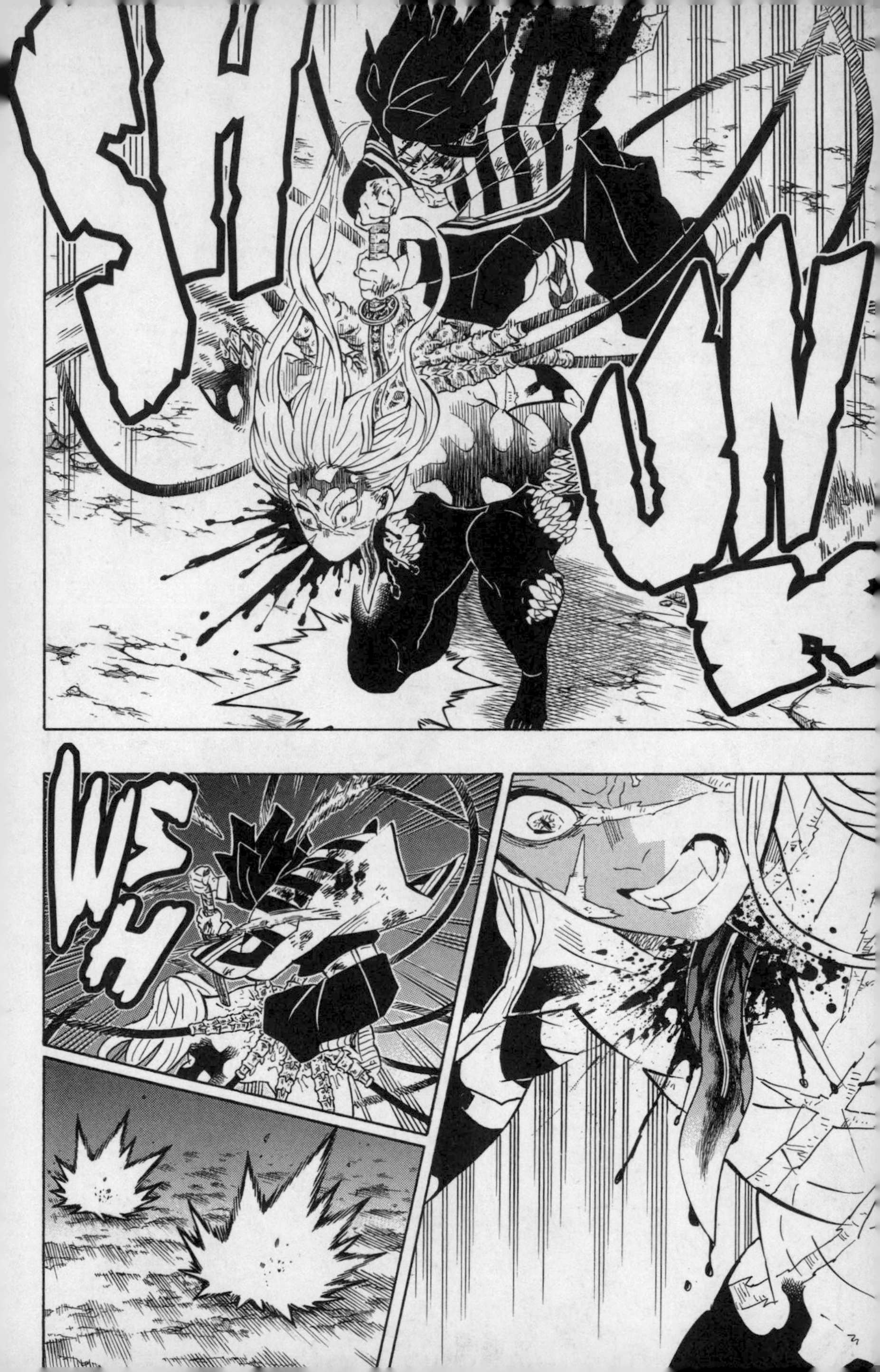
SHUNK
WSH

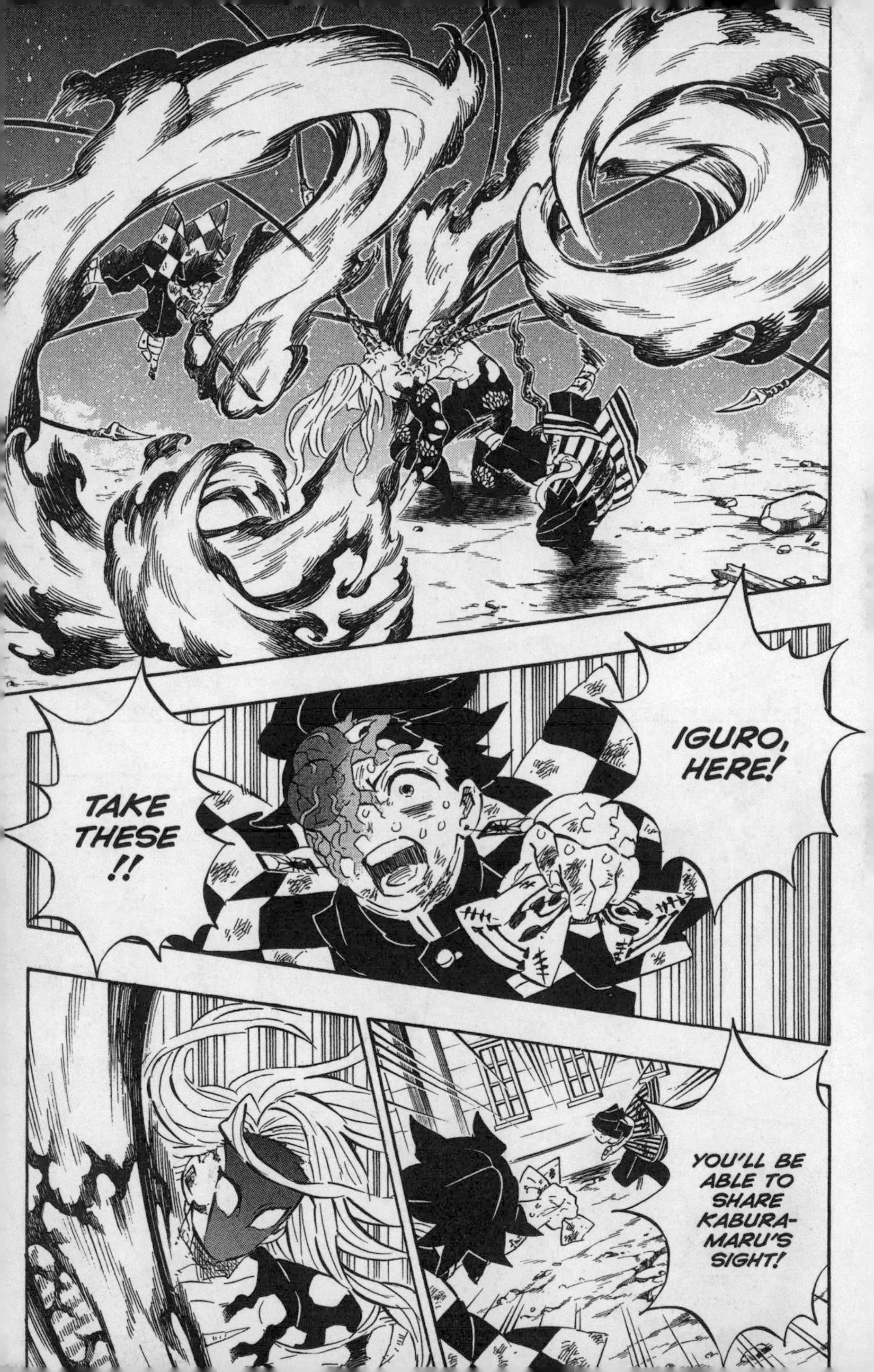
IGURO, HERE!
TAKE THESE !!
YOU'LL BE ABLE TO SHARE KABURA-MARU'S SIGHT!

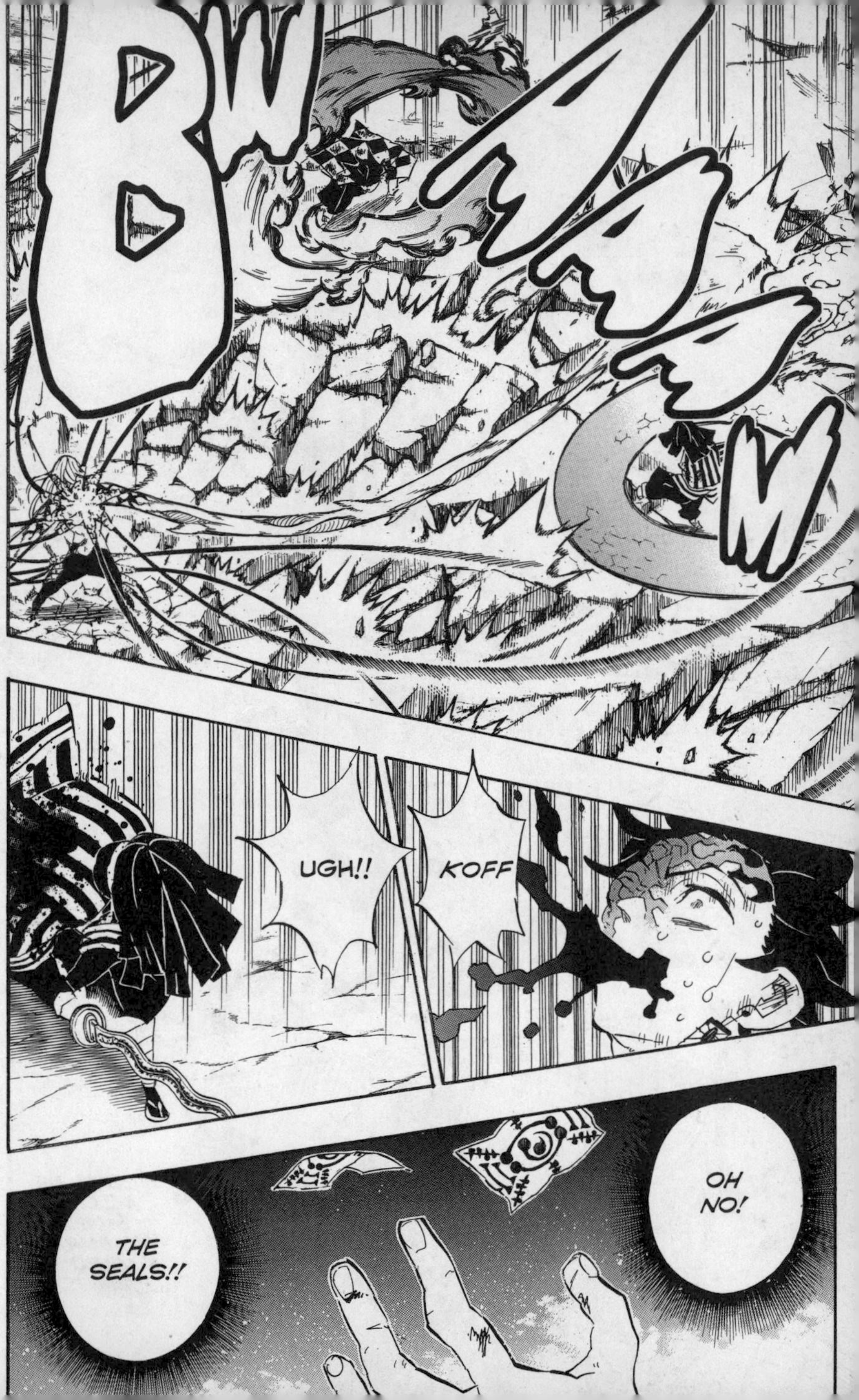
BWAAM
KOFF
UGH!!
OH NO!
THE SEALS!!

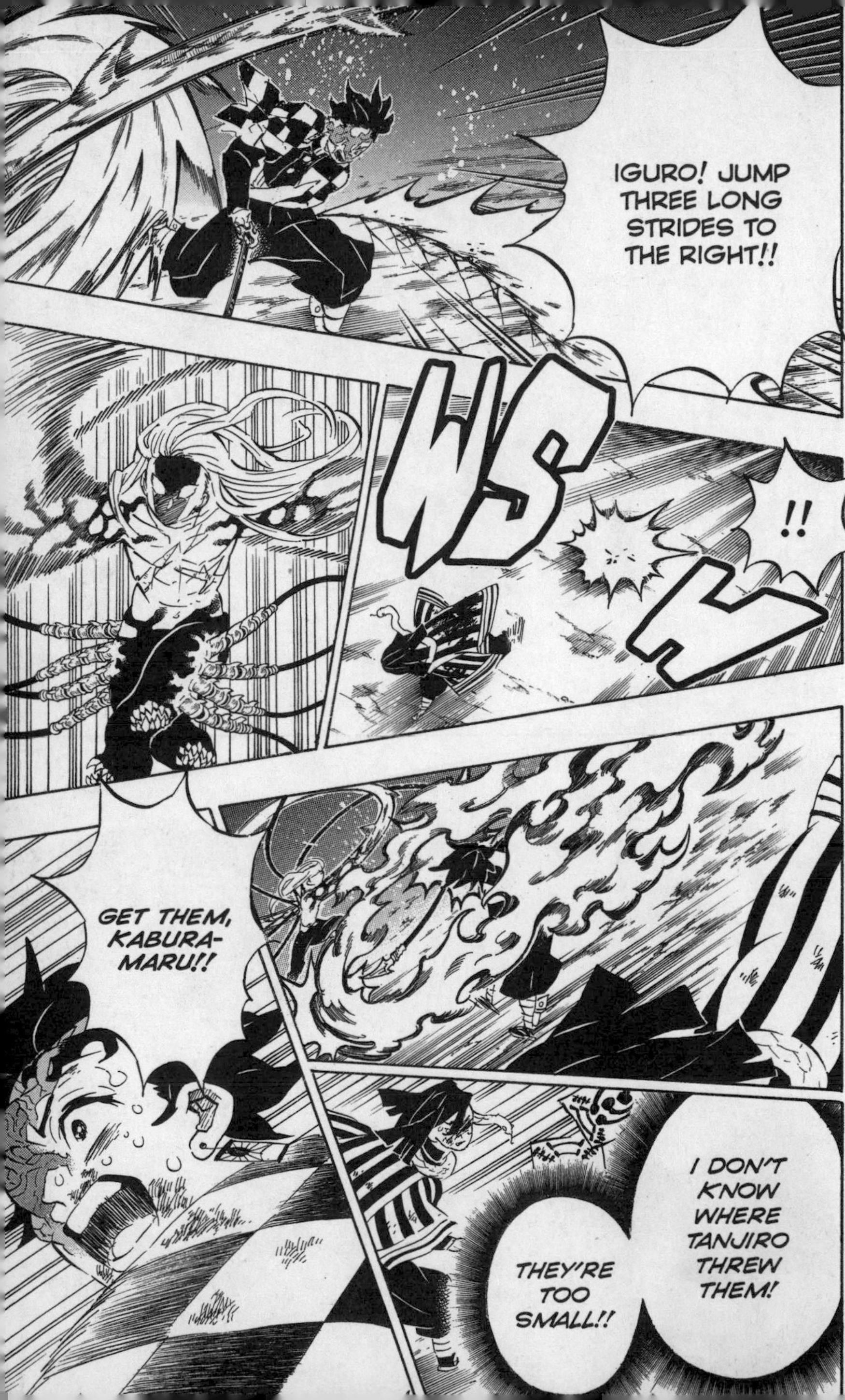
IGURO! JUMP THREE LONG STRIDES TO THE RIGHT!!
WSH
!!
I DON'T KNOW WHERE TANJIRO THREW THEM!
THEY'RE TOO SMALL!!
GET THEM, KABURA-MARU!!

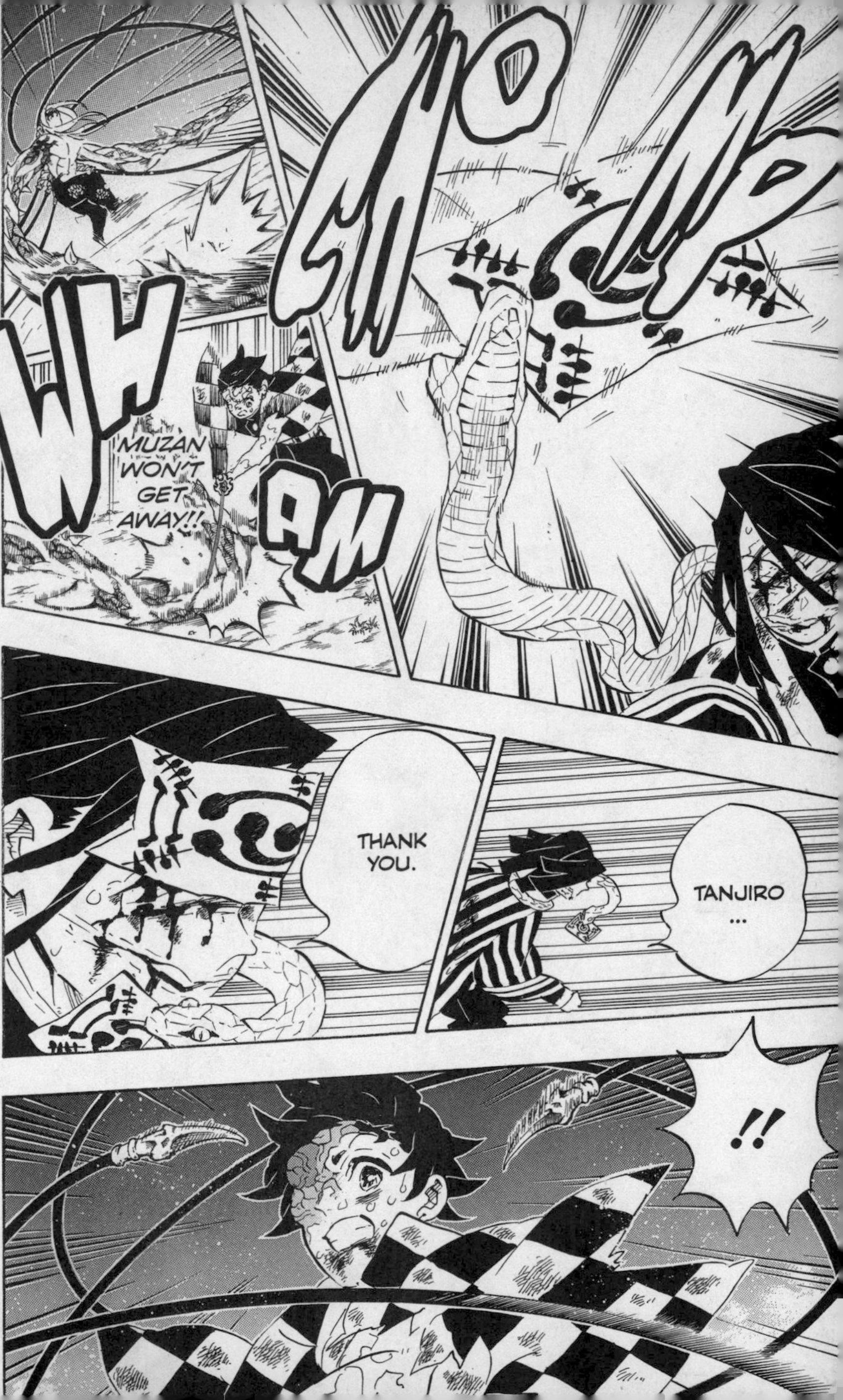
MUZAN WON'T GET AWAY!!
WH AM
TANJIRO ...
THANK YOU.
!!

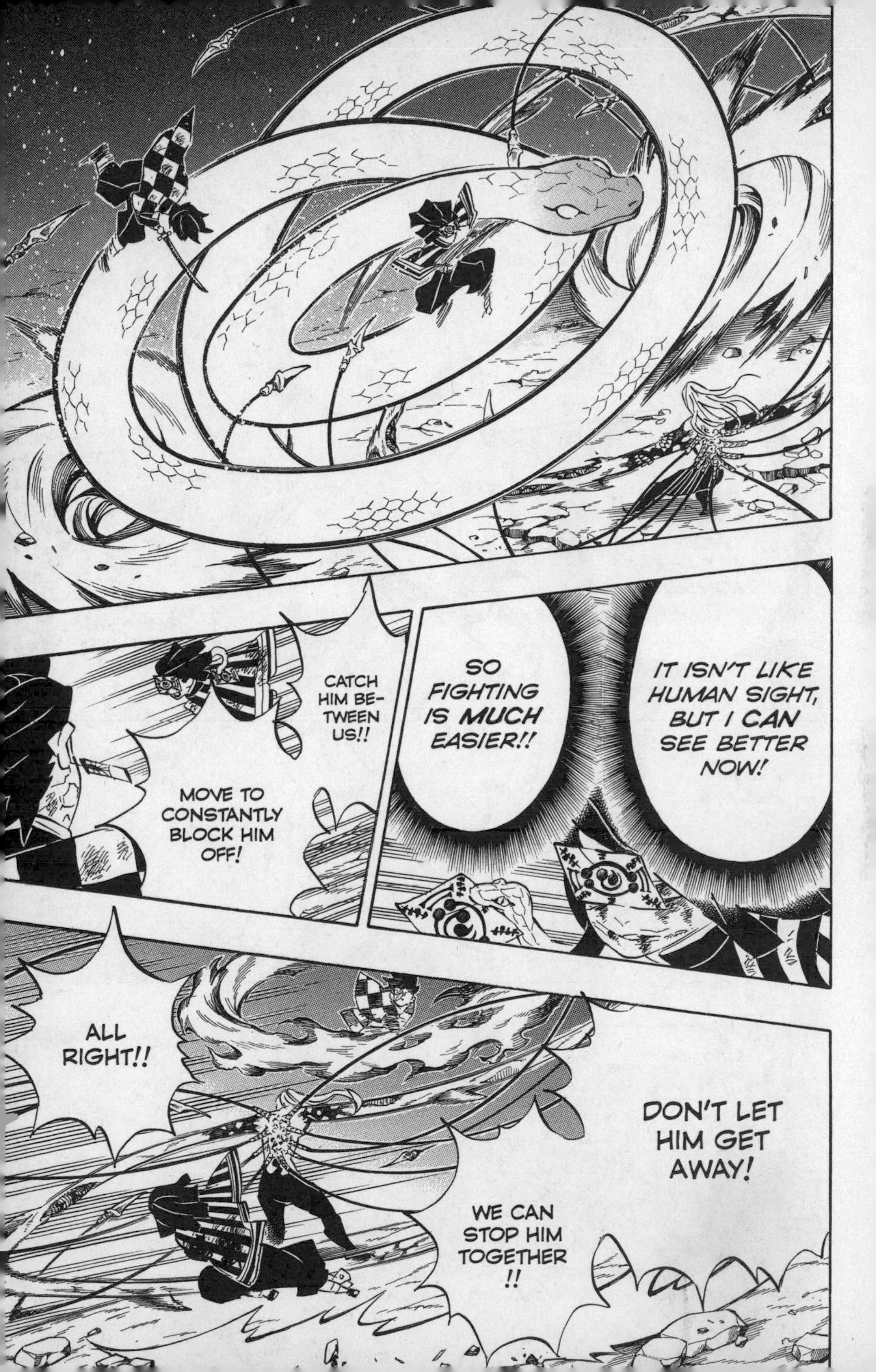
IT ISN'T LIKE HUMAN SIGHT, BUT I *CAN* SEE BETTER NOW!
SO FIGHTING IS *MUCH* EASIER!!
CATCH HIM BE-TWEEN US!!
MOVE TO CONSTANTLY BLOCK HIM OFF!
DON'T LET HIM GET AWAY!
WE CAN STOP HIM TOGETHER !!
ALL RIGHT!!

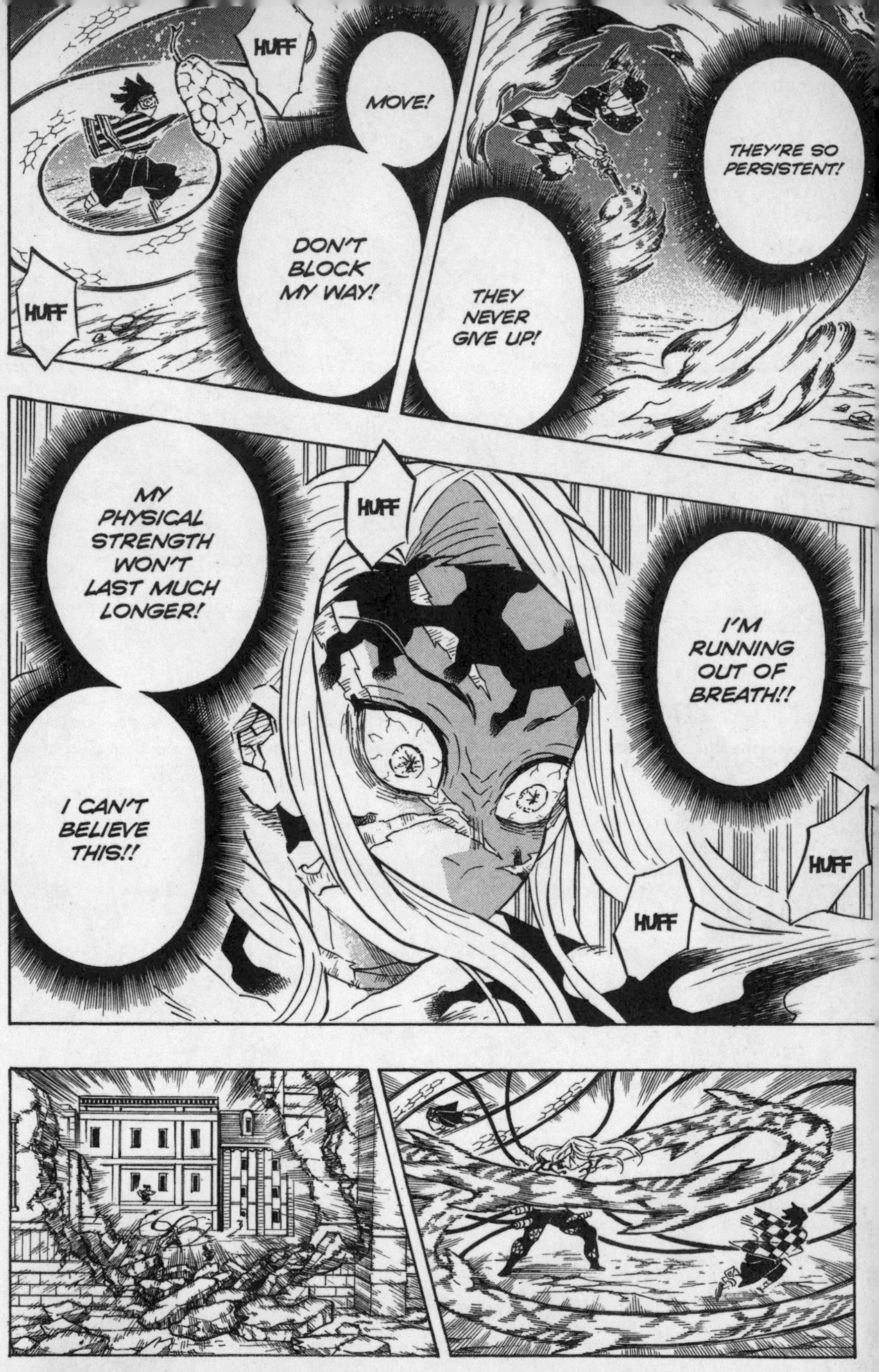
THEY'RE SO PERSISTENT!
THEY NEVER GIVE UP!
HUFF
MOVE!
DON'T BLOCK MY WAY!
HUFF
HUFF
I'M RUNNING OUT OF BREATH!!
MY PHYSICAL STRENGTH WON'T LAST MUCH LONGER!
HUFF
HUFF
I CAN'T BELIEVE THIS!!

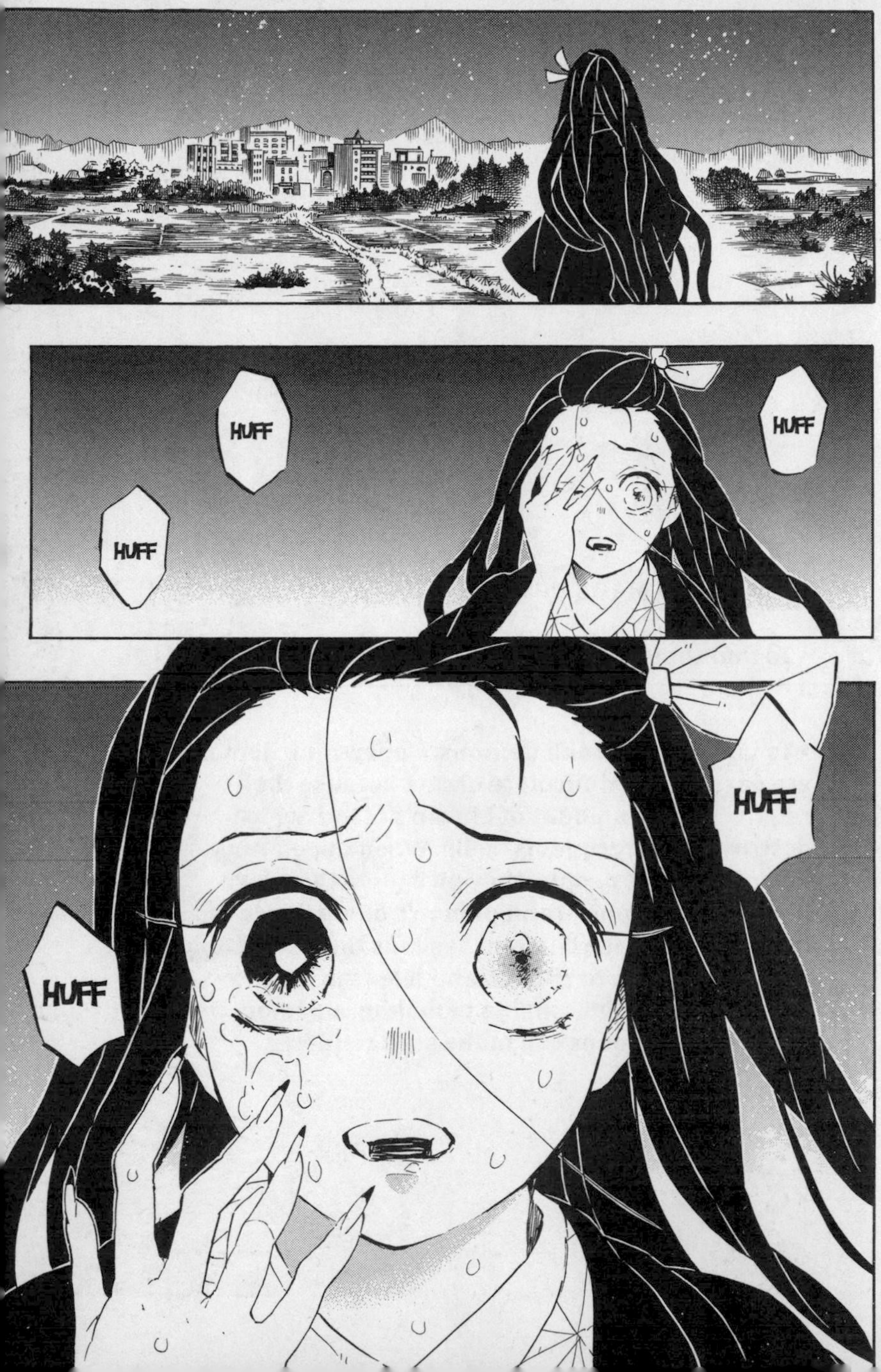
HUFF
HUFF
HUFF
HUFF
HUFF

WHY MUZAN MADE DEMONS

• To find someone capable of withstanding sunlight as a demon.

• To make upper-rank demons. Upper-rank demons are particularly difficult to create because they require a large amount of Muzan's blood, which destroys most recipients' cells. When upper-rank demons recruit people, they give them their own blood, but an upper-rank demon's blood doesn't have the ability to make demons. It sends their intention of making a demon to Muzan, and if Muzan approves, it changes into blood capable of making a demon. Only upper-rank demons can make such requests.

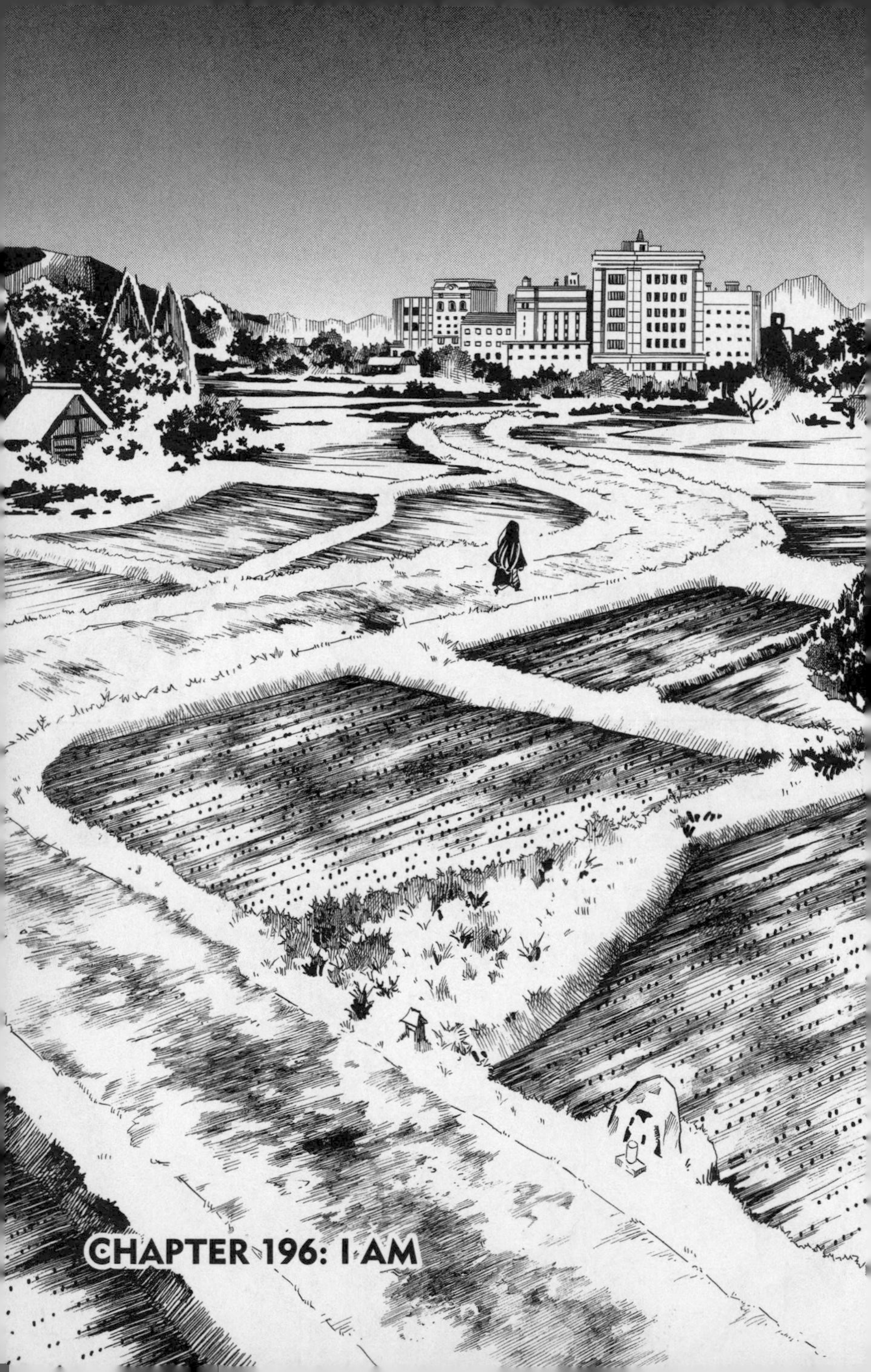
CHAPTER 196: I AM

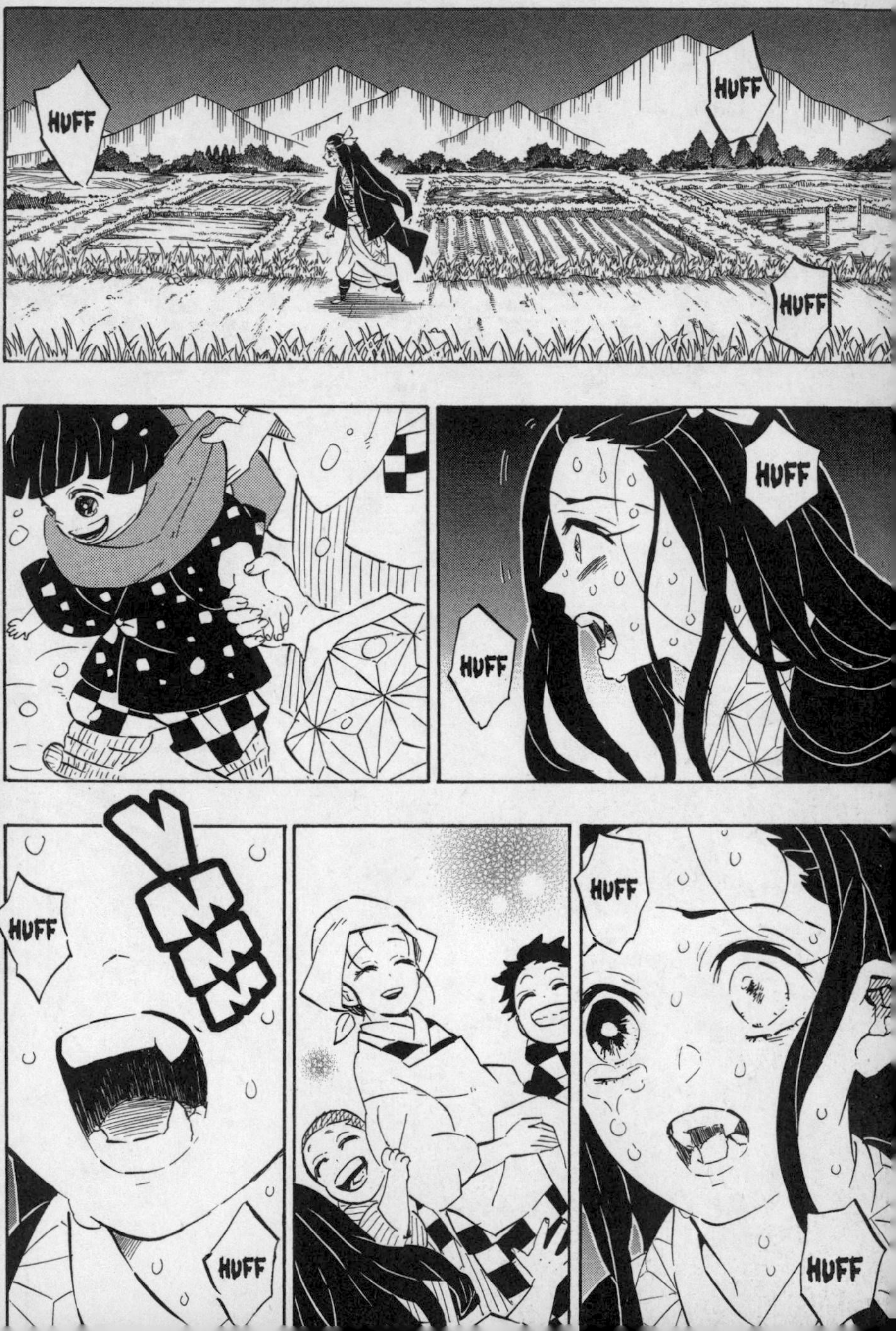
HUFF
HUFF
HUFF
HUFF
HUFF
HUFF
HUFF
HUFF
HUFF

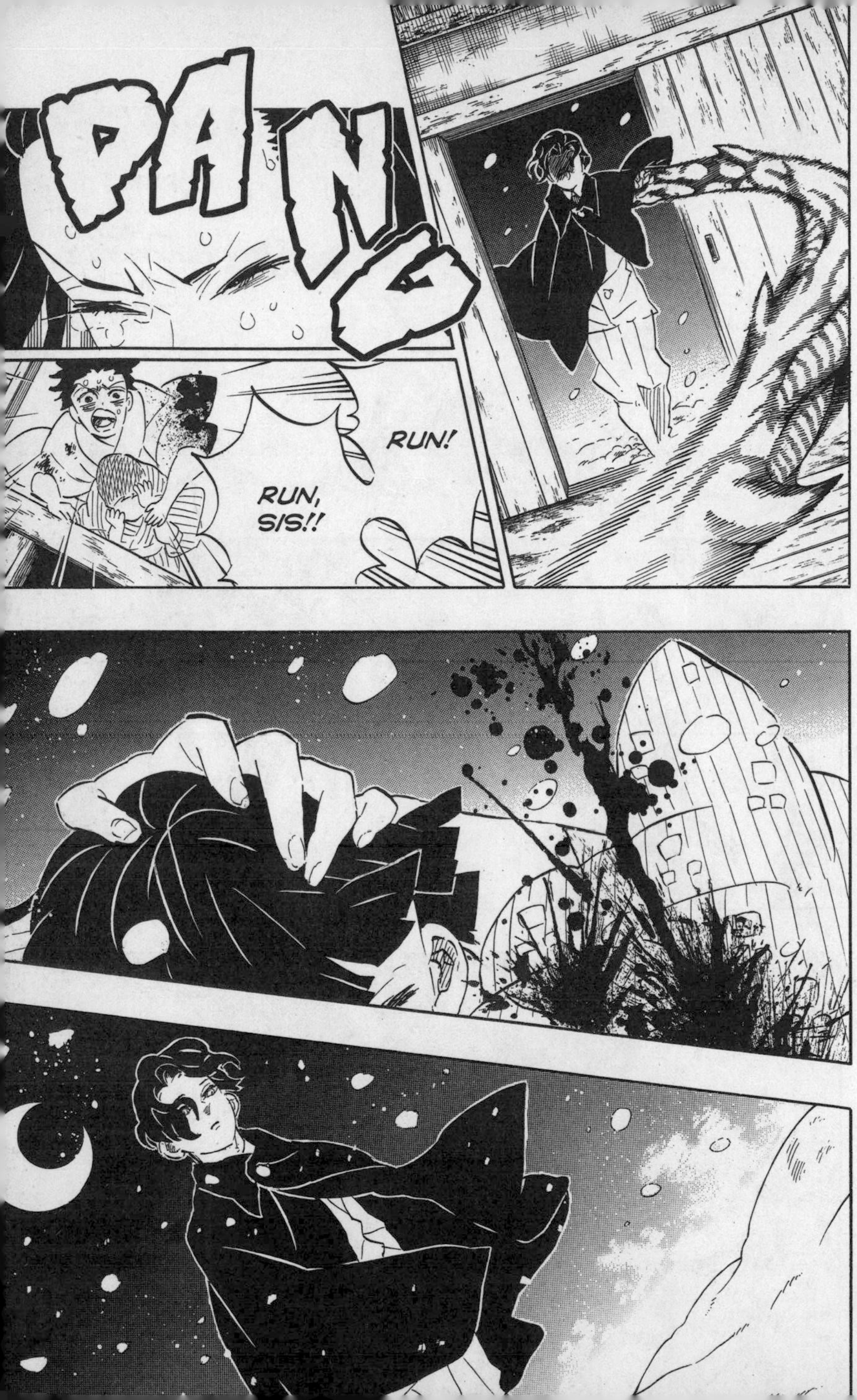
PANG
RUN!
RUN, SIS!!

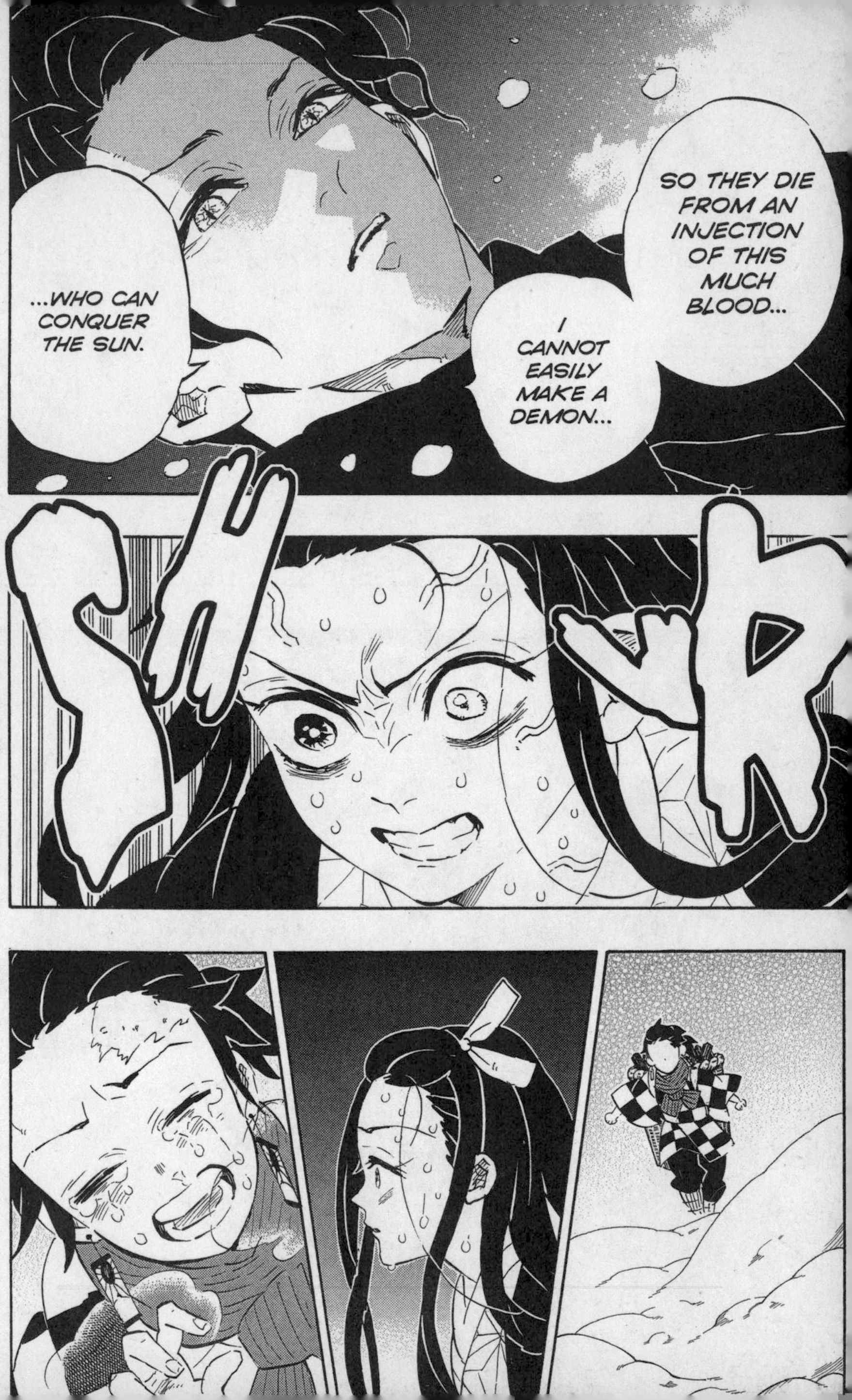
SO THEY DIE FROM AN INJECTION OF THIS MUCH BLOOD...
I CANNOT EASILY MAKE A DEMON...
...WHO CAN CONQUER THE SUN.

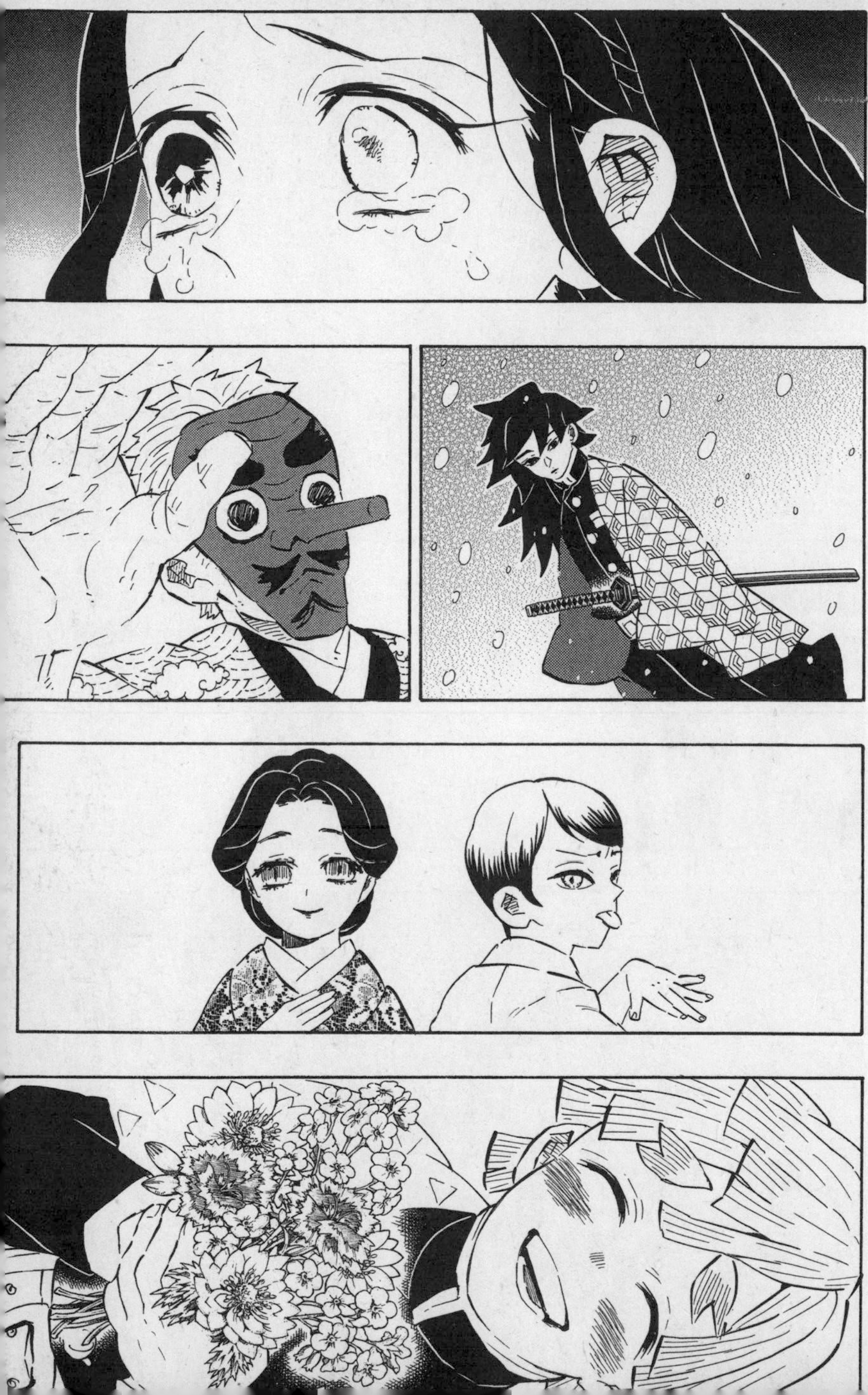

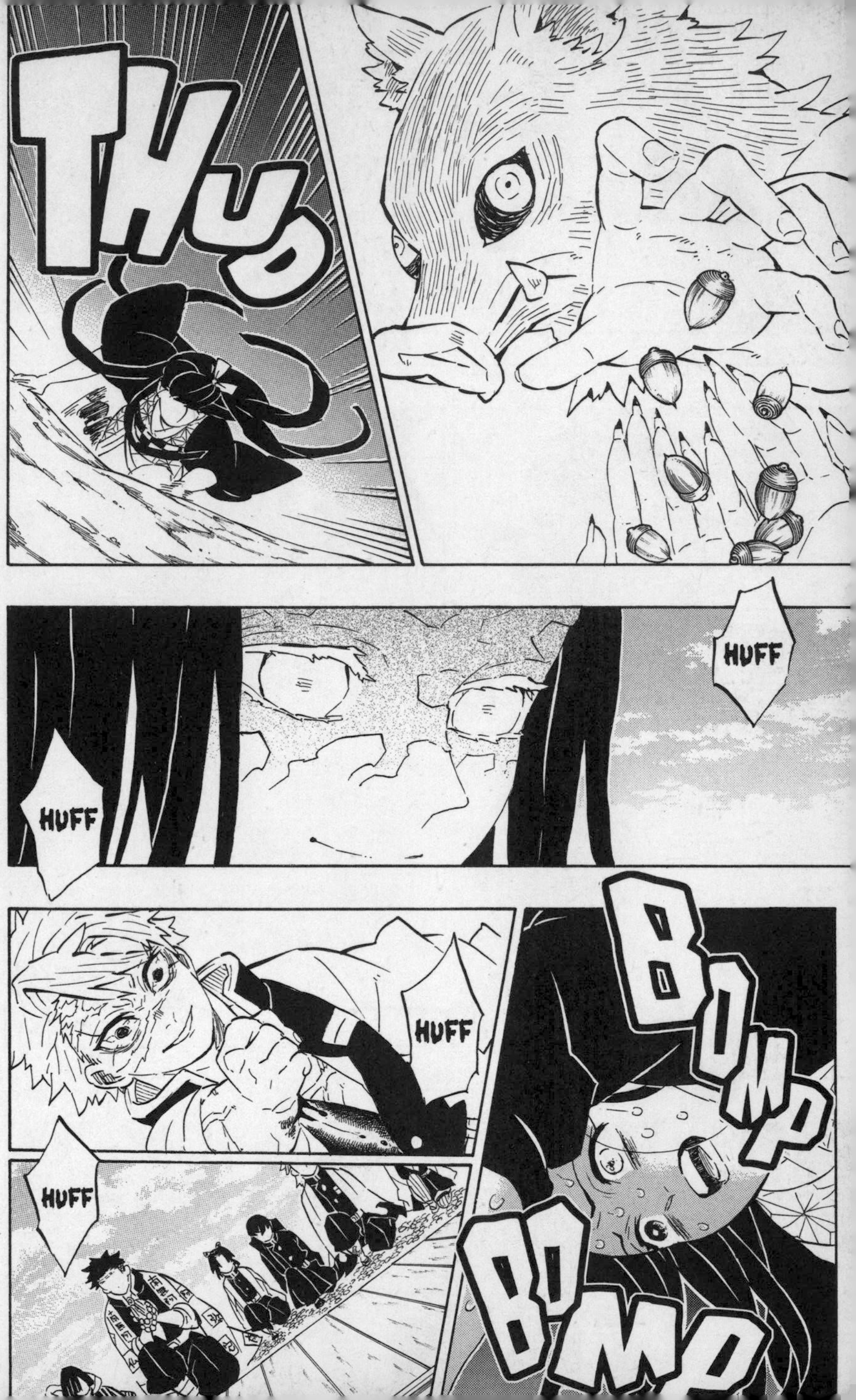
THUD
HUFF
HUFF
BOMP
BOMP
HUFF
HUFF

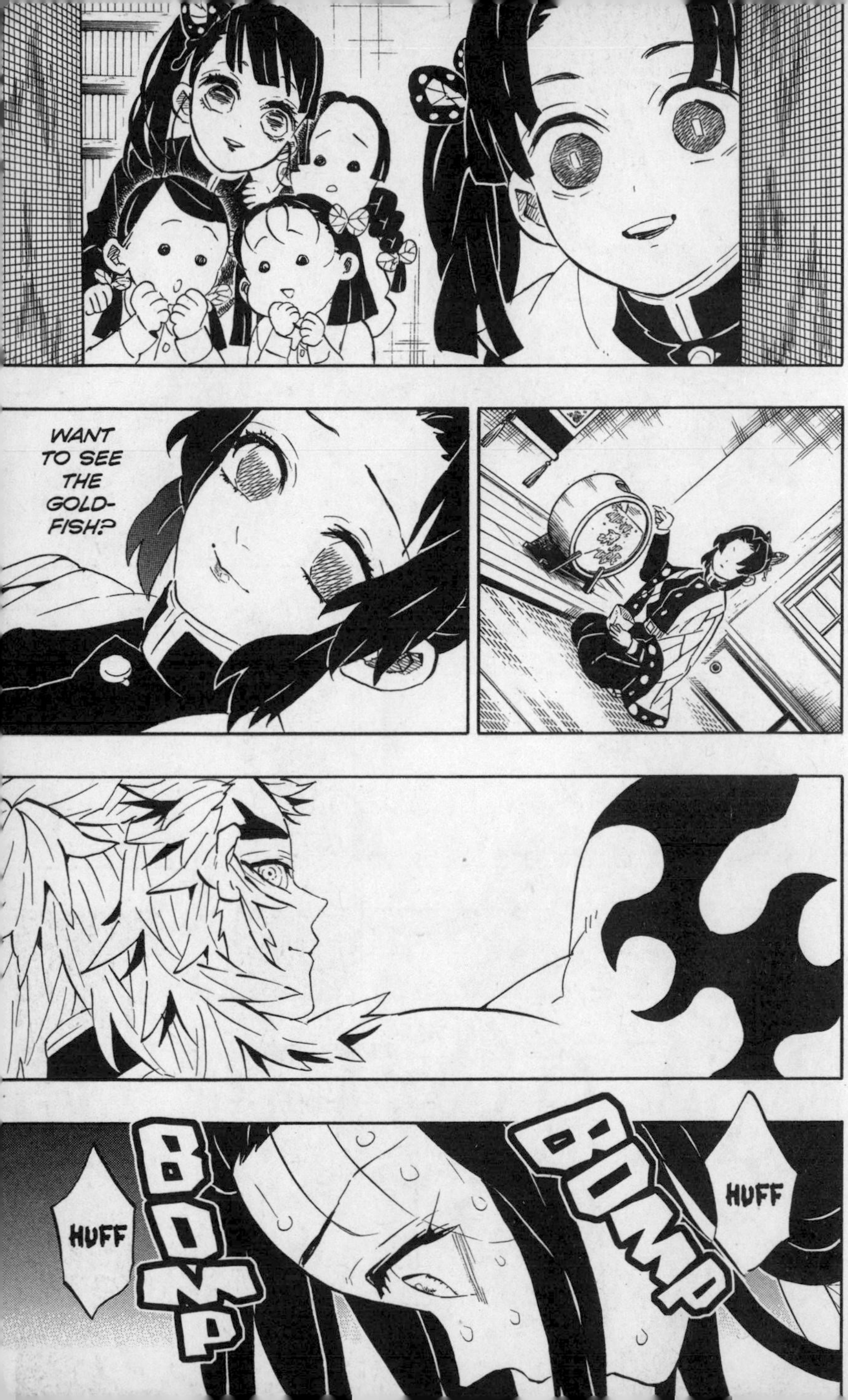
WANT TO SEE THE GOLD-FISH?
HUFF
BOMP
BOMP
HUFF

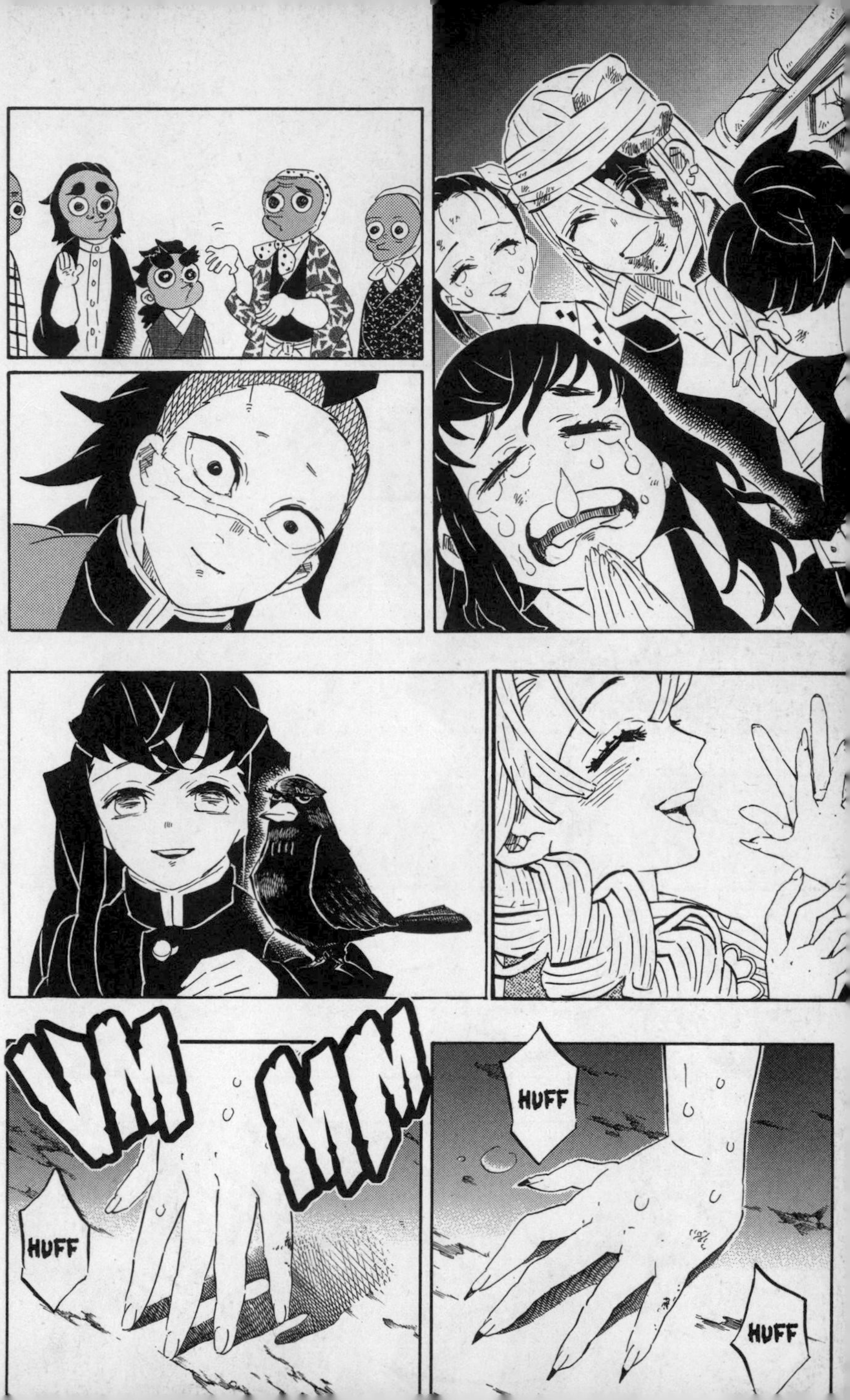
HUFF
HUFF
VM
MM
HUFF

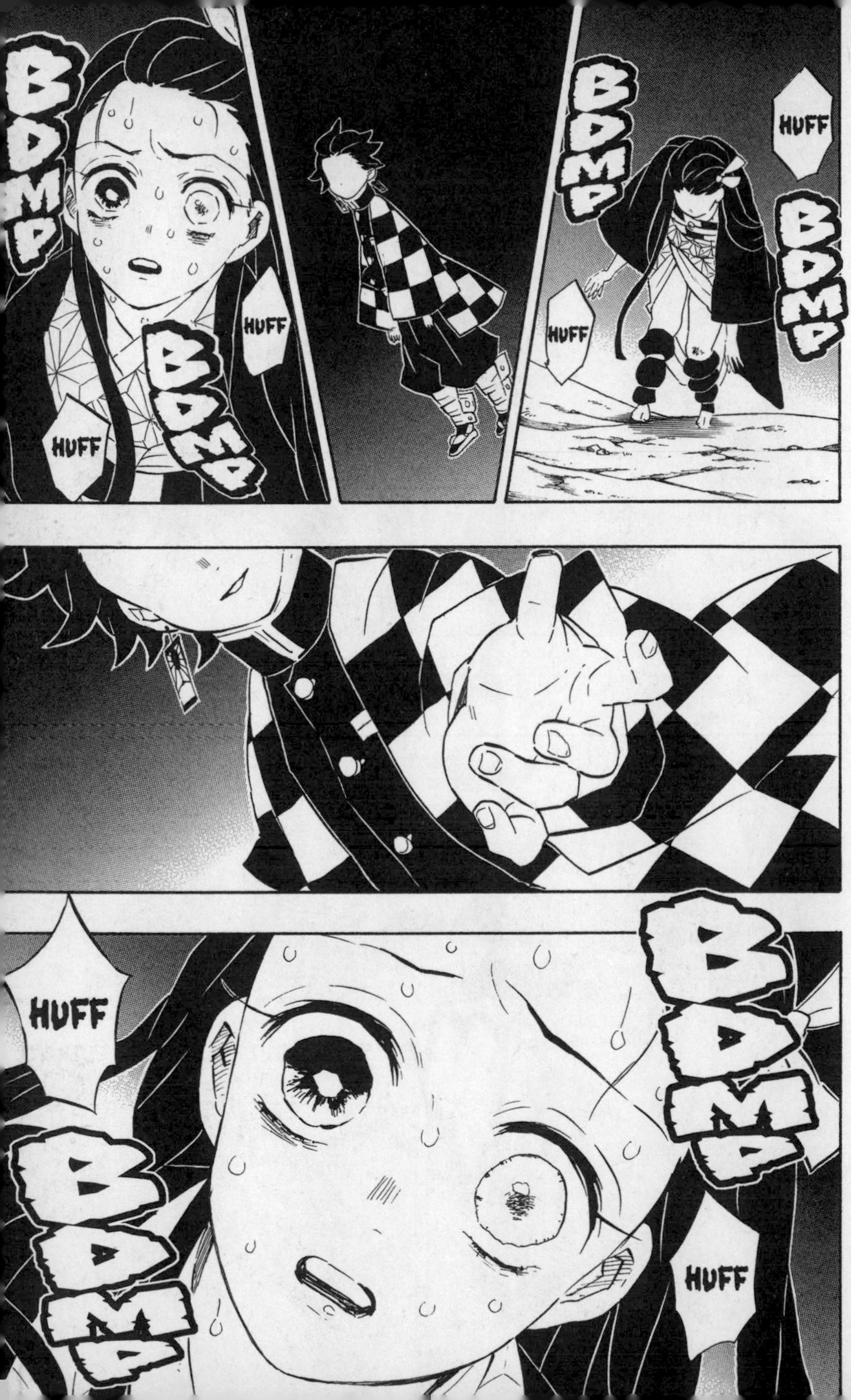
HUFF
BDMP
BDMP
HUFF
BDMP
HUFF
BDMP
HUFF
BDMP
HUFF
HUFF
BDMP

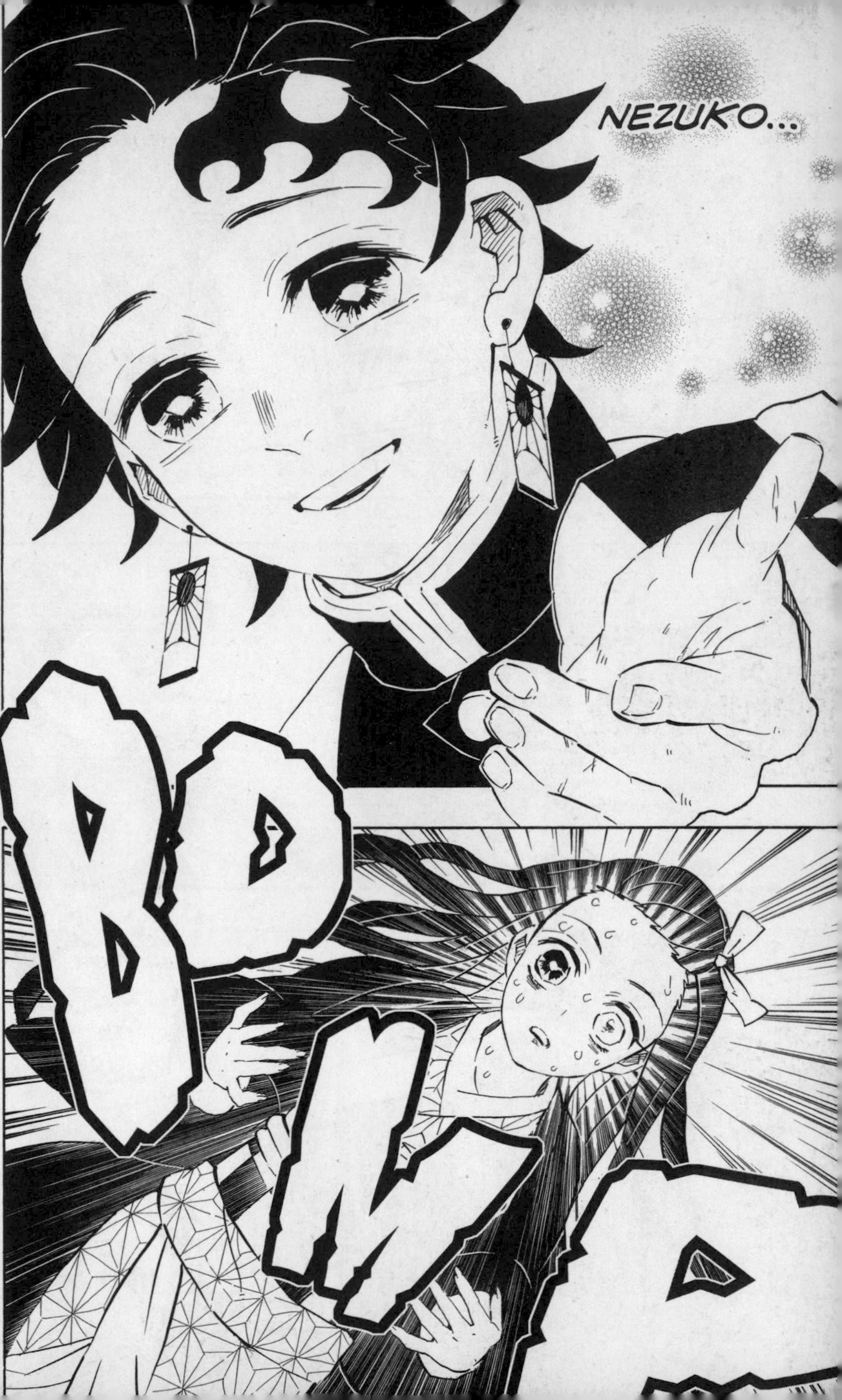
NEZUKO...

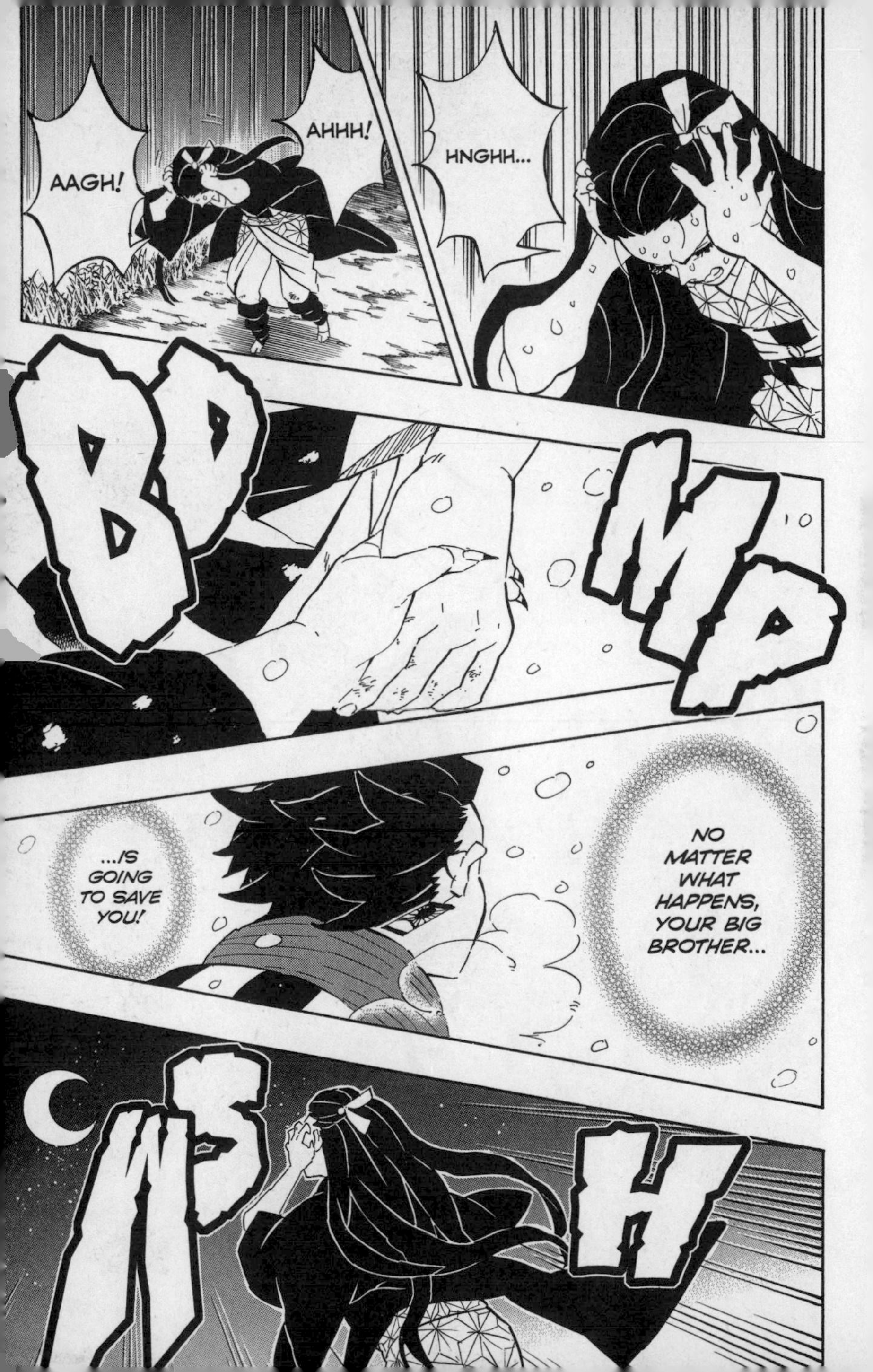
HNGHH...
AHHH!
AAGH!
BOMP
NO MATTER WHAT HAPPENS, YOUR BIG BROTHER...
...IS GOING TO SAVE YOU!
WSH

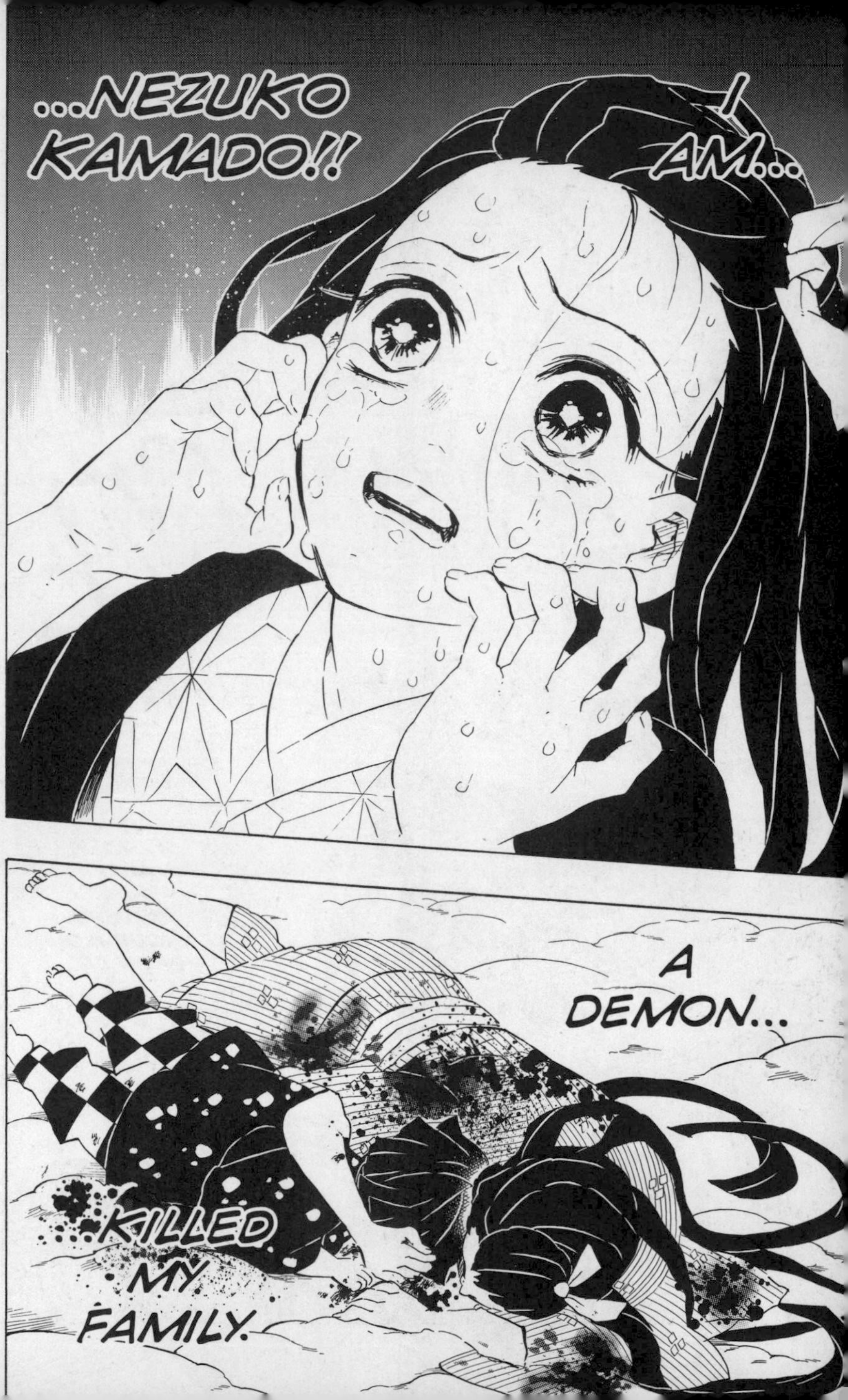
I AM...
...NEZUKO KAMADO!!
A DEMON...
KILLED MY FAMILY.

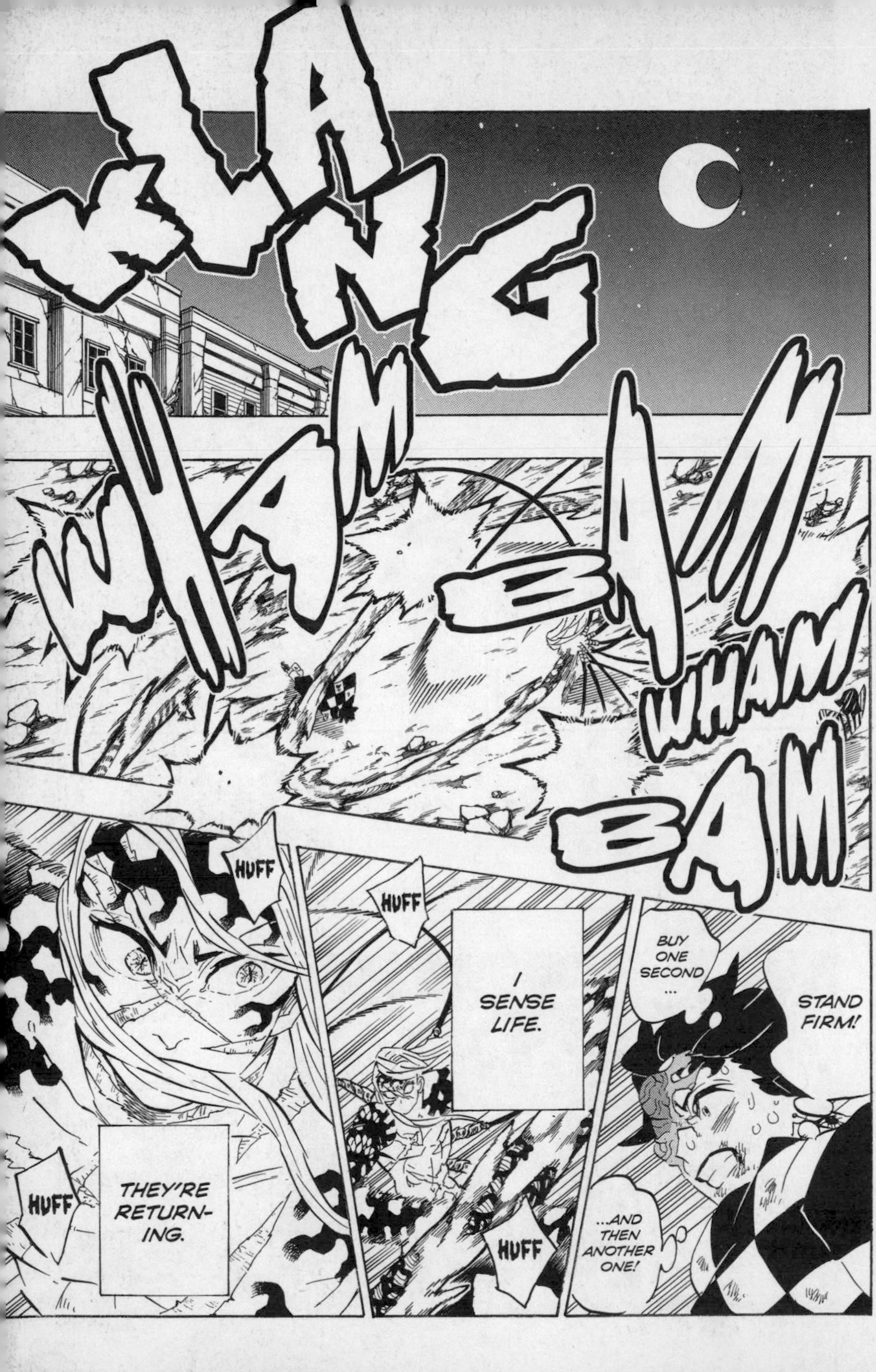
CLANG
BAM
WHAM
BAM
WHAM
BUY ONE SECOND...
STAND FIRM!
...AND THEN ANOTHER ONE!
HUFF
I SENSE LIFE.
HUFF
HUFF
HUFF
THEY'RE RETURN-ING.

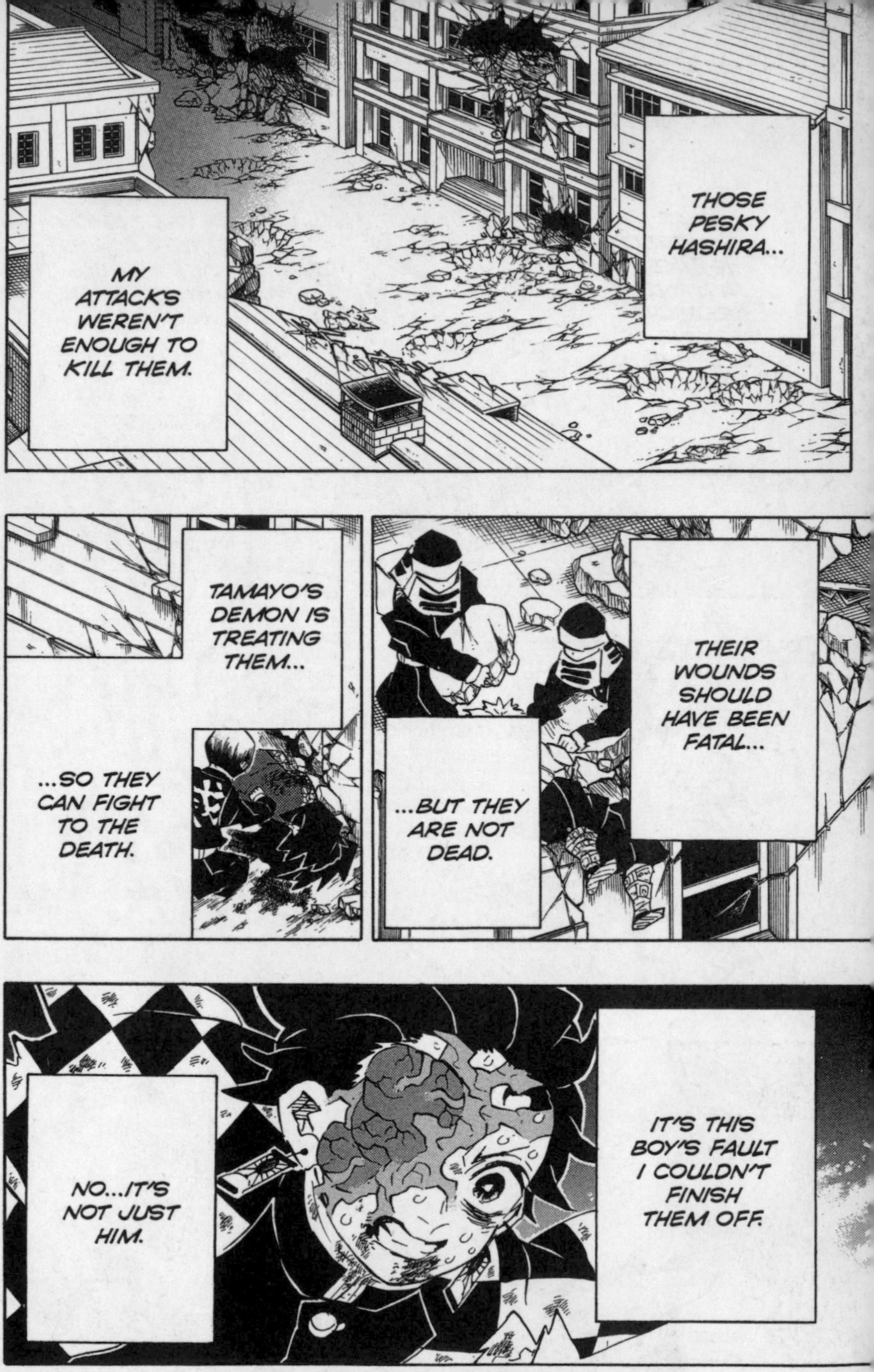
THOSE PESKY HASHIRA...
MY ATTACKS WEREN'T ENOUGH TO KILL THEM.
THEIR WOUNDS SHOULD HAVE BEEN FATAL...
...BUT THEY ARE NOT DEAD.
TAMAYO'S DEMON IS TREATING THEM...
...SO THEY CAN FIGHT TO THE DEATH.
IT'S THIS BOY'S FAULT I COULDN'T FINISH THEM OFF.
NO...IT'S NOT JUST HIM.

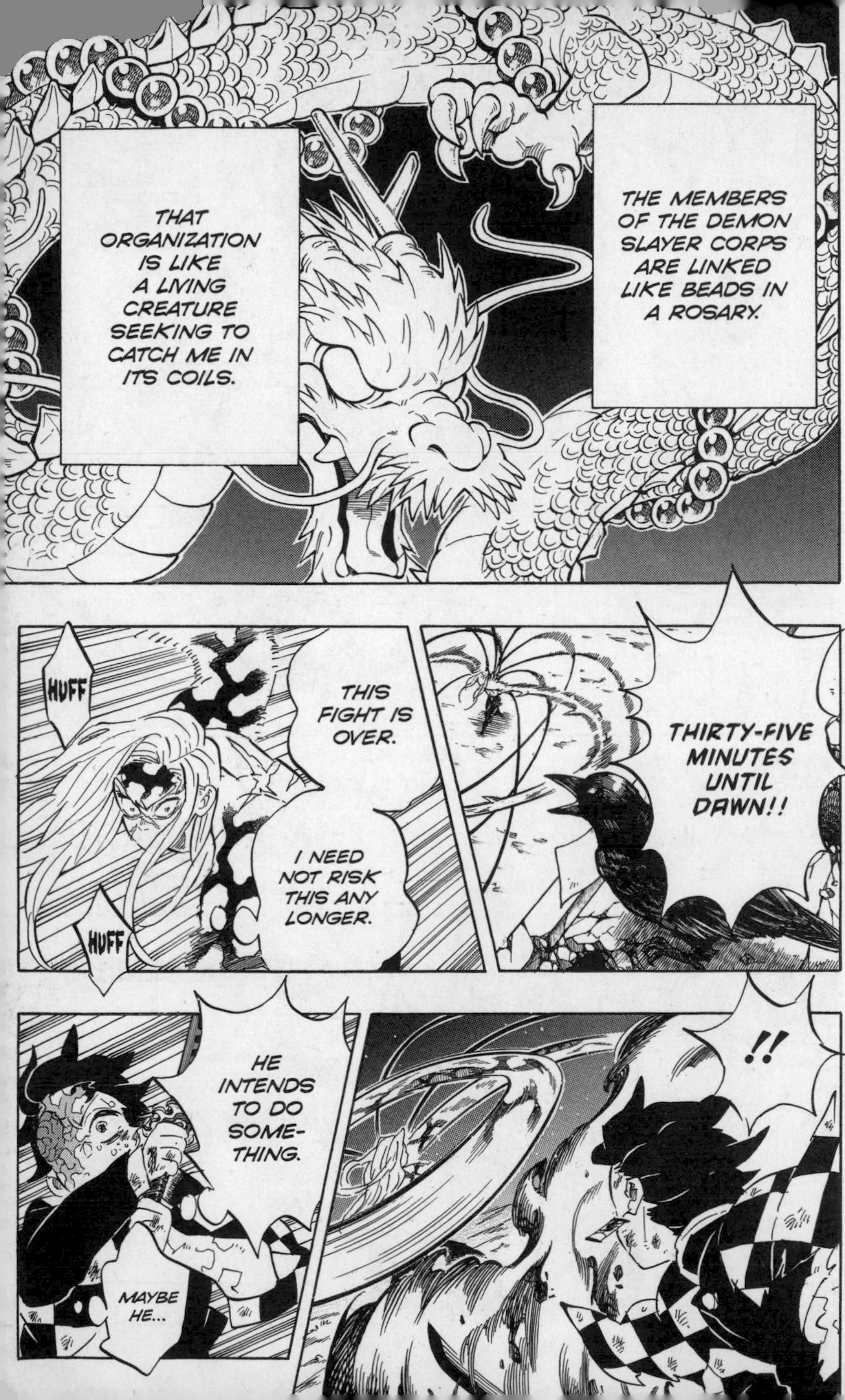
THE MEMBERS OF THE DEMON SLAYER CORPS ARE LINKED LIKE BEADS IN A ROSARY.
THAT ORGANIZATION IS LIKE A LIVING CREATURE SEEKING TO CATCH ME IN ITS COILS.
THIRTY-FIVE MINUTES UNTIL DAWN!!
HUFF
THIS FIGHT IS OVER.
I NEED NOT RISK THIS ANY LONGER.
HUFF
!!
HE INTENDS TO DO SOME-THING.
MAYBE HE...

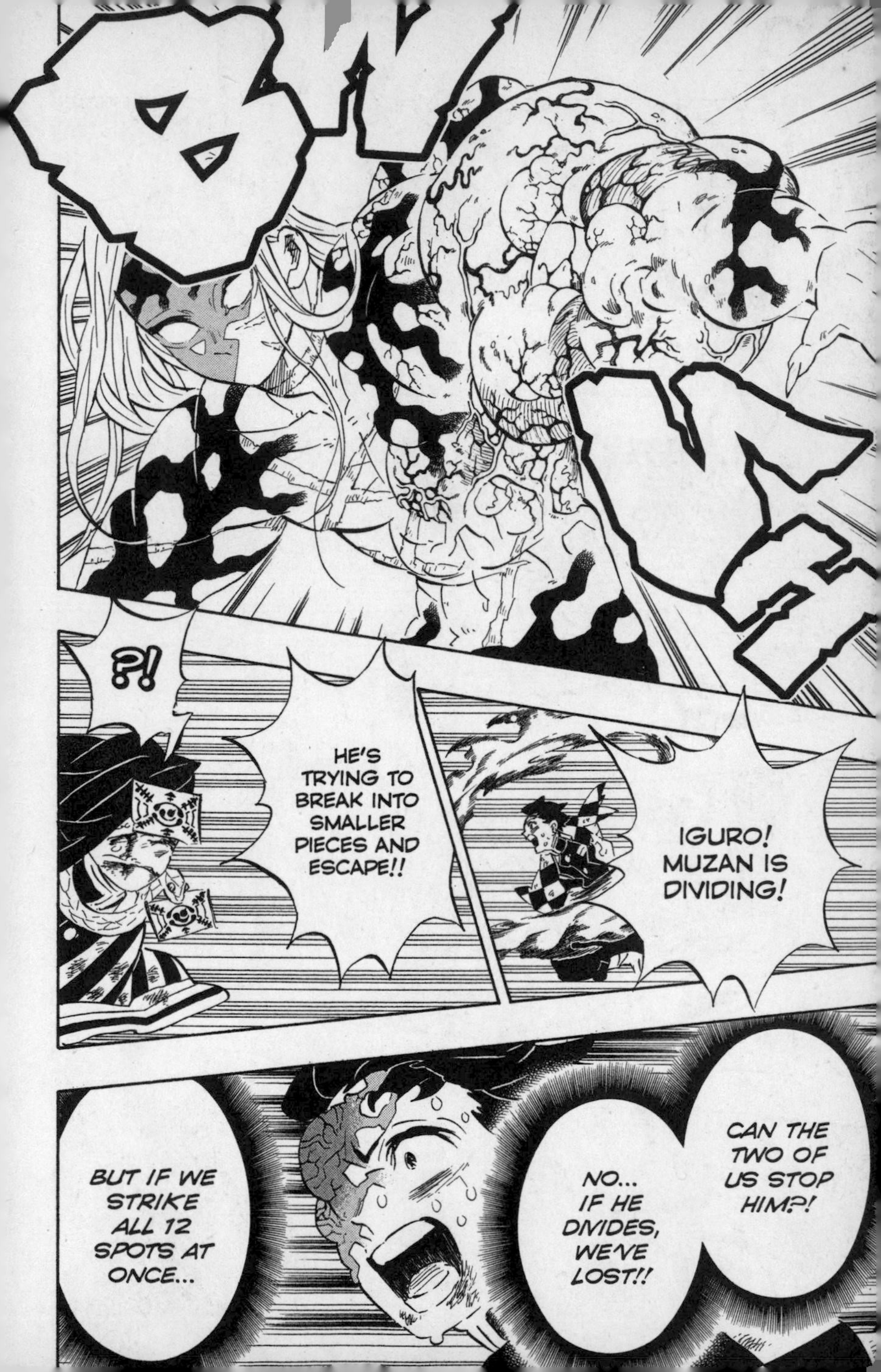
IGURO! MUZAN IS DIVIDING!
?!
HE'S TRYING TO BREAK INTO SMALLER PIECES AND ESCAPE!!
CAN THE TWO OF US STOP HIM?!
NO... IF HE DIVIDES, WE'VE LOST!!
BUT IF WE STRIKE ALL 12 SPOTS AT ONCE...

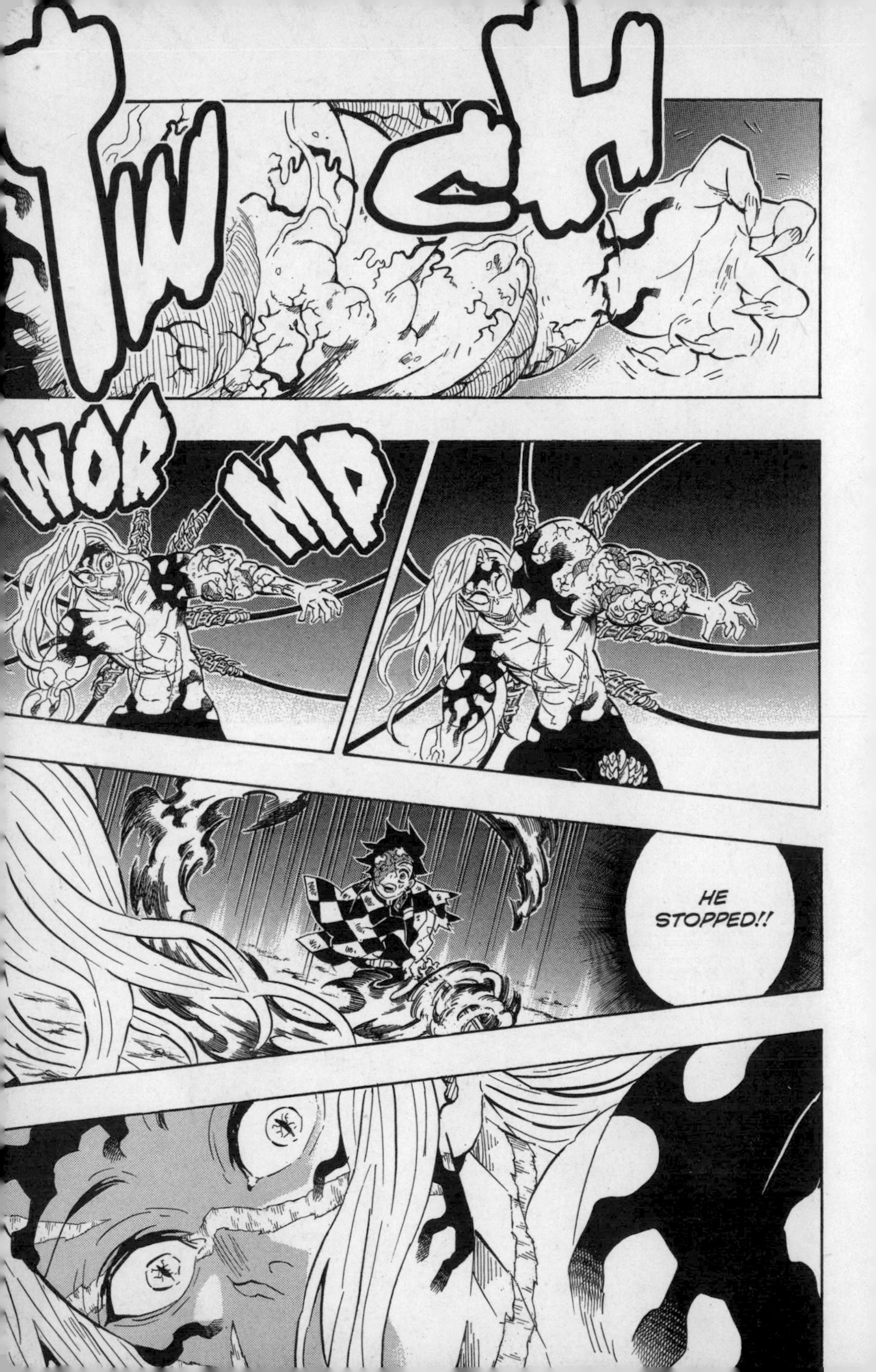
WOR
MP
HE STOPPED!!

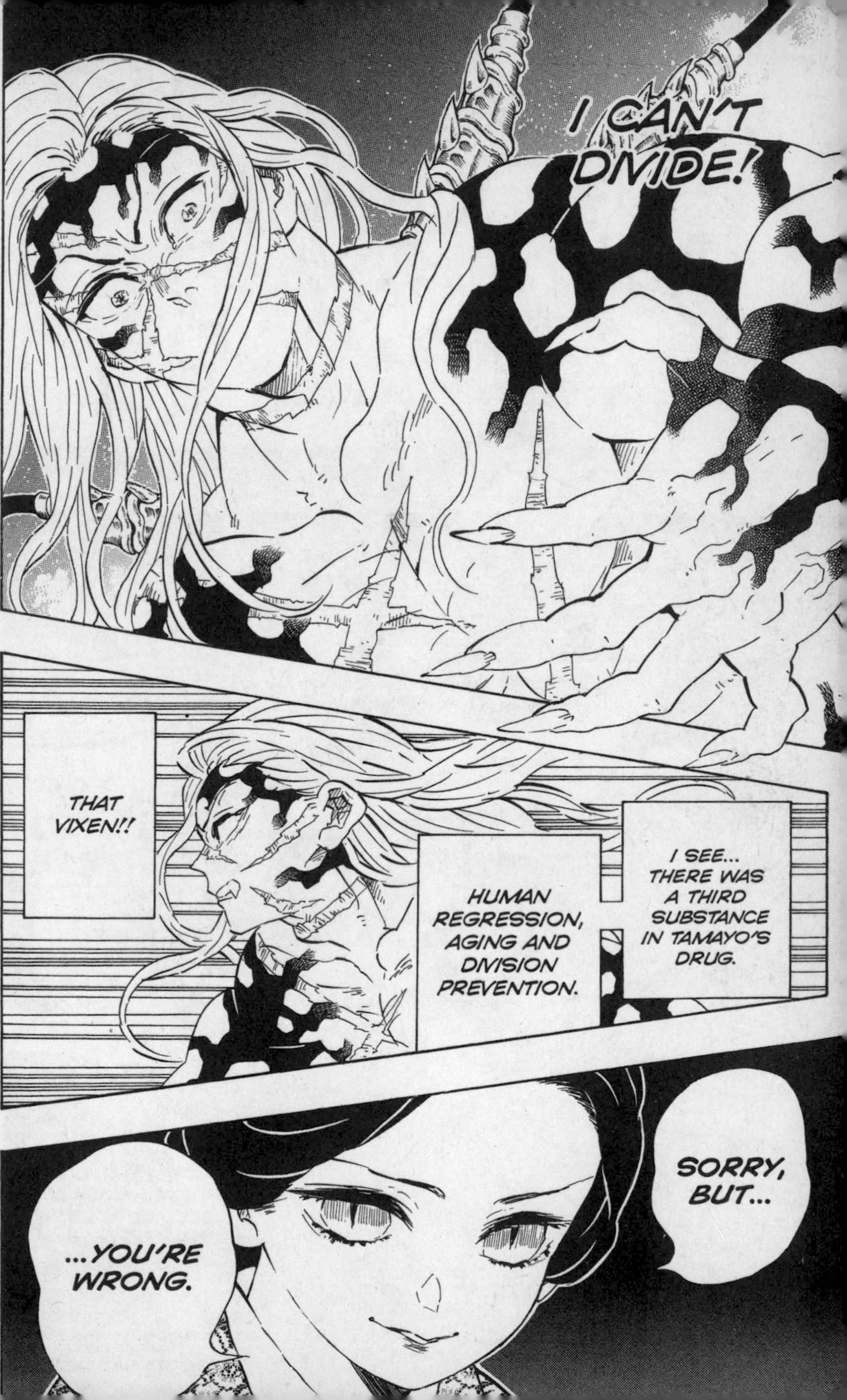
I CAN'T DIVIDE!
I SEE... THERE WAS A THIRD SUBSTANCE IN TAMAYO'S DRUG.
HUMAN REGRESSION, AGING AND DIVISION PREVENTION.
THAT VIXEN!!
SORRY, BUT...
...YOU'RE WRONG.